THE NEW JEWISH EXPERIENTIAL BOOK

D1522081

By
BERNARD REISMAN
and
JOEL I. REISMAN

With Editorial Contribution by
SIMON KLARFELD

KTAV PUBLISHING HOUSE, INC.

Library of Congress Cataloging-in-Publication Data

Reisman, Bernard.
 The new Jewish experiential book / by Bernard Reisman and Joel
Reisman.-- 2nd ed.
   p. cm.
 ISBN 0-88125-709-5
 1. Jewish religious education--Teaching methods. 2.
Jews--Identity--Study and teaching. I. Reisman, Joel. II. Title.
 BM103 .R43 2002
 296.6'8--dc21

                          2002075737

        Manufactured in the United States of America
KTAV Publishing House, 926 Newark Avenue, Jersey City, NJ 07306
             Email: info@ktav.com

To my wife of over 50 years, Elaine,
our four children, their spouses,
and our eight grandchildren.

CONTENTS

Preface and Acknowledgements   vii

Introduction to Activities in the Book   xi

1   Contemporary Context and Population Trends   1

2   Informal Education: Principles   14

3   Informal Education: Some Tools and Techniques   34

4   Icebreakers/Mixers   63

5   Antisemitism/Holocaust   106

6   Israel and Israel-Diaspora Relations   125

7   Family and Lifecycle   153

8   Issues Confronting the Community   183

9   Leadership   207

10 Personal and Professional Values   239

11 Religion and Culture   273

12 Pluralism   345

13 Jewish Identity   376

14 Informal Education: Practitioners' Perspectives   407

PREFACE AND ACKNOWLEDGEMENTS

I am pleased to welcome you to *The New Jewish Experiential Book*. The original *Jewish Experiential Book* was published in 1979. It was well received and has since then gone through a number of printings. A generation has now passed. The last 25 years have seen considerable changes in issues facing the American Jewish community. The acceptance of Jewish experiential education has increased considerably since publication of the first edition. Finally, I have continually been developing and collecting new experiential activities. All these factors made it clear—first to my publisher, Bernard Scharfstein of KTAV Publishing House, and then to me—that a new edition would be of great interest.

At first I was not sure I was ready to muster the time and energy to take on the task. I was quite busy and satisfied with my teaching and research duties at Brandeis University. Then came June 1, 2001—my formal retirement after 34 years of teaching at Brandeis University. Now there was no excuse for not getting the new book underway. Still, I found other activities to engage me until my publisher urged me to get started. Once I got rolling I was grateful to him for the push.

I have amassed a large number of new experiential activities. A significant source was the hundreds of Brandeis graduate students who took courses with me when I was teaching in the Hornstein Program in Jewish Communal Service. The major student assignment of my course on informal Jewish education was to create new experiential activities, which were later assembled into a book distributed to all the students. These activities, composed by a new generation of Jewish leaders that has emerged since the original publication, provide a fresh perspective.

Another significant influence has been the growing body of educators and other communal professionals who employ experiential activities. When the first edition was published, informal Jewish education was a new field. Over the past two decades, I have benefited from sharing experiences and perspectives with many committed, creative practitioners in this field. It is my hope that the activities in this book will show the range of backgrounds and styles of the many educators who have shaped the field of Jewish informal education over the last 25 years.

❀   ❀   ❀

In describing the genesis of *The New Jewish Experiential Book*, I must quickly move beyond the first person. I had several collaborators in the conceptualization, development and production of this manuscript. Foremost is my son Joel I. Reisman, who made vital contributions in every phase of the writing. Joel is a graduate of Harvard College and works as a quantitative healthcare analyst for the U.S. Veterans Administration in Bedford, Massachusetts. Simon Klarfeld, a former student of mine, contributed text and activities that appear throughout the book. Simon received a master's degree from the Hornstein Program and, among many contributions to the Jewish community, organized the Genesis summer program for teens at Brandeis University. Currently, he is the Vice President of the Andrea and Charles Bronfman Philanthropies in New York City.

My daughter Robin Reisman Maltz did much of the typing and also helped by giving periodic nudges to get the book finished. Joshua Stein, a former student of mine who received a master's degree from the Hornstein Program, bore major responsibility for researching and organizing the quotations that appear throughout the book. My daughter Sharon Reisman Conway proofread the finished manuscript.

Alan Teperow contributed the chapter on Pluralism. He is Executive Director of the Synagogue Council of Massachusetts. He, too, is a former student of mine, and received a master's degree from the Hornstein Program in 1976.

Zohar Raviv contributed an original article for this book that centers on an activity at the Massada site and that appears in the chapter on Informal Education. A graduate of the Hornstein Program in Jewish Communal Service at Brandeis University, he is now a doctoral candidate in Near Eastern and Judaic Studies at the University of Michigan. Mr. Raviv has taught at the Institute for Informal Education at Brandeis and the Florence Melton Adult Mini-School in West Bloomfield, Michigan.

We are most grateful to the staff of *Sh'ma* and the individual authors for permission to reprint the articles comprising the chapter "Informal Education: Practitioners' Perspectives". In particular, thank you to Susan Berrin, the editor, and Yosef I. Abramowitz, the publisher of the journal.

It is gratifying to be able to publish the efforts of my students and colleagues and see my teaching reflected in a new generation. To all of my students whose activities have been incorporated in this book, I say "Thank you." Contributors are identified by name at the end of each activity.

My deepest appreciation is reserved for my wife Elaine S. Reisman. She has always been a wonderful partner to me and was a source of emotional support and encouragement throughout production of this book. It may be more than coincidence that this book appears during the year of our 50th wedding anniversary.

INTRODUCTION TO ACTIVITIES IN THE BOOK

The standard format used to describe each activity includes the following elements:

Purpose:

A summary of the objectives of the activity, issues addressed, and special methodological considerations.

Group:

The age-group and number of participants recommended for the activity. Groups larger than what is indicated can usually be accommodated by breaking into smaller groups and providing each group with its own leader and meeting space.

Setting:

The nature of the room or place in which the activity is to occur, with appropriate physical arrangements.

Materials:

Necessary supplies and equipment.

Time:

The amount of time recommended for conducting the activity.

Instructions:

Guidelines, listed sequentially, for the leader to conduct the activity.

Variations:

Additional activities on a related theme.

Notes to Leader:

Supplemental guidelines and, where appropriate, cautions in conducting an activity.

TERMINOLOGY

In the humanistic literature, the person who conducts experiential activities has been referred to with several designations: facilitator, teacher, professional, trainer, and group leader. Similarly, activities are alternately referred to as structured experiences, games, exercises, strategies, instruments, and techniques. All these terms are appropriately descriptive, and most can be used interchangeably.

There were many different authors and many sources for the activities appearing in this book. Some attempt has been made to clarify or update activities, but by-and-large the original wording and tone of the activity were kept intact. Accordingly, some instructions are addressed in the second person (e.g. "You should divide the group . . .") while others are in the third person (e.g. "The leader should divide the group . . .") Terms for informal education concepts, such as leader and participant, have not been made uniform. Usage with regard to specialized terms or words in Hebrew or Yiddish follows the preference of each author. In particular, spelling of the name of the Deity either as "G-d" or "God" reflects each author's use.

At the end of each chapter there are quotations relevant to the chapter. Quotations were chosen so as to provide a wide range of viewpoints and in some instances to be provocative. This material can be used to illustrate major themes or as a starting point for discussion. For a structured way to make use of this material, see the activity "Jewish Quotes" in Chapter 3, "Informal Education: Some Tools and Techniques."

I

CONTEMPORARY CONTEXT AND POPULATION TRENDS

Issues affecting Jews must be seen in the context of social and political forces, trends in secular culture, and relations between Jews and the larger society. An understanding of those forces frames discussion on topics such as anti-Semitism, relations with Israel, family life, feminist issues such as ordination of women as rabbis and counting women in the *minyan*, and Jewish identity and continuity.

There is a sense of peoplehood and connectedness that binds together Jews as much as religion and culture. All Jews have a stake in issues affecting other Jews and Jewish communities around the world. Israel occupies a unique place. The fate of Jews in particular countries, such as the former Soviet Union, has also occupied the attention of Jews in general. Awareness of these and related issues is a prelude to offering effective and appropriate leadership to the Jewish community of the 21st century.

Population Trends

Questions of the size and distribution of the Jewish population have long been of interest and concern for Jewish leaders. Most importantly, the sheer number of Jews is directly related to the prospects for Jewish survival. In contemporary America there are some notable trends having to do with where Jews choose to live; these factors have major consequences for the types of community organization that are needed.

There are 13,191,500 Jews in the world. (See Table 1.) North America, i.e. the United States and Canada, constitutes close to half the population, Israel comprises over a third, and the remainder are scattered elsewhere, mainly in Europe.

The size of the world Jewish population was affected drastically by the Holocaust. Roughly one-quarter of the population was lost between 1935 and 1945. Since then the population has been increasing but at a slow rate. (See Table 2.)

The fate of the North American Jewish community has a vital bearing on Jews worldwide. Besides being home to almost half the world's Jews, North America occupies a position of leadership for world Jewry. North America and Israel are equal and complementary partners. Jewish life in North America is vibrant, rich and diverse. North America stands as a model of what can be achieved in a diaspora community.

The U.S. Jewish population is 5,700,000. (See Table 5.) The number grew steadily in the early part of the 20th century because of a large influx of immigrants from Europe. Recently, population growth has been slow. In fact, the current birth rate is less than the 2.1 children per female that would be necessary to maintain the present population. A low birth rate is associated with populations that are better educated and better off financially. Assimilation and intermarriage have decreased the number of people who are considered Jews. The proportion of Jews in the United States has been declining steadily in recent decades and now stands at 2.3%. Nonetheless, the influence of U.S. Jews is disproportionate to their numbers, as has often been noted.

U.S. Jews have experienced high levels of success, influence and acceptance. They are characterized by a high degree of education and representation in professional occupations. In fact, Jews are one of the most highly educated population groups in the U.S. The proportion of Jews having a college degree or more is 48%, as compared to 21% in the general population. Similarly, the proportion of Jews who work as professionals or managers is 49%, as compared to 31% in the general population. (From David Singer, Ed. *American Jewish Yearbook 2001*, NY: American Jewish Committee, 2001.) The thorough integration of Jews into North American culture is the culmination of a process that began with a major period of immigration three generations ago. Gradually, anti-Semitism and distrust on the part of the larger culture have diminished, as has Jewish parochialism.

Jews on the Move

As with the general population, Jews in the U.S. have become highly mobile. It is no longer necessary or expected to live close to one's family or where one grew up. Historically, Jews lived in areas of high Jewish density, typically urban areas of the Northeast. Jews are now comfortable living in all parts of the U.S. There has been a consistent pattern over the last 30 years for the proportion of Jews living in the Northeast to decrease, while the proportion increases in the South and West. (See Table 8.) Jews no longer only seek traditionally Jewish areas and are moving increasingly to states that have small Jewish populations and little in the way of organized religious or communal life. This phenomenon is documented at length in the aptly titled book *Jews on the Move* by demographers Sidney and Alice Goldstein of Brown University.

Among the areas of the country that typify the phenomenon of "Jews on the move" is Alaska. In 2000, the Jewish population of the state was 3,600. Conditions in Alaska would seem ripe for assimilation. Most Alaskan Jews live far from family; many came to Alaska to escape their traditional upbringing; the culture is decidedly non-Jewish; and there are only three conventional synagogues in the state, Reform and Lubavitch synagogues in Anchorage and a "liberal" synagogue in Fairbanks. And yet, the significant majority of the Jews of Alaska manage to come together for holidays, worship, study and communal gatherings. Committed individuals in a dozen towns have formed Jewish community groups, without aid from formal institutions. Levels of religious observance are comparable to those of Jews in the U.S., as a whole. The success of Jewish life in the state bodes well for other remote, low-density regions. (See Bernard Reisman and Joel I. Reisman, *Life on the Frontier: the Jews of Alaska*, Cohen Center for Modern Jewish Studies, Brandeis University, Waltham MA, 1995.)

Intermarriage is prevalent, accounting for half of the married households. At least in terms of numbers, however, intermarriage results in a net population gain. There are more non-Jews who identified as Jews after marriage than Jews who subsequently identified with their spouse's religion.

As the phenomenon of "Jews on the Move" continues, places

like Alaska will represent a greater share of the Jewish population. There are heartening implications from the success of Alaskan Jews in withstanding the forces of assimilation, disaffection, and intermarriage and in creating new institutions.

Optimism and Pessimism

It has been common to be pessimistic about prospects for Jewish survival in North America. Adherents of this view point to the high rate of intermarriage, the low birth rate, and the large number of people born Jewish who abandon their identity or do not pass it on to their children. This view is in line with a philosophy for motivating the Jewish community through fear for the survival of the Jewish people. Critics have termed this "the Lachrymose Approach."

In the authors' opinion there is reason for guarded optimism. Granted, the rate of intermarriage is high and unlikely to change. The National Jewish Population Survey conducted in 1990 found that 52% of the households married in the prior five years were mixed marriages. However, intermarriage in itself is not a problem. What matters is the Jewish identity of the household and of the children in it.

Whether someone is a Jew should be a matter of self-identification or behavior. It should not require formal conversion or matrilineal descent, i.e. the *halakhic* requirement that a person must have a Jewish mother to be counted as a Jew. If we are prepared to view all members of a mixed household as potentially Jewish, our response can focus constructively on efforts to make Jewishness more salient for them. With that view, intermarriage can be seen as a series of opportunities and challenges. In the case of Alaska, cited above, the net effect has been favorable for Jewish continuity.

The low birth rate is a source of concern. Its impact will be felt more strongly as the population continues to spread to areas of low Jewish density.

North American Jews are receptive to what being Jewish has to offer. While they are highly acculturated and worldly, they are also aware of their needs for spirituality and community. Being Jewish affords a viable and attractive option for meeting those needs.

Again, the example of Alaska is a hopeful sign that assimilation is not inevitable; indeed, people will take initiative to maintain their Jewish identities in areas having none of the familiar supports for Jewish community.

One way in which community leaders can help is to stop their criticism of mixed marriage and, instead, to reach out to such households and encourage them to identify as Jews. Another way is to offer Jewish programming that responds to the full age spectrum and to families as units. Yet another way might be to encourage families to have more children, while realizing that economic factors and personal preferences are likely to be the strongest determinants of the decision to have children. Most important, leaders can make being Jewish more appealing by taking a more positive view of what it has to offer and by placing faith in its ability to adapt constructively to social change.

TABLES OF POPULATION DATA

The tables that follow will provide group leaders with key facts about Jewish population that may be relevant to activities about Israel-Diaspora relations, Jewish identity and continuity, or issues confronting the Jewish community. Information from the tables could be the basis for a quiz or the starting point for a discussion, for example on the subject of where Jews choose to live.

TABLE 1
World Jewish Population, 2000*

	Population	% of Total
TOTAL WORLD	13,191,500	
Diaspora	8,309,500	63.0
Israel	4,882,000	37.0
MAJOR REGIONS:		
Americas	6,483,900	49.2
Europe	1,583,000	12.0
Asia		
Israel	4,882,000	37.0
Asia excl. Israel	50,900	0.4
Africa	89,800	0.7
Oceania	101,900	0.8

Source: David Singer, Ed. *American Jewish Yearbook 2000*, NY: American Jewish Committee, 2000.

TABLE 2
Trend in World Jewish Population*

Year	Population
1935	15,250,000
1945	11,000,000
1955	11,800,000
1965	12,500,000
1975	12,742,000
1985	12,871,000
1995	13,020,000
2000	13,191,500

Source: David Singer, Ed. *American Jewish Yearbook 2001*, NY: American Jewish Committee, 2001.

TABLE 3
Distribution of World Jewish Population, 1968 and 2000*

	1968		2000	
	Population	% of Total	Population	% of Total
Diaspora	8,391,200	64.1%	8,309,500	63.0%
United States	5,869,000	44.8%	5,700,000	43.2%
Israel	4,701,600	35.9%	4,882,000	37.0%
TOTAL	13,092,800	100%	13,191,500	100%

Source: David Singer, Ed. *American Jewish Yearbook 2000*, NY: American Jewish Committee, 2000.

TABLE 4
Ten Countries with Largest Jewish Population, 2000*

Country	Population	% of World
1. United States	5,700,000	43.2
2. Israel	4,882,000	37.0
3. France	521,000	3.9
4. Canada	362,000	2.7
5. Russia	290,000	2.2
6. United Kingdom	276,000	2.1
7. Argentina	200,000	1.5
8. Ukraine	100,000	0.8
9. Brazil	98,000	0.7
10. Australia	97,000	0.7

Source: David Singer, Ed. *American Jewish Yearbook 2000*, NY: American Jewish Committee, 2000.

TABLE 5
Trend in U.S. Jewish Population*

Year	Population
1900	1,058,000
1910	2,044,000
1920	3,602,000
1930	4,228,000
1940	4,770,000
1950	5,000,000
1960	5,531,000
1970	5,870,000
1980	5,800,000
1990	5,981,000
2000	6,136,000

Source: David Singer, Ed. *American Jewish Yearbook 2001*, NY: American Jewish Committee, 2001.

TABLE 6
Ten U.S. States with the Largest & Smallest Numbers of Jews, 2000*

	Largest Number of Jews		
State	Jewish Population	State Population	% of State
1. New York	1,651,000	18,197,000	9.1%
2. California	967,000	33,143,000	2.9%
3. Florida	637,000	15,111,000	4.2%
4. New Jersey	465,000	8,143,000	5.7%
5. Pennsylvania	282,000	11,994,000	2.4%
6. Massachusetts	274,000	6,175,000	4.4%
7. Illinois	270,000	12,128,000	2.2%
8. Maryland	216,000	5,172,000	4.1%
9. Ohio	144,000	11,257,000	1.3%
10. Texas	124,000	20,044,000	0.6%
TOTAL	5,030,000	141,364,000	3.6%

Smallest Number of Jews

State	Jewish Population	State Population	% of State
1. South Dakota	350	738,000	0.05%
2. Wyoming	400	480,000	0.08%
3. North Dakota	700	641,000	0.11%
4. Montana	800	879,000	0.09%
5. Idaho	1,000	1,210,000	0.08%
6. Mississippi	1,400	2,731,000	0.05%
7. Arkansas	1,600	2,523,000	0.06%
8. West Virginia	2,400	1,812,600	0.13%
9. Alaska	3,500	609,000	0.57%
10. Utah	4,500	2,059,000	0.22%
TOTAL	16,650	13,683,000	0.12%

Source: David Singer, Ed. *American Jewish Yearbook 2000*, NY: American Jewish Committee, 2000.

TABLE 7
Regional Distribution of U.S. Jewish and General Populations, 2000*

Region	Jewish Population		General Population	
	Population	% of Total	Population	% of Total
Northeast	2,812,000	46.4%	51,830,000	19.0%
South	1,280,000	21.1%	96,468,000	35.4%
Midwest	701,000	11.6%	63,242,000	23.2%
West	1,268,000	20.9%	61,150,000	22.4%
TOTAL	6,061,000	100.0%	272,690,000	100.0%

Source: David Singer, Ed. *American Jewish Yearbook 2000*, NY: American Jewish Committee, 2000.

TABLE 8
Regional Distribution of U.S. Jewish Population, 1900 to 2000*

	% of Total		
Region	*1900*	*1968*	*2000*
Northeast	58%	64%	46%
South	12%	10%	21%
Midwest	24%	13%	11%
West	5%	13%	22%

Source: David Singer, Ed. *American Jewish Yearbook 2000*, NY: American Jewish Committee, 2000.

QUOTES

Before the beginning of the nineteenth century all Jews regarded Judaism as a privilege; since then most Jews have come to regard it as a burden.

Rabbi Mordecai Kaplan
(1881–1983)

American Jews are like the messenger who has forgotten the message.

Rabbi Abraham Joshua Heschel
(1907–1972)

The role of the Jews, the inventors of western culture, is singular: there is simply no one else remotely like them; theirs is indeed a unique vocation.

Thomas Cahill, *The Gifts of the Jews:*
How a Tribe of Desert Nomads
Changed the Way Everyone Thinks
and Feels, 1998

Jews view their historic experience of continuity in the face of overwhelming obstacles as suggesting the divine—a rumor of angels.

Peter Berger, sociologist, 1969

A people dying for thousands of years means a living people. Our incessant dying means uninterrupted living, rising, standing up, beginning anew.

Simon Rawidowicz (1897–1957),
"Israel: the Ever-Dying People"

The Jews are a particular people. In age after age, they have been expected to disappear and yet they persist.

Rabbi Arthur Hertzberg, July 1998

A person of faith will be abundant in blessings.

Proverbs 28:20

To maintain tradition does not mean to conserve ashes, but to keep the spark alive.

Otto von Bismarck (1815–1898)

Come writers and critics
Who prophesize with your pen
And keep your eyes wide
The chance won't come again
And don't speak too soon
For the wheel's still in spin
And there's no tellin' who
That it's namin'.
For the loser now
Will be later to win
For the times they are a-changin'.

Bob Dylan (1941–)

Human history is a race between education and catastrophe.

H.G. Wells (1866–1946),
English author

Alone a Jew is nothing. But if he is with other Jews, he's a force. Because then automatically he inherits all the strengths and all the tears, all the despairs and all the joys of his ancestors. A Jew alone cannot be Jewish. A Jew can be Jewish only if he's part of the community.

Elie Wiesel (1928–), 1977

What would the Jew be without his community? In joy as in sorrow, a Jew is never alone.

Elie Wiesel (1928–), 1977

Why has the Messiah not come either yesterday or today? Because we are today just as we were yesterday.

Rabbi Menachem Mendel of Kotzk
(1787–1859)

If we are not better tomorrow than we are today, why have a tomorrow?

Rabbi Nachman of Bratslav
(1772–1811)

Choose life, that you and your offspring may live.

Deuteronomy 30:19

The wilderness is not just a desert through which we wandered for forty years. It is a way of being. A place that demands being open to the flow of life around you.

Rabbi Lawrence Kushner (1943–)

The transformation of Jewish individuals will require the transformation of Jewish institutions, which will, in turn, require transformations in the relationships among institutions, all aimed at crating a "community of communities."

Jonathan Woocher, 1986

Don't trust anyone over thirty.

Slogan of the 1960's

As a rallying cry, "Will our grandchildren be Jewish?" seems more likely to provoke policy prescriptions than personal change. Thus although concern for the future is undoubtedly a powerful motivating force for today's efforts, it is not, I would argue, a sufficient basis on which to ground them and may in fact, lead us somewhat astray.

Jonathan Woocher, 1986

The contemporary American Jewish community is undergoing a major transformation, the outcome of which will be the religious conversion of American Jews to Christianity by the year 2015.

Professor Samuel Klausner

The American Baby Boomers have come of age. They are a generation of seekers . . . turned away from the bland religious establishments of their youth.

Wade Clark Roof, A Generation of
Seekers, 1993

Jews age 35–44 are no less ritually active than their elders age 55–64.

Professor Steven M. Cohen

The lady doth protest too much, me thinks.

William Shakespeare (1564–1616)

2

INFORMAL EDUCATION:
PRINCIPLES

This chapter appeared as Chapter 2 in the first edition of The Jewish Experiential Book. *In this chapter, the term "experiential education" is synonymous with "informal education." The next
chapter serves as a supplement offering more practical guidance
on conducting experiential activities.*

What is experiential education? Where has it come from? To what
kinds of educational objectives does it apply? How can one function effectively as an experiential educator? These questions serve
as a point of departure for defining experiential education and its
applicability to Jewish life today.

EXPERIENTIAL EDUCATION: ORIGINS AND PRINCIPLES

Experiential education, as the term indicates, is an approach to
education based on the experience of the learner. The underlying
assumption is that meaningful learning will ensue to the extent
that a learner is directly (i.e., personally) linked to the content or
subject matter. This principle was initially propounded by John
Dewey as one of the basic tenets of progressive education. In 1916,
Dewey described the link between experience and learning:

> To learn from experience is to make a backward and forward connec-
> tion between what we do to things and what we enjoy or suffer from
> things in consequence. Under such conditions, doing becomes trying:

an experiment with the world to find out what it is like; the undergoing becomes instruction—discovery of the connection of things.[1]

A related rationale for linking educational approaches to the experience of the learner arose from the work of the social psychologist, Kurt Lewin. Lewin's experiments during the 1930s and 1940s were concerned with ways of changing attitudes and behavior. He found that the key dynamic in change was the direct involvement of people in the process of change itself: "This result [change] occurs when the facts become really *their* facts [as against other people's facts]. An individual will believe facts he himself has discovered, in the same way he believes in himself."[2] Lewin's work also gave impetus to another key principle of experiential education: the importance of the small group as the vehicle through which basic attitudes can be shaped. The interaction of a small group of peers, with the subject matter and among each other, constitutes a significant dynamic in the communication of content and the effecting of personal change.

The link to experience enables the individual to understand in his/her own terms the subject under consideration, and when this process occurs in a personalized small group, there is an additional enhancement of learning as a result of the broadened perspective and support provided by one's peers. The experiential approach makes subject matter accessible to the learner as it filters through his/her own needs and interests, and at his/her own pace. These properties of an experiential approach to learning increase the likelihood that the learning will be sustained in behavior beyond its point of instruction.

Emerging from the underlying principles, the basic two operational components of experiential education are: (1) *creative activities*, or games, which seek to link the subject matter to the experiences and interests of the participant; and (2) *a learning community* which consists of the use of the personalized small

1. John Dewey, *Democracy and Education* (New York: Macmillan, 1964), p, 140.
2. Kurt Lewin, quoted in Alfred Marrow, "Events Leading to the Establishment of the National Training Laboratories," *Journal of Applied Behavioral Science* 3 (1967): 114–50.

group as the fundamental educational unit so as to encourage peer learning and emotional support.

DIFFERENCES BETWEEN EXPERIENTIAL AND TRADITIONAL EDUCATION

In traditional educational programs, the teacher/leader assumes full responsibility for organizing and presenting the subject matter. The role of the student/member is essentially a passive one—to absorb the information presented by the teacher.

The role of the experiential teacher/leader is a more nondirective one. S/he does not assume the interest and attention of the student; more typically, the opposite is assumed. Accordingly, it becomes the appropriate responsibility of the teacher/leader to stimulate and help sustain the motivation of the learners. This objective is pursued through the use of a program of experiential activities designed to connect up with the specific interests and capacities of the students. Further, the teacher/leader works to create an educational environment in which the learners share responsibility for both the learning agenda and the maintenance of a supportive emotional climate. The function of the experiential educator is essentially that of a facilitator: s/he structures and orchestrates the several components of the educational experience—his/her own role, the design of the experiential activities, the physical setting of the classroom or meeting room, and the network of interpersonal relationships—in order to optimize the achievement of learning objectives.

DIFFERENCES WITHIN EXPERIENTIAL EDUCATION

In making the distinction between traditional and experiential approaches to education, it was pointed out that the former is almost exclusively focused on content, or the *cognitive* component, while experiential education addresses itself to emotions, or the *affective* component, as well as the cognitive one. It is important to note that variations exist within the field of experiential education. These variations stem from different prescriptions for a balance of cognitive and affective emphases. At one extreme are those approaches which emphasize individual needs and personal growth: that is, the benefits to the individual from active participation and interpersonal interaction are seen as a sufficient educational rationale. Formal content serves as a vehicle for the achievement of affective goals. The process becomes an end unto itself while the content or product is viewed as a means. In a related approach, a clarification of the participants' values is defined as the content of the educational experience. Here, too, the emphasis is placed more on the process by which the participants acquire values than on the values themselves. In the first book about value clarification, and still one of the most influential works on the subject, Raths, Harmin, and Simon represent this position: "We shall be less concerned with the particular value outcomes of any one person's experiences than we will with the process that he uses to obtain his values."[3] At the other end of the experiential education continuum, greater concern and attention are focused on the cognitive component. The experiential approach is utilized mainly as a means of attaining a specific educational objective: either to influence personal attitudes or to convey subject matter (e.g., history, literature, philosophy, Jewish identity, etc.). One approach in which an affective orientation and methodology are blended with a clear cognitive objective is *confluent education*.[4] In confluent education, and similar methods, effectiveness is measured in terms of the achievement of a specific cognitive goal for the class or group. This view of experiential education begins with a specific educational content objective— the achievement of which is enhanced through the appropriate personal involvement of the participants and the creation of a supportive learning community.

The reader should be aware of this author's methodological bias, which brings him closer to the approach of confluent educa-

3. L. E. Raths, Merrill Harmin, and Sidney Simon, *Values and Teaching* (Columbus: Charles E. Merrill, 1966), p.28.

4. The basic text in confluent education is George Brown, *Human Teaching for Human Learning* (New York: Viking Press, 1971). The applicability of confluent education to Jewish education is addressed in William Cutter and Jack Dauber, "Confluent Education in the Jewish Setting," *Pedagogic Reporter*, June 1972.

tion than to the more personal growth/process-oriented approaches. This preference does not imply a denial that the affective processes lack intrinsic validity; it arises, rather, from the conviction that a cognitively focused method is more appropriate to the subject of Jewish identity. In the ensuing material in this book describing the experiential activities, the reader will note a commitment to the basic affective components of participant involvement, use of creative techniques, and generating a supportive learning community, *but* within the context of contributing to an overarching cognitive objective. This involves communicating information about the Jewish experience or affecting Jewish attitudes and values.

Experiential education has been utilized in a wide range of settings for both formal and informal educational purposes. In addition to being used in classrooms for formal Jewish education, experiential education has been applied in a variety of social welfare and informal educational settings (e.g., federations, community centers, youth groups, college Hillel programs, synagogues, etc.) for programs such as workshops on Jewish identity, adult education, family-life education, Jewish-consciousness raising, community development, leadership development, staff training, and fund-raising.

RECENT SOCIAL FORCES ASSOCIATED WITH THE EMERGENCE OF EXPERIENTIAL EDUCATION

Why is it that experiential education and related approaches have recently attracted attention in the American Jewish community? As with any social phenomenon, the answer lies in an understanding of changing societal forces that have generated new needs and interests, which in turn require new responses. Experiential education has emerged as one such response. Its appeal can be explained in terms of its congruence with the needs of contemporary American Jews. Three areas of congruence can be identified.

1. Quest for Jewish Life-Style

The last decade has witnessed an abatement in the earlier assimilative trend in American Jewish life and a resurgence of interest in

Jewish identity. This renaissance is related to three contemporary socio-historical developments which have a particular bearing on American Jews: the achievements of the State of Israel, culminating in a dramatic victory of the Six Day War; the rise of ethnic consciousness and pride in America, superceding the concept of the melting pot; and the disillusionment of American Jews with two of the major ideological systems which had been important modern sources of belief for them: the "American Dream" and liberalism.

Immigrant Jews at the turn of the century were attracted to America's secular culture and aspired to shed "old country" ways in favor of what their new country offered. In short order, the secular society became the immigrant's prime frame of reference. By the middle of the twentieth century, Jews had achieved a high level of education and sophistication in the broader open society. At the same time, however, their level of Jewish knowledge and Jewish competence was gradually diminishing. Now, as many Jews seek to revise this condition so as to make Jewishness more prominent in their lives, they encounter a cultural lag.

Responding to the earlier assimilative trend in Jewish life, most Jewish educational approaches developed in recent decades have been based on the premise that Jews would only pursue Jewish activities if they were exhorted to or were cajoled. This meant that the initiative for Jewish learning and behavior came to reside with rabbis, Jewish educators, and other recognized professionals. The style of Jewish behavior for most Jews had become a vicarious one. Virtually the only sphere in which Jews were seen to have any competence to function autonomously was in secondary, instrumental activities, such as helping to build and maintain cathedral-like synagogues and the elaborate network of Jewish social welfare institutions. With respect to Jewish learning and customs, however, the average Jew had become essentially illiterate.

Such a pattern ceases to be functional at the point at which Jews decide, of their own volition, that they want to become more directly involved with their Jewishness. The vicarious style was neither well suited to nor well received by a motivated, now highly educated, and sophisticated Jewish community. Most Jews today are not being challenged in proportion to their interests and capacities. They are reluctant to settle for instrumental or vicarious definitions of their Jewish identify. Instead, contemporary American Jews are seeking a return to the essence of Judaism, to learn how this religious tradition could shape a style of life.

Jewish experiential education shifts much of the responsibility and initiative for Jewish learning and action from the rabbi, educator, and social worker to the people themselves (congregants, students, members). In this kind of framework, the professional serves as a resource to nourish and expand on the interests of the people as they seek, through direct participation, to clarify the meaning which the Jewish tradition holds for their own lives.

2. Secularization of Authority

Attitudes toward authority have changed dramatically in recent decades. In earlier generations it was generally accepted that the authority figure—parent, teacher, employer, etc.—was the source of all wisdom relevant to his/her role and, as the occupant of the authority role, was entitled to awe and respect. As this concept of authority has eroded, it has resulted in the increased power of the formerly dependent member of the social unit—the child, student or employee. This transition generally translates into a greater readiness and expectation for people to be actively involved in shaping their destiny. In educational terms, this means a receptivity to more individual participation, the use of small groups, and nonauthoritative leadership styles—all of which are essential characteristics of experiential learning.

3. Heightened Individualism

As learners' expectations have been raised, the issue of motivation has assumed a more significant role in the educational process. Teachers can no longer assume that their task is merely to present content, which students are obliged to absorb. Not only does the student expect to be recognized and responded to as an autonomous individual, but s/he has also been conditioned—via the media—to expect ideas to be represented interestingly and dramatically. Thus, the modern teacher must consider not only the "what" of his/her subject, but "how" it can be creatively presented so as to elicit the interest of the student. Further, the teacher must be aware of the varying personalities of his/her students—individually and collectively.

Contemporary values reflect a distrust of large institutions and the formalized human relations they engender. They are seen as repressive and constricting of human potential. There is a preference for structures and approaches which give free rein to individuals to pursue their own interests. In experiential education, this value orientation is expressed through the learning community, with its encouragement of individual participation and peer learning. Because the concept of the learning community is compatible with contemporary values, it enhances the individual's receptivity to the educational objectives of the experiential program.

ELEMENTS OF EXPERIENTIAL EDUCATION

To be an effective practitioner in any applied social or physical science requires an understanding of the primary assumptions and principles which underlie the discipline. Lacking such knowledge results in rote or mechanical functioning: one applies techniques without fully understanding why or how they work. Operating with a shallow conceptual grounding limits the effectiveness of the practitioner: s/he lacks the flexibility to adapt the routine in the face of changing or unanticipated circumstances. Above all, inadequate background limits the sense of assuredness which the practitioner has in the methodology, which inevitably is perceived by the participants and results in a corresponding loss of confidence in the service.

The major elements of experiential education can be subsumed under four categories: the setting in which it occurs, the use of the small group, the program, and the role of the leader.

1. The Setting

Effective experiential approaches involve a carefully structured environment—physical and psychological. Since universal and active participation is a key requisite of experiential programs, the format and setting should be designed in order to facilitate that objective. If the number of participants is large, this will require dividing the participants into several smaller discussion groups. Typically, the determination of the size and style of the discussion group frequently occurs by default, i.e., as a result of how maintenance personnel set up the meeting room—usually, one large assembly of chairs in rows.

A room with movable, plain, single chairs (rather than larger upholstered chairs or school desks) and little else by way of furniture offers the greatest flexibility for an experiential program. This arrangement affords ease of movement in changing both physical formats and the size of the groups used for different activities. For example, one should be able to switch easily from a circle activity for small groups to an activity requiring dyads or triads, and then to a session in which the total group assembles together.

Ample space is necessary to assure privacy of discussion, especially when several units are meeting in the same room. It is well to avoid intrusions by passers-by and other distractions; this helps to sustain the focus on work and to assure the aura of confidentiality in the deliberations. A blackboard or an easel with newsprint sheets allows for providing clear instructions and for summarizing discussions. For some activities, background music sets an appropriate tone. Posters with pertinent slogans placed around the meeting room can be used to create the desired atmosphere. Many experiential activities call for posting signs or sheets of newsprint on the walls. It is preferable, therefore, that the room not be so elaborately decorated as to preclude affixing things to the walls.

Finally, attention should be paid to maintaining a comfortable room temperature and adequate ventilation. These days, the question of smoking inevitably arises. In the spirit of participation and autonomy, the leader may choose to deflect the smoking issue to the group. The leader would do so on the double assumption that not only are the participants the ones most able to find a resolution to this thorny issue, but also that the achievement of a resolution will contribute to their emerging sense of community. A different procedure is indicated for a conference or retreat which occurs on Shabbat. Here, the leader must anticipate the smoking issue and raise it in advance with the sponsors. If a policy of no smoking on Shabbat is decided upon, this should be clearly communicated to all the participants prior to the session.

Beyond the physical environment, a psychological ambience

needs to be fostered that provides a supportive context for the achievement of experiential objectives. Initially there is the interpretation that while the leader assumes responsibility for overall structure, the actual work at the sessions resides mainly with the participants. Active participation is the by-word rather than passivity or dependency. This is best communicated with a minimum of explanation and a quick entry into a first experiential activity—one designed to establish the participatory mode.

Two other things can be said about the flavor of the participation:

a. *Open and Forthright.* Participants should be encouraged to express themselves honestly and forthrightly. A sufficient openness is sought to enable participants to feel free to ask the "stupid question" or to express unpopular points of view. It is likely that the learning agenda, with such an atmosphere, will accurately reflect the interests and pace of the participants—a requisite for effective learning and/or behavioral change. A critical ingredient in the attainment of this atmosphere is a nonjudgmental attitude on the part of the group leader. Despite his/her nondirective posture, the leader is still the authority figure, and group members will be attentive to any indication of his/her views. To the extent that the leader, either explicitly or implicitly, communicates a point of view, s/he is apt to stifle some degree of expressivity among the participants. This is not to say that the leader should never take a position, but if done, it should be done thoughtfully and with the following three considerations in mind: first, it is best for the leader to reserve the expression of his/her own positions for a later point in the discussion; second, the leader should make a clear distinction between when s/he is providing objective facts and when s/he is offering his/her own subjective opinions; and finally, while the leader may disagree with a participant, s/he should never do so in such a way as to demean the individual with whom s/he is disagreeing.

b. *Risking.* Another preparatory tone important to establish is that of risk-taking. A central objective of the experiential approach is the encouragement of a greater expansiveness among participants. This objective stems from the assumption that most people function cautiously and in stereotypic ways. Herbert Otto has suggested that "healthy humanity is operating at 10% to 15% of its potential," and to fulfill more of this potential "represents the

major challenge and the major promise of this age."[5] Participants
are presented with an attractive model in the leader who assumes
initiative for organizing the experiential session in a nontypical
and creative way. Further, as participants broaden their insights
and achieve personal gratifications from their active role in the
experiential program, they reinforce their capacity to function
autonomously and to pursue other new frontiers.

2. A Personalized Small Group

Earlier the point was introduced that experiential activities are
designed for small groups in order to maximize participation. The
fewer the individuals in a learning constellation, the greater are
the opportunities for individual "air-time." For general discussion
purposes, a group of 8–10 participants seems to offer the right
balance between optimal participation and that critical mass necessary for diversity and the sense of being part of a significant
unit. Not all experiential activities, however, involve small-group
discussion. Some activities call for a solitary involvement, others
call for the use of dyads or triads, and others still for a plenary
session involving a large number of participants. Although the
total number of participants in a class or workshop is fixed, the
number of people included in any particular segment of the program can and should be varied based on the requirements of the
activity. As with modification of the physical environment, the
arrangement of different-sized units demonstrates adaptability and
responsiveness—attributes which are integral to effective experiential education.

A personalized flavor should be established, irrespective of the
constellation in which participants are grouped. To establish this
flavor, the leader and group members must come to know and
refer to one another by name. The objective here is for each person
to arrive at the feeling that s/he is recognized and valued as a person in his/her own right and is not seen as an anonymous unit.
The personalized flavor is often experienced as such a contrast to
the more typical, impersonal associations to which people have

5. Herbert A. Otto, *Explorations in Human Potentialities* (Springfield:
Charles C. Thomas, 1966), p. xv.

become accustomed that it can elicit an almost exhilarating response in participants. This positive affect can transfer to the work of the group, providing it with a source of energy and motivation.

In addition to providing emotional support, the personalized sense of community interprets and enhances a crucial educational dimension of the experiential approach—peer learning. Each individual in the collectivity is seen as a vital source of information. One learns from the ideas and experiences of one's colleagues in addition to learning from authorities. The process of peer learning is not a new phenomenon in Jewish life. It is aptly described in *Pirke Avot (Sayings of the Fathers)*, where Rabbi Ben Zoma observes: "Who is wise? He who learns from every man"(4:1).

When there is a recognition of the inherent wisdom residing in a group's members, it makes sense to utilize small, personalized groups and for the leader to function so as to optimize participation and interaction. Instead of feeling that s/he, as the group leader, must provide all the answers, the leader defines his/her role as to encourage maximum participation by the group's members. The leader gives encouragement through recognition of contributions and by posing questions; also, by being disciplined in the constraint of his/her own verbal participation. In short, the leader "trusts the process": s/he is assured that people, when given appropriate encouragement, will function thoughtfully and will contribute to one another's growth and learning.

3. The Program

It would be an error to assume that the experiential program requires less advance preparation because the role of the group leader is much less directive than is the case in a traditional educational approach. In fact, since the leader's role during the actual sessions is a less active one, his/her influence emerges largely from the type of structure and atmosphere s/he is able to create—effects determined mainly through advance planning of the program.

The objectives which the group seeks to accomplish are the prime determinant of the program objectives. The need to clarify the group's objective calls for some form of advance contractual discussion between the leader and the group members or its representatives. In these preliminary negotiations, the leader should inform participants of his/her plans to use an experiential approach. The outcome of these early discussions should be shared with all the participants. Preferably participants should receive formal written communication so that they can come to the opening session with an awareness of the purpose of the meeting and the style of functioning to be utilized.

With the clarification of objectives and other data gathered from the initial contracting, the leader can then proceed to design a program which will take into account the age and number of participants, the nature of the meeting room, and the available time. It is well to overplan: have more activities available than are needed, and allow for alternatives should one or another activity not be well received. All necessary supplies and equipment should be anticipated, arranged for, and readied. The leader's thoroughness in planning will decrease the likelihood of delays during the program which may diminish participants' concentration. Above all, the leader's sense of organization contributes to the group members' confidence in the enterprise, and their willingness to experiment with this new venture.

When the leader meets with the full group at its first session, a discussion of the goals and a plan of work should ensue. The substance of this discussion should be consistent with the advance deliberations and with the written announcement of the class or workshop. The purpose of such a discussion is to engage all the group members—even if only tacitly—in a collective determination of what is to occur. This engagement is particularly important in an experiential approach because of the vital expectation of member participation. It is usually sufficient for the leader to clearly and succinctly present the purposes and schedule of the activities, and to request everyone's cooperation in being responsive to the experiential mode of work, i.e., that everyone participate and that everyone be candid and expressive of his/her feelings. When a group is familiar with the proposed agenda, it is appropriate that members be involved in a more extended discussion of the proposed plan. More typically, however, participants are individually and collectively at a beginning stage of awareness regarding both the subject matter and/or ways of defining a plan for addressing the group purpose. It is suggested, therefore, that efforts aimed at achieving a more substantive involvement occur when they can actually lead to a more meaningful exchange, and not when they are made as mere gestures. In any event, at the outset of the session, even if a thorough discussion is not generated, it is important that participants be asked to endorse the leader's proposed outline.

Explanations of the rationale underlying an experiential methodology should be kept to a minimum, lest they distort the essence of an experiential approach. As soon as the main points in the contracting process have been covered, the first activity should be immediately introduced. Extended discussion belies one's conviction of the utility of the approach and only serves to increase the apprehension of participants.

In designing a program, the sequence of activities should allow for a natural flow, in terms of both subject matter and the type of group constellations employed. For example, if the program includes two activities which both utilize a small-group format of people seated in a circle, it is wise to plan these back-to-back. An objective is to avoid the disruptions caused by too many physical or substantive changes. On the other hand, some variation in content and style is appropriate for the full coverage of a subject, as well as for maintaining the interest of participants. Throughout, the leader should be attentive to the issue of timing, concluding activities before they have ceased to hold the members' interest.

A concluding, summary discussion is necessary to bring substantive aspects of a program into focus for the participants. Because of the creative flavor of the activities, it is quite possible that an entire program could take place that would be engrossing for the participants but in which no internalization of learning objectives occurred. The cognitive message can be subtly camouflaged by the appealing format. Thus, in the concluding session of the program, the leader should make connections between the original objectives and what emerged during the several activities. By establishing the link between the affective medium and the cognitive message, one not only provides a broadened perspective on the substantive content, but also further interprets the utility of the experiential methodology.

The summarizing function is often forsaken, usually with the rationale that for the leader to assume this role would be contrary to the nondirective, nonauthoritative stance implicit in the experiential approach. More likely, it is forsaken simply because it is a difficult task. To summarize well obliges a leader to be fully attentive, during the course of the group deliberations, to the many points registered, and then, with little lead time, to be able to join these together in a coherent and concise manner. Knowing that s/he is to make a concluding summary aids the leader in effectively fulfilling the function of discussion-leading during the session: listening attentively (a critical discipline) and keeping the group discussion focused. For group members, the summary highlights learnings and/or actions to be taken. To reiterate, a summary is an unexpendable element of effective experiential education.

4. Role of the Group Leader

It soon becomes apparent that there are several paradoxes inherent in the leader's role in experiential education. Given the emphasis on fostering active participation and responsibility on the part of group members, and given the accompanying prescriptions for a low-profile role for the leader, one would be apt to conclude that leadership is not an important consideration in experiential education. This is not so; in fact, of all the elements of experiential education which we have been examining, the quality of leadership is the major determinant of effective practice.

The term *facilitator* has often been used to characterize the role of the leader of an experiential group. It is a fitting designation because it captures the overarching function of the group leader: to structure the elements of the educational experience—the setting, the program, the personalized group, as well as the leader's own role—so as to achieve a blend which is conducive to optimal learning and growth. The facilitative role, therefore, involves a coordinating function, but only in part, because there is also a more direct role, in that the leader him/herself is a key component in the mix. This distinction parallels Robert Vinter's two aspects of group leadership: *indirect* means of influence, those acts of a leader which seek to shape a context conducive to the achievement of group goals; and *direct* means of influence, those sources of influence which stem from the leader as a personality and from his/her direct interventions with the group members.[6]

6. Robert D. Vinter, "The Essential Components of Group Work Practice,"

The indirect means of leader influence have been addressed in the earlier sections dealing with the *setting* and *program*. Now a more detailed analysis of the direct means of influence available to the leader will be explored.

a. *A Symbol of Authority.* However nonauthoritarian or democratic a leader's style may be, as the formal occupant of the leader's role s/he symbolizes authority for group members. In Vinter's terms, the leader serves as "the object of member identification and drives."[7] In the first instance, the leader is a potential model with whom members may choose to identify; in addition, the leader is the recipient of the emotions and energies of members' psychological attitudes to authority. Within this reservoir of members' emotional reactions to the leader lies a significant potential for influencing the outcome of the educational experience. To the extent that a leader is perceived as a positive authority, s/he can serve as a personal model for students/participants. If the leader is perceived negatively, this sets into motion participant reactions which impede learning; they reject the leader and his/her comments. If carried to an extreme, this leads to a rejection of the total learning experience.

b. *A Balance of Task and Socio-Emotional Requirements.* Robert Bales has pointed out that groups have two sets of requirements which must be fulfilled in order to attain effective group functioning; the *task* to be achieved, and the *socio-emotional*, or moral, needs of the group members.[8] The leader must be responsive to both requirements, even though this may appear to call on him/her to assume contradictory roles. Meeting group task requirements demands leader acts directed toward sustaining the group members in work: prodding, initiating, limiting, focusing. The socio-emotional requirements demand another set of leader acts: nurturing, distracting, easing tension, and giving approval and recognition. An astute leader recognizes that the two requirements are,

in *Individual Change Through Small Groups*, ed. Paul Glasser, Rosemary Sarri, and Robert Vinter (New York: Free Press, 1974), pp. 18–32.

7. Ibid., p. 19.

8. Robert F. Bales, *Personality and Interpersonal Behavior* (New York: Holt, Rinehart & Winston, 1970).

indeed, mutually reinforcing—as members experience a sense of achieving their task, their morale is bolstered, and to the extent that the morale of group members is high, they have more energy to invest in their work. A skillful leadership style is responsive to both task *and* socio-emotional group requirements.

c. *A Facilitative Leadership Style.* Another tension confronting the experiential leader consists of finding a balance between the nonauthoritarian leadership style necessary to foster autonomy and participation and his/her status as a knowledgeable teacher/ resource. The need for a nonauthoritarian leadership stance calls upon the leader to be able to listen, reflect, and generally shift the focus of attention away from him/herself and to the members. As the occupant of a position of authority, however, one's inclination—usually well supported by members' expectations—is to move to center stage and function as the expert, providing answers and proffering solutions to the less knowledgeable. To the extent that a leader yields to such pressures, s/he weakens the dynamic of experiential learning. The leader has then fallen victim to what Paul Tillich described as the fatal pedagogic error: "To throw answers like stones at the heads of those who have not yet asked the questions."[9]

In the face of conflicting pressures to function nondirectively or as an authoritarian expert, a resolution consistent with the principles of experiential education is afforded through the conception of the leader as a facilitator. The facilitator encourages people to use their own resources and to move at their own pace in dealing with the subject matter. In exercising the discipline to contain his/ her proclivity to "do for" group members, the leader is simultaneously making possible the expression of potential within the group. The source of this potential lies in people's natural curiosity and their desire for mastery and achievement. Once the leader discovers that group members will, indeed, respond, take initiative, and mobilize sound resources, s/he is reinforced for "trusting the process."

d. *Appropriate Leader Affects.* The novel format of the experiential approach, along with its expectations for the personal

9. Paul Tillich, quoted in George Isaac Brown, *Human Teaching for Human Learning* (New York: Viking Press, 1971), pp.15–16.

involvement of the participants, inevitably generates some anxiety—both for the leader and the participants. The manner in which the leader deals with this anxiety is an important determinant of the outcome of the program. If the leader deftly responds to the anxiety, s/he demonstrates the efficiency of the experiential approach and will elicit the trust of the participants. They recognize that in the course of the program they have experienced a transformation of their anxiety into a sense of well-being, even excitement. They move from apprehension and doubt to curiosity and eagerness for engagement.

A key ingredient in achieving and sustaining the transformation of anxiety is the affect communicated by the leader. By conveying a sense of his/her confidence in and enthusiasm for the experiential approach, the leader energizes the inclination of the participants to risk themselves and become involved, rather than to be cautious and remain passive. This is not a matter of inspirational leadership; it is a reflection of the leader's assuredness in what s/he is doing.

The assuredness of the leader communicates to participants the message that they can trust the leader and safely venture with him/her into uncharted territory. Trust in the leader is further promoted through his/her sensitivity to people—his/her ability to recognize and respond to the varying rhythms and needs of individuals as well as their collective uncertainties.

Caveats. The increasing availability of detailed descriptions of experiential activities plus the range of people who have used the approach make it appear that anyone can conduct experiential educational programs. This is not the case. When the approach is used by inadequately trained leaders, the likelihood is that its potential will be only partially tapped or, at worst, result in a negative experience. The most common danger with poor leadership results in a trivialization of the activities—using them as a sophisticated form of parlor game. Even with trained leaders, there are common traps which can undermine the success of the experiential method. These potential hazards, and suggestions for minimizing them, are described in the following four caveats:

a. Because the style of the experiential approach is informal and the activities are likely to be "fun," participants might tend to view an experiential program as an entertaining and distracting but not serious educational effort. This will occur when the leader's planning has not included a clear educational objective. The participants might initially respond favorably to the program, but upon reflection are apt to view it as nothing more than a series of interesting, although unrelated, activities. The antidote obviously lies in grounding the experiential activities in a learning/action objective. Utilization of advance or concurrent readings aids in focusing receptivity to the educational content; in addition, it helps the learner place his/her own personal experience in a broader social and historical context.

b. Experiential education is not the appropriate educational methodology for all phases and aspects of Jewish learning. It is a particularly useful technique for motivating learners and for making concepts come alive through the link to the participants' own experience, but it cannot by itself guarantee a well-rounded Jewish education. For example, the mastery of Jewish texts, the Hebrew language, and Jewish history all require formal teaching and diligent individualized work of an extended sort. If experiential activities are utilized wisely, they can serve to whet people's interest in their Jewishness and thereby lead them to augment their learning.

c. Experiential programs deal with the attitudes and feelings of people only as far as these relate to the subject matter under consideration, but not to explore interpersonal or intrapersonal relationships. These latter foci would be appropriate to deal with in an encounter or T-group, but not in an experiential education program. Provided the leader is clear on the issue, participants usually have little problem with this distinction. In the course of the group's proceedings, some participants are liable to become emotionally upset. This is a sign that the program is working—people are personally involved. It is unnecessary—even inappropriate—for the leader to seek to curtail the expression of feelings; instead s/he may seek to help people focus their feelings on issues rather than on other individuals.

d. For an experiential program to work well, spontaneity and creativity are important ingredients. Sometimes leaders become so comfortable with a particular program format that they indiscriminately use it for every group with which they work. This distorts the essence of experiential learning; the emphasis has inappropriately been placed on the activity and not on the process of personalized learning—the leader is operating mechanically, and his/her energies and interests are with the activity and not with the people with whom s/he is working. Activities can be categorized, but people cannot. All groups are different—they have different objectives, and the people who comprise the groups have different rhythms and different interests. Moreover, if a leader adheres repetitively to a fixed routine, his/her creativity and spontaneity are inevitably dulled, and this undesirable affect is transmitted to the group. It may just have to be accepted, as a burden of the method, that to work well in an experiential vein calls for developing a separate design for each new situation. One way to assure this freshness of approach is to be diligent about involving participants in the advance and ongoing stages of program planning.

SUMMARY

At a first glance, experiential leadership appears deceptively simple: present an experiential activity (according to the numbers) as described in the instruction book and then expect that a dramatic impact will inevitably follow. While it has been noted that there is significant potential in the use of experiential methodology, it has also been emphasized that its coming to fruition is not automatic and is dependent, rather, upon skillful application. The skill of experiential leadership is a function of achieving a subtle balance among a series of paradoxes and tensions; it requires both conceptual understandings and a disciplined use of oneself. In a sense, effective experiential leadership is a combination of science and artistry. It is the systematic application of knowledge, uniquely expressed to reflect the emotional commitment and personal style of the leader.

Notwithstanding the caveats here noted, experiential education is an effective means of communicating with people. It can be particularly useful for broadening the repertoire of approaches available in the Jewish community to more fully tap reservoirs of unused Jewish and human potential among individuals and organizations.

3

INFORMAL EDUCATION: SOME TOOLS AND TECHNIQUES

"People are the heart and the spirit of all that counts. Without people, there is no need for leaders. Leaders can decide to be primarily concerned with leaving assets to their institutional heirs, or they can go beyond that and capitalize on the opportunity to leave a legacy which provides greater meaning, more challenge, and more joy in the lives of those whom leaders enable."
—Max De Pree, *Leadership is an Art*, 1989. Max De Pree is Chairman of the Board of Directors of Herman Miller, Inc. and author of *Leadership Jazz, Leadership is an Art*, and *Leadership Without Power*.

          ❀   ❀   ❀

This chapter provides tools and techniques that will help the informal education practitioner. In particular, the methodologies given here will assist the practitioner in fulfilling the function of an enabler, a presence and force that can capture the interests and attention of people and help them, individually and collectively, learn from one another. What follows are an overview of conducting experiential activities taken from the first edition of this book; technical advice on topics including leadership style, dividing into subgroups, and conducting discussions; activities concerned with basic functions of groups; and a detailed treatment of one activity that illustrates distinctive aspects of experiential learning.

INTRODUCTION TO ACTIVITIES
(Reprinted from first edition)

DIFFERENT MODES OF EXPERIENTAL ACTIVITY

Among the various creative modes used in the experiential activities to engage the participants and to generate information or attitudes are the following: (1) *rankings and priorities*—forms or schedules which ask individual participants to determine preferences from among an array of value or behavioral options; (2) *role playing*—activities in which participants act out a structured or self-designed vignette; (3) *questionnaires and quizzes*—instruments designed to explore and extend substantive knowledge; (4) *expressive*—activities utilizing one of the artistic media (music, art, dance, drama) to create a mood or an experience; (5) *fantasy*—activities which encourage use of the imagination to provide new perspectives and insights; (6) *external stimuli*—use of objects, materials, or symbols to stimulate participant reactions; and (7) *lecturettes*—formal substantive presentations on some aspect of the group's agenda by the leader or other resource.

In all the experiential activities, there is a basic educational formula involving three components. First is *generating data*—the curiosity, concerns, and reactions evoked by the creative technologies. Second is *processing the data*—discussing participants' affective and cognitive reactions to the content. Finally, consideration is directed to *implications*—what principles and patterns have emerged, and in what ways do these affect the participants (individuals and organizations)?

Several different constellations of participants are prescribed in the activities, each with a somewhat different objective. These include: (1) *the individual*—many activities call for individual participation to encourage independent responses prior to the group give-and-take, and also, in concluding, to allow for considering personal implications; (2) *an intimate cluster*—such as a dyad, triad, or quartet—is an appropriate unit to provide stimulation and support for extending personal involvement in a subject with minimal risk; (3) *a small group*—usually comprising 5–12 participants—offers the advantage of a representative expression of views while still allowing for active participation and a personalized flavor; and (4) *a plenary session*, which brings all participants together for initial contracting, for introducing or concluding a unit of study, and for giving full rein to the diversity of ideas and values represented in that community.

THE AUDIENCE

The experiential activities are directed primarily at two audiences: *Jewish professionals* who might use the activities in their work with members of Jewish communal and religious organizations, and *Jewish learning communities*, self-directing units within the Jewish community that meet for programs of Jewish study, celebration, and fellowship (e.g. havurot, study groups, and informal collegial networks). Most of the experiential activities included in this book have been designed for use with some organizational entity within the Jewish community. They assume a critical mass in terms of numbers of participants and diversity of points of view. However, it is also possible for many of the activities to be used meaningfully by individual family units. Some activities may require adaptations for family use.

1. In the Beginning: Warm-ups and Tone-setting Activities.

The central objective of an opening activity is to set a tone which will facilitate the involvement of participants in a program. The opening activity seeks to counteract the initial anxiety people feel when coming to a new situation. Characteristically, on such occasions people are apt to be unsure of themselves, awkward about meeting others, and, accordingly, quite self-focused. As a result, little energy is available to be directed at learning new content. Further, their uncertainty leads the newcomers to be particularly dependent on the authority figure (leader) and to expect him/her to assume responsibility for whatever transpires.

This beginning set is not conducive to effective learning. The first activity seeks to move participants beyond their initial anxiety and passivity into a more active stance—one in which they are involved in the agenda of the program, and one in which they assume direct responsibility for their own learning.

The following are important components of a beginning activity.

1. *Introductions.* Since experiential approaches rely on the participants themselves as a vital ingredient in the learning, it is important that participants should get to know each other at the outset. As "strangers" get to talk, much of their initial tension and uncertainty dissipates. The participants begin to experience some trust in others and a sense of shared purpose. A learning community is launched. Also, to the extent that participants feel more secure in their environment, they have more energy available to them for investment in their learning objectives.

2. *A Participatory Environment.* A good first activity moves people from passive skepticism to active participation. To accomplish the goal of full participation, the activity should provide an opportunity for each person to do something—speak, write, or move physically. Many people are accustomed to attending classes or meetings where they never speak. They defer either to the teacher/leader or to more verbal fellow participants. An effective experiential opener is designed to provide an opportunity for everyone to participate. Once the "ice is broken," the typical nonparticipant finds it easier to sustain a more active role.

3. *"Throwaway" Subject Matter.* The subject matter of beginning activities ought to be simple and noncontroversial. In fact, given the primary objective of fostering a participatory flavor, it is appropriate that the content of the activity be of a "throwaway" nature. That is, no effort is invested in extracting substantive learning from this activity. Rather, the content serves as a medium for interaction and tone-setting. Leave a more substantive orientation for later activities.

4. *A Creative Ambience.* First impressions often determine the way people perceive an experience. Dr. Saul Wachs, professor of Jewish education at Gratz College in Philadelphia, has likened the beginning of a class or other learning experience to people sitting down to watch television. They turn the set on: if the program which appears seems interesting, they watch it; if not, they flip to another channel and watch it for a few seconds to decide whether it is interesting; if not, on to the next channel, and so on through the several channels. In a matter of 30 seconds they may cover the full range of offerings and then make the decision to either watch a particular program or turn off the set.

The objective of a first experiential activity is to "turn on" the participant—to whet his/her appetite for involvement. This heightening of interest is most likely to occur if the first activity captures the attention of the participant. The introduction of an experiential opener should make it apparent to participants that theirs will not be a routine class or meeting, with the teacher/leader doing all the talking and the participants settling into a passive state. Through their involvement in the activity, their interest is stimulated and their imagination is challenged. Moreover, since the ultimate purpose of a program is to help participants extend themselves intellectually and emotionally, the creative, nonroutine flavor of the opening activity sets a pattern for pursuing new insights and resolutions.

5. *A Jewish Environment.* A Jewish ambience contributes to fostering a sense of community; therefore, it is well that a Jewish component be introduced at the outset to blend with the other goals for a first activity. People can relate easily to others with similar backgrounds and interests; moreover, they share a common agenda—concern for meaningful Jewish continuity—the pursuit of which can be advanced by their work together. To the extent that a Jewish component enhances the objectives of an opening activity, it increases the receptivity in the remaining activities. In a broader sense, as Jewishness is effectively interwoven in the program, it interprets for the participants an organic approach to Jewishness—one in which the Jewish component is not seen as a burdensome "add-on," but rather as an authentic, integral, and enriching experience.

6. *Methodological Considerations.* Two variables to be considered in choosing a first activity are: (1) the size of the group, and (2) how well the participants know each other.

Concerning size: if a group has fewer than 25 participants, a single-circle activity in which each person presents some information about him/herself is appropriate. Such a format becomes awkward for larger groups. A single-circle activity is unsuited because it takes too much time, people become uncomfortable presenting themselves to a large group, and it is difficult to remember that many names. Accordingly, for larger groups it is preferable to use beginners that divide up the groups into subunits. This means that further introductions may need to be addressed in a later activity. However, if the group is so large and no extended contact of the participants is contemplated, one accepts that only a segment of the population can be personalized.

When a group is composed of strangers, beginning introductions seem appropriate and natural. When a group comes together whose participants know each other, introductions appear to be unnecessary, even foolish. Experience indicates that even people who have "known" each other for years may actually know little about one another personally. Therefore, it is useful to include personal introductions even with groups of acquaintances. The one variation in such cases would be to avoid having acquaintances present obvious descriptive information, and instead seek less typical, personal background facts and experiences. One final methodological consideration: An ideal amount of time for a beginning activity is 30 minutes—with 45 minutes for larger groups. The point is that a beginning activity is a tone-setter—an activity to help prepare participants for work on the agenda; it is not the major focus at the session. A potential problem with a beginning activity—especially those in which participants go around in a circle and tell something about themselves—is that the activity may become too extended if group members get carried away by the opportunity to talk. For example, in a group of 20 people, if each person took 5 minutes, the activity would run for over an hour and a half. Two suggestions for avoiding such an eventuality:

a) The leader is explicit about time limits in his/her instructions ("each person should speak briefly—a maximum of 2 minutes"). Also, the leader indicates a general outline of the rest of the agenda so the participants know that other activities are forthcoming (with possible listings of time allotments.)

b) A more structured approach is for the leader to ask for a volunteer timekeeper. This person's instructions are to use a watch to allow each speaker a maximum of 2 (or whatever) minutes time. The timekeeper announces when 2 minutes are up. Because the timekeeper is also a member of the group, his/her intrusions are accepted by the others, thereby avoiding a situation in which the leader is forced to limit participants.

7. *The Leader's Role.* Proceeding with innovative learning experiences imposes a burden on a leader. To begin with, the learners raise an inevitable initial resistance to getting involved. In a traditional educational approach, not much is expected of the learners—they can slide into their chairs and wait for the teacher/leader to assume the initiative and responsibility. When the leader decides on an experiential approach, s/he has also committed the learners to a role of active participation. How do the learners feel about this? Are they resentful? Will they agree to participate?

In choosing an innovative approach, the risk for a leader is further extended by the possibility of failure. If the leader functions traditionally, little attention is focused on failure, largely because ineffectual educational experiences are not uncommon. When s/he breaks from the mainstream, however, this draws attention to the methodology and if it does not work, the responsibility for its failure rests fully with the leader.

This burden is particularly felt by a leader as s/he is about to embark on an experiential program. At that juncture, the temptation is great to avoid the risk and "go straight." Several considerations are helpful to the leader in coping with the fears attendant upon launching an experiential program. It is well to remind oneself of two basic facts of human nature: most people get greater satisfaction from being active rather than passive, and most people welcome opportunities to be linked with other people. Further, knowing in advance that uncertainty is intrinsic to introducing the experiential process can help the leader maintain his/her resolve. This becomes easier after several outings and the reinforcement of favorable outcomes. But even individuals with considerable experience with the methodology continue to experience uncertainty at the outset of a program. Previous experience affords the advantage that one is not surprised when doubts emerge, and one can automatically set into motion the predetermined strategy: pursue the original approach despite any last-minute reservations which may arise.

Doubt and tentativeness on the part of the leader are highly contagious. If group members sense uncertainty, it serves to activate their own apprehensions and make them more wary of getting involved. On the other hand, to the extent that participants sense that their leader is assured and competent, they are encouraged to follow his/her lead, and are encouraged themselves to risk moving into new territory. Once helped to "leap" into the first activity, the participants will receive gratification from their active involvement that will, in turn, provide the momentum for the rest of the program. All of this is to highlight the importance of the conviction and assuredness with which the leader introduces the first activity—despite an awareness of underlying doubts.

NOTES TO ACTIVITY LEADERS: IMPORTANCE OF FLEXIBILITY

A good leader operates with confidence in the planned activities, faith in the wisdom of informal education, and optimism about the disposition and capabilities of the group. Even so, the leader must be ready and willing to change when circumstances demand it. Numerous things may happen: more or less attendance than expected, change in weather conditions affecting an outdoor activity, a change in mood or loss of interest within the group. The leader should be familiar with the material, know how to adapt it, have back-up plans, and in general be willing to deviate from a pre-determined program.

Every program must be tailored to the personal characteristics, knowledge, experience and expectations of the particular group. A straightforward example of this principle is the quiz in "The Shabbat Table" activity. The quiz is not an end in itself, intended to convey a fixed body of content, but rather one component of an activity that has other, experiential components. Thus it is important that the questions be attuned to the level of Jewish knowledge within the group. Another example pertains to the mood of the group. If energy is low or members of the group appear resistant to the concept of experiential learning, a role play may not be an appropriate activity.

Selecting and designing effective activities calls for flexibility on the part of the leader. Most of the activities in this book come with explicit instructions. However, the leader is not bound to conduct them exactly as described. Indeed, an almost unlimited variety of activities could be formed by adapting the different techniques of informal education illustrated in this book to other educational content and needs as appropriate. Following are guidelines for adapting a program to meet the needs of a particular situation, taken from *Jewish Youth Sourcebook*.

"Your organization is a unique place given its geographic location, population, size, facilities, resources, and leadership. It undoubtedly has its own 'personality' and a particular role it has carved out in the community. Your Youth Program also differs in important ways from other Youth Programs. Given these unique qualities, it is vital to consider how a program idea should be modified to fit the particulars of your teens and your organization.

"The ideas presented here are *starting points* from which to develop programs most suitable for your situation. Programs can be adapted in a number of ways:

1. Keep the general technique but change the specific content.
2. Keep the theme but change the methods and activities.
3. Keep the program but adapt to a different audience.
4. Keep the program but re-design for a different setting.
5. Change a single activity into an on-going program.
6. Scale programs up or down to match resources.
7. Expand the program by building creative connections to other groups, organizations, agencies and resources in your community.
8. Enhance the program by seeing it as an opportunity to further Jewish learning." (Simon Klarfeld and Dr. Amy Sales, *Jewish Youth Sourcebook*, Waltham, MA: Jewish Community Center Association and Cohen Center for Modern Jewish Studies, Brandeis University, 1996.)

DIVIDING THE GROUP

A large number of informal or experiential education activities are conducted in small groups. Small groups, ideally between 5 and 10 people, afford a greater degree of participation and increase people's interest in the task at hand. They are large enough to provide diversity of viewpoints and small enough so that everyone feels directly involved. Thus, a small group is a natural vehicle for experiential learning. It engages the students/group members directly in the subject being addressed, and thereby enhances their learning and capacity to internalize and/or take action on the subject.

The teacher/leader can use the task of dividing into groups as an opportunity to capture group members' attention and encourage them to take risks. Instead of dividing people based on some neutral attribute—e.g., alphabetical order of names or where people are seated—the leader might choose an arbitrary category, for instance, favorite ice cream flavor or sports team. Group members are asked to form a group with others who state the same preference. Establishing groups in this way may instill in group members the feeling that they already have something in common and reinforce their identity as a group with a shared mission.

This approach works best when the leader is not too concerned about the number or sizes of groups. When that is the case, the leader may predetermine categories and assign people to different groups by distributing slips of paper with the names of the groups. Choosing groups from an appealing category, e.g., Jewish holidays, will have a beneficial effect on group identity.

GROUND RULES FOR USEFUL DISCUSSIONS

This presentation of "Ground Rules for Useful Discussions" is taken from a publication of Study Circles Resource Center. Address: 697 Pomfret St., P.O. Box 203, Pomfret, CT 06258–0203. Telephone: 860–928–2616. Web address: www.studycircles .org.

Whether you are talking with close friends or casual acquaintances, effective communication requires that you respect others and take their ideas seriously—even when you think they're dead wrong.

Talk about public issues can bring out strong emotions, because many of our beliefs are a large part of how we identify ourselves. You can respect another's feelings without necessarily agreeing with the conclusions that person has come to.

There are no sure-fire rules, but applying some basic principles will make your conversations more productive, satisfying, and enjoyable. Though many of these ground rules seem commonsensical, we all know that in practice they are not so commonly applied!

- Listen carefully to others. Try to really understand what they are saying and respond to it, especially when their ideas differ from you own. Try to avoid building your own arguments in your head while others are talking.
- Think together about what you want to get out of your conversations.
- Respect the confidential nature of personal stories.
- Be open to changing your mind; this will help you really listen to others' views.
- When disagreement occurs, keep talking. Explore the disagreement. Search for the common concerns beneath the surface. Above all, be civil.
- Value one another's experiences, and think about how they have contributed to group members' thinking.
- Help to develop one another's ideas. Listen carefully and ask clarifying questions.

JEWISH QUOTES

Purpose:

To stimulate people's thinking about various aspects of the Jewish experience by exposing them to key ideas about the Jewish people or Judaism, which have been articulated in basic Jewish texts by Jewish writers, thinkers, and statesmen, and by non-Jews.

Group:

Junior high school and older; groups of any size are possible, since the activity is conducted in small clusters.

Setting: An open room with movable chairs to allow for different groupings.

Materials:

Individual quotes can be prepared in advance either on slips of paper to be distributed to participants or on signs to be posted on the wall. Each participant is given paper and a pencil.

Time: Depending on the number of quotes used, the activity can sustain interest for up to 1½ hours.

Instructions:

1. The group is divided up into small discussion groups of 6–8 people. One quote is presented to the group-either distributed on a slip of paper or as a sign posted on the wall. Each person is asked to think about his/her reactions to the statement and to make notes. (This is done to encourage each individual to come up with his/her own ideas before interacting with others.)
2. Participants are asked to share their reactions with others. This can be done in small units-dyads or triads-followed by a discussion in the larger unit of 6–8 people, or the discussion can initially be conducted in the 6–8 person group. The leader serves as a discussion leader: keeping focus, limiting overly verbose participants, trying to involve people who haven't spoken, and summarizing when the discussion has run its course.
3. Other related quotes can be used following the same procedure.
4. If there are several concurrent groups, the leader may choose to convene the full group for a summary discussion of the insights generated by the quotes.

Notes to the Leader:

There is an extensive selection of quotes at the end of each chapter. The leader can choose from this list to weave the quote(s) into the planned experiential program.

Variations:

A. AN EXCHANGE. The leader may encourage the expression of different opinions with respect to the quotes. This can be done by asking the participants to divide up on the basis of their reactions to the ideas represented by the quote. One approach, appropriate with a small group (18 or fewer) and with quote material where there might be differences of opinion, is to have the group split into two subgroups: those who are essentially in agreement with the views expressed, and those who disagree. The two groups should be asked to assemble on either side of the room, and then to meet in their separate groups to discuss their thinking on the issue. This can lead to a cross-discussion in which both sides exchange their views, or it can be structured more formally, in a debate. For a debate, each side chooses two persons to represent its arguments, and they proceed, taking turns to argue their positions.

With larger groups (over 18 people), the leader prepares in advance four signs—*strongly agree, agree, disagree, strongly disagree*—which are posted in the four corners of the room. After the quote is presented, the participants are asked to move to the corner which most closely represents their views on this subject. At the corners they exchange ideas and then the leader calls for an open discussion across the four positions.

B. PROJECTIONS. Particularly with younger groups or with family units, the groups are asked to respond to the quote by depicting what the quote means to them, using an artistic medium (e.g., a tableau, a short play, or a graphic representation made with arts and crafts materials). This is followed by a discussion of the different interpretations.

C. THEMES. Several quotes covering a broad historical time span and with related ideas are given to participants. They are asked to find a common theme in the quotes. This is especially effective with such themes as: the distinctiveness of the Jew, the centrality of Zion in the thought of the Jew, anti-Semitism, and the "chosen people" motif.

ACTIVE LISTENING

Purpose:

To teach participants how to listen constructively to another person.

Active listening is a skill that benefits both speaker and listener. The person who needs to speak has the chance to speak freely with no interruption. Mirroring back what the listener just heard shows the speaker that they were not only heard, but that they were understood.

Often, when we are talking to each other, things that the person says brings forth an association that the natural course of conversation allows us to share. The skill of active listening consists in setting aside our association or judgemental response, so that the person speaking can be the center of attention, focusing both the speaker and listener on whatever problem or issue they are discussing.

Materials:

A watch or timer.

Instructions:

1. The leader states that the aim of this activity is to help participants become better listeners. The group is divided into pairs. One person in each pair should be designated an "A" and the other a "B."
2. Within each pair the A talks to the B for one-and-a-half minutes about an experience s/he had that day. (The leader should be strict about keeping the time.) The B should focus all his/her energy on listening. Then, the B repeats in his/her own words the story that s/he has just heard. The A may correct the B until the story is repeated correctly. After this, the B should relate what s/he experienced during the retelling of the story. Comments should begin with the phrase "It sounds like . . ." For instance, "It sounds like this was a difficult time for you." Or, "It sounds like you wished you were in Hawaii instead of the Caribbean."
3. The process is repeated with B's speaking and A's listening and mirroring.
4. The leader re-assembles the group for a discussion of the experience in pairs. Questions to address include:
   - What did it feel like to speak without interruption?
   - What did it feel like to hear what you had said told back to you?

- How was it to correct the person who was repeating your
  story to you?
- What did it feel like to sit silently and listen without adding your own experience into the story?
- What was it like to listen knowing you were going to have
  to repeat back what you just heard?

5. Finally, the group should engage in a general assessment of
   how they felt and what they learned.

THE LARGE GATHERING

Purpose:

To provide awareness of how the individual functions in group
settings and to encourage empathy with how other people may
feel.

Group:

Participants in a leadership development program.

Instructions:

1. The leader reads the following scenario.

   "You are about to enter a large gathering of people. You are
   nervously anticipating this event. Will you know anyone? Most
   people have friends who will be coming to this gathering. They
   are members of one of several clubs. The members of the clubs
   all wear a distinctive badge indicating the club to which they
   belong.

   "Unfortunately, you are not a member of any club. You feel
   very much alone. You don't really know anyone at the large
   gathering and you feel like an outsider. While there may be
   several other non-club people present who are also outsiders,
   you really don't want to have anything to do with them.

   "If one of the clubs would be willing to have you, you would
   be very pleased. But you don't want to push yourself. You
   watch from the sidelines to see if any of the clubs give you a

sign of welcome or encouragement. If not, you might just stand around and watch quietly, or if you want to take a chance and can mobilize the courage, you might reach out to one of the clubs to see if they would welcome you into their ranks. However, you certainly want to avoid putting yourself in the position of being rejected.

"It may be that you will remain a loner throughout the gathering watching with some envy the activities of the clubs."
2. The group reflects on and discusses reactions to the scenario.
   • Have you ever experienced a similar situation?
   • Did anyone reach out to welcome you?
   • How did you feel in that situation?
   • Are you someone who would notice a newcomer and be likely to reach out and welcome that person?

MASSADA—WHERE WOULD *YOU* STAND?
An Interactive Interpretation of Site and Story

The following article was written by Zohar Raviv for inclusion in this book. First, he presents a theoretical basis for the function of narratives and setting in experiential education. Second, he presents an activity concerned with the martyrdom at Massada which provided the impetus for the theoretical discussion.

Preliminary Thoughts on Experiential Education

A conventional class-setting educational process relies primarily on thought and analysis, as no immediate connection necessarily exists between the studied topic and the physical arena the participants are in, namely the classroom. An experiential educational process, on the other hand, engages all senses to promote its agenda and exposes the student to an environment that corresponds—and ultimately supports—its respective educational goals. By surrounding the participant with a complex and immediate physical arena, it furnishes a broad range of stimuli with which our senses interact, and to which both intellect and emotions respond.

An educational endeavor based on an experiential process,

relies therefore on a complex environment that corresponds with an equally complex set of cognitive, emotional, and motivational sensibilities of individuals. Hence, I shall call such an educational setting a "Corresponding Environment."

As educators, two preliminary points should integrate and underline our approach, if we wish for our corresponding environments to *support*, rather than *interfere with*, our educational rationale:

1) Assess the nature of our educational goals at any given program. What are the messages we wish to promote? These need to be kept simple and well-articulated.
2) Orchestrate our chosen environments to *adequately* correspond with the educational goals to which we expose our students: Make sure that the physical arena, as well as all other educational means used (texts, props, etc.) support, give rise to and enhance the messages we try to convey.

With the above in mind, I wish to approach the following Massada program.

Massada

Massada surely stands as one of the most popular and well-known historic sites in Israel. Located in the Judean desert, the majestic table-mount evokes awe and carries one's mind to a history that should not easily be forgotten. Massada, indeed, is the sort of site that can carry its own weight without the help of the educator and/or tour guide. Nature at its best and the memory of a mythic narrative offer a powerful experience to the explorer who walks its trails. Everyone knows of Massada, yet very few actually learn to meet it face-to-face and struggle with its multi-layered enigma.

The above reasons might actually present Massada as one of the hardest sites to lead and teach. As our students come to the site with a set of pre-conceived assumptions and a well-constructed romantic view of the historical narrative (good vs. evil, heroism in its classic form, Judaism at its bravest moments, independence etc.), we—the educators—need to carefully examine the ways by which such views can be balanced with a sounder understanding of the subject matter. In that respect, we should aim to furnish our audience with an experience that is both grounded in the textual bodies of evidence (in this case only one—a powerful message in and of itself), while utilizing the site as a corresponding environment with which the "spirit of the story" can be experienced. A healthy combination of these two aspects may allow us a structured environment that challenges our audience and pushes them toward a more careful analysis of Jewish history, its literary expression and above all the relevance of their relationships with such narratives.

Telling a Story vs. Entering a Story—The Four Dimensions of the Text

A conventional approach to text-study usually looks at the text in its apparent two-dimensional form; black letters on white paper or parchment. The text, even if interesting and intriguing, cannot be seen as a representation of a human voice, a spirit that gives it rise. Moreover, since the text is not perceived as a testimony to the living souls of our past, so is the spirit of the reader not fully corresponding with its deeper realms.

In fact, we should strive to present our texts in a four-dimensional format: The *author*, the letters, the sheets and the *reader*. Out of these four, it is the author and the reader who actually possess the ability to connect present with past in a powerful way: Allow our present students a gate into the soul behind the texts and, by extension, re-affirm their own souls as the important vehicles through which the story can be understood, questioned and challenged. They are the recipients of the story and their souls should adhere to that of the author(s). In such a manner the text itself becomes a bridge between the soul of the past and that of the present—a bridge that allows our students to understand how history, in all its magnitude and overwhelming complexity, is a web of *human* interactions, thoughts and deeds. Humans, with flaws and fears, joys and laughter, deep beliefs and harsh skepticism . . . humans, like we all are!

It is through the art of connecting souls that the real potential and beauty of our texts comes to surface. The text becomes the *Shofar* that echoes a real sound, a two-dimensional world that hides within it the tear of a man, the joy of a child, the fear of pain, or the beauty of life. But more than anything, when we allow the text a living soul and enter the narrative rather than simply tell it, we should also listen to its untold stories.

Massada is a classic example.

Massada—The Untold Story

Being such a well-known story, there is no need for us to retell the events of Massada in their entirety here. It is a story that has all the ingredients of a classic Hollywood movie (which indeed it has become.) This program shall focus on one aspect of this highly acclaimed, albeit highly controversial, story: the mass suicide at Massada, starting with the speech by the leader of the Zealots, Elazar Ben Yair, exhorting his followers to commit suicide rather than be taken by the Romans.

Contrary to popular understanding, Elazar Ben Yair's speech is in fact *two* speeches, being divided by an interim stage of contemplation (and hesitation) on the part of his listeners. The two speeches, arguably, can be considered to reflect Ben Yair the military leader vs. Ben Yair the spiritual-religious leader.

The following activity focuses on the time between the two speeches—the time when each one of the 967 Jews on top of Massada needed to decide how to respond to Ben Yair's powerful first speech. Although that moment is quite obscure in the unfolding of our story, it was of supreme importance to those present. It thus has great potential to function as a *bridge of souls*.

Massada—Where would *You* Stand?

Goals and Objectives

Each educator should create his/her own focus and aims. The following is a summation of goals for the activity stemming from the philosophy elaborated above.

1) Allow a meaningful encounter with the people of Massada through the process of decision-making in response to Ben Yair's demand.

2) Allow a better understanding of the Massada story and, by

extension, to raise awareness of the complexity of any historical narrative.

3) Allow a well-informed involvement with textual materials that
are relevant to our subject matter (suicide, killing, sanctifica-
tion of G-d's name, etc.)

4) Structure an environment through which the people of Massada are seen as human beings rather than heroes (or not) in a
simple/romantic form.

5) Create a learning atmosphere through which participants can
explore issues, values and beliefs in a manner relevant to their
own lives.

6) Allow participants a sense of ownership over the subject
matter.

7) Create a learning environment that redefines the nature of
"study" and "text".

8) Expose the participants to the richness of Jewish thought
regarding the relevant issues raised in this program: Questions
regarding the sanctity of life, the permission (or lack thereof)
to take one's life, etc.

Setting and Preparations

1) Location: Preferably Massada, although it can be done as preparation for a visit or—with some modification—in a camp or
other educational setting.

2) Time: 1½–1¾ hours.

3) Timing within the Program: If done at Massada, use it as the
concluding piece of your visit. (Do not tell participants about
Ben Yair's speech beforehand.)

4) Suitable Age for Participants: 14 and up, suitable for adults of
all ages.

5) Preliminary Preparations:
   (a) A shady location for the sub-groups. (There are some good
   spots next to the Roman Bath House or next to the Hero-
   dian Western Palace.)
   (b) An Elazar Ben Yair costume. (Be creative.)
   (c) Elazar Ben Yair speeches—Divide between the two.
   (d) Sub-groups—Between 3 and 5 participants in each.
   (e) One participant (preferably with natural leadership skills)

to be prepared in advance for the role of Ben Yair, to deliver the first speech.

(f) Appoint (from staff or participants) a moderator for each sub-group. They should be prepared in advance and be familiar with the goals and objectives illustrated above.

(g) Pens and papers—Given to each sub-group or each participant.

(h) Textual sources for discussions. (See Supplement.)

Structure of Program

1) Situate the entire group in one place. They should be, at this point, familiar with the site and the different historical events that had taken place there. They should not (as of yet) be told about the end of Massada.

2) 10–15 Minutes: Create the right mood for the story about to be told. You may either use Josephus Flavius' own account *The Jewish Wars* (the only text that actually refers to Massada) or present the story in a way that suits you. In any event, the story should be told so as to prepare the stage for the entrance of Elazar Ben Yair and his first speech.

3) 5 Minutes: Elazar Ben Yair's first speech: This should be staged carefully, for it may "make or break" the program. You may want to hide "Ben Yair" and allow a more dramatic entrance, or use any method you deem suitable. Be advised, however, not to take this phase lightly.

4) 5–10 Minutes: After the speech, present the participants with the core questions. "Where do *you* stand?" "How do *you* react to this demand (not only as teenagers, but also as [potential] parents, as Jews, etc.)?" "What is your answer in this case, understanding that you have to back it up with actions?" Each sub-group should return with an answer to Ben Yair's first speech. Allow participants to ask you questions or provide time for clarifications regarding the task.

5) Give each group moderator the materials needed (pens, paper, a copy of Ben Yair's first speech and the added textual sources.) Send each sub-group to a location of its own. It is recommended not to send them too far from each other, yet at the same time allow them the needed space for a distraction-free discussion.

6) 30 Minutes: Group discussions in relation to the different texts. Circulate among the sub-groups and note to yourself some of the main points raised by the different groups.
7) 30 Minutes: Sub-groups reassemble. Each presents its conclusions and remarks. The educator's role here is of utmost importance: Encourage discussion between sub-groups, juxtaposing different views and clarifying some of the similarities between the various groups.
8) 5 Minutes: Elazar Ben Yair's second speech.
9) 5 Minutes: Conclusion of main points and a summation of main goals and objectives of the program.

Supplement—Textual Sources

"And I shall hold each soul responsible for its blood. Every living creature I shall hold responsible and from every human I shall claim the human soul. He who spills the blood of a fellow human, his blood shall be also spilled, for the human was created in the image of G-d." (*Genesis* 9:5–6)

"And the [Jewish] courts of law are warned not to allow a compensation from a murderer for the soul of the victim . . . for the soul of the victim is only G-d's possession. And there is no matter that the Torah has been as strict about as the spilling of [human] blood." (Maimonides, *Mishneh Torah*, "The Laws of a Murderer")

"[A man] is not allowed to strike his fellow man, even should the latter ask him to do so. For a man has no right whatsoever over his [fellow man's] body, to hit him, nor to put him to shame, nor cause him any sorrow." (Maimonides, *Mishneh Torah*, "Laws Regarding Harming Body and Soul")

"And one Rabbi was slaughtering many [Jewish] babies at the time of the great [Roman] persecutions, fearing they might be converted. And there was with him another Rabbi who got angry and yelled at him, 'Murderer.' And trying to prevent [the first Rabbi] he continued to rebuke him and said, 'Maybe if you didn't kill them the persecutions would have stopped and they could have been saved.'" (Beit Yosef, *Yoreh De'ah*, 157)

"And the righteous man should not love the life in this world. For it is only a step by which he can elevate himself to the life to come, not simply for itself. (And why was the human heart given the love of this world?) Only to prevent a man from killing himself when trouble came into his path." (*The Book of Beliefs and Concerns*, Rabbi Sa'adiya Gaon, 10th essay, 11)

"When a 'star worshiper' [meaning a pagan] forces a Jew to either violate any of the commandments of the Torah or to die, [the Jew] must violate the Torah and not die. For it is said, 'And you shall live by it.' Live and not die. And if [the Jew] prefers to die, he is condemned. . . . And the exceptions are *idolatry, incest*, and *shedding blood*." (Maimonides, *Hilchot Yesod Torah (The Laws of the Torah's Foundations)*, 5th chapter, A)

"For the human was created only to work for his creator, and whoever doesn't surrender his body for the work of his master is not a good servant. [And if we find] people giving their souls for their masters, wouldn't it be moreso for the commandment of the Holy One, Blessed be He?!" (Aharon Zalhah, *The Book of Education*, 268)

"If the Gentiles come to a group of Jews and demand that a random Jew will be given to them to be killed, otherwise they will all die—they should all die and not surrender a soul of Israel. But if the Gentiles have demanded a specific person, the Jews should surrender that person instead of all die." (*Toseftah, Tractate Berachot*, 80)

"A one-day-old infant . . . he who kills him must be punished, for he is like a groom in his wedding to his father, mother and his entire family." (*Mishnah, Nidah*, 85, 43)

QUOTES

Effort is our own reward. We are here to do. And through doing to learn, and through learning to know; and through knowing to experience wonder; and through wonder to attain wisdom; and through wisdom to find simplicity; and through simplicity to give attention; and through attention to see what needs to be done . . .

Pirkei Avot 5:27

Not study, but practice is the main thing.

Rabbi Shimon ben Gamliel,
Pirkei Avot 1:17

Let your practice keep step with your knowledge.

Chinese fortune cookie saying

Learning is great, because learning leads to action.

Talmud Kiddushim 40b

Only parable can express the full complexity of our times. If you define your subject too precisely you'll stifle its living richness. But if you tell a story, then your listeners will sense everything that the story may contain . . . This is the way to make ideas grow.

Rene Dubos (1901–1982), French-born
American bacteriologist

Example is not the main thing in influencing others. It is the only thing.

Albert Schweitzer (1875–1965)

The trouble with using experience as a guide is that the final exam often comes first and then the lesson.

Anonymous

The country is your classroom.

Israeli t-shirt slogan

A child educated only at school is an uneducated child.

George Santayana (1863–1952)

I hear it and I forget; I see it and I remember; I do and I understand.

Confucius (551–479 B.C.E.)

A good idea without discussion is like a hidden treasure from which nothing is extracted.

Rabbi Solomon ibn Gabirol
(1020–1057)

I see no more than you, but I have trained myself to notice what I see.

Sherlock Holmes, fictional character created by Arthur Conan Doyle
(1859–1930)

Only learning that is enjoyed will be learned well.

Judah Ha-Nasi (135–219)

Messages that come from the heart, go to the heart.

Talmud

People want to be amused, not preached at, you know. Morals don't sell nowadays.

Louisa May Alcott (1832–1888),
Little Women, 1868

The fatal pedagogic error is for the teacher to throw answers, like stones, at the heads of those who have not yet asked the questions.

Paul Tillich (1886–1965)

You know more than you think you do.

Dr. Benjamin Spock (1903–1998)

It is for our own good that we learn Torah and forget it; because if we studied Torah and never forgot it, the people would struggle with learning it for two or three years, resume ordinary work, and never pay further attention to it. But since we study Torah and forget it, we don't abandon its study.

Kohelet Rabbah I 13:1

Minds are like parachutes, they only function when open.

Bumper sticker

The essence of faith is in the power of imagination, because whatever the intelligence understands has no connection to faith.

Rabbi Nachman of Bratslav
(1772–1811)

Imagination is more important than intelligence.

Albert Einstein (1879–1955)

If you wish to see the valley, climb to the top. If you desire to see the mountain, rise into the clouds. But if you seek to understand the clouds, close your eyes and think.

Kahlil Gibran (1883–1931)

Whoever is ashamed to ask, will diminish in wisdom among men.

Moses Ibn Ezra (11th c.), *Shirat Yisrael*

Whoever is not ashamed to ask, will in the end be exalted.

Samuel ben Nahman (3rd c.),
B.T. Berachot 63b

A wise person's question is half the answer.

Solomon Ibn Gabirol (1020–1057)

The truly wise question the wisdom of others because they question their own wisdom as well, the foolish, because it is different than their own.

Rabbi Leopold Stein (1810–1882),
Journey into the Self

The wise man is astonished by anything.

Andre Gidé (1869–1951)

What is a human being after all but a question? One is here to ask and only to ask, to ask honestly and boldly, and to wait humbly for an answer.

Rachel Varnhagen (1771–1833),
German salon leader

Letter to Adam von Müller, December 15, 1820

Our little children know how to ask good questions. We evade answering them.

Israel Eldad (1910–1996), "The Victory
of the Wise Son," *Hegyonot Chazal*

Unless you call out, who will answer the door?

Ethiopian proverb

It is an old saying: Ask a Jew a question, and the Jew answers with a question. Every answer given arouses new questions. The progress of knowledge is matched by an increase in the hidden and mysterious.

> Rabbi Leo Baeck (1873–1956),
> *Judaism and Science*, 1949

Hillel would say: the bashful pupil cannot learn and the pedantic (overly strict, quick to anger) teacher cannot teach.

> *Pirkei Avot* 3:5

A theology student once asked Martin Luther, "What did God do before He created the world?" And his answer was, "God was making Hell for those who are inquisitive."

> Martin Luther (1483–1546)

Men's curiosity searches past and future . . .

> T.S. Eliot (1888–1965)

Curiosity is one of the permanent and certain characteristics of a vigorous intellect.

> Samuel Johnson (1709–1784)

The important thing is never to stop questioning.

> Albert Einstein (1879–1955)

Make for yourself a teacher and acquire for yourself a friend.

> *Pirkei Avot* 1:6, Rabbi Yehoshua
> ben Perachya

. . . the teacher is the creator of the future of our people . . .

> Rabbi Abraham Joshua Heschel
> (1907–1972)

The education of children must never be interrupted, even to rebuild the Temple.

> *Talmud Shabbath* 119b

Rabbah bar Hanah said: "Why are the works of Torah likened to fire, as in the verse, 'Is not My word like as fire? Saith the Lord.' (*Jeremiah* 23:29)? To teach you that just as fire does not ignite of itself, so the words of Torah do not abide in him who studies by himself."

T.B. Ta'anit 7a

Learning is achieved only in company.

Talmud Berakoth 63

Don't say, "When I have leisure, I will study." Perhaps you will never have leisure.

Pirkei Avot, Hillel 2:5

Move to a place where there is learning; you can't expect learning to move to you.

Pirkei Avot 4:5

Education is a companion which no misfortune can depress, no crime can destroy, no enemy can alienate . . . At home a friend, abroad an introduction, in solitude a solace, and in society an ornament.

Joseph Addison (1672–1719)

A room without books is like a body without a soul.

Cicero (106–43 B.C.E.)

BOOKS AND ARTICLES ON INFORMAL AND EXPERIENTIAL EDUCATION

1. Almond, Richard, *Dynamics of the Therapeutic Milieu*, New York: Jason Aronson, 1974.
2. Band, Adrianne and Ron Wolfson (eds.), *First Fruit: A Whizin Anthology of Jewish Family Education*, Los Angeles: Shirley and Arthur Whizin Institute, 1998.
3. Elkins, Dov Peretz, *Jewish Guided Imagery: A How-to Book for Rabbis, Educators and Group Leaders*, Princeton, NJ: Growth Associates, 1996.
4. Frankel, Mindy and Nancy Nelson (eds.), *Informal Jewish Education Activities*, Waltham, MA: Hornstein Program, Brandeis Univ., 1995.

5. Glasser, Paul, Rosemary Sarri, and Robert Vinter, *Individual Change through Small Groups*, New York: The Free Press, 1974.
6. Lieberman, Morton A., Irvin D. Yalom and Mathew B. Miles, *Encounter Groups: First Facts*, New York: Basic Books, 1973.
7. Phillips, Gerald M., Douglas Pedersen and Julia T. Woods, *Group Discussion: A Practical Guide to Participation and Leadership*, Chapel Hill, NC: Houghton Mifflin, 1979.
8. Reisman, Bernard, *The Jewish Experiential Book: The Quest for Jewish Identity*, New York: KTAV Publishing House, 1979.
9. Shumofsky, Julie (ed.), *Highlights of Informal Jewish Education Activities*, Waltham, MA: Hornstein Program, Brandeis Univ., 1998.
10. Siegel, Richard and Carl Rheins, *The Jewish Almanac: Traditions, History, Religion, Wisdom, Achievements*, New York: Bantam Books, 1980.
11. Siegel, Richard, Michael Strassfeld and Sharon Strassfeld, *The Jewish Catalogue*, Philadelphia: Jewish Publication Society, 1973.
12. Simon, Sidney, *Caring, Feeling and Touching*, Niles, IL: Argus Communications, 1976.
13. Simon, Sidney B., Leland W. Howe and Howard Kirschenbaum, *Values Clarification: A Handbook of Practical Strategies for Teachers and Students*, New York: A & W Visual Library, 1978.
14. Strassfeld, Sharon and Michael Strassfeld, *The Second Jewish Catalogue*, Philadelphia: Jewish Publication Society, 1976.
15. Yankelovitch, Daniel, *New Rules: Searching for Self-Fulfillment in a World Turned Upside Down*, New York: Random House, 1981.

4

ICEBREAKERS AND MIXERS

Any experiential education program should begin with activities designed to prepare participants for the work at hand. The opening activities of a program serve many purposes, among them, introducing participants to each other, giving people energy for the tasks that follow, assisting people to overcome their fear or resistance, fostering a sense of group identity and purpose, and establishing a tone where people are comfortable participating.

The term "icebreaker" brings to mind a frozen sea and a ship opening a passage through the ice. It is an apt term for activities that assist participants in breaking through barriers posed by anxiety, fear of the unknown, and accustomed routine. "Mixers" are activities whose primary purpose is to introduce people.

Opening activities perform a critical function in introducing participants to the style of experiential education. These activities will be participants' first exposure to the expectations of experiential education. At the core of learning is the concept of *risking*, approaching routine tasks and roles in new ways. The group leader can facilitates awareness of this concept by modeling it in his/her own behavior. As the students observe their teacher employing a non-traditional, informal mode of teaching, they are emboldened to try out new ideas and attitudes themselves.

Another function of opening activities is to welcome people and provide an opportunity for group members to meet one another. The exchange may be a simple introduction by name or may extend to information about personal characteristics or interests that reflect the uniqueness of each person. Even when participants already know each other or work together, a mixer is valuable. In such a setting, a mixer ensures that every person is introduced and that existing patterns of interaction based on social ties or working relationships are replaced with democratic interaction among all group members. As participants learn about others in the group, so does the group leader. The information gained may help the leader adjust the content and pace of the educational program.

Another function is to create an environment that fosters active and creative participation by the group members/students. The opening activities should set a tone that captures the attention of participants and makes it likely that they will assume an active learning role.

Related to this is establishment of "safe space". Experiential education often involves sharing ideas, memories or personal information that might seem difficult to speak about openly in a group, particularly among strangers. Therefore it is important to build a climate where people feel comfortable with others in the group, the nature of the activities, and their participation in them. Presence of a safe space reassures group members that they will be accepted, supported and embraced as they take part in the educational process.

Although the activities in this chapter do not necessarily contain Jewish content, they can play a significant role in setting the stage for the success of subsequent activities.

❀   ❀   ❀

BREAKING THE ICE

This is an activity designed to help overcome awkwardness and unfamiliarity at the beginning of a meeting, conference, or social gathering.

The leader distributes a list of questions to each individual. (See below for examples of questions.) As the opening activity, the group leader asks each individual to think about and respond briefly to the questions.

Adequate time should be allotted for people attending the workshop or meeting to think about the questions posed. Then people should be told to gather in small groups. Within the groups, members take turns answering questions. The leader convenes the total group and asks them to assess the dynamics of the opening activity.

Since people up to this point have only met those in their small discussion group, there remains the task of introducing the people from the other small groups. At this point it would be wise to use a simple introductory activity, so that the full group could begin to address the substantive component of the conference or meeting.

INTRODUCTORY QUESTIONS

1. Why did you choose to come or why were you invited to this program or meeting?
2. What word or phrase best describes how you felt as you entered this meeting room?
3. What word or phrase best describes how you expect to feel as the meeting ends and you are ready to return home?

CREATIVE QUESTIONS TO START A MEETING

1. Where were you born? Where do you now live?
2. What makes you proud to be a Jew?
3. What one word best characterizes:
   a) Your Jewish organization?
   b) The American Jewish community today?
   c) Your views of the State of Israel?
4. What do you see as the core interests/needs of American Jews today?

CREATIVE "QUICKY" OPENERS

The following are 14 examples of opening questions which might be posed and for which each person would offer their responses.
1. My favorite quotes/words of wisdom
2. My hero
3. Individuals who have influenced my life
4. Key historical events
5. World leaders who have shaped human history
6. Famous couples in politics
7. Famous couples in literature
8. My favorite subject when I was in school
9. My most valuable material possession

10. My favorite hobby
11. My most embarrassing moment
12. My favorite relative
13. My best friend
14. If I could start my life over again, what would I do differently?

TEN QUESTIONS TO REVIEW THE PAST YEAR: LOOKING BACK SO THAT YOU CAN MOVE FORWARD

This is an activity which is especially appropriate to use at the end of a year to help people review key events, societal or personal.

As Shakespeare observed, "What is past is prologue." If we fail to learn from what went before, we are likely to repeat the errors of those who preceded us. That perspective applies to each of us as individuals and no less to us as members of the larger society.

In that spirit of reflection, I have posed ten questions to encourage you to reflect on the past year. These questions will enable you to assess key issues, problems and achievements; extract relevant insights; and integrate these revelations into your own life-style.

Such a process of reflection will surely add to your own growing insight and values and the determination that you will learn as you age, and that you will not repeat the errors of those who preceded you. Rather, you will learn from those errors and benefit personally and also contribute to a better society.

To begin the process of reflection, proceed to answer the following *Ten Questions*.

1. What do you consider the single most important event affecting society in general in the past year?
2. What do you consider the single most important event affecting the Jewish people in the last year?
3. Which individual had the most impact on the course of events in the United States during the past year?
4. Which individual had the most impact on the Jewish people in the past year?
5. Reviewing the past year, what is one insight you achieved about the "human drama"?
6. What was the most impressive, creative work you experienced

in the past year: a) book, b) concert, c) movie, d) show, e) or . . . ?

7. What was your most memorable personal event or experience of the past year?
8. What is one wish/hope you would project for next year?
9. What is one societal problem you would like to try to improve in the coming year?
10. What can your religious beliefs or values contribute to this process of reflection and social change?

BUMPER STICKERS

Among the sources by which American culture is transmitted are the bumper stickers found on the backs of cars. Bumper stickers are often pithy, clever and humorous, and often reflect current social or political concerns. Below is a short representative list.

Participants are asked to describe their favorite messages, either used on their own car or seen elsewhere. Then the group considers how bumper stickers are used as a means of personal expression or identification.

BUMPER STICKERS: A RANDOM SAMPLE

Question Authority
What Would Jesus Do?
I'm Pro-Choice and I Vote
God is coming—and is She pissed
A woman's place is in the House—and the Senate
If you want peace, work for justice
You can't hug a child with nuclear arms
Don't blame me, I'm from Massachusetts [the only state to favor George McGovern over Richard Nixon in the 1972 presidential election]
You'll take my gun away when you pry it from my cold dead fingers
Visualize world peace

PLAY THE JEWISH NUMBERS GAME

Don't let the title give you the wrong impression: this activity has nothing to do with gambling. It consists of a short quiz that can start people actively using their Jewish knowledge.

The quiz below asks people to identify the number associated with each of the clues. Different clues could be provided to make a harder quiz.

This quiz can be used as a way for individual participants to occupy time while waiting for other participants to arrive or to complete an assigned task. It might be available on the tables at a large meeting, to be completed by participants while waiting for the next order of business to begin. Offering a Jewishly relevant filler activity can help keep the focus serious during a break period and might in fact encourage social interaction.

One educational challenge would be to require elaboration on the clues, for example, not merely to state the number of Matriarchs but to name them. Another challenge would be to think of other Jewish concepts associated with the numbers 1 through 10 or other numbers. The numbers 13, 18, 36 and 40 all have evident associations.

JEWISH NUMBERS GAME

Match the numbers 1 through 10 with the clues given here.

(In practice, the order of clues should be mixed up so that the answers are not in numerical order.)

a) God is . . .
b) Tablets of the Law
c) Patriarchs
d) Matriarchs
e) Books of Moses
f) Orders of the Mishnah or Workdays in the Week
g) Blessings of the Marriage Ceremony
h) Days of Chanukah
i) Tishah B'Av
j) Plagues

Answers

a) God is . . . : 1
b) Tablets of the Law: 2
c) Patriarchs: 3
d) Matriarchs: 4
e) Books of Moses: 5
f) Orders of the Mishnah or Workdays in the Week: 6
g) Blessings of the Marriage Ceremony: 7
h) Days of Chanukah: 8
i) Tishah B'Av: 9 (9th of Av)
j) Plagues: 10

FAMOUS COUPLES

Below is a listing of famous couples, real and fictional. They are identified by the name commonly used to describe the duo. See how many you recognize. Can you supply last (or first) names?

This activity can be used either as an opening activity or as a change of pace. Participants may wish to think up their own famous couples.

Mickey and Minnie (Disney characters)
Tom and Jerry (TV cartoon)
Jack and Jill (nursery rhyme)
Hansel and Gretel (fairy tale)
George and Martha (Washington, president and first lady)
John and Jackie (Kennedy, president and first lady)
Franklin and Eleanor (Roosevelt, president and first lady)
Bill and Hillary (Clinton, president and first lady)
Adam and Eve (Biblical couple)
Cain and Abel (Biblical brothers)
Abraham and Sarah (Biblical figures)
Laurel and Hardy (Stan and Oliver, comedy team)
Abbot and Costello (Bud and Lou, comedy team)
John and Yoko (Lennon and Ono, member of The Beatles and wife)
Simon and Garfunkel (Paul and Art, singing duo)
Bonnie and Clyde (Parker and Barrow, outlaws)
Tarzan and Jane (hero and heroine of jungle adventures)
Fred and Ginger (Astaire and Rogers, dance team)

Mork and Mindy (TV sitcom)
Lone Ranger and Tonto (doers of justice in the Old West)
Alice and Ralph (Kramden, "The Honeymooners")
Lucy and Desi (Arnaz, TV sitcom)
Rodgers and Hammerstein (Richard and Oscar, song-writing team)
George and Ira (Gershwin, song-writing team)
Holmes and Watson (Sherlock and John, detective and companion)

THE PERFECT MATCH

"The Perfect Match" icebreaker is a wonderful way to get people talking to each other and working together. It also gives them a chance to move around and become energized; it therefore is well-suited for the start of a meeting or conference. The activity starts by pairing people and proceeds to form people into quartets.

Instructions:

1. In advance of the activity, assemble pairs of objects that have a logical connection. The connection need not be obvious. However, objects should be selected so that each object clearly goes with just one other choice. Possible examples include the following:
   watch—clock; black paper—white paper; tie—tie tack; bagel—cream cheese; nut—bolt; dictionary—thesaurus; Israeli flag—American flag; baseball—baseball glove; "Adam" name tag—"Eve" name tag; coffee beans—sugar; red AIDS ribbon—pink Breast Cancer ribbon.
2. As participants enter the room, give them each an object. Do not explain what the object will be used for; curiosity will stimulate involvement. Be sure that both objects in a pair are distributed, but not to people who arrive together. Once everyone has been given an object move quickly to the next step.
3. Tell the participants that somewhere in the room there is a "perfect match" for each person. Now they must search for that person. When members of a pair find each other, they are

to sit down together. Some pairs may be more difficult to identify, but the matches will gradually become evident by process of elimination.

4. Once all matches have been made, instruct pairs to join with any other pair. Within the quartet the challenge is to think of a way to relate the four objects brought by the participants. The way of relating the objects can be something they have in common, a way of sequencing them, or a brief story that uses them as props. Particularly creative would be finding a connection that had something to do with the shared work or organization of the participants.

5. Assemble the entire group. Have each quartet present its objects and how they relate. Concluding remarks should touch on the success of the group task, in words such as, "We were able to take unrelated things and work together," or, "We can overcome obstacles . . ."

Note to Leader:

When there is an uneven number of participants the leader or other staff members may need to participate so that every participant can be paired. When groups of four are formed, if there is one pair left over it can join one of the quartets.

(Submitted by Mindy J. Frankel and Melissa Millman)

FIND A RELATIVE

Purpose:

To divide the group into pairs while learning about the relationships among various persons mentioned in the Bible.

Group:

Age 10 and older; between 12 and 20 participants.

Setting:

A room with chairs set in a circle.

Time:

15–20 minutes.

Materials:

One copy of a Bible passage for each participant. Each passage should be one half of a vignette that features two individuals. Together, the two halves will enable two participants to form a pair. Each passage should be labeled with the name of the featured character and whether this is the beginning or end of the vignette.

Instructions:

1. Participants spend a little time familiarizing themselves with their story so that they understand their character.
2. One participant who has a beginning passage reads it aloud. Then, the participant who is a relative of the reader's character gets up and sits next to the reader. That person reads his/her passage, thus completing one story.
3. Then another participant reads a beginning passage. The process continues until everyone has read.

Variation:

This activity can readily be modified to divide participants into groups of three or four. Narratives that mention three or four related individuals will be used.

Note to Leader:

Texts can be chosen that are relevant to the theme of the overall program. For example, pairs of such as Abraham-Isaac or Rebekah-Jacob would be relevant in a parent-child workshop. Discussion can follow about the similarities or differences among the pairs that are formed.

(Submitted by Iren Kaganova)

HUMAN TREASURE HUNT

In this mixer activity, participants discover some of the "human treasures" within the group. The purpose is to circulate and have contact with many people.

Each participant is given a list of characteristics to look for among members of the group. The participant goes around trying to find someone with certain desired characteristics. When s/he finds someone, the two people briefly introduce themselves and tell where they are from. Then, the participant looks for someone having another characteristic.

Activity can stop when there has been a sufficient amount of mingling and introduction.

HUMAN TREASURE HUNT

Find one or more people with these characteristics:

1. Their first name starts with the same letter as yours.
2. Their favorite Jewish holiday or custom is the same as yours.
3. They have been to Israel.
4. They *daven* regularly.
5. They exercise or work out regularly.
6. They were born in the same city (or state or country) as you.
7. They have a birthday within this month.
8. They were born in the same year as you.
9. They share interest in a hobby of yours.
10. They attended the same college as you.

MEAL TIME

Purpose:

To create a situation for people to meet and share personal information with each other.

Group:

Any age group. 12–30 people. Ideally, the number of participants would be a multiple of 6, as activity calls for forming groups of exactly 6 people.

Setting:

An open space conducive to mingling. Chairs should be available for discussions in pairs and later in groups.

Time:

30 minutes.

Materials:

Recipes for appetizers, main courses and desserts, either photocopied or cut out of newspapers or magazines; large index cards; glue; scissors; pencil; paper bag.

Instructions:

1. Obtain copies of recipes. There should be the same number of each category, with the total number of recipes half the size of the group. Glue each recipe onto an index card. Then cut the recipe in half between the ingredients and the cooking instructions. On the back of each half, write the appropriate letter "A", "M" or "D" for appetizer, main course or dessert. In a paper bag, mix up thoroughly.
2. Instruct the group that this is a mixer that will tell a little about the "ingredients" of the group. Hand each member of the group half of a card. When the leader says to start, each participant looks for the person who has the other half of the recipe. When they find each other, they sit down, introduce themselves, and talk on a specified personal topic for a few minutes.
3. Instruct the group that they now need to help make a "meal" by finding the other "courses". The letter on the back of each card indicates the course. Thus, an "A" pair would seek an "M" and a "D". When these groups of 6 are formed, the group talks on a specific topic related to the theme of the program.
4. The wrap-up should touch on the important contribution made by each person and the benefits of mixing in different combinations.

WHERE DO WE BELONG?

Purpose:

To enable a large group of people to become acquainted with each other through an association with Jewish subject matter and to divide into groups that will be suitable for a subsequent discussion and/or activity.

Group:

Junior high and older, 50–150.

Setting:

An unobstructed space large enough to accommodate the movement and conversation of the entire group.

Materials:

Newsprint or posterboard, marking pens, tape or tacks, and slips of paper on each of which is written the name of one member of a Jewish category.

Time:

20–30 minutes, with more time needed for larger groups.

Instructions:

1. Based on the group size and the plan of activities, the leader determines the desired number of subgroups and a suitable subgroup size for the next activity.
2. The leader chooses an appropriate number of categories (see list at end of activity), based on the number of subgroups, with a corresponding and appropriate number of members per category. S/he then prepares a sign for each category and a slip of paper for each of the members of all the categories chosen. The category signs are posted throughout the setting, and the slips are placed in a hat, paper bag, shoe box, etc.

3. Either participants randomly pick slips or they are directly distributed by the leader. The leader explains that everyone has received the name of a member of a Jewish category and that all of the category titles are posted around the setting. Members are instructed to determine which category they belong in; then the participants proceed to their category location and introduce themselves to the other members of their category.

Variations:

A. BLIND CATEGORIES. This is essentially the same activity except that participants are given the additional challenge of determining a title for their category, which adds a dimension of group interaction. Consequently, this variation is suggested for use with more Judaically sophisticated groups. Participants are told that there are supposed to be x number of members per category. Participants are instructed to introduce themselves to each other in order to both discover what category they constitute and to assemble all of its members. Once the requisite number of members is gathered and everyone agrees as to their category title, a member of the group goes to the leader for a marking pen. Participants then write on a blank sign what they think the title of their category should be, and the group members assemble under their sign.

B. JEWISH NUMBERS. This beginning activity offers a good problem-solving task for a group of 15–30 individuals. As participants address the task, they not only get to know the other members of the group, but also gain a sense of collective achievement. Each person is given a slip of paper with a brief description of some aspect of Jewish tradition which represents or describes a number (e.g., the questions asked at the Passover Seder-4; or the number of days of Chanukah-8). The task of the group is to line up, single file, so that the full group is ordered in progressively higher numbers (e.g. 1, 2, 4, 7, 8, 10 . . .). A list of Jewish numbers is included with the list of Jewish categories. Several people may be given different descriptions for the same numbers. They should stand together in the ordered line.

CATEGORIES

Patriarchs (3)
Abraham
Isaac
Jacob

Matriarchs (4)
Sarah
Rebecca
Rachel
Leah

12 Tribes (12)
Benjamin
Joseph
Naphtali
Judah
Simeon
Gad
Reuben
Zebulon
Dan
Issachar
Levi
Asher

Prophets (15)
Isaiah
Jeremiah
Ezekiel
Hosea
Joel
Amos
Obadiah
Jonah
Micah
Nahum
Habakkuk
Zephaniah
Haggai

Zechariah
Malachi

Kings (10)
Saul
David
Solomon
Ahab
Jeroboam
Manasseh
Hezekiah
Abimelech
Omri
Rehoboam

Books of Moses (5)
Genesis
Exodus
Leviticus
Numbers
Deuteronomy

Hebrew Months (12)
Tishrei
Cheshvan
Kislev
Tevet
Shevat
Adar
Nisan
Iyyar
Sivan
Tammuz
Av
Elul

Jewish Writers (18)
Elie Wiesel
Bernard Malamud

Philip Roth
Joseph Heller
Cynthia Ozick
Solomon Ibn Gabirol
Arthur Miller
Nelly Sachs
Fran Liebowitz
Saul Bellow
S. Y. Agnon
Chaim Nachman Bialik
A. B. Yehoshua
Amos Oz
Mendele Mocher S'forim
I. B. Singer
Franz Kafka
Sholom Aleichem

Jewish Fast Days (6)
Tzom Gedaliah/Fast of
Gedaliah
Yom Kippur
Fast of the Tenth Month
Ta'anit Ester/Fast of Esther
Fast of the Fourth Month
Tisha B'Av

Jewish Victims (11)
Ethel and Julius Rosenberg
Alfred Dreyfus
Edgar Mortara
Leo Frank
Mendel Beilis
Anne Frank
Col. Efim Davidovitch
Walter Rathenau
Janusz Korczak
Anatoly Sharansky
Shylock

Anti-Semites (12)
Haman
Joseph de Gobineau
Alfred Rosenberg
Torquemada
Bogdan Chmielnicki
Joseph Stalin
Father Coughlin
Houston Stewart Chamberlain
George Lincoln Rockwell
Henry Ford
Adolph Hitler
Julius Streicher

Zionists (13)
Chaim Weizmann
Henrietta Szold
Theodor Herzl
Vladimir Ze'ev Jabotinsky
Berl Katznelson
David Ben-Gurion
A. D. Gordon
Louis Brandeis
Moses Montefiore
Joseph Trumpeldor
Ahad Ha'Am
Ber Borochov
Moses Hess

Rabbis/Teachers (18)
Rambam
Israel Salanter
Rashi
Isaac Luria
Solomon Schechter
Abraham Joshua Heschel
Mordecai Kaplan
Baal Shem Tov

Vilna Gaon
Yochanan ben Zakkai
Stephen S. Wise
Judah L. Magnes
Hillel
Shammai
Alexander Schindler
Joseph Dov Soloveitchik
Menachem Mendel Schneerson
Sandy Sasso

Jewish Artists (10)
Chaim Gross
Marc Chagall
Amedeo Modigliani
Jacques Lipschitz
Jacob Epstein
Jo Davidson
Wassily Kandinsky
Alfred Steiglitz
Roman Vishniac
Ben Shahn

Jewish Musicians (11)
Isaac Stern
David Oistrakh
Itzhak Perlman
Jascha Heifetz
Artur Rubinstein
Gary Graffman
Leonard Bernstein

Vladimir Ashkenazy
Darius Milhaud
Ernest Bloch
Aaron Copland

Historical Situations
A. The Dreyfus Affair (5)
Alfred Dreyfus
Theodor Herzl
Émile Zola
Major Esterhazy
Devil's Island

B. Purim (6)
Ahasuerus
Vashti
Haman
Esther
Mordecai
Shushan

Philanthropists (9)
The Rothschilds
Baron de Hirsch
Jacob H. Schiff
Judah Touro
Hyam Salomon
Moses Montefiore
Felix M. Warburg
Julius Rosenwald
Oscar S. Straus

Jewish Numbers (22)
   1—God is One
   2—Number of tablets
   3—Patriarchs; Daily Services; Moses' Discourses; Meals of
      Sabbath; Pilgrimage Festivals
   4—Sons in the Haggadah; Corners of Tsitsith; Questions at
      Pesach Seder
   5—Books of Moses
   6—Levitical Cities of Refuge; Orders of Mishnah

7—Sabbath; Sabbatical Year; Commandments of Noah;
   Blessings of Marriage Ceremony
8—Days of Chanukah
9—Ninth Day of Av
10—Commandments; Plagues; Minyan
12—Tribes of Israel
13—Attributes of Divine Mercy; Bar/Bat Mitzvah Year; Articles
   of Faith of Maimonides
18—Blessings in Shemoneh Esrei
30—Days of Mourning
36—Righteous Men
40—Years of Desert Exile
49—Jubilee Year
50—Sephirah-Counting of Omer
70—People in Sanhedrin
120—Age of Moses at Death; Members of Israeli Knesset
613—Commandments
967—Martyrs at Masada

Other Suggested Categories
Jewish Diplomats
Jewish Philosophers
Biblical Commentators
Hasidim
Famous Jewish Women
Jewish Members of Congress
Mattathias' Five Sons
Six Orders of the Mishnah
Ten Commandments
Angels
Jewish Places of Importance
Jewish Nobel Prize Winners

THAT'S ME

Purpose:

To make participants comfortable with actively participating, to
provide physical stimulation, and to furnish the leader with information about the makeup of an unfamiliar group.

Time:

2–5 minutes.

Instructions:

The leader reads various statements. For each statement, every person to whom it applies stands up, throws his/her arms in the air and exclaims, "That's me!" Statements at the beginning should be simple, such as "I am female" or "I am originally from Boston." Later statements can be lighthearted—"If I don't have coffee first thing in the morning, my day is ruined;" interesting—"I have been in a synagogue outside the United States or Israel;" or informative—"I speak Hebrew fluently." Choice of statements is arbitrary, though the final few should lead into the topic of the program.

(Submitted by Jay Lewis)

STEP FORWARD

Purpose:

To allow a large group to become acquainted with the Jewish identity of group members and to divide into subgroups for the next activity.

Group:

Adults; 20–30.

Materials:

Masking tape and black tape; three signs marked "Sukkot", "Purim", and "Pesach".

Setting:

A space large enough to accommodate three discussion groups. On the floor, two parallel lines of tape, one of masking tape and one of black tape, about 12 feet apart. Around the room the three signs are posted.

Time:

10 minutes.

Instructions:

1. Leader welcomes the participants and asks them to stand at the white line (masking tape) and face the black line.
2. Leader reads the statements below, one at a time. For each statement, all participants to whom it applies step forward to the black line and turn to face the white line. At a signal from the leader, such as a hand clap or saying "Thank you," everyone goes back to the white line. This is repeated for each statement.
3. After the last statement, the group counts off starting at one end of the line. In turn, participants say "Sukkot", "Purim", "Pesach". Each group defined by a holiday assembles under its sign, as a transition to the next activity.

Variation:

A. STEP FORWARD WITH DISCUSSION. Each subgroup discusses the following questions about what has been learned about the entire group's Jewish identity:
   a) What did you learn about the people in the group?
   b) Were there any surprises?
   c) What are the difficulties in defining what a Jew is?

RECOMMENDED STATEMENTS TO USE

The following statements may be used. They range from simple facts to matters of belief and personal identity.

1. As a teen I went to a Jewish camp.
2. I went to a supplementary Hebrew school or day school.
3. I was bar/bat mitzvahed.

4. As a teen I was active in a Jewish youth group.
5. When I was growing up my parents kept kosher in their home.
6. As a teen I went to services at least twice a month.
7. I obey the laws of Kashruth.
8. I have learned to read Hebrew.
9. I can speak Hebrew.
10. I do not ride on Shabbat.
11. My parents hung a mezuzah on our door.
12. I went to Israel as a teen with a youth group.
13. I went to Israel as an adult.
14. I would eventually like to make *aliyah*.
15. The Beauty of Nature reminds me of God.
16. I believe in God.
17. I feel I am spiritual.
18. I feel a strong closeness with *Klal Yisrael*, the Jewish People.
19. I am an American Jew.
20. I am a Jewish American.
21. I feel I have two homes, my native country and Israel.
22. I am a Zionist.
23. I am a Jew of the world.

(Submitted by Nancy Nelson)

A NAME TAG WITH ESSENCE

The typical name tag prepared in advance for a large meeting or conference includes dry information such as name, home community and organizational affiliation. You might encourage use of a more creative and expansive name tag.

Individuals might prepare their own name tags, decorating them or providing some personal information such as:

1. Nickname.
2. A relevant professional achievement.
3. A special skill that would be helpful to the group.
4. The title of a lecture or article delivered on the subject the group is addressing.
5. A favorite quotation and its author.

Inclusion of such items projects values of depth and creativity, as well as allowing people to know more about those with whom they are collaborating.

WHAT IS YOUR EPITHET?

This is a good opening activity for a workshop, conference, or family gathering in which people will be together for half a day or more. It allows people to introduce themselves, learn each other's names and discover something vital about each other. It thus creates a favorable atmosphere for the group's subsequent deliberations.

The activity is introduced as follows.

"Your friends, relatives, neighbors, and work colleagues are planning a major event at the biggest hotel in town to honor you for being such a wonderful person. They have commissioned an artist to produce a large banner on which your epithet will be painted. You are invited to select your own epithet, the one word or phrase that best describes the essence of you, and of which you could feel justly proud as you look at the banner located boldly in your office or home."

After everyone has selected their epithet, they should print it with a marking pen on a large sheet of paper. Then each person should present his or her epithet and its rationale. Finally, all the epithets are posted on the wall in the meeting space.

IF A PICTURE IS WORTH A THOUSAND WORDS . . .

Purpose:

To assist participants in getting to know something about one another, in order to make people feel comfortable to move on to the next activity.

Group:

10–25

Setting:

A large, open space, where people can spread out on the floor, and later sit in a circle.

Materials:

Pictures on a variety of subjects taken from magazines or other sources. There should be more pictures than people to allow everyone a good selection.

Time:

20–25 minutes.

Instructions:

1. Before the arrival of the participants, the pictures should be spread out on the floor.
2. During the first five or ten minutes, as people start coming into the room, instruct them to look through the pictures for one that reflects who they are.
3. When everyone has selected a picture, participants take turns explaining in one or two sentences why they chose their picture.

Variations:

A. FOCUS. This activity can be focused by having all the pictures pertain to the same theme, e.g., Israel. Another way to focus the activity is by having the explanation be more specific, e.g., "Tell what this picture means to you as a Jew," or "Choose a picture that reflects your relationship with G-d." The set of pictures must be chosen accordingly.
B. EXTENSION. Each person passes their picture to the person on their left. Then the group takes turns giving responses to the new pictures.

(Submitted by Amy T. Golubtchik)

ABOUT MY NAME

Introductions in large groups tend to provide more information than a person can absorb. This activity allows people to introduce themselves in a way that makes it easier for others to remember who they are. The leader explains that the objective is for people to learn each other's first name. Each person is asked to tell their first name and one or two related pieces of information. Additional information might include for whom they were named, whether they prefer to use a nickname, and how they feel about their name.

Variation:

A. THE PERSON TO MY RIGHT IS . . . Each person introduces himself and then repeats the name of the person who was introduced previously. For example, "My name is Harry. The person to my right is Jennifer." This approach to reinforcing what was just said can be used with any introduction activity where it is important for participants to be able to use the information they learn about others.

KING AND I POKER: GETTING TO KNOW YOU

Purpose:

To facilitate participants learning about each other.

Group:

High-school age and older; groups of 5–7.

Setting:

The participants should gather in a circle, either in chairs or sitting on the floor. Small tables would be helpful.

Time:

10–15 minutes.

Materials:

A deck of cards and a handout for each group.

Instructions:

Each participant draws five cards. Participants then go around sharing information corresponding to one of their cards. (Refer to the handout "King and I Poker Rules".) Sharing continues until all cards have been presented. Participants can draw more cards if desired.

KING AND I POKER RULES

Please share pieces of information corresponding to the card(s) that you have drawn.

Ace	a personal goal
2	a favorite book
3	an accomplishment you are proud of
4	an embarrassing moment
5	someone you admire and why
6	a childhood memory
7	an unusual skill or interest
8	three adjectives that describe you
9	one thing about yourself that you would like to change
10	your definition of friendship
Jack	(wild card—it's up to you)
Queen	a pet peeve
King	a fear or phobia
Joker	the funniest joke you know

(Submitted by Allison Leigh Reilly)

AT THIS TIME I FEEL

Purpose:

This is an opening activity for a conference, retreat or institute that is scheduled to meet for several days. The objective is to encourage the participants to think about, and then express honestly, their feelings at this moment of beginning. Most people will have some apprehension or uncertainty about their participation in a meeting or workshop where they will be expected to be actively engaged. Providing the opportunity at the outset for participants to share these feelings will diminish the level of anxiety, help people feel that the environment is safe and sensitive to their concerns, and foster more honest and creative participation in the larger agenda that lies ahead.

Group:

10–25.

Instructions:

1. At the beginning the leader puts up a sign or writes on a blackboard the phrase, "At this time I feel ... " The leader then asks each person to think about the question and to report honestly on their feelings, preferably with just a word or phrase that captures these feelings. The leader writes those words or phrases on the blackboard or a sheet of newsprint.
2. After everyone has responded, the leader conducts a brief (10–15 minutes) discussion addressing common themes.

Variation:

AT CONCLUSION. A related activity might be used, several days later, at the concluding session of the retreat/institute. The leader would pose the same question as before and elicit responses. After everyone has responded, the leader asks the participants to assess the rationale and effectiveness of these paired sessions and to compare feelings at the beginning and end of the retreat/institute.

Note to Leader:

It would be possible to employ this activity after a simple opening mixer. The advantage is that people might then feel safer in speaking honestly about their feelings. The disadvantage is that the opening mixer might diminish initial anxiety without allowing those feelings to be reported or discussed.

A CIRCLE OF FRIENDS

This activity is designed for a group that interacts on an ongoing basis, such as the staff of an organization or a group of students who are part of one academic program. Through sharing personal information in a creative manner, this activity offers a model of interaction that the group can follow during its regular activities.

First, each person is given a piece of paper on which they are asked to draw a likeness of themselves as well as clearly print their name. The name sheets are prepared with strings attached so that people can wear their picture around their neck as a "name tag."

After each person completes the name sheet, the leader assembles the group in a circle. With more than 25 people, the group should be divided into two separate smaller groups.

The group leader asks a series of questions that reveal something about the individual. (See below for suggestions.) For each question, each person in the circle has one minute to answer.

Then it would be well to take a ten-minute break. When the group reassembles in the circle, the group should process their impressions of the opening activity and their feelings about the group and its prospects.

SUGGESTED QUESTIONS FOR "A CIRCLE OF FRIENDS"

1. What was your family name in "the Old Country" before our ancestors came to the United States? What is it now? How do you feel about it?
2. What is your fondest memory of a *bubbeh* or *zaydeh* (grandmother or grandfather)?
3. Whom do you consider today as your role model(s), and why?
4. You are given the power to go back in time and change one event in history. What event would it be, and why?
5. If you could invite five people, living or dead, to a Passover seder, whom would you invite?
6. As you review history, which three people would you single out as evil or bad?
7. What is your favorite Jewish or non-Jewish holiday, and why?
8. If you could spend a day with one biblical figure, whom would you select, and why?
9. What is something you would really like to learn to do?
10. If you could change one thing about yourself, what would it be?

(Source: Adapted from *Is Your Dog Jewish?*, by Leo Dworker.)

TWO CIRCLES

Purpose:

To allow group members to get to know each other quickly and to instill a participatory mindset. This activity also serves to divide a large group into small groups ready to work on a subsequent experiential activity. "Two Circles" is the activity that the author has used most frequently in beginning experiential workshops.

Group:

Junior high school and older; conducted in small groups of 10–14, of which any number can operate simultaneously.

Setting:

A room with sufficient space to accommodate all the small groups. Straight-back chairs are set up in two concentric circles containing the same number of chairs. Chairs in the inner circle face out, and those in the outer circle face in. This diagram illustrates the physical arrangement for a group of 12:

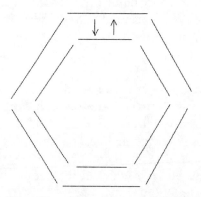

Time:

35–40 minutes.

Instructions:

1. Participants fill up the prearranged chairs. If there is a large group, one should separate mates and people who know each

other well into different small groups. For very large groups (over 50), it is desirable that people be preassigned to the small groups.

2. The leader explains that the activity will involve a series of brief conversations (of about 3 or 4 minutes duration) on subjects to be assigned by the leader, for each of the couples sitting facing each other. Prior to commencing the conversation, the two persons are asked to introduce themselves. The leader then announces the question (see list at end of instructions) and asks both persons to speak to the question within the assigned time. Participants are asked to stay on the subject and, if needed, to prod their partner to obtain a full response.

3. Following the conclusion of the discussion on the first question, the leader asks the people in the outer circle to move one chair to their right. (For variety, people from the inner circle can be asked to move one chair to the left.) The new pair introduce themselves, the leader assigns a new question, and the pair converse. This continues until every pair has conversed on an assigned question.

4. Since members of the same circle have not had a chance to talk with one another, the leader suggests that members of the inner and outer circles move around and introduce themselves to the others in their circle.

5. At this juncture the participants are aware of a dramatic contrast between their initial anxiety and the warm afterglow generated by the series of personal conversations. This leaves them with a sense of trust for their new colleagues and receptive to continue the process of personal sharing.

Notes to the Leader:

1. The reason for suggesting small-circle groups of 8–14 (4–7 in each of the two circles) is twofold: (a) 4–7 conversations is an appropriate number before the activity hits the point of diminishing returns; (b) groups of 8–14 members are a good size for dealing with other tasks in future experiential activities.

2. Since people generally get seriously involved in their conversations, it is sometimes difficult to conclude the conversations, The leader, in advance, should prepare the participants for the

fact that s/he will be interrupting their conversations. In addition s/he should point out that s/he will stand up in the middle of the circle about 30 seconds before announcing time to conclude a conversation and to change partners. This will prepare the partners for the fact that the conversation is about to end.

3. It is important to realize that the questions which go along with this activity are not meant to be processed by the group, i.e., that they are "throwaway" questions and have no intrinsic value beyond their use in setting a tone of expressivity and participation. The questions provided below are listed in random order. The leader is encouraged to choose among them and to modify them according to his/her sense of the needs of his/her particular group.

QUESTIONS FOR TWO CIRCLES
(OR RELATED ACTIVITIES)

1. How do you feel at this moment?
2. What really bothers you?
3. What is there about your personality that most people aren't apt to know?
4. Describe an instance in which you were especially aware of being Jewish.
5. Describe a person who you feel exemplifies a good Jew.
6. What do you really expect from this meeting? (workshop? summer camp? program? etc.)
7. What would you most like to change about yourself?
8. What is a special skill or talent that you have?
9. What is there about the work of your organization that you like most (least)?
10. Which person who you have known has had the most impact on your life as a Jew?
11. What do you value most about being Jewish?
12. Whom do you most admire?
13. When you were young, what was your secret aspiration?
14. What do you recall as an especially positive (negative) experience since you have been at your organization?
15. What do you like most (least) about yourself?
16. What do you hope to achieve in your lifetime?

17. How close to your life aspiration do you believe you will come?
18. What do you most fear?
19. Are you different today than you were 5 (10) years ago?
20. What do you find most (least) satisfying about your job?
21. In what way would you most like your life to be different?
22. Recall an early experience of success (failure).
23. What are your memories of first entering school?
24. What things do you have to do that you least like doing?
25. Tell about something that usually makes you uncomfortable.
26. What were your first impressions of the people in this group?
27. In what situations do you feel alienated from other people?
28. What is the image of yourself you would like people to have?
29. What is the image of yourself you think people actually have?
30. What most helps you relax?
31. What makes you most tense?
32. What book that you have read has had the most impact on you?
33. What do you think you will be doing 5 (10) years from now?
34. What is the thing that "bugs" you most on your job?
35. If you could change your job tomorrow, what would you choose to do?
36. Describe the type of person you have the most difficulty getting along with.
37. What is your favorite place?
38. Who is the historical figure whom you most admire?
39. What historical event has had the most significance for you?
40. What do you do that gives you the most satisfaction?
41. What kind of Jew makes you feel most uncomfortable?
42. What kind of Jew makes you feel most proud?
43. What is something you have to do that you have been avoiding?
44. What is a particularly difficult decision which you recently made?
45. Who would you most like to tell off?
46. If you wanted someone to confide in about a personal matter, to whom would you turn?
47. What is particularly upsetting to you these days?

48. What is the thing you like most (least) about your synagogue?
49. What is the thing you like most (least) about your rabbi?
50. To you, what were the "good old days"?
51. Why did you choose to live where you are now living?
52. How many different homes have you lived in?
53. What do you like most (least) about the neighborhood where you live?
54. Where do you think you would most like to live, and how likely is it that you will ever live there?
55. What is something you did recently about which you were proud? (ashamed?)
56. What was the most significant thing you did this past week?
57. Did you ever help someone who was in need?
58. In what ways do you feel you waste time?
59. What vacation do you remember as most outstanding?
60. If you came into unexpected wealth, what would you buy?
61. Which individual has helped you the most?
62. Did you ever hate anyone?
63. When you were a child, were you ever teased about anything?
64. Tell about something that you have kept as a secret.
65. Tell about an incident in which you were frightened.
66. What is the strangest thing that has ever happened to you?
67. Who is the best teacher with whom you have studied?
68. Who is the most famous person you have personally known?
69. Describe a situation in which you were embarrassed.
70. If you could choose a different first name, what would it be?
71. What do you worry about most?
72. What incident from your childhood do you remember warmly (unpleasantly)?
73. What is the most beautiful sight you have ever seen?
74. Tell about a "peak experience" you have had.
75. What gift that you have received has meant the most to you?
76. What is the most dangerous thing you have ever done?
77. What is the subject you most (least) liked in school?
78. What is the most physical pain you have experienced?
79. Whom do you consider your best friend?
80. What do you like most about your best friend?

81. What is one quality you expect in a friend?
82. At what time in your life did you feel most happy?
83. What is something you experienced that you would not wish your own children to go through?
84. Is there an issue on which you have changed your views?
85. What are you proud of in relation to your family?
86. When you were a child, what bothered you most about your parents?
87. What is your most prized material possession?
88. When do you remember feeling very sad?
89. Is there anything unconventional about you?
90. Can you tell about a time which you might consider a turning point in your life?
91. Do you think you are a better parent for your children than your parents were for you?
92. What habit would you like to change?
93. What is the most serious illness or accident that you have had?
94. What do you consider to be your greatest success?
95. What role do you usually take in groups?
96. Tell about a missed opportunity in your life.
97. Which section of the Sunday newspaper do you read first?
98. To whom are you important?
99. How important is it for you to "get to the top"?
100. If one speaks of "we and they," for you, who would be "we" and who would be "they"?
101. What is a prejudice you have?
102. What is success for you?
103. What is the most important decision you ever made?
104. Have you ever felt embarrassed about being a Jew?
105. When was the last time you cried?
106. What thoughts come to your mind when you think of Christmas?
107. Where did "your people" come from?
108. What are your memories on first starting to work for this organization?

QUESTIONS FOR CHILDREN

1. Do you wish you had a smaller or larger family, or is your family the right size as it is now?

2. If you could be any age, what age would you be?
3. If it were fully up to you, would you attend religious school?
4. Do you believe in God?
5. What would you like to learn to do very well?
6. Did you ever think about running away from home?
7. If you were a parent, would you raise your children differently from the way your parents are raising you?
8. Would you marry someone of a different religion?
9. Who is the person with whom you can talk most freely about your personal feelings and concerns?
10. If you could choose one foreign country to visit, which one would you choose?
11. Do you like it better when adults are strict or easygoing?
12. If you were the principal of your school, what is the first change you would make?
13. What school subject do you find to be most boring? difficult? interesting?
14. What really scares you?
15. What do you think you will be doing 10 years from now?
16. What bothers you about your friends?
17. What is something you are proud of concerning your school? your family? your country? your religion? your neighborhood?
18. Is there someone you really respect?
19. What was the most satisfying thing you did in this past week?
20. Do you think you will get married?
21. What is your favorite holiday?
22. Who is the person that you knew the best who has died?
23. If it were up to you, how would you prefer to spend most of your time?
24. If there were only one food you could eat, what food would you choose?
25. When can you remember feeling very happy?
26. Have you ever really hated someone?
27. What was the worst punishment your parents ever gave you?
28. Tell about a time when you felt no one understood you.
29. If you could watch only one TV show, which would it be?
30. How do you think this world could be better?

31. Tell about another young person about your age you would like to be like.
32. What is a question that you have always wanted to ask but haven't?
33. Tell about a time when you felt you were being left out of a group.
34. Talk about a teacher who really frightened you or hurt your feelings.
35. Describe how your life might change if there were no TV.

CIRCULAR LAP SIT

This activity utilizes a physical challenging task—having people arranged in a circle sitting on each other's laps.

The activity starts by getting participants in groups of six to eight individuals and having them create a tight circle where they all stand facing the same way. Then each person crouches down attempting to sit on the lap of the person behind them. The challenge is to see which circle can remain intact the longest, with no one falling on the ground and no external support. The activity continues with all the groups coming together to attempt a circular lap sit with the entire group.

It might be of interest to see how long the circle groups remain without falling. If "Circular Lap Sit" is repeated over time with an organization that meets regularly, the challenge at each meeting would be to break the organization's lap-sitting record.

LINE-UP

This activity gives participants the experience of interacting and functioning as a team. "Line-Up" calls for communication and cooperation. Participants are asked to line up according to a specified rule, e.g., alphabetically by name, by age, by length of time spent in Israel. The activity could be repeated a few times using different rules, depending on the group.

Variation:

A. NON-VERBAL LINE-UP Participants must line up without talking. Consider an appropriate rule such as by height or weight.

(Adapted from an idea submitted by Jay Lewis)

WHO ARE WE?

Purpose:

To help group members get to know each other, especially a group where members will be working together for an extended period.

Group:

Elementary school age and up; size of group: up to 50.

Setting:

Any open meeting room in which signs can be posted on the walls.

Materials:

4 signs to be posted in corners of the room (see below) and a list of questions.

Time:

30–40 minutes.

Instructions:

1. In each of the four corners of the room, the leader posts one of the following signs:
   Definitely yes
   Yes, most of the time
   Not usually
   Definitely no

2. The leader reads a statement (see the list below) and asks the participants to move to the corner of the room which most accurately describes their response to that item. Participants are encouraged to be spontaneous in making a choice and are reminded that there are no "right" or "wrong" answers—only personal preferences.
3. When people get to their corners, they introduce themselves and then exchange experiences and factors related to their respective reactions to the subject.
4. The leader continues the activity for at least 6 statements and/or enough time to insure that all participants have conversed with each other.

LIST OF STATEMENTS

a. I enjoy(ed) going to Hebrew school.
b. I like matzoh ball soup.
c. I enjoy having a pet.
d. I enjoy eating cheeseburgers.
e. My favorite place is Israel.
f. I enjoy reading our community's Jewish newspaper.
g. In our family we celebrate Shabbat.
h. I go to religious services at synagogue regularly.
i. I prefer to read a good book than to watch TV.
j. I like to stay up late.

Leaders are encouraged to make their own statement lists.

QUOTES

A good laugh is sunshine in the house.

William Thackeray (1811–1863)

A merry heart is a good medicine; but a broken spirit drieth the bones.

Proverbs 17:22

To look out at this kind of creation and not believe in God is, to me, impossible.

John Glenn (1921–), senator
and astronaut

Abolish the lust for money and the Messiah will come.

> Rabbi Nachman of Bratslav
> (1772–1811)

How pitiful is the miser: He lives with poverty in order to die with wealth.

> Rabbi Yehezkel of Shinova

There are lies, damn lies, and statistics.

> Mark Twain (1835–1910)

I wouldn't want to join any club that would have me as a member.

> Groucho Marx (1890–1977)

When I use a word . . . it means just what I choose it to mean— neither more nor less.

> Lewis Carroll (1832–1898)

The test of a first-rate intelligence is the ability to hold two opposed ideas in the mind at the same time and still retain the ability to function.

> F. Scott Fitzgerald (1896–1940)

One must, it is true, forgive one's enemies—but not before they have been hanged.

> Heinrich Heine (1797–1856)

We are what we pretend to be.

> Kurt Vonnegut Jr. (1922–)

In the halls of justice, the only justice takes place in the halls.

> Abbie Hoffman (1936–1989)

No one should ever see how men make laws or sausages.

> Otto von Bismarck (1815–1898)

Everyone has his day and some days last longer than others.

> Winston Churchill (1874–1965)

A fanatic is someone who will not change his mind and refuses to change the subject.

Winston Churchill (1874–1965)

We make a living by what we get; we make a life by what we give.

Winston Churchill (1874–1965)

History teaches us that man learns nothing from history.

Georg Wilhelm Friedrich Hegel
(1770–1831)

It takes an endless amount of history to make even a little tradition.

Henry James (1843–1916)

They are as sick that surfeit with too much, as they that starve with nothing.

William Shakespeare (1564–1616)

The Jew is that sacred being who has brought down from heaven the everlasting fire and has illuminated with it the entire world.

Leo Tolstoy (1828–1910)

Coming together is a beginning; keeping together is progress; working together is success.

Henry Ford (1863–1947)

The greatest use of life is to spend it for something that will outlast it.

William James (1842–1910)

Let us not take it for granted that life exists more fully in what is commonly thought big than what is commonly thought small.

Virginia Woolf (1882–1941)

Essential things have great power to touch the heart of the beholder—I mean such things as a man plowing the field, or sowing, or reaping; a girl filling a pitcher from a spring; a young mother with her child.

Max Beerbohm (1872–1956), 1918

The chief product of an automated society is a widespread and deepening sense of boredom.

Cyril Parkinson (1909–1993)

The only thing we have to fear is fear itself.

Franklin D. Roosevelt (1882–1945)

Courage is being scared to death—and saddling up anyway.

John Wayne (1907–1979)

The illusion that times that were are better than times that are has probably pervaded all the ages.

Horace Greeley (1811–1872)

There is nothing more permanent than change.

Samuel Rogers (1763–1855), 1792

The good life is not a passive existence where you live and let live. It is one of involvement where you live and help live.

Isaac Bashevis Singer (1904–1991)

If you will it, it is no dream.

Theodor Herzl (1860–1904)

Nothing great was ever achieved without enthusiasm.

Ralph Waldo Emerson (1803–1882)

Ninety percent of success is simply showing up.

Woody Allen (1935–)

Success is never permanent. Failure is never failure. The only thing that really counts is to never, never, never give up.

Winston Churchill (1874–1965)

Dare to dream, and when you dream, dream big.

Henrietta Szold (1860–1943)

Man is not the creature of circumstances. Circumstances are the creatures of men.

Benjamin Disraeli (1804–1881)

A man's reach should exceed his grasp, or what's a heaven for?
Robert Browning (1812–1889)

Not to know is bad.
Not to want to know is worse.
Not to hope is unthinkable
Not to dare is unforgivable.
Ibo (S.E. Nigerian) proverb

The myth of the impossible dream is more powerful than all of the facts of history.
Robert Fulghum (1937–)

If you take a step and it feels good, you must be headed in the right direction.
Linda Weltner (1939–)

Freedom is not worth having if it does not connote freedom to err.
Mohandas K. Gandhi (1869–1948)

Be hopeful, but not foolishly hopeful.
Morris Schwartz (1917–1995),
Tuesdays with Morrie, 1997

To travel is better than to arrive.
Robert Louis Stevenson (1850–1894)

The proper office of a friend is to side with you when you are in the wrong. Nearly anybody will side with you when you are in the right.
Mark Twain (1835–1910)

Part of the secret of success in life is to eat what you like and let the food fight it out inside.
Mark Twain (1835–1910)

It is only the superficial qualities that last. Man's deeper nature is soon found out.
Oscar Wilde (1854–1900)

Men resemble their own times more than those of their fathers.

Arabic proverb

What has been long neglected cannot be restored immediately. Fruit falls from the tree when it is ripe. The way cannot be forced.

Buddha (565–483 B.C.E.)

It's a funny thing about life; if you refuse to accept anything but the best, you very often get it.

W. Somerset Maugham (1874–1965)

Quiet progress does not make news; raucous conflict and humiliating failures do.

Stephen Bailey, a professor of education
writing about efforts at educational
reform.

You will always find those who think they know your duty better than you know it.

Ralph Waldo Emerson (1803–1882)

We are all in the gutter, but some of us are looking at the stars.

Oscar Wilde (1854–1900)

What is a weed? A plant whose virtues have yet to be discovered.

Ralph Waldo Emerson (1803–1882)

Man will occasionally stumble over the truth, but most times he will pick himself up and carry on.

Winston Churchill (1874–1965)

The voices of silence are more elevated than the sounds of speech.

Baal Shem Tov (1698–1760)

I like the silent church before the service begins better than any preaching.

Ralph Waldo Emerson (1803–1882)

"Some day I will do it" is self-deceptive. "I want to do it" is weak. "I am doing it" is the right way.

Rabbi Menachem Mendel of Kotzk
(1787–1859)

None are more hopelessly enslaved than those who falsely believe they are free.

Johann Wolfgang von Goethe
(1749–1832)

It isn't the horse: it's the oats that pull the wagon.

Russian proverb

5

ANTI-SEMITISM AND THE HOLOCAUST

Anti-Semitism and the Holocaust are unpleasant realities of Jewish existence. An experiential approach can enable people to face what they would otherwise intellectualize, commit to a routine, or not think about at all.

What insights does the Holocaust offer in regard to the deadly and wide-reaching threats of terrorism that permeate the world? What can we learn from the Holocaust beyond an appreciation of our own, often tragic, history? Are we to learn about issues of racism, anti-Semitism and xenophobia? Are we to reflect on our own stereotypes, prejudices and hostile behavior? Can we improve relations within the Jewish community?

As with other sensitive topics, these topics raise difficult questions for educational planners. While recognizing the importance of the Holocaust to Jewish experience, planners need to evaluate the centrality of the Holocaust in comparison with other elements of Jewish identity. How can we derive strength and inspiration from our long history of persecution while preserving a sense of the joyous and life-affirming aspects of our religion? How can we use the lessons of history to look realistically at current events? Of particular importance to educators are questions relating to age sensitivity in programming around the Holocaust. How young is too young to start engaging children in these questions? Finally, there is the question of emotionally charged programming versus programming that is intellectual and neutral. We do not want to be creating, after all, Jews who are only aware of the Holocaust affectively. At the same time, to create a purely fact-driven understanding of the Holocaust would take away its spiritual and emotional power.

Similarly, anti-Semitism is a subject that will be of concern to many. The question becomes how we as a community respond to incidents of anti-Semitism. While recognizing the importance of public acts of education, advocacy and community relations, there is also need for Jews to talk with each other about their own experiences and responses. Do we provide safe space within the community for such conversations to take place? Can we provide guidance to move beyond emotional response to effective action and personal empowerment?

The following activities are designed to help participants consider and clarify their responses to anti-Semitism and the Holocaust. Activities address both historical and hypothetical expressions of hostility.

LIGHT ONE CANDLE
(A preparation for studying the Holocaust)

Purpose:

To introduce the study of the Holocaust, a Holocaust museum, classroom history section, or Yom Ha'shoah and to provide a powerful, age-appropriate activity that brings a group closer together

Group:

People who are similar in age; 30–50 participants.

Setting:

A room that can comfortably accommodate 11 groups of 3–5 each.

Materials:

12 candles; tin foil.

Time:

20 minutes, consisting of 5–10 minutes song session, 2 minutes lights out, 10 minutes conclusion.

Instructions:

1. The success of this activity depends on the mood created at the beginning. It is important to approach this program as if it is just another group meeting or song session.
2. Participants divide themselves into 11 equal groups of 3–5 members in size before entering the room. It is important to ensure that people do not enter with large groups of friends.
3. As each group enters, hand it one lighted candle and instruct the members to sit around the candle on the floor. While groups are filing in, create a joyous communal mood (sing songs, play the guitar, sing cheers, or do anything else that is universally known in the group.)
4. Once all groups are seated and a joyous mood is created, abruptly turn off the lights and create a verbal commotion by yelling for quiet. During the commotion, go around and blow out seven of the eleven candles. Once the group is silent, say "And only a third survived." Allow 30 seconds or longer for the group to think about that sentence. Then turn the lights back on. Ask the group what they thought when they heard the sentence. Explain that what just happened was a poignant representation of the change brought about in the population of Jews in Europe by the Holocaust.
5. Re-light the candles that were extinguished to stress that we are the survivors . . . and that we are a community. Use this as a springboard into a short discussion of thoughts and feelings that were generated by the activity.

(Submitted by Joe Levin)

PROGRAM ON THE HOLOCAUST

Purpose:

To appreciate the loss of 6 million Jewish lives; to understand that the Holocaust has implications for every facet of life: philosophy, politics, personal relations, etc.

Group:

Teenagers to adults, preferably a large group.

Setting:

A large, quiet room that is dark except for the light of a single burning candle.

Time:

At least 1 hour, about ½ hour for Introduction and at least ½ hour for Discussion and Processing.

Instructions:

1. Enter the darkened room. People should come into the room without speaking and stand or sit on the floor. The leader sets a mood by reading the following words:

   "You are about to enter a very different world. It is a dark world where evil reigned for twelve long years. It is a world that was created by people in order to murder other people.

   The Holocaust was the attempt by the Nazis and their accomplices to totally annihilate the Jewish people. Their attempt ultimately failed. But before the systematic killing stopped, six million Jews—fully one third of the Jews in Europe—were murdered. This was the genocide of the Jewish people.

   The world that was European Jewry is gone forever, cut off and destroyed in the Holocaust. There is barely a family amongst us that wasn't touched, in some way, by the Holocaust. We are the Jewish world that remains; each of us is part of those branches that were left."

2. Choose a member of the group to read a selection from *Night* by Elie Wiesel (New York: Bantam Books, 1982, pp. 95–96.)

3. Choose another member of the group to read the following:

   "Today we are going to learn about a different world. There are three actors on the stage of the Holocaust. Firstly, the perpetrators—the Nazis, people who hated the Jews to the extent that they manufactured death machines to murder. Secondly, the bystanders—the world, people and governments in the rest of the world for whom it was not a priority to rescue Jews. And thirdly, the victims—the Jews; people who were unable to defend themselves. These three groups make up the complicated story of the holocaust.

'Tomorrow belongs to me,' sang the youth of the S.S. In the end tomorrow didn't belong to them but in many ways the scars they left do make our world a darker place."

4. Use your own short memorial ceremony to conclude. Music or singing would be appropriate.
5. Allow the group some time to reflect and absorb the impact of the forgoing activity.
6. You can follow up with a factual presentation, discussion, or expressive activity to respond to the Holocaust as past, present or future construct. Some themes to consider are: how to preserve memory of the Holocaust; the decision to resist; examples of physical or spiritual resistance; where was God?
7. The leader should stress that it may be difficult to fully resolve issues raised or to reach clear conclusions. The notion that there are no simple answers is a valuable learning. This activity identifies many roles that were played out during the Holocaust, and that are played out in any situation of oppression. It is hoped that we, as Jews and as human beings, will never become perpetrators, never become bystanders, and never again become victims. The leader should conclude on a reassuring note.

ASSEMBLY OF PRENYA SING

Purpose:

To help participants achieve an insight into the dynamics of "we-they" differences. By involving people in an experience in which some people become an in-group and others an out-group, we enable them to be more sensitive to the processes of exclusion and alienation. These processes occur in contemporary Jewish life along several dimensions, e.g., denominational differences, Ashkenazic and Sephardic background, differences in level of Jewish literacy, converts, synagogue and federation affiliation, etc.

Group:

High school age and older; 15–30 participants.

Setting:

A space large enough to isolate one group out of hearing range of another; enough straight-back chairs to accommodate each person.

Materials:

Assembly of Prenya Songsheets (see below), one per person; an arbitrary seating pattern that will exclude one person per row, or about one-quarter of the participants.

Time:

45 minutes.

Instructions:

1. Note: leader should maintain a fairly authoritative stance throughout. Leader enlists group assistance in arranging chairs in several rows, as one person per row will have a special part to play (see step 4.)
2. Leader asks participants to be seated and come to order.
3. Leader gives firm instruction that s/he will pass out a songsheet which should be kept strictly to oneself and not shared with one's neighbor.
4. Leader passes out songsheets *individually*, excluding one person per row according to the leader's predetermined design.
5. Everyone without a songsheet is asked to leave the room. Taking them out of earshot of the assembly, the leader advises them that they will be sent for at a later time. It is important

that the leader give them no instructions as to how to spend their time. The tone here is nothing more than official.

6. Leader begins a coaching session with those who received songsheets, telling them that during the course of the sessions they are free to mark up their sheets if it will help them to remember what they learn, but not to share that information with the returning group. The coaching session comprises the tasks below:

   a. A read-through of the songsheet, establishing a commonly understood pronunciation, and giving the information that all diacritical marks are to be ignored, and that all *g*'s are silent.

   b. Assigning tunes to each of the three stanzas, the opening measures of "Oh What a Beautiful Morning," "I've Been Working on the Railroad," and "Ol' Man River".

   c. Giving the complete order of the stanzas: 1, 2, 3; 1, 2, 3; 2, 3.

   d. Assigning the place of two rise-and-sits, and an ending gesture. (Suggested rise-and-sits: rise during last two lines of first stanza, first time through; and during second stanza, second time through. Suggested ending gesture: extend right arm and curl right forefinger.)

   e. An abbreviated talk-through, including movements and gestures, then a quiet sing-through complete.

   f. Instructions that when the leader returns with the isolated members, the group should be mingling freely, spicing their conversations with a familiar use of one or two words from their newly learned vocabulary.

7. Leader calls in the excluded group, again taking care not to be anything more than official in tone.

8. After being back in the room together for one or two minutes, the leader calls everyone back to their chairs, asking off-handedly of one of those who had been isolated whether or not they have received a songsheet.

9. Once all the participants are in their places, the leader hastily passes out songsheets to those who did not get them originally, and forthrightly commences with the song. It will be helpful here if the leader enthusiastically conducts the singing, while also taking part.

10. Immediately at the conclusion of the singing, the leader requests participants to arrange the chairs in a full circle. From this point on, the leader acts first as a facilitator in the exploration of people's feelings, paying special attention to the cues, the onset and intensity of feelings of inclusion and exclusion, and how these feelings affect perception of the "other." Next, the leader acts as a discussion guide: helping people to relate their experience to ways in which exclusion occurs in Jewish communal life.

ASSEMBLY OF PRENYA SONGSHEET
(All rights reserved, Assembly of Prenya, 1977)

Merdaline tellerup naikleg,
rishmatin lexazset limson;
fongdue câwds bluran creenic,
bocudrew tankeymen vip

vipra porjay sivee ektapince
gnedrap hinktee prenya prenya

Lotspinchel aglunt,
Versapiné aglunt -
mingya putski nadóo:
prenya prenya prenya.

(Submitted by Eliezer Margolis)

STEREOTYPES AND PREJUDICE

Purpose:

To enable people to examine on two levels the processes of stereotyping and group prejudice: (1) general principles, and (2) personal reactions. The activity gives sanction to stereotyping and the free expression of feelings about different constellations of people. The expectation is that in a nonjudgmental, open environment, the participants are apt to bring forth stereotypical images and prejudiced attitudes to other religious and ethnic groups. The objective is not to give approval to stereotyping or bigoted attitudes, but rather, by bringing latent feelings to the fore, to help people better understand the dynamics of prejudice and thereby be in a position to cope with it in a realistic and responsible manner.

> *Caution:* Since this activity encourages the expression of negative attitudes and feelings, it is especially important that it be used only when conducted by a skilled, experienced group leader.

Group:

Ages 16 and older; 15–40 participants.

Setting:

Any open room which has space for several smaller groupings to meet separately.

Materials:

Sheets of newsprint, markers, tape.

Time:

1½ hours.

Instructions:

1. The leader chooses in advance several pairs of groups whose relationship has been characterized by conflict or tension (e.g., Blacks and Whites, Arabs and Jews, Jews and Christians, Orthodox Jews and Secular Jews, Catholics and Protestants.) The number of pairs chosen depends upon the number of people participating in the activity. For each pair of groups there should be 10 people, five assigned to each group. Thus for 30 participants three pairs would be required. In order that the assignment of participants to groups is perceived as random,

the leader should write the predetermined group names on slips of paper which participants then draw from a hat.

2. The participants meet first in their groups of 5, and they are encouraged to spend a few minutes getting acquainted with their fellow group members. The leader then brings together the two halves of the pair. S/he introduces them and explains that traditionally there has been tension and hostility between these two groups. The objective, at this point, is not to ignore or seek to resolve any negative group attitudes or feelings, but rather to bring them to the surface. Accordingly, the appropriate flavor for achieving the objectives of this activity is honesty and forthrightness. People should try to be fully expressive, not censoring any ideas or thoughts which come to mind.

3. The leader gives each group a sheet of newsprint and a marking pen. Each group should have adequate space so it can work privately. The groups are given two tasks, both focusing on their opposite group in the pair. First, they are to free-associate with respect to the other group, listing on the sheet of newsprint their uncensored reactions. Second, they should develop a skit which highlights the most blatant stereotypes of the other group.

4. When the groups have completed their lists and skits, the leader reassembles the full group. S/he again notes that for purposes of the activity, it is fully appropriate to give expression to negative, even distasteful, ideas and expressions. S/he notes that the pairs will take turns presenting their materials. Participants are not to comment or interrupt the presentations. Discussion time will follow after the several pairs present their lists and skits. The leader chooses one pair and has both subgroups move center-stage and sit opposite each other. Each presents its list and skit. Then the next pair presents its material, etc. The lists of each of the subgroups in a pair are taped on the wall alongside each other.

5. Discussion is held off until all the presentations are completed, so as not to focus the reactions on the first pair and thereby diminish the impact of the subsequent presentations. Also, allowing for the full presentation brings forth a diverse range of intergroup relations and, accordingly, provides more comprehensive data on the dynamics of stereotyping and prejudice.

6. The assumption is that after the presentations are completed, the participants will have many ideas and feelings to express. Therefore, the leader should not intrude into the discussion, except perhaps to serve as a "traffic cop." It is important that the participants identify how they felt in giving free rein to stereotypes and prejudices. Therefore, if this does not arise spontaneously in the discussion, it should be sought out by the leader.

7. By way of concluding the activity, participants should be asked what they have learned about stereotyping and prejudice and, based on this learning, what positive steps or programs they would propose to help improve intergroup relations. The key principle underlying this activity is that the basis for positive intergroup relations begins with a recognition of attitudes as they are, which is a necessary prelude to any subsequent attitudinal change.

Variations:

A. STEREOTYPES AND PREJUDICE PLUS OBSERVERS. This variation proceeds as the basic Stereotypes and Prejudice activity described above, except for the presence of a group of observers. So, this variation would have 5 people assigned to each of the two conflicting groups in the pair, plus a group of 5 people serving as observers. The role of the observers is to bring a stance of detachment and objectivity to the deliberations. In the instructions, the observers are asked to remain neutral and to concentrate on the dynamics of the interactions between the two conflicting groups. While the two subgroups are acting out their stereotypes, the observers observe, although remaining silent, only participating verbally when the concluding discussion begins.

   A modification of the task for each of the two subgroups might be tried in this variation. The subgroups are each given two sheets of newsprint. On one they list their stereotypes of the other group; on the second they list the attitudes or stereotypes they think the other group has of them. Following the presentation by the two subgroups of their newsprint materials, the observers are asked to share their observations. The issue to be explored in this summary discussion is the extent to which people's attitudes and perceptions of "social reality" are determined by their circumstance—even when it is artificially and temporarily defined.

(Adaptation of ideas submitted by Benita Gayle, Jeanne Maman and Barry Judelman)

B. JEWS AS MINORITY. The intent of this variation is to encourage Jews to explore their feelings about the non-Jewish world. Jews live as a minority in a society primarily shaped by the values and culture of the non-Jewish majority. How do Jews feel about their status? The exploration of this question is the purpose of this activity. Using pencils and paper provided by the leader, participants free-associate with a list of pairs of culturally significant words and phrases. Each pair comprises a Jewish concept and a non-Jewish counterpart. However, so as not to be obvious, the two related words or phrases are not read one after the other. Examples of the words to be read by the leader include: rabbi-priest; Chanukah-Christmas; Passover-Easter; goy-kike; mogen david-cross; brisket-baked ham; Moses-Jesus; "Hatikvah"-"Star Spangled Banner"; synagogue-church; tefillin-rosary beads; Old Testament-New Testament; gefilte fish-shrimp. For each word or phrase, the participants are asked to write down their first reaction. After the lists are completed, the leader divides the large group into smaller units of 5 or 6 to discuss their lists. In a summary session, the leader raises with the entire group the extent to which they were aware of a different level of response to the Jewish-non-Jewish dimension of the words presented. What does the activity illustrate with respect to how Jews feel about their minority status, and their attitudes towards the Christian majority?

(Adaptation of an idea submitted by Jeanne Maman)

C. IMAGES. This variation is an adaptation of an activity developed by the family therapist Virginia Satir. The group is divided into pairs, and each pair asked to find a place where they can sit together, apart from the other pairs. A few minutes are devoted to the couple getting to know each other. Then the leader asks the pairs to close their eyes and relax.

The leader continues: "I would like you and your partner to concentrate your thoughts on a category of people which I will suggest. Think that the person sitting opposite you is a representative of that category. Keeping your eyes closed, let your imagination express itself fully as you think about that person. S/he is a _____." (The leader chooses from the categories of people s/he would like the people to react to—e.g., Nazi, rabbi, minister, nun, Hasidic Jew, self-hating Jew, Quaker, etc.)

The leader continues: "Spend the next few minutes, with your eyes remaining closed, thinking about this designated person sitting opposite you. Try to picture him/her in your mind. What emotions do you feel? Are you aware of any physiological reactions? Think for another few minutes about the person, allowing any images or ideas to emerge."

After a few moments of silence, the leader asks the partners to slowly open their eyes. They are asked to share their reactions.

The leader repeats the activity for a total of four or five categories of people, and then asks the full group to come together to discuss the experience.

❀ ❀ ❀

QUOTES

Remember what Amalek did unto thee . . . as ye came forth out of Egypt . . . Thou shalt blot out the remembrance of Amalek from under heaven; thou shalt not forget.

Deuteronomy 25:17,19

First they came for the Communists, but I did not speak out because I was not a Communist. Then they came for the Socialists and the Trade Unionists, but I was neither so I did not speak out. Then they came for the Jews, but I was not a Jew so I did not speak out. And when they came for me, there was no one left to speak out for me.

Pastor Martin Niemoeller (1892–1984)

There is no sense trying to convince the non-Jews by all sorts of inferences that we are equal, for their behavior does not have its roots in the mind.

Albert Einstein (1879–1955)

It is not the Jewish character that provokes anti-Semitism, but rather it is the anti-Semite who creates the Jew.

Jean-Paul Sartre (1905–1980)

Anti-Semitism is independent of its object. What Jews do or fail to do is not the determinant. The impetus comes out of the needs of the persecutors.

Barbara Tuchman (1912–1989), 1979

Those who say they want to kill me because I am Jewish would find other reasons if I were not Jewish. I mean, I think if there were no Jews or Catholics, or if everyone was white or German or American, if the earth was one country, one color; then endless new creative rationalizations would emerge to kill "other people"—the left-handed, those who prefer vanilla to strawberry, all baritones, any person who wears saddle shoes.

Woody Allen (1935–), 1991

The Holocaust is the final decisive refutation of diaspora existence.

A. B. Yehoshua (1936–)

All the Protocols tell the same tale of malice, revenge, cupidity and murderous hate against Christians and Christianity. Judaism is Satanism; and no amount of ritual and Kabalistic camouflage can hide this fact.

Protocols of the Learned Elders of Zion,
originally circulated in the late 1800's
(translated from the Russian of Serge
Nilus by Victor E. Marsden, Russian
correspondent for *The Morning Post*, a
British newspaper)

There is a certain people scattered abroad and dispersed among the peoples in all the provinces of thy kingdom; and their laws are diverse from every people, neither keep they the king's laws; therefore it profiteth not the king to suffer them. If it please the king, let it be written that they be destroyed.

Esther 3:8 (Haman to King Ahasuerus)

The Jewish people was a pretty barbarous people. It butchered without pity all the inhabitants of an unfortunate little country (Canaan) to which it had no more right than it did to Paris or London.

Unknown

The religion of the Jews was, during their period of wandering and during the period of their kings, nothing but a confused and contradictory collection of the rites of their neighbors.

Voltaire (born Francois Marie Arouet)
(1694–1778)

Money is the jealous God of Israel, beside which no other god may exist. The bill of exchange is the real God of the Jews.

Karl Marx (1818–1883)

Hence today I believe that I am acting in accordance with the will of the Almighty Creator: by defending myself against the Jew, I am fighting for the work of the Lord.

Adolph Hitler (1889–1945),
Mein Kampf, 1925

Every practicing Hebrew worthy of that name is obliged even now, in conscience, to use in food, in drink, in circumcision, and in various other rites of his religious and civil life the fresh or dried blood of a Christian child, under the pain of infringing his laws and passing among his acquaintances for a bad Hebrew.

La Civilta Cattolic, March 4, 1882

Zionism is a form of racism and racial discrimination.

UN Resolution, October 17, 1975

The Jews are an elite people, sure of itself and domineering.

Charles de Gaulle (1890–1970), 1968

I say to the Jewish people and to the Government of the United States of America: The present state called Israel is an outlaw act. It was not done by the almighty God nor was it done by the guidance of the Messiah. It was your cold naked scheming, plotting and planning against the lives of a people there in Palestine. Now you have taken the land and you called it Israel and you pushed out the original inhabitants, making them vagabonds in the earth. You have lied and said this was a promise made by God to you.

Louis Farrakhan (1933–)

Wenn Judenblut von Messer spritzt -
Dann geht's nochmal so gut!
[When Jewish blood spurts from the knife,
then all goes doubly well.]

Chant of executioners at German con-
centration camps, 1940's

The Jewish race is being exterminated, but it will never be mentioned publicly. It is a glorious page of history never to be written.

Reichsführer Heinrich Himmler (1900–
1945), speaking to SS troops, 1943

RESOURCES FOR INFORMATION AND SUPPORT ON ISSUES RELATED TO ANTI-SEMITISM

For further information on the organizations mentioned below, consult the most recent edition of the *American Jewish Year Book*, published by the American Jewish Committee, New York, NY.

1. *Anti-Defamation League*, 823 United Nations Plaza, New York, NY 10017; *www.adl.org*
2. *American Jewish Committee*, 165 E. 56th St., New York, NY 10022
3. *American Jewish Congress*, 15 E. 84th St., New York, NY 10028
4. *Jewish Council for Public Affairs*, 443 Park Avenue So. 11th Floor, New York, NY 10016
5. In almost every intermediate to large city thre is a local Jewish Community Relations Council (usually part of the city's Jewish federation).
6. *Yad Vashem—The Holocaust Martyrs & Heroes Museum*
    Yad Vashem in Jerusalem, Israel is dedicated to documenting the events associated with the Nazi driven Holocaust and the destruction of six million Jews from 1933–1945. Its mission is

symbolized by its motto: "Recalling the past, realizing the future." It seeks to provide a memorial to the victims of the Holocaust and to educate future generations so that such a tragedy is never repeated. Yad Vashem is also a valuable resource for publications, lectures, workshops, and other information about the Holocaust and expressions of anti-Semitism.

They can be reached at: Yad Vashem, P.O. Box 3477, Jerusalem 91034, Israel. Telephone: 00-972-2-643400; Fax: 00-972-2-6443443; *general.information@yad-vashem.org.il;* *www.yadvashem.org.*

7. *United States Holocaust Memorial Museum*
Center for Advanced Holocaust Studies
100 Raoul Wallenberg Place, SW
Washington, DC 20024-2126
202-488-6162
www.ushmm.org

The *U.S. Holocaust Memorial Museum* maintains displays and oral histories of Holocaust survivors, as well as offering a wide range of lectures and symposia on the most systematic and deadly expression of anti-Semitism in history: the Nazi destruction of six million Jews in Europe during World War II.

READINGS ON ANTI-SEMITISM

Note: Publications are arranged by date of publication.

Carroll, James, *Constantine's Sword: The Church and the Jews—A History.* Boston, MA: Houghton-Mifflin, 2001.

Chanes, Jerome A., *A Dark Side of History: Anti-Semitism Through the Ages.* New York, NY: Oxford Univ. Press, 2001.

Blakeslee, Spencer, *The Death of American Anti-Semitism.* Westport, CT: Praeger, 2000.

Zakim, Leonard P., *Confronting Anti-Semitism: A Practical Guide.* Hoboken NJ: Ktav Publishing House, 2000.

Audit of Anti-Semitic Incidents. New York NY: Anti-Defamation League 1999.

Chazan, Robert, *Medieval Stereotypes and Modern Anti-Semitism.* Berkeley, CA: Univ. of California Press, 1997.

Goldhagen, Daniel Jonah, *Hitler's Willing Executioners: Ordinary Germans and the Holocaust.* New York, NY: Alfred A. Knopf, 1996.

Bohnen, Michael J., "Anti-Semitism Couldn't Destroy Us, But Apathy Might", in *At the Crossroads: Shaping Our Jewish Future.* Combined Jewish Philanthropies and Wilstein Institute of Jewish Policy Studies, Boston, MA, 1995.

Chanes, Jerome A., *Anti-Semitism in America Today: Exploding the Myths.* Secaucus, NJ: Birch Lane Press, 1995.

Frank, Barney, "Pushing Back the Boundaries of Anti-Semitism", in *At the Crossroads: Shaping Our Jewish Future.* Combined Jewish Philanthropies and Wilstein Institute of Jewish Policy Studies, Boston, MA, 1995.

Rabb, Earl, "The Riddle of the Defensive Jew", in Seymour Martin Lipset and Earl Rabb, *Jews and the New American Scene.* Cambridge, MA: Harvard Univ. Press, 1995.

Dinnerstein, Leonard, *Anti-Semitism in America.* New York, NY: Oxford Univ. Press, 1994.

Lipstadt, Deborah E., *Denying the Holocaust: The Growing Assault on Truth and Memory.* New York, NY: The Free Press, 1993.

Nicholls, William, *Christian Anti-Semitism: A History of Hate.* Northvale, NJ: Jason Aronson, 1993.

Dundes, Alan (ed.), *The Blood Libel Legend.* Madison, WI: Univ. of Wisconsin Press, 1991.

Gould, Alan (ed.), *What Did They Think of the Jews?* Northvale, NJ: Jason Aronson, 1991.

Wistrich, Robert S., *Antisemitism: The Longest Hatred.* New York, NY: Pantheon Books, 1991.

Langmuir, Gavin I., *Toward a Definition of Antisemitism.* Berkeley, CA: Univ. of California Press, 1990.

Foster, Arnold, *Square One.* New York, NY: Donald I. Fine, 1988.

Tobin, Gary A. with Sharon L. Sassler, *Jewish Perceptions of Anti-Semitism.* New York NY: Plenum Press, 1988.

Prager, Dennis and Joseph T. Telushkin, *Why the Jews? The Reasons for Anti-Semitism.* New York NY: Simon & Schuster, 1983.

Krefets, Gerald, *Jews & Money.* New Haven, CT: Ticknor & Fields, 1982.

Flohr, Paul R. Mendes and Jehuda Reinharz, *The Jew in the Modern World*. New York, NY: Oxford Univ. Press, 1980.

Trotsky, Leon, "Anti-Semitism in Soviet Russia", in Eliezer L. Ehrmann, *Readings in Modern Jewish History*. New York, NY: Ktav Publishing House, 1977.

Glassman, Bernard, *Anti-Semitic Stereotypes Without Jews*. Detroit, MI: Wayne Univ. Press, 1975.

Foster, Arnold and Benjamin R. Epstein, *The New Anti-Semitism*. New York, NY: McGraw-Hill, 1974.

Poliakov, Leon, *The History of Anti-Semitism*. New York, NY: Schocken Books, 1974.

Sartre, Jean-Paul, *Anti-Semite and Jew*. New York, NY: Schocken Books, 1973.

Glock, Charles Y. and Rodney Stark, *Christian Beliefs and Anti-Semitism*. New York, NY: Harper & Row, 1969.

Samuel, Maurice, *Blood Accusation: The Strange History of the Beiliss Case*. New York, NY: Alfred A. Knopf, 1966.

Flannery, Edward H., *The Anguish of the Jews: Twenty-Three Centuries of Antisemitism*. New York, NY: Macmillan, 1965.

Poliakov, Leon, *The History of Anti-Semitism*. New York, NY: Vanguard Press, 1965.

Livingston, Sigmund, *Must Men Hate?* Cleveland, OH: World Publishing, 1945.

(Compiled with the help of Charles Cutter, Judaica and Special Collections Librarian, Brandeis University, Waltham, MA and Earl Rabb, sociologist of contemporary Jewry, San Francisco, CA.)

6

ISRAEL AND ISRAEL-DIASPORA RELATIONS

The State of Israel has always played an important role in the identity of most American Jews. Indeed, for a large number, expression of Jewishness has come primarily through Israel-related activities. American Jews have been active in fundraising and lobbying on Israel's behalf. A large number have visited Israel in youth groups or as adults, often finding the trip a formative experience. Israel and its achievements have been a source of pride and its mere existence seen as vital for Jewish survival.

Yet, Israel has become a very different state from what it was at the time of the first publication of *The Jewish Experiential Book*. The threats are greater. Overshadowing all else is the heated conflict between Israeli Jews and Palestinians. Israel has been grappling with questions relating to the role of religion in shaping national policy. There is bitter debate over questions of who is a Jew and the religious legitimacy of the non-Orthodox.

In America, as well as other parts of the Diaspora, Jews are seeking ways of defining themselves that have more to do with personal or family life. The possibility exists that this large and vibrant Jewish community should be seen as the equal of Israel as a source of leadership to world Jewry.

The complexities of the relationship between Israel and the Diaspora are captured in an intriguing question: Is Israel the center of the Jewish world or merely one vital component of it? The alternative perspectives were aptly illustrated by Simon Rawidowicz (1897–1957), a scholar who wrote on the continued importance of a vibrant diaspora even after the emergence of the modern State of Israel in 1948. In the traditional or Zionist perspective, the Jew-

ish world has one center, Israel, whence intellectual and spiritual
leadership emanates. Diaspora communities are on the periphery. In
the two-centered perspective both Israel and Diaspora are centers.
(Referring to the two greatest ancient centers of Jewish learning,
Rawidowicz terms this relationship "Jerusalem and Babylon".)
The mutual interaction and support of the two centers enriches the
entire Jewish world. While the two centers are of equal importance, at any time one or the other may be in the ascendancy.
(See Simon Rawidowicz, "Two That Are One," in Benjamin Ravid
(Ed.), *Israel: the Ever-Dying People and Other Essays*, Ruther-
ford, NJ: Fairleigh Dickinson University Press, 1986.)

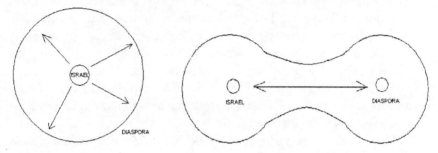

Traditional Perspective   *Two-Centered Perspective*

How do we feel towards Israel? What is an appropriate means
for being involved—making *aliyah*, fundraising, advocacy, or is it
better not to interfere? Is there a viable future for Jews outside of
Israel? How is that future specifically affected by what happens
to the American community? To address these questions requires
examining our values, views and passions. Experiential Jewish
education can play a part in affording people the opportunity to
sort out feelings as well as examine the political realities. The
activities in this chapter are structured toward that goal.

DISCUSSION ON SURVIVAL IN EXILE
AND JEWISH CONTINUITY

The following quotations from the writings of the Jewish theolo-
gian Yehezkiel Kaufmann (1889–1963) focus on the phenomenon

of Jewish continuity. He highlights the fact that Jews are the only people who have sustained themselves as a nation living in exile outside of their own national land. In this state of exile, he notes, the Jews have not only maintained their distinctive identity but also made significant contributions to the larger society.

1. "The singular history of the people of Israel consists of the unique combination of two factors: the national and the religious."
2. "There is another unique phenomenon which we find in the history of Israel (the people) and no other people: the existence of the people of Israel in its dispersion and exile."
3. "There is no other people in the world which was scattered among other nations, adopted their languages, and nevertheless continued to exist."

(From "On the Fate and Survival of the Jews" by Yehezkiel Kaufmann, in Nahum Glatzer (ed.), *Modern Jewish Thought*, North Stratford, NH: Ayer Co. Publishers, Inc., 1977.)

In contrast, traditional Zionist thinkers view life outside of Israel as a place of peril. Israel is viewed as the only secure place for Jews, the center of Jewish life, and the heart of its culture.

1. "Spiritual slavery under the veil of outward freedom." (Description of the Jewish community in France in 1891.) Ahad Ha'am (1856–1927)
2. "The Jews have one way of saving themselves—a return to their own people and emigrating to their own land." Theodor Herzl (1860–1904)
3. "Now that the mission of the Wandering Jew is completed, he must discard the knapsack and cease to be an accomplice in his own destruction." Arthur Koestler (1905–1983)

A fruitful discussion can be had using these contrasting sets of quotations as a starting point. The activity could start with participants considering Kaufmann's affirmation of life in the Diaspora. How do people evaluate the state of Jewish life and culture in America today? Is the American Jewish community likely to continue and to flourish? Then, participants could consider the other set of quotations. Is it bad to live in *galut*? Since living in Israel is a practical possibility, is it better to shift the focus of Jewish life to there?

A HEARING ON ISRAEL-DIASPORA RELATIONS

Purpose:

To explore key issues concerning Israel-Diaspora relations; to demonstrate both the variety of beliefs within the Jewish community and the practical problems this poses for arriving at a consensus.

Group:

High school to adult; 12–30 participants.

Setting:

An open room with adequate space for separate group discussions.

Materials:

Questionnaires on Israel-Diaspora Relations (see below); pencils, newsprint, markers.

Time:

1–1½ hours.

Instructions:

1. The leader explains that the topic to be dealt with is that of Israel-Diaspora relations. S/he announces that before proceeding s/he would like the participants to fill out a questionnaire. Participants are encouraged to be honest and need not identify themselves on the questionnaire.

2. The leader passes out questionnaires and asks participants not to share their answers.
3. After the questionnaires are completed, each participant scores his/her answers in the following way: strongly agree = 2 points; agree = 1 pt.; uncertain = 0 pts.; disagree = − 1 pt.; strongly disagree = − 2 pts.
4. Scores for the group should be tallied. On the basis of the distribution of scores, the leader should divide participants into three groups: (1) those with the highest scores represent a strongly Zionist-oriented group; (2) those with the lowest scores represent a group that is committed to Jewish life in the Diaspora; (3) those whose scores are in the middle range will function as the Policy-making Committee of the Council of Presidents of the Major American Jewish Organizations. (Some explanation of the Council should be provided by the leader.)
5. The leader explains that groups 1 and 2 have been invited to send a delegation to the Policy-making Committee of the Council of Presidents of Major American Jewish Organizations. The two groups are instructed to develop five policy statements in relation to Israel which they believe will represent the feelings of the American Jewish community. They are instructed to choose a chairperson to present their statements. Statements are to be recorded on newsprint. The Policy-making Committee meets to prepare themselves for the hearing which is to follow. They should define the issues on which policies need to be defined and the criteria to be met before they can endorse any policy positions. (Approximately 25 minutes should be allowed for the three groups to prepare themselves.)
6. The leader calls the three groups together and has groups 1 and 2 sit on opposite sides with group 3, the Policy-making Committee, in the middle. One member of group 3 serves as chairperson and conducts a hearing, allowing each of the two groups up to 10 minutes to present their case and to be questioned by other members of the Policy-making Committee. The activity concludes with the committee taking a preliminary vote on the policies they will recommend to the Presidents' Council. If they are unable to reach a consensus, their report may include majority and minority reports, or they may choose to list questions for which further study is required.

7. The leader concludes the activity by summarizing the major issues raised with respect to Israel/Diaspora relations and also by commenting on problems which may have arisen in the attempts to define community policies.

QUESTIONNAIRE ON ISRAEL-DIASPORA RELATIONS

Key: SA = strongly agree; A = agree; U = uncertain; D = disagree; SD = strongly disagree

1. _____ Identification with Israel is the single most important part of my Jewishness.
2. _____ The State of Israel makes me proud to be Jewish.
3. _____ Every Jew has a moral obligation to support Israel.
4. _____ One cannot really be a Jew in the full sense in the Diaspora.
5. _____ All Diaspora Jews should be encouraged to make Aliyah.
6. _____ All Jews should consider themselves Zionists.
7. _____ I am a Jew first and an American second.
8. _____ Without Israel the American Jewish community would fall apart; Israel is the key to meaning and cohesion in the American Jewish community.
9. _____ The first priority of American Jewish communal funds is to help Israel.
10. _____ Israel should receive undivided support from American Jews so that we appear united in the eyes of our enemies.
11. _____ We must strive to influence U.S. foreign policy to support Israel—even if we are criticized for it by non-Jews, the press, Arabs, etc.
12. _____ Israel should receive undivided support from American Jews since we can assume that the policies of a Jewish state will be sound.
13. _____ After we send money to Israel, we have no right to control the allocation of those monies.
14. _____ We have no right to dictate policy to the Israeli government, for example, regarding occupied territories.
15. _____ Israel is the cultural center of world Jewry.
16. _____ Israel is the spiritual center of world Jewry.

17. _____ Russian, South African, and South American immigrants should go to Israel and not other countries in the West.
18. _____ Religious (Jewish) law must be maintained as predominant in Israel.
19. _____ Israel has a right to keep all the territories conquered in past wars.
20. _____ "If I forget thee, O Jerusalem, let my right hand wither and lose its cunning." Jerusalem is ours.

(Adapted from an idea submitted by Fran Ginsburg)

ATTITUDES TOWARDS ISRAEL

Purpose:

To consider attitudes towards Israel and to determine differences in attitudes between participants and their families or youth group.

Group:

Teenagers who are members of a youth group or other Jewish organization; 10–25.

Materials:

Many small stickers of red, blue and green. There should be at least 60 for each participant. Alternatively, colored pens of suitable colors. Questionnaires (see below). One large copy of the questionnaire for posting.

Time:

1 hour.

Instructions:

1. Start with a warmup exercise about Israel. One possibility is to find one word beginning with each letter of the alphabet that is

associated with Israel. For example, A is "ancient", B is "bold", etc.

2. Have participants fill in the questionnaire. Every square should be filled with a sticker representing the rating of importance. (Red = Desirable, Blue = Neutral, Green = Undesirable.) Each row should receive three responses. Participant should answer for him/herself in Myself column, and answer for what they believe to be the attitude of their family or youth group in the other columns.

3. Post a large sheet containing a copy of the questionnaire. Each participant comes to this sheet and places stickers on it reflecting their questionnaire responses.

4. Conduct a discussion focusing on the differences among the three groups of attitudes. In particular, How have our attitudes changed from our families'? Do we agree on what we perceive as the attitudes within our group? Why or why not?

5. Other topics that make use of the summary of attitudes are possible.

EXPRESSING ATTITUDES TOWARDS ISRAEL

	Myself	*My Family*	*My Group*
Taking special note when Israel is on the TV or in the newspaper.			
Being especially concerned and worried if Israel was involved in a war.			
Giving regularly to an Israel charity.			
Considering making *aliyah* (going to live in Israel).			
Viewing Israel as the home for all Jews.			
Viewing Israel as a refuge for persecuted Jews.			
Making special effort to celebrate Yom Ha'atzmaut (Israel Independence Day).			

Following Israel's soccer and basketball teams.			
Taking an interest in Israel's internal politics.			
Viewing Israel as a religious Jewish country.			

Note: Red = DESIRABLE   Blue = NEUTRAL   Green = UNDESIRABLE

PROVOCATIVE STATEMENTS

Purpose:

To structure and encourage lively discussion about the role of Israel through use of strong statements.

Instructions:

1. The leader marks out a scale from 0 to 100 across the length of the room. (This may be done physically, by taping lines on the floor, positioning chairs at each end, or merely by pointing out the ends of the scale.) The scale measures agreement with selected statements about Israel and Zionism (see below), with 0 meaning totally disagree and 100 meaning totally agree.
2. For a particular statement, participants position themselves on the scale according to their degree of agreement. People should take a moment to observe the distribution of agreement.
3. The group is divided into two sides for a debate, with participants located at 0–49 arguing against the statement and at 50–100 arguing for it. Each side is given a few minutes to state their case.
4. Participants are asked to reflect on the content of the debate and again to position themselves on the scale. Have people's views changed? Did one side win the debate?

Note to Leader:

Participants on each side in the debate get to articulate their own views. It is also possible to have each group make their best effort at arguing the *opposite* side. This may help avoid spouting of rhetoric.

Variations:

A. PARTNERS WITH SIMILAR VIEWS. The leader prepares a separate sheet for selected statements and posts them around the room. When people come in, they write their name on the three sheets whose statements they most strongly agree with. Then, the group is divided into pairs, matching people as closely as possible according to their expressed views. Each pair sits together and spends five minutes working out an argument for one of the statements on which they agree. The whole group comes together and each pair presents its argument.

B. RANKING OF STATEMENTS. The leader chooses ten statements that span a range of feelings towards Israel and Zionism. Participants are divided into small groups of 5 or 6 people. Each subgroup is to develop one ranking that reflects, as well as possible, the attitude of the group. This is an exercise in teamwork that will require attention to group process.

   The group reconvenes and each subgroup reports on their experience of developing the ranking. How did each subgroup decide on their order: by voting, compromise or authority?

STATEMENTS ABOUT ISRAEL AND ZIONISM

1. All Jews should live in Israel.
2. All Jews should work for the Jewish community.
3. All Jews should speak Hebrew.
4. Israel is the only place you can be a non-religious Jew.
5. There should be a Jewish State no matter where that state is.
6. Israel must fulfill Torah Law to be a Jewish State.
7. Israel must be exclusively for Jews.
8. All Jews should be allowed to live in Israel.
9. Only religious Jews should be allowed to live in Israel.
10. It is enough to support Israel without living there.
11. It is not enough just to live in Israel; one must build a Jewish future there.
12. We must support Israel, whatever it does.
13. The Jewish State must set an example for the rest of the world.
14. *Aliyah* is more important than anything Jews can do outside Israel.

15. The land of Israel is more important than what happens there.
16. The land of Israel is more holy than any other land.
17. Jews can never live securely outside Israel.
18. It is just as dangerous for Jews to live in Israel as outside.
19. Israelis who emigrate are Jewish traitors.
20. All Soviet Jews should go to Israel.
21. It is worse for an Israeli to emigrate than for me not to make *aliyah*.
22. No part of the Holy Land can be given back to the Arabs.
23. The Holocaust was the ultimate proof that we are not meant to live outside Israel.
24. In the Jewish State everyone must be equal.
25. Zionism means Kibbutz.
26. Israel can be a state like any other state.

CHANGES IN ATTITUDES OF
AMERICAN JEWS TOWARD ISRAEL

Among American Jews, the fervor and material support for Israel that existed since the establishment of the State of Israel appear to be waning. Israel is no longer central for American Jews in defining their Jewish identity. Three scholars and commentators on contemporary American Jewish life recently offered their observations on this change.

Daniela Deane, writing in *USA Today* (May 1, 1998) reports, "Israel's 50th anniversary finds the world's largest Jewish community, American Jews, caring less about the Jewish homeland and more about the future of their culture at home . . . For decades, American Jews equated Judaism with political and financial support for Israel. Today's Jews separate religion from Zionist commitment."

In the same article, Professor Jonathan Sarna of Brandeis University observes, "There's been an enormous change in the American Jewish community. The Zionist era in American Jewish history has ended."

A third comment comes from Yosef Abramowitz, editor of the magazine *Jewish Family Life*: "In nearly every dimension of American Jewish life that has been associated with Israel—from advocacy to fundraising to education—Israel has lost its centrality."

Instructions:

1. Participants are asked to consider whether their attitudes toward Israel have changed. The questionnaire "Changes in Attitudes Toward Israel" may be distributed to aid in this reflection.
2. The group discusses how and why attitudes have changed in the past few years. Questions for participants regarding the nature of the change are:
   a) Has the change resulted from things happening in or to Israel?
   b) Have other aspects of Judaism or Jewish life become more salient? If so, what aspects?
   c) Have other non-Jewish activities or involvements become more salient? If so, what are they?
   d) How do you feel about this change?

CHANGES IN ATTITUDES TOWARD ISRAEL

1) Have your feelings about Israel changed in the past few years?

   _____ Yes

   _____ Somewhat

   _____ No

2) If so, how has the intensity of your feelings changed?

   _____ Stronger

   _____ About the same

   _____ Weakcr

3) If so, what is the direction of change?

   _____ Much more positive

   _____ More positive

   _____ More negative

   _____ Much more negative

4) What are the reasons for this change?

   _____

❀   ❀   ❀

THE PERFECT(?) STATE

Purpose:

This activity is particularly geared to young people who have recently participated in a trip to Israel—to encourage youth to reflect on what they learned about Israel, and to discuss their ideals for a Jewish state and how these may be compromised by the problems and political realities which confront Israel.

Group:

High school or college age; 15–40 participants.

Setting:

Either one large room so that small groups may meet without interference or one large room with smaller workrooms adjacent.

Materials:

Index cards, pencils, newsprint, markers, tape.

Time:

1–1½ hours.

Instructions:

1. The leader divides the group into discussion groups of 8–10 people and explains that the purpose of the session is to explore their attitudes to Israel in the wake of their recent trip there.
2. The leader passes out index cards and pencils. S/he asks each participant to answer the following questions without discussion:
   a. List 5 aspects of Israel or Israeli life that made you happy and/or proud.
   b. List 5 aspects of Israel or Israeli life that disappointed you.
3. After the lists are completed, the participants are asked to share their responses and feelings (approximately 20 minutes).

4. The leader tells the discussion groups that each one is a political party in Israel. They are asked to develop a political platform which incorporates the positive factors which were on their lists, and also tries to correct the problems they listed. The platform should have a maximum of ten positions or statements. The party must be guided by the political reality that its platform will only be instituted if it wins the election. Along with the platform, the group should choose a name for their party which is consistent with their views. The party's name and policies should be written on a sheet of newsprint (30–40 minutes).
5. The leader calls the full group together and asks a representative of each discussion group to explain and defend its platform. The newsprint is taped to a wall for all to see.
6. After representatives speak, the facilitator calls for an election by show of hands or ballot. Participants are not allowed to vote for their own party and are given color-coded ballots.

(Submitted by Fran Ginsburg)

THE WORLD ZIONIST CONGRESS

This activity is a game designed to expose participants to the lives of nine great figures from Zionist and Israeli history and to dramatize the considerations and political forces that went into crafting the Jewish State. There are three stages to this game, each taking half an hour. First, participants are assigned to a "Zionist group" corresponding to one of the figures. Each group drafts a policy statement consistent with their assigned figure. Second, "commissions" are formed to study each of four policy areas and make recommendations. Third, the entire group meets in a "Congress" to develop a strategy for establishing the Jewish State.

Following are the instructions presented to each participant.

INSTRUCTIONS

What is about to take place is the most important debate in the modern history of the Jewish people. A World Zionist Congress is being held to create/establish the Jewish State (as at the Basel

Congress, 1897.) Every one of you will have a le to play in deciding the future direction of our nation.

STAGE ONE (30 minutes):
You are one of the great Zionist thinkers/activists. Time is very short: in a matter of minutes the World Zionist Congress will be convened. You must see that your beliefs are represented, that the World Zionist Congress creates the kind of Jewish State that you can support. From the information you are given about your ideology (i.e., the enclosed biography) you must prepare a policy statement of not more than 250 words in the form of:

I, [name of Zionist thinker], BELIEVE IN . . .
I NOTE . . . [any relevant information about the current situation for Jews]
I RESOLVE . . . [what you want to do for the Jewish people and the creation of the Jewish State]

The issues that you should decide policy on are:
DEFENSE
THE ARAB QUESTION
LAW OF THE LAND
JEWS IN THE DIASPORA

A commission will be set up to study each of these areas. The group should appoint at least one representative to serve on each commission.

STAGE TWO (30 minutes):
Hand a copy of your policy to the leader of the activity who will post each declaration around the room.

The commissions consisting of a representative from each Zionist group are called together to discuss each policy area. Each commission must summarize the different arguments and come up with a compromise position on the issue.

STAGE THREE (30 minutes):
All commissions come together to form a World Zionist Congress, where they discuss and debate the issues and draw up a clear strategy for establishing the Jewish State. A concluding discussion has

participants step out of their characters and compare the strategy that they developed with what actually occurred in the formation of the State of Israel.

WHO'S WHO

Begin, Menachem (1913–1992)

He was Prime Minister from 1977–1983. He was born in Brest-Litovsk, Poland and graduated from the Warsaw University Law School. He joined Betar (youth movement of the Revisionists) and became its head in 1938. He was imprisoned in Siberia. He came to Palestine in 1942 where he was head of Irgun Zvei Leumi (IZL), a militant underground group fighting for establishment of the State of Israel, from 1943 to 1948. He then formed the Herut Party and just before the Six-Day War joined the new Government as minister-without-portfolio. He founded the Likud (coalition) in 1973 and in 1977, as head of the Likud, became Prime Minister. He signed the Camp David Peace Treaty with Egypt in 1978, and retired from politics in 1983.

Ben Gurion, David (formerly Gruen) (1886–1973)

He was the Israeli Labor leader, politician and the first Prime Minister of Israel. He was born in Russia where he attended a modern Hebrew language school. In 1906 he immigrated to Palestine and became involved in the Socialist-Zionist Po'alei Zion. In 1921 he was elected Secretary-General of the Histadrut, which he led for 13 years. From 1935 to 1948 he was chairman of the Jewish Agency Executive Council. On Independence Day, May 14, 1948, Ben Gurion became Israel's first Prime Minister and declared, "Israel will be a light unto all other nations." He later served as Minister of Defense. Ben Gurion resigned twice from office: in 1953 and again in 1963 when he retired to the Kibbutz S'de Boker. He finally retired from politics in 1970 and died in 1973.

Ben Yehuda, Eliezer (formerly Perlman) (1858–1922)

He was a widely acclaimed Hebrew author and lexicographer. He was born in Lithuania and completed his Jewish and secular education in a Yeshiva in Plotsk, after which he studied medicine in France. In 1880 he settled in Palestine. He was by now deeply involved in the revival of the Hebrew language and he edited and published many Hebrew journals and articles. In 1912 he founded the first Hebrew daily newspaper *Doar Hayom* (*Daily Post*).

He believed that the revival of the Hebrew language as the spoken language of the Jews was of ultimate importance to the Zionist cause since it would be the link between the religious concepts and the establishment of the Jewish State of Israel. His greatest work was a 16-volume comprehensive dictionary, in which he introduced many new Hebrew words that he invented to deal with aspects of modern life. Ben Yehuda died in 1922 having only reached the letter "mem" in his dictionary. His memory is honored throughout Israel, where many towns have streets named after him.

Ben Zvi, Yitzchak (formerly Shishelevich) (1884–1963)

He was the founder of Zionist Socialism and the second President of the State of Israel, as well as a noted historian of Palestine. Ben Zvi was born in the Ukraine and educated at a *heder* and at a government secondary school. He organized the Po'alei Zion (Workers of Zion) Party in the Ukraine. He settled in Palestine in 1907 and helped found "Hashomer" for self-defense of the Jews in 1909. He was expelled by the Turks in 1914 and went with Ben Gurion to the U.S. where they formed "Hechalutz" (the Pioneer Movement) and the Jewish Legion. Ben Zvi returned to Palestine after the First World War and helped establish the Histadrut, the Knesset of Israel and the Vaad Leumi (National Committee of the Jewish community in Mandate Palestine), the latter of which he was chairman of from 1944 to 1949. In 1953 he became President and he died in 1963.

Eshkol, Levi (formerly Shkolnik) (1895–1969)

He was Israel's Labor leader and eventually became Prime Minister. He was born in Russia where he attended a Hebrew secondary school in Vilna and joined the first Zionist movement. He settled in Palestine in 1914. Eshkol worked in several communes, served in the Jewish Legion and became a founder of Kibbutz Degania Bet. Between 1937 and 1951, he directed the Mekorot Water Company and from 1948 to 1963, he led the Jewish Agency Land Settlement Department which established 370 new villages, nearly all of which were moshavim settled by olim without any prior knowledge of farming.

In the 1940s he was in charge of the Haganah financial office and in 1949 was appointed Treasurer of the Jewish Agency. He was elected to the Knesset as a member of Mapai (the Workers' Party) in 1951. Between 1952–1963 he had cabinet posts first as Minister of Agriculture and then Minister of Finance. Under his guidance, Israel made significant economic progress. He succeeded Ben Gurion as Prime Minister in 1963 and was in office during the Six-Day War in 1967. Among his several achievements in office were closer ties with America, an increase in immigration from the Soviet Union and maintenance of good relationships between political opposition groups during and after the Six-Day War.

Ginsberg, Asher Hirsch (better known by his pen name **Ahad Ha'am**) (1856–1927)
He was a Hebrew author, Zionist theoretician and leader of Hibbat Zion. He believed that Zionism's chief task was the revival of the Jewish cultural and spiritual center of Palestine ("cultural Zionism"), rather than the creation of a Jewish State there. He was one of the earliest Zionists to warn against ignoring the Arab question. He was born in the Ukraine. After receiving a Hebrew education, he studied other languages and literatures. In 1886 he became involved in the Jewish national movement Hibbat Zion in Odessa. He was convinced that the majority of Jews would always remain in the Diaspora and he said about his ideal of a cultural center of Jewish life, "What we lack above all is a fixed spot to serve as a national spiritual center, a safe retreat, not for Jews, but for Judaism, for the spirit of our people."

After the first World Zionist Conference in 1897 he was engaged in vehement public arguments with Herzl and Max Nordau over the merits of diplomatic, i.e., political, Zionism. He contended that only through a cultural/spiritual Jewish revival could the Diaspora be safeguarded from assimilation and the proper foundations be laid for another Jewish homeland. He moved to Palestine in 1922 and advocated a Jewish majority there as the only way to actualize Zionism. His writings are still widely read, though they are not as influential as in the past generation. His pen name, Ahad Ha-am, was specifically chosen since it means "One of the people".

Herzl, Theodor (1860–1904)

He was the founder of "political" Zionism and of the World Zionist Organization. He was born in Budapest, Hungary, where he received little Jewish education as a child. When 18, he studied law at the University in Vienna. It was there that he became aware of and involved in the troubles and suffering of the Jewish people. At 35 he was well-known as Paris correspondent for the famed Viennese newspaper, the *Vienna Neue Freie Presse*. Herzl covered the Dreyfus Affair, the story of a Jewish officer in the French Army who was falsely accused of being a spy. By now, Herzl had come to terms with the depth of French anti-Semitism. His conclusion, as expressed in his short book *Der Judenstaat (The Jewish State)* issued in 1896, and in his convening of the First World Zionist Congress in Basel in 1897, was that the Jewish people should return to their own homeland, a Jewish State, preferably in Palestine.

Between 1896 and 1904, he traveled widely in Europe as well as visiting Istanbul and Palestine several times in an attempt to enlist the financial and/or diplomatic support of Jews and government officials. He was opposed by most religious leaders while he gained increasing popularity among the Jewish masses of Europe, particularly in the Pale of the Settlement. He was elected first President of the WZO (1897–1904) and spent the last brief period of his life in further diplomatic and fund-raising efforts and in the making of the WZO an ultimately effective agent for these methods of achieving his dream. In 1949 he was reburied on Mt. Herzl in Jerusalem near the Herzl museum. Both of his books on Zionism, the second being *Altneuland (Old New Land)*, have been translated into English as well as *The Diaries of Theodore Herzl* (1960). The Hebrew anniversary of his death, 20th of Tammuz, is a national memorial day in Israel.

Meir, Golda (formerly Meyerson) (1898–1978)

She was an Israeli Labor leader, politician and Prime Minister. She was born in Kiev, Russia, moved to Milwaukee and was educated as a teacher. She made *aliyah* in 1921, having become involved in

Zionist activities. In 1934 she joined the Executive Committee of the Histadrut and became active in Labor Zionism. In 1946 she was made head of the Jewish Agency Political Department and met with King Abdullah of Transjordan in efforts to reach an agreement on Palestine's future.

In 1948 she became the first Israeli minister to Russia. She was a member of the Knesset from 1949 until her death. She served as Minister of Labor in successive governments until 1956, when she became Foreign Minister and represented Israel at the United Nations. In 1966 she was made General Secretary of Mapai (the Workers' Party) and finally Prime Minister in 1969, following the death of Levi Eshkol. Her prestige and health were gravely undermined by the strain and tension of the early days of the Yom Kippur War and she retired a few months later. "Golda", as she was universally known, published her collected papers under the title *This is our Strength* in 1962 and an autobiography *My Life* in 1975.

Szold Henrietta (1860–1945)

She is known as the "Mother of Youth Aliyah". She was born in Baltimore, where she was trained as a teacher and got early experience assisting with integration of Jewish immigrants. She became active in publishing, first as Secretary of the Jewish Publication Society and later as Associate Editor of the *Jewish Year Book*. In 1912, Szold founded Hadassah, the Women's Zionist Organization of America. In 1927, she became the first woman member of the Zionist Executive and was responsible for the education and health of the Yishuv in Palestine.

She was a woman of great vitality and wisdom and had tremendous sympathy and understanding for individual children. In 1930, she became Director of Social Welfare of Vaad Leumi and in 1934, was responsible for settling the first group of children who had fled Nazi terror. She then became an active leader of Children and Youth Aliyah, which saved thousands of Jewish children. She also worked to create friendly relationships between Jews and Arabs. The Hadassah Hospital in Jerusalem is funded by the organization which she founded. She died in 1945.

(Submitted by Simon Klarfeld)

QUOTES

For the Jews, Jerusalem symbolizes the fact that we have come home. Tel Aviv is a modern city. Jerusalem reminds us that we are 3,000 years old.

David Hartman (1931–)

The State of Israel . . . will be based on freedom, justice and peace as envisaged by the prophets of Israel; it will ensure complete equality of social and political rights to all its inhabitants irrespective of religion, race or sex . . .

Declaration of Independence
of Israel, May 14, 1948 (5 Iyyar, 5708)

There are few countries which have played so central a role in world history as the land of Israel.

David Ben-Gurion (1886–1973), 1965

A nation does not receive a state on a silver platter.

Chaim Weizmann (1874–1952)

As long as in the heart the Jewish spirit yearns
With eyes turned eastward looking toward Zion
Then our hope, the hope of two thousand years, is not lost;
To be a free nation in our land, the land of Zion and Jerusalem.

"Hatikvah"

. . . the comfort level for American Jews is such that they look less and less toward Israel—especially now, when the Orthodox Establishment that controls religious life in Israel seems intent on demeaning the religious practices of most American Jews.

Craig Horowitz, in *New York*
Magazine, 1997

For the Jew there are only three paths open:
1. To remain as we are, in our present condition, to be oppressed forever.
2. To abandon Judaism . . . but still to suffer debasement and derision for many, many years . . .

3. To begin our effort for the rebirth of Israel in the Land of its
   fathers, so that our next generation may attain a normal
   national life in every sense of the word. . . .
Make your choice.

Moshe Leib Lillenblum
(1843–1910), *Diaries*

If the husband wishes to go to Palestine but his wife refuses, she
may be compelled to go; if she refuses to comply, she may be
divorced and forfeits her marriage contract. If she wishes to go,
while he refuses, he may be compelled to go; if he refuses he is
compelled to divorce her and pay her marriage contract in full.

Ketubot 110b

The air of Israel makes one wise.

Rabbi Zeira-Baba Batra 158b

Do you want to behold God's presence during this life? Then study
Torah in the Land of Israel.

Midrash Tehillim 105:1

Even the comments of inhabitants of people in Israel in the street
are Torah.

Vayikra Rabba 34:7

In the imagination of the world the people of Israel occupy considerably more space than they do on the geographic map. Since time
immemorial Israel has been richer in drama than in physical
dimensions.

Shimon Peres (1923–), 1979

Jewish males get restored to masculinity and vigor in Israel where
the powerless, the scattered, the impotent Jews of the Diaspora are
restored to potency by nationhood.

Philip Roth (1933–), 1986

The Promised Land, where we can have hooked noses, black or
red beards, and bow legs, without being despised for it. Where we

can live at last as free men on our own soil and where we can die peacefully in our own fatherland.

Theodor Herzl (1860–1904),
Private Diaries

We have learned: Until the people of Israel entered the Land all songs of praise to God could be rendered in any place; once Israel entered the Land, songs of praise to God could be rendered in no other place. Until the Land of Israel was chosen, prophetic communication could occur in any place; once the Land of Israel was chosen, prophetic communication could occur in no other place.

Midrash Yalkut on *Ezekiel* 1

My heart is in the East and I am at the edge of the West. Then how can I taste what I eat? How can I enjoy it? How can I fulfill my vows and pledges while Zion is the domain of Edom and I am in the bonds of Arabia? It would be easy for me to leave behind all the good things of Spain. It would be glorious to see the dust of the ruined shrine.

Yehuda Halevi (before 1075?–1141)

The world makes many images of Israel, but Israel makes only one image of itself: that of being constantly on the verge of ceasing to be, of disappearing.

Simon Rawidowicz (1897–1957),
"Israel: the Ever-Dying People"

Why are we not allowed to say that after the emergence of the State, a Zionist is only he who packs his bags and comes to Israel?

Golda Meir (1898–1978)

Zionism has to be redefined so as to assure a permanent place for Diaspora Judaism.

Rabbi Mordecai Kaplan (1881–1983)

Now the Lord said unto Abram: "Get thee out of thy country, and from thy kindred, and from thy father's house, unto the land that I will show thee. And I will make of thee a great nation, and I will bless thee, and make thy name great and be thou a blessing. And I will bless them that bless thee, and him that curseth thee will I curse; and thee shall all the families of the earth be blessed." So Abram went, as the Lord had spoken unto him.

Genesis 12:1–4

Thus said the Lord: I have returned to Zion, and I will dwell in Jerusalem. Jerusalem will be called the City of Faithfulness, and the mount of the Lord of Hosts the Holy Mount. Thus said the Lord of Hosts: There shall yet be old men and women in the squares of Jerusalem, each with staff in hand because of their great age. And the squares of the city shall be crowded with boys and girls playing in the squares.

Zechariah 8:3–5

In Basel I founded the Jewish state. If I said this aloud today, I would be answered by universal laughter. Perhaps in five years, and certainly in fifty, everyone will agree.

Theodor Herzl, (1860–1904) (writing in
his diary about first Zionist Congress in
Basel, 1897)

The Hebrew language is the only language which can unite the Jewish world.

Menachem Ussishkin
(1863–1941), 1905

The Jews of America cannot live without English but will not survive without Hebrew.

Rabbi Solomon Schechter (1847–1915)

My approach to Zionism was through Americanism. In time, practical experience and observation convinced me that Jews were by reason of their traditions and their character peculiarly fitted for the attainment of American ideals. Gradually, it became clear to me that to be good Americans, we must be better Jews and to be better Jews, we must become Zionists! I began gradually to realize, that these 20th century ideals of America, of democracy, of social justice, of longing for righteousness, were ancient Jewish ideals . . . that that which I was striving for as a thing essentially American, as the ideals for our country, were the Jewish ideals of thousands of years.

Louis D. Brandeis (1856–1941)

Our aim is the kingdom of Heaven. . . . We take Palestine by the way. But we must take it with clean hands; we must take it in a way as to enable the Jewish people. Otherwise, it will not be worth having.

Louis D. Brandeis (1856–1941), 1921

It is not necessary to be crazy to be a Zionist, but it helps.

Chaim Weizmann (1874–1952)

We have fought our way through to liberty, equality and fraternity; no one shall rob us of these gains. . . . We Jews of America have found America to be our Zion. Therefore, I refuse to allow myself to be called a Zionist. I am an American.

Henry Morgenthau, Sr.
(1891–1967), 1940

If you place in one hand all the ideals of the Jewish people, and in the other hand the survival of Israel—if it ever comes to a matter of choice—I will choose survival, for the dead do not praise God.

David Ben-Gurion (1886–1973), 1950

We fight, therefore we are.

Menachem Begin (1913–1992)

I am first and foremost a Jew—and only then an Israeli. I implore you to teach your children Judaism. I know you give them love and devotion. But that is not enough. You are enjoined, you are required, you are commanded to bring them up as Jews.

Moshe Dayan (1915–1981), 1978

What you do know is that there is one fact of Jewish life unchanged by the creation of a Jewish state: you cannot take your right to live for granted. Others can; you cannot. This is not to say that everyone else is living pleasantly and well under a decent regime. No, it means only that the Jews, because they are Jews, have never been able to take the right to live as a natural right.

> Saul Bellow (1915–),
> *To Jerusalem and Back*

We consider ourselves no longer a nation, but a religious community, and therefore expect neither a return to Palestine, nor a sacrificial worship under the sons of Aaron, nor the restoration of any of the laws concerning the Jewish state.

> "Pittsburgh Platform of the Reform
> Movement", 1885

The restoration of unity to the world must be accomplished through exile. . . . One must remember that it was Babylonia (and not Israel) that gave birth to the entire Oral Tradition.

> Tzeddik Ha Cohen of Kublin,
> *Pri Tzaddik*, 1934

The essential nature of Judaism resists the idea of a Jewish state with borders. . . . Nationalism will cause severe inner damage to Judaism.

> Albert Einstein (1879–1955), 1938

The Diaspora is the reservoir from which the Jewish homeland must be fed.

> Hyam Greenberg, 1943,
> American Zionist

I am in favor of Jews becoming assimilated with and absorbed by the countries in which they live. I think it is high time to liquidate this anachronism of a separate community all over the world, which cannot be defined either as a separate race or nation or religious sect, and whose insistence on remaining in one way apart has led to an unparalleled chain of massacres, persecutions and expulsions for fifteen thousand years.

> Arthur Koestler (1905–1983), 1946

The time has come for us to proclaim the enduring legitimacy of the Diaspora on a spiritual level.

> Rabbi Gershon Cohen, 1973

Diaspora is more characteristic of the Jewish people than the State.

Nahum Goldmann, 1977

Anybody who cares seriously about being a Jew is in Exile and would be in Exile even if that person were in Jerusalem. That Exile results because our Jewish ideal is unrealized anywhere in the world. . . . For us, Exile specifically means being willing to take upon oneself the burdens of being an individual in relationship to one's faith and fighting for the welfare of the Jewish people, most of whose members are largely indifferent and don't care.

Rabbi Eugene B. Borowitz, 1980

I don't believe for one single moment that I live in Exile. I never teach it to my children or to any other children. I wouldn't teach that to anybody. I don't live in Exile. I live in a Jewish Diaspora and I'm perfectly content to live in a Diaspora. I think the emphasis on *aliyah* is nonsense for American Jewry.

Rabbi Balfour Brickner, 1980

It is time to recognize that Israel and the Diaspora are two different answers to the question: what is it to be a Jew? Israel is the national answer: to be a Jew is to live in a Jewish state. The Diaspora is the religious answer: to be a Jew is to live by the Jewish faith anywhere in the world.

Chief Rabbi Jonathan Sacks, 1994

While continuing to lend philanthropic support to their fellow Jews who live in the land of our remote ancestors, Reform Jews might now begin to devote themselves again to the deepening and strengthening of a progressive Judaism in America, which is and will remain fiercely independent of ephemeral political constellations in another country.

Rabbi Jakob Petuchowski
(1925–1991), 1981

Many non-Orthodox Jews in America are prepared to accept any enormity from Israel without challenging it, even if a similar enormity in the United States would send them into the streets.

Rabbi Jakob Petuchowski
(1925–1991), 1981

It was 30 centuries ago that Samaria and Judea broke off from one another and then were separately destroyed. The alienation of Jewish communities from one another is never beneficial. Yet there is danger of such a separation, brought about by clerical-political arrogance in Israel and growing disillusion on the part of American Jews.

Rabbi David Polish (1910–1995), 1981

The future of the Jews is in Israel. . . . We know what mixed marriages can bring. From a demographic point of view, Israel is the only place. I urge you to make Israel your home.

Ezer Weizman (1924–), former
President of Israel, 1993

It's time to say that America is a better place to be a Jew than Jerusalem. If ever there was a Promised Land, we Jewish Americans are living in it. Here Jews have flourished, not alone in politics and economy, but in matters of art, culture and learning. Jews feel safe and secure here in ways that they do not and cannot in the State of Israel. And they have found an authentically Jewish voice—their own voice—for their vision of themselves.

Jacob Neusner (1932–)

America is different—because no Hitler calamity is going to happen here. America is different—because it has no long-established majority ethnic culture, but is still evolving a composite culture to which Jews, too, are privileged to make their characteristic contributions. America is different.

Professor Ben Halpern, 1958

In Israel, people have their roots in the Diaspora, and that is an interesting sociological and historical development. So I start out with a very important premise: *we are a world people*. If we don't start out with that premise, then the communities in the Diaspora have a very inferior reality, and if we accept that self-image, we cannot grow, we cannot be what we want to be.

Rabbi Sherwin T. Wine, International
Institute for Secular Humanism, 1993

7

FAMILY AND LIFE CYCLE

In the Jewish community, as in the larger American society, there are diverse conceptions of what constitutes a family. There is no longer a single norm defining expectations and roles within the family. Among the factors affecting family composition are divorce and remarriage, later age of marriage or child-bearing, adoption (particularly of children from other cultures), ease of mobility away from one's family home, and acceptance of "alternative lifestyles" such as gay and lesbian relationships. Of particular significance to Jewish family life and continuity is the high rate of intermarriage.

The Jewish community can best respond by recognizing that diversity and developing institutions, settings and programming that are relevant to non-traditional units as well as to "traditional families". The degree to which the community accepts members of non-traditional units and responds to their needs will influence whether they remain connected to the community.

Several activities in this chapter allow members of families to explore, appreciate, and be comfortable with the unique relationships in their own family. The non-judgmental and egalitarian qualities of experiential education are conducive to honest exploration. Those activities also provide an opportunity for communication within a family, allowing all family members to be heard.

Those same virtues of experiential education apply to the activities concerned with relations between generations and with aging.

A FAMILY CREST

Purpose:

A particularly good opening activity for a family program or retreat. This activity can serve to introduce families to each other and also to begin to get family units working together. It can also be used for individuals to present themselves as a beginning activity.

Group:

Family units; up to 20 family units.

Setting:

An open, spacious room in which family units can spread out and comfortably work with crafts materials.

Materials:

A sheet of newsprint and markers for each family unit; tape.

Time:

45–60 minutes.

Instructions:

1. The leader posts in the front of the room a large example of a family crest and the categories of information needed to complete it.

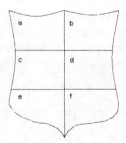

Categories
a. The family name and its meaning and/or earlier versions
b. First names of family members in English and Hebrew
c. Countries of origin of grandparents

d. Occupations of adults
e. Greatest family achievement
f. Favorite family activity

2. Each family is given a sheet of newsprint and markers. Family members discuss how they would respond to the above six categories in completing the family crest and work together in making their family crest.
3. Families take turns introducing themselves by presenting their family crest. All the family crests should be posted on the walls of the meeting room, where they remain until the end of the program, when families are encouraged to take home their crest.

Variation:

A. FAMILY MOGEN DAVID. Instead of the crest use a Mogen David (Star of David) to present the several facts about the family. This can be done by having the family draw a Mogen David on a sheet of newsprint and fill in the six pieces of information called for in the Instructions (above) in each of the six triangles of the star. In the middle space fill in the family name. Additional categories for providing information include: family hobbies, a Jewish organization to which you belong, favorite food, a special family vacation, favorite biblical figure, favorite childhood story, a favorite TV show, and a Jewish cause or issue in which you are involved.

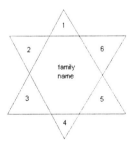

A more elaborate way of constructing the Mogen David is for the leader to prepare in advance equal-size triangles in different colors. Enough triangles should be prepared so that each family can have six different-colored triangles on which they creatively respond to the six categories of information requested for their family. The family then assembles the six triangles on a sheet of poster board to form a Mogen David.

(Adapted from ideas submitted by Hannah Handler and Mark Weinberg)

❀   ❀   ❀

GROUP MURAL

Purpose:

"Group Mural" is an especially good activity to use as a first activity at a family workshop, or one in which there is a mixture of different groups of people. The objective of this activity is to provide an opportunity for a family or any other small cluster of people with a common identity to get to know other, similar units. In addition to introducing the separate units and providing them with an opportunity to enhance their own group-pride, the activity begins the process of linking the smaller groups into a larger whole.

Group:

Mixed age groups: children through adults; up to 15 families or other units.

Setting:

A large, open space with floor and walls that can accommodate craft activity.

Materials:

Assorted craft supplies in sufficient supply for the size of the group; a large strip of brown wrapping or butcher paper, 3 feet wide (length is determined by the number of units: allow approximately 8 feet per unit for the individual murals).

Time:

50–60 minutes, approximately 30 minutes for completing the mural and 20 minutes for the units to introduce themselves.

Instructions:

1. The leader stretches out the mural paper and marks sections for each family or unit. (Alternative: cut up segments of the mural paper and give each unit a separate strip which they can work on, and later all the separate murals are taped together in one large mural.) Each unit is asked to use the crafts materials to do a graphic presentation that tells some salient facts about their unit and will serve as the basis for introducing them to the other units.
2. After all groups finish their unit murals, the full mural is taped up on the wall, and each unit introduces each of its members via their artistic representation.
3. The mural can remain hanging during the subsequent activities of the program and can be referred to by the leader at the conclusion of the program to remind the participants of where they were at the outset and where they are after their work together.

FOLK WISDOM

Every culture accumulates words of wisdom, which are passed on from generation to generation, without attribution to any author. The following sayings are likely to be familiar to most Americans. They may serve to recall similar sayings, and to set into motion shared reminiscing.

Purpose:

To generate an intergenerational dialogue as an icebreaker or means of improving communication between generations.

Group:

Most effective with a group comprised of several generations, possibly a family reunion.

Setting:

Any room where conversation can occur comfortably.

Materials:

Newsprint and markers or blackboard and chalk.

Time:

5–30 minutes.

Instructions:

The leader hands out printed sheets of the following examples of folk wisdom or has group members offer their own contributions which the leader can record on newsprint or a blackboard. The leader divides the group into intergenerational pairs of a young and old member and encourages conversation about the meaning of the sayings. The leader may encourage participants, especially the older ones, to recall personal associations with the sayings.

EXAMPLES

The shortest distance between two points is a straight line.
Keep thy shop and thy shop will keep thee.
Truth is stranger than fiction.
Where there's smoke, there's fire.
A friend in need is a friend indeed.
A penny saved is a penny earned.
Don't put off to tomorrow what you can do today.
He who hesitates is lost.
Haste makes waste.
A stitch in time saves nine.
Honesty is the best policy.
When it rains, it pours.
He is a fool that cannot conceal his wisdom.
Seek and you shall find.

❀ ❀ ❀

FAMILY WORDS OF WISDOM

Purpose:

To help people to get a sense of the important values which are passed on to them by their families. While this activity has the same content as "Folk Wisdom," the emphasis here is on the individual's experience of learning from his/her forebears.

Group:

High school and older; any size, since the activity will be done in smaller units.

Setting:

A space large enough to allow the full group to break up into small-group discussions.

Materials:

5 × 7 cards and pencils for each person; newsprint and masking tape.

Time:

1–1¼ hours; more time if done as an intergenerational activity.

Instructions:

1. Each person is asked to try to remember any key phrases heard frequently in childhood. These are statements which might have been repeated by parents or grandparents as important words of advice for the child.
2. Each participant receives a 5 × 7 card and is asked to write down the one or two phrases that were the most important pieces of advice they received from their families.

3. Form pairs, trios, or quartets so participants can share this advice with each other. Group members should be asked to relate the meaning the advice had for them: As a child, how did he/she feel about the advice? What are his/her feelings about it now? Does the advice contain a Jewish element?

4. The leader asks each of the subgroups to report the most frequent pieces of advice, which are then listed on a sheet(s) of posted newsprint. The full group assembles to discuss the implications of the value-messages transmitted to them by the previous generation.

5. The participants are then asked to think about advice, statements, or phrases which they often repeat (or have repeated) to their children. (If a participant has no children, what might be the type of advice s/he would be inclined to pass on?) These key statements should be written on the reverse side of the 5 × 7 card. The same subgroups reassemble and share their responses.

6. As before, the leader asks the discussion groups to report their most typical statements, which are listed on a sheet of posted newsprint. Are there apparent differences in the content and extent of advice given by the two generations? Are there differences in the place accorded to Jewish values in the advice?

Variation:

A. FAMILY ADVICE: A GENERATIONAL PERSPECTIVE. This activity can be used as a basis for parent-child discussion. The parents and children are asked to think about, and write down, the words of advice they (parents) give or receive (children). First, the parents and children should meet separately to discuss their collective responses and to draw up summary newsprint sheets. Then, small groups of parents and children (not of the same families) should be convened to share perspectives. A summary session for all participants would highlight general considerations and different perspectives across generations. As a conclusion to this activity, children and parents of the same family should share their observations.

THE FAMILY VALUES QUESTIONNAIRE

Purpose:

To help families identify and articulate their personal values.

Group:

Family units.

Setting:

A comfortable room with seating for everyone.

Materials:

Paper and pencils.

Time:

1 hour.

Instructions:

1. The Questionnaire could be a basis for a meeting, which is part of a Jewish Family Education program. Having children as well as parents present makes it possible to compare and discuss responses both of children and adults as groups, and then to have members of individual families compare their responses.
2. Once the data are generated on the items in the Questionnaire, they can be saved by the group leaders to be used as comparisons with other entities within the organization, as well as other populations, and also with the same or similar populations in the future.

THE FAMILY VALUES QUESTIONNAIRE

I. Please answer each of the 5 questions below with your prefered choice on a scale from 1 to 5.

	Strongly agree	Agree	Neutral	Disagree	Strongly disagree
1. All members of a family should be prepared to give up personal plans for special family gatherings.					
2. Jews should marry only other Jews.					
3. Jews should try to be like rather than unlike other Americans.					
4. All Jews should have a special loyalty to the state of Israel.					
5. Being Jewish is a very important part of my life.					

II. Think about your own family life. If there is one thing you could change about how your family operates, what would it be?

III. ADVICE: What is really important to you? If you had to give only one piece of advice to your children, what would it be?

ADVICE: FROM PARENTS TO CHILDREN

Purpose:

This is an activity designed to help people think about the issues and tensions in rearing Jewish families in the 21st century. It will facilitate and focus dialog between adults and children on transmitting Jewish identity and values within the family.

Group:

Children high-school age or older and their parents.

Setting:

A comfortable setting with seating for all members.

Materials:

Printed questionnaires and writing materials or newsprint and/or blackboard.

Time:

30–60 minutes.

Instructions:

1. The leader introduces the activity by explaining that parents are a critical influence on whether a child will make Judaism an important part of their adult lives. What is important is not only what the parents try to do but how it is perceived by the child. Each generation may exert both positive and negative influence on the next generation's attitudes toward religion and cultural heritage.
2. The leader either hands out a sheet with the following questions or has them posted in advance on a blackboard or newsprint.
3. Depending on size of the group, it may be necessary to divide participants into groups. These may be within generation or across generation according to needs of the program. Each group discusses the questions.
4. The groups then reconvene to report what they share and what is unique to each generation. The leader can record on newsprint the generational influences that are reported.

INFLUENCE OF PARENTS ON JEWISH IDENTITY

1a. (IF YOU ARE A CHILD) What is one piece of advice you would give your parents about how they could be better Jewish parents?

1b. (IF YOU ARE A PARENT) What is one piece of advice you would give your child/ren as to why and how they should be Jews as they grow up?

2a. What is one piece of GENERAL advice or wisdom you received from your parents that has influenced your values and how you have conducted your life?

2b. What is one piece of JEWISH advice or wisdom you received from your parents?

2c. What are the two most important messages, positive or negative, that your parents passed on to you?

2d. How would you evaluate YOUR PARENTS as role models for you, in terms of their behavior and values they stood for?
___ Excellent ___ Good ___ Fair ___ Poor

2e. (IF YOU HAVE CHILDREN) How would you evaluate YOURSELF as a role model for your child/ren, in terms of your behavior and values you stand for? (IF YOU DON'T HAVE CHILDREN BUT THINK YOU MIGHT, ANSWER HYPOTHETICALLY.)
___ Excellent ___ Good ___ Fair ___ Poor

2f. As you review the above questions, what insights have you gained about how Jewish parents can and should function?

GRANDPARENTS: TRANSMITTERS OF WISDOM?

This is an activity which focuses on the role of grandparents today. It has two components: to ask people to reflect on their reactions to their own grandparents and to ask people to anticipate the prospect of their becoming grandparents in the not too distant future.

ME AS A GRANDCHILD

Grandparents have traditionally been thought of as bearers of the "wisdom of the generations". Does that piece of traditional wisdom still pertain in this era of Post-Modernity? Ideally, if the parents of both your mother and father lived long enough for you to have known them, you would have known four grandparents.

Reflect on your interaction with your grandparents. The first question to think about is whether you had enough (or any) interaction with your grandparents for them to have made any impression on you. Do you feel you have now, or in the past, received wisdom from your grandparents? Then, please share one or two special memories of experiences or ways in which any of your grandparents influenced you or your values. Try to be objective in reporting on the influence of your grandparents, recognizing the possibility of either no impact or, even a negative impact, and of course, of positive experiences.

ME AS A GRANDPARENT?

Finally, given the great advances in medical technology, the fastest growing age group today is the age 70 and over population. Therefore, it is realistic to expect that most of you will indeed become grandparents, and likely sooner than you think. So, the final phase of this activity is to ask you to think about yourself as a grandma or grandpa.

What are your spontaneous thoughts on becoming a grandparent? Is that a depressing or a positive idea for you? Think about these questions and write down some of the thoughts and feelings which emerge as you anticipate yourself as a grandparent.

To conclude this process of reflection we will arrange for people to meet in small groups of 5 or 6 people and share with one another your thoughts on becoming a grandparent. Is this something you have thought about before? What are your emotions as you anticipate yourself as a grandparent?

INTERGENERATIONAL PROGRAM

Purpose:

To bring senior citizens and children together for an activity. To have participants share what is like to be a child now and what it was like before. To tell about an important person in their lives.

Group:

A mixed group of senior citizens and children aged 9–11. The activity works best with a roughly equal number from each age group.

Setting:

This activity should take place around tables.

Materials:

Participants should be instructed to bring a 4 × 6 picture of some-one who is important to them. Leaders should provide 4 × 6 plastic frames and materials with which to decorate them, e.g., fabric paint, buttons, sequins, stickers, glue.

Time:

    5 minutes for introduction
    10 minutes for interviewing
    10 minutes to present pictures
    20 minutes to decorate frames
    5 minutes to wrap up

Instructions:

1. Welcome participants to the program. If the group is small, say less than 15, go around the room and have everyone introduce themselves. If group is larger, participants will introduce themselves when they get into smaller groups.
2. Divide into smaller groups. Groups should be made before the program as to insure that in each group there are some senior citizens and youth. Place numbers on the tables so that participants will know where to go.
3. Within each smaller group, divide into pairs consisting of one senior citizen and one child. It is okay if there are a group of three as long as there is at least one senior and one youth. In the pairs, they should interview each other. The following is a list of questions. (Questions should be typed and passed out at the start of this part.)

   Questions for senior citizen to ask child:
   a) Name
   b) School
   c) Favorite Sport

d) Parents' occupations
e) Any siblings
f) Any pets
g) Favorite ice cream flavor
h) Favorite movie
i) Free-time interests

Questions for children to ask senior citizens:
a) Name
b) Any children and grandchildren
c) Where they grew up
d) Childhood memories
e) Occupation
f) Favorite movie
g) Free-time interests
h) Any pets
i) What their biggest worry was when they were the child's age

4. Pairs should come back together into the large group. Then each person should go around and share their picture, explaining who is in the photo and why they chose to bring that photo.
5. Participants will then decorate frames for their pictures.
6. Wrap-up: Leader can focus the discussion on what each generation has learned about the other or any other feedback offered by participants.

(Submitted by Shannon Stein)

SENSITIVITY TO AGING WITHIN THE JEWISH COMMUNITY

Purpose:

To promote understanding of life changes that occur with aging and, in particular, to deepen sensitivity toward the issues and needs of the senior population.

Group:

This exercise is especially geared to the teenager population. It is a great program to do for teenagers who will be working as volunteers with senior adults. There should be between ten and fifteen people who will participate in this program. The rest of the teens will be an audience who will watch the presentation and discuss their reactions.

Setting:

This program should take place indoors. There should be a row of chairs arranged in a straight line (one chair per participant.) There should be another chair which is placed in the center facing the line of chairs.

Materials:

Eight signs made out of cardboard or paper to be used as age cards. Each sign bears an age (20, 30, . . . , 90) written large enough for an audience to see.

Time:

35 minutes.

Instructions:

The leader begins by stating that the introduction and directions to this exercise will take five minutes to explain, the exercise itself will take twenty minutes, and the wrap-up session will take ten minutes. Next, the leader gives the following introduction to the teenage participants:

"This is an experiential exercise that will give you a better understanding as to what it is like for a Jewish person to grow old and become frail. It will enable you to become more sensitive to this population within the Jewish community. It is important for you to remember that no one wakes up as ninety. These people have all experienced the same joys, hopes, and fears, and sorrows as all of us. The difference is all of the losses the elderly people have suffered as they have aged. These losses may not be just physical, like losing hearing or vision. Many seniors have lost close friends and family. All of these individuals were once children, teenagers, and young adults. Many married, had families, homes, and productive jobs. You will each have the opportunity to see the loses that the elderly population have suffered so you will have a greater understanding of them and be more sensitive to their aging process."

The leader then asks for a volunteer to be the individual who "ages." This individual will be seated in the center chair, the one that faces the audience. Next the leader asks for eight more volunteers. These volunteers will hold up the different age cards. The age cards are distributed to these participants, who sit in the single row that faces the individual who ages.

The exercise begins with the leader explaining that the person in the "aging" chair will age from 20 to 90 in the next 20 minutes. As the leader tells a story, which was prepared in advance, the participant acts out the appropriate age; this story follows the life of a 20-year-old named Daniel. The volunteer with the age-20 card is asked to come to the front, stands behind Daniel, and holds the card above his head.

Age Twenty:
The leader then tells a story about the twenty-year-old Daniel. For example, "Well Daniel—you are a bright handsome, young man. You are active in the Young Jewish Singles Society at your synagogue. You are finishing your undergraduate degree at an Ivy-League college where you are majoring in pre-med. You own your own car and are living in an apartment on campus which you share with two other young men. You are very popular and have an active social life. You have a mother, father, grandparents (all four on both your mother's and father's side), and two sisters. You have a large group of friends. Your life is great and your health is excellent."

Age Thirty:
Now ten years later . . . The person holding the age-20 sign sits down and the person holding the age-30 sign takes that person's place. The leader goes on to discuss Daniel's life at thirty.

"Daniel is married, he graduated from Einstein medical school and is doing his residency at Mount Sinai in New York City. His wife is pregnant with their first child. Both of his older sisters are now married and they each have two children. Daniel is the president of the Society for Jewish Resident Doctors in NYC. His family is a member of the JCC and synagogue."

Age Forty:
The exercise continues in this manner throughout Daniel's life. At forty he has three children, he has a big home in Westchester, he is the chief heart surgeon at Beth Israel Hospital in NYC, he is active in the brotherhood at his synagogue, his grandparents have all passed away, etc.

Age Fifty:
His mother develops cancer, he becomes Treasurer of his synagogue, etc.

Age Sixty:
His children are all in college, his mother passed away, his father is in a nursing home due to a stroke that left him unable to care for himself, Daniel is forced to pay for his father's expenses in this home, Daniel's mortgage is paid off, etc.

Age Seventy:
His father died, he is now a grandparent, his wife develops breast cancer and dies, he retires from the hospital and begins teaching at Einstein.

Age Eighty:
Both of his sisters have passed away, he has retired from teaching, his closest two friends from childhood have died, his eyesight is deteriorating and he is no longer able to drive. He begins to feel helpless and that he is no longer productive. He is no longer active in Jewish life. The last few years have been hard for him.

Age Ninety:
He is in a nursing home. He fell and broke his hip and can no longer care for himself. All of his friends have died and his children have moved out of state. He feels all alone.

This is the end of the activity.

Wrap-up session:
Everyone is asked to take seats in a circle. The leader opens the wrap-up session with a question. "What does Daniel's life look

like now? What is he left with?" The following questions can be asked and discussed in the wrap-up session.

1. What losses has Daniel suffered over the years?
2. How do you think he feels?
3. What might he be like if you met him now for the first time?
4. What are some of the things that this exercise helped you think and learn about in relation to the elderly population?
5. What do you think are the main issues that individuals face while growing old?
6. What role does the Jewish community play in caring for the needs of our seniors?
7. Do you ever think about your own process of aging? If so, what are some of the feelings you experience?

(Submitted by Melissa Braverman)

CHILDHOOD MEMORY

Purpose:

To introduce members of the group and to discuss memories from childhood.

Group:

15–30 people of any age.

Setting:

Space adequate for pairs to converse and for the group to assemble.

Materials:

Participants bring baby photos or items representing a childhood memory. The leader provides a large plastic bag or other container for holding these items.

Time:

30 minutes.

Instructions:

1. Potential participants are notified in advance of the activity to bring a baby photo of themselves or an item representing a childhood memory. A followup reminder may be appropriate.
2. When the activity is conducted, the leader introduces it as an opportunity both to get to know other participants and to express something meaningful about oneself. Exactly half of the participants place their items in the bag. The other half hold onto their items.
3. Each person who is holding an item takes another from the bag and displays it. The person who contributed that item comes forward; and the two become a pair. Within pairs, the two people introduce themselves, relate where they were born and grew up, and share a childhood memory related to their item.
4. After ten minutes, the pairs reassemble in the larger group. In turn, each person introduces his/her partner to the other participants, describes the partner's item, and summarizes the partner's special memory.

(Submitted by Nina Bloomstein)

GENDER IN PICTURES

Purpose:

To facilitate discussion about gender roles and our society. This activity is designed to help the youth understand that they are not alone in their confused feelings and to empower them to understand and deal with gender stereotypes and barriers.

Group:

Senior Youth groups of any size

Setting:

A large room that allows for the students to spread out and work alone, in addition to two separate areas for discussion groups.

Materials:

Magazines (ask the students to bring old magazines to the activity, the more the better and the more variety the better), glue, scissors, construction paper, markers.

Time:

1 hour.

Instructions:

Mixer:

Each person takes a turn stating their name and favorite childhood toy. Someone should record answers according to gender. At the end of the program, this makes an interesting wrap-up statistic and may serve to emphasize themes brought up during the activity.

Collage making:

Have everyone make a collage that represents who they are. Collages will be constructed from pictures cut out of the magazines by gluing pictures onto construction paper. (Mix up the magazines so that each participant gets a variety.) Participants may also draw with markers if they can't find an appropriate illustration; but, stress that the pictures should be the main focus of the collage.

Discussions about collages:

- When everyone is finished, put them into pairs. Ask them to pretend that the collage really represents an important **female** figure in their lives—a teacher, mother, sister, older friend, etc . . . and have the people in each pair talk to each other about what in the collage would suit this figure and what would not.
- Have everyone take a new partner, and do the same exercise substituting an important **male** figure.
- Have everyone take a new partner, and ask them to identify what they consider to be typically **female** characteristics in their collage.
- Have everyone take a new partner, and ask them to identify

what they consider to be typically **male** characteristics in their collage.

Gender discussions:

Split the group into male and female subgroups, and have a brief discussion about the activity.

- What stereotypes did this activity bring to light?
- Which pictures supported these stereotypes?
- Were there pictures that made you uncomfortable?
- Has the media affected any of your thoughts? How?

Summary:

Bring the students back together for a wrap-up. Ask for any final comments, read the list from the mixer, which should show them how in tune they are with society's standards. Explain to them how important it is that they are aware of gender stereotypes and roles, and how they need to work together as a group to be sensitive to one another.

(Submitted by Liz Kaufman-Taylor)

KEY TO A HAPPY MARRIAGE

Purpose:

This activity is meant to consider factors which are likely to contribute to a happy marriage. The point of departure for this projected review is the list, "Key to a Happy Marriage". Such a discussion on marriage could be an activity, by itself, or as part of a broader forum on the subject of marriage.

Group:

Teens ages 16 and over, on through adults of all ages. Activity would be conducted differently with married couples.

Instructions:

1. The activity would begin with the leader explaining that the purpose of the activity is to encourage participants to share

their perspectives on the factors which would contribute to a "happy" or "good" marriage. The leader should consider two alternative ways to utilize the "Key to a Happy Marriage" list. One approach is to ask the group participants initially to come up with a list of ten factors which they believe would contribute to a happy marriage. When they have come up with their own lists, participants receive printed copies of the "Key to a Happy Marriage" list, and subsequent discussion would allow for group members to compare their own lists both with the other group members and with the printed "Key to a Happy Marriage" list.

2. An alternative approach would be to have the participants begin by reading the "Key to a Happy Marriage" list and then to indicate the extent to which they agree with the ten items listed. They might also be asked to rank the ten listed items in order of importance they believe each of the ten items has for assuring a happy marriage.

3. The activity would conclude by asking the participants to try to achieve a consensus on a list in which the ten items are listed in rank order of importance. Another variation would be to ask the participants to come up with two or three new criteria for "A Happy Marriage" and to substitute these for two or three of the current items.

4. A final question for the participants is the extent to which the "Key to a Happy Marriage" list was helpful to them in assessing their marriage, or their ideas about what it takes to develop "A Happy Marriage."

KEY TO A HAPPY MARRIAGE

1) Never both be angry at the same time.
2) Never yell at each other unless the house is on fire.
3) If one of you has to win an argument, let it be your mate.
4) If you have to criticize, do it lovingly.
5) Never bring up mistakes of the past.
6) Neglect the whole world rather than each other.
7) Never go to sleep with an argument unsettled.
8) At least once every day try to say one kind or complimentary thing to your life's partner.

9) When you have done something wrong, be ready to admit it and ask for forgiveness.

10) It takes two to quarrel, and the one in the wrong usually is the one who does the most talking.

FINAL DISTRIBUTION

Purpose:

As the saying goes, "In this world nothing is certain but death and taxes." Though death is inevitable, most people prefer to avoid considering the topic. This activity requires participants to think realistically about the prospect of their death, by considering how their possessions should be distributed. This aspect of death is not particularly deep; and it is hoped that this easy introduction to contemplating one's death will encourage participants to give further, realistic thought to the subject.

Group:

Middle-aged or older adults.

Setting:

A comfortable room with seating for everyone.

Materials:

Paper and pencils.

Time:

30 minutes.

Instructions:

1. Participants write down an inventory of their most important possessions, then rank them by perceived value. It is important

to include items that have personal, sentimental value as well as those that have objective value. Some examples of items of sentimental value would be: family photos, awards or prizes, school report cards, one's first ballet slippers or baseball glove, and mementos of relatives or friends.

2. Then, participants are asked to envision the scenario, "What if you were to die tomorrow?" In response, participants indicate for each listed possession either the person to whom they would like it given or the fact that there is no preference.

3. Group discussion begins with participants describing what they found most satisfying about inventorying their possessions. This is followed by comments about the plans for distribution, e.g., whether things were distributed to one person or several, and whether the disposition of sentimental possessions was important. Discussion can proceed to address the significance of the inventory as a final statement in a person's life.

4. In summarizing, the leader should note the value of a planning exercise such as this in reducing squabbles over the inheritance, particularly among family members. On a broader level, it is valuable to be realistic and open in facing the reality of death.

Note to Leader:

The leader should be sensitive and prepared to respond to the strong feelings that may be engendered by this activity.

QUOTES

You're only young once, and if you work it right, once is enough.
Saying on a Lipton tea bag

Youth is wholly experimental.
Robert Louis Stevenson (1850–1894)

Teach your child Torah, a trade and how to swim.
Kiddushim 29a (also 30b)

And you shall teach [the Torah] to your children, and shall speak of it, when you sit in your house, when you walk on the road, when you lie down and when you rise up.

Deuteronomy 6:7

Teaching Torah to a child is analogous to giving him life.

Talmud Sanhedrin 19b

A child is not a vessel to be filled, but a flame to be kindled.

Anonymous

Train a child in the way he should go. And even when he is old, he will not depart from it.

Proverbs 22:6

The youth of a nation are the trustees of posterity.

Benjamin Disraeli (1804–1881)

He who has no wife cannot be considered a whole man.

Yebamot 63a

A virtuous woman is a crown to her husband.

Proverbs 12:8

Whoso findeth a wife findeth a great good and obtaineth favor of the Lord.

Proverbs 18:22

Marriage, if one will face the truth, is an evil, but a necessary evil.

Menander (342–291 B.C.E.)

There is no more lovely, friendly and charming relationship, communion or company than a good marriage.

Martin Luther (1483–1546)

Marriage is a noose.

Miguel de Cervantes (1547–1616)

Hasty marriage seldom proveth well.

William Shakespeare (1564–1616)

Though marriage makes man and wife one flesh, it leaves 'em still two fools.

William Congreve (1670–1729)

Keep your eyes wide open before marriage, half shut afterwards.

Benjamin Franklin (1706–1790)

Marriage to women as to men must be a luxury, not a necessity; an incident of life, not all of it. And the only possible way to accomplish this great change is to accord the women equal power in the making, shaping and controlling of the circumstances of life.

Susan B. Anthony (1820–1906)

Marriage is like life in this—that it is a field of battle and not a bed of roses.

Robert Louis Stevenson (1850–1894)

Marriage has many pains but celibacy has no pleasures.

Samuel Johnson (1709–1784)

Judaism considers sex God's gift and procreation His command. It considers marriage the proper context for intercourse and makes it a prescribed religious duty.

Rabbi Eugene B. Borowitz, 1969

Honor your father and your mother as the Lord your God has commanded you so that your days may be many and so that it may go well with you in the land which the lord your God is giving you.

Deuteronomy 5:16

There are three partners in the creation of man: God, father, mother. When a man honors his parents, it is as though God dwelt in their midst and was honored.

Kiddushim 30a

The love of parents goes to their children, but the love of these children goes to their children.

Talmud Sotah 49a

A father once came to the Rabbi Baal Shem Tov (the founder of the Hasidic movement) with a problem concerning his son. He complained that the son was forsaking his Jewish religious practices and morality, and asked the Rabbi, "What can I do? He is destroying my life, he is destroying everything I've stood for." The Rabbi answered: "Love him more."

Hasidic Saying

The center of Judaism is in the home. In contrast to other religions, it is at home where the essential celebrations and acts of observance take place—rather than in the synagogue or temple . . . the synagogue is an auxiliary . . . A Jewish home is where Judaism is at home, where Jewish learning, commitment, sensitivity to values are cultivated and cherished.

Rabbi Abraham Joshua Heschel
(1907–1972)

The strength of a nation derives from the integrity of the home.

Confucius (551–479 B.C.E.)

Woe to a man who has no home.

Friedrich Nietzsche (1844–1900)

Judaism imposes a vital task on a parent: To tell the child his people's story. What the child does with this past no parent can decree. Parents provide their children with luggage. Whether the children will open up the suitcases and use their contents is beyond the reach of parents. We have no right to enter the child's future. The parents must instill memories that haunt the child an entire lifetime; their bequest is the weight of generations: an awareness that one's biography began with Abraham.

Rabbi David Hartman, 1978

A person is part of a family. There is no fulfillment of one's duties or one's pleasures as an isolated individual. If a man is not a husband and father, then "he is nothing." A woman who is not a wife and mother is not a "real" woman.

Mark Zborowski and
Elizabeth Herzog, 1962

There may be quarrels and misunderstandings, but in time of crisis a family hangs together and cares for its own. If parents cannot give their children the support and help that is their due, other members of the family are expected to step in. Perhaps an uncle, an aunt, a grandparent, or even a more remote relative will take responsibility.

Mark Zborowski and
Elizabeth Herzog, 1962

Home is the place where, when you have to go there, they have to take you in.

Robert Frost (1874–1963)

A family is a circle of friends who love you.

T-shirt slogan

It is regrettable but true that family ties as well as other close relationships can fall apart because of jealousy, pride, anger, greed, money, incompatibility, an unkind word spoken, or for no known reason at all.

T. E. Lawrence (1888–1935)

The day your horse dies and your money is lost . . . your relatives turn into strangers.

Chinese proverb

Forty is the age of youth, fifty is the youth of old age.

Saying on a Lipton tea bag

You shall rise before the aged and show deference to the old; you shall fear your God: I am the Lord.

Leviticus 19:32

You can't help being your age, so . . . put it out of your mind and appreciate the moment. After all, it isn't a very nice way to respond to the gift of life by being vexed . . . about its ending.

John Updike (1932–)

Old folks have ambitions and dreams, too, like everybody else and why don't they work for them? Why don't they go for it? Don't sit on a couch someplace, that's my attitude.

John Glenn (1921–)

For the unlearned, old age is winter; for the learned, it is the season of the harvest.

Hasidic saying

You can be young without money, but you can not be old without it.

Tennessee Williams (1911–1983)

Old age is a shipwreck.

Charles De Gaulle (1890–1970)

Old is no longer an age category, but a state of mind.

Leonie Gordon, Editor, Harvard Institute for Learning in Retirement

There is a time for departure even when there's no certain place to go.

Tennessee Williams (1911–1983)

The art of dying is the art of living.

Dr. Sherwin B. Nuland (1930–)

Learn how to live and you'll learn how to die and you'll know how to live.

Morris Schwartz (1917–1995)

8

ISSUES CONFRONTING
THE COMMUNITY

This chapter focuses on the Jewish community as a society. Every society has formal organizations and social institutions that provide services, maintain order, and lend cohesion. Every society has an internal dynamic that is the result of differing needs and interests of the constituents.

The activities in this chapter are concerned with establishing and pursuing objectives for the community as a whole, while appreciating that preferences of subgroups or individuals vary. As opposed to many of the activities in later chapters, these activities emphasize collaboration and awareness of the responses of all participants. Some activities are concerned with establishing priorities for communal institutions. The direction of communal institutions is a significant factor in the Jewish community's surviving and remaining distinctive. Other activities are exercises in the processes of decision-making and coming to consensus within an organization.

These activities will be relevant to all people, whether or not they are in positions of leadership. All participants will benefit from the experience of expressing opinions that might shape the course of the Jewish community.

AN INTERGROUP SCORECARD

Purpose:

To explore reactions of Jews to different elements in the Jewish community and to non-Jews. Do Jews have more in common and are they more comfortable with other Jews than with non-Jews? Are there differential attitudes and feelings across the range of Jewish identification?

Group:

High school age or older; 12 or more participants; with large groups the activity can be conducted in subunits.

Setting:

Adequate space and chairs for the participants to work individually and in small groups without disruption.

Materials:

An Intergroup Scorecard (see below) and pencil for each participant.

Time:

35–45 minutes.

Instructions:

1. Each person is given an Intergroup Scorecard and asked to complete it (5–10 minutes). Small discussion groups (5–8 people) are formed, preferably with people from different backgrounds or perspectives.
2. The members of the discussion groups tally their scorecard responses by adding up the totals by columns for each of the categories. Two copies should be made of the group totals— one to serve as the focus for the small group to discuss their responses; the other to be given the leader to aggregate the totals from all the discussion groups. A low score consistently indicates a positive emotional response, while a high score consistently indicates a negative response.
3. In the discussion, the participants explore the reasons for their emotional reactions to the several groups, What are the differ-

Intergroup Scorecard

For each of the six *Questions* (left column), choose one of the *Alternative Responses* (center column) for each of the eight *Groups* (right column). Enter a 1, 2, or 3 in the columns for each group, depending on which response most accurately represents your reactions to that group.

> **GROUPS**
>
> H—Hasidic Jews
> C—Catholics
> AB—American Blacks
> U—Unitarians
> JD—Jews who deny their Jewishness
> IR—Israelis-Religious *(Dati)*
> IN—Israelis-Non religious *(Lo-dati)*
> NA—North African Jews

QUESTION	ALTERNATIVE RESPONSES			GROUPS							
	1	2	3	H	C	AB	U	JD	IR	IN	NA
1. My first reactions to this group?	Favorable	Neutral	Unfavorable								
2. What I think they think of me	"	"	"								
3. The extent to which we have something in common?	Very much	Moderate	Very little								
4. How I would feel if my child married one?	Wonderful	Indifferent	Terrible								
5. If I were in trouble, could I count on them for help?	Definitely	Maybe	No								
6. If one of them was in trouble, would I feel obliged to help?	"	"	"								
TOTALS											

❀ ❀ ❀

ences between the Jewish and the non-Jewish groups? What are the differences among the several Jewish groups? Is there evidence to support the notion that Jews, regardless of their differences, recognize that they share a common destiny with their fellow Jews?

4. The activity concludes with a coming together of the full group and an examination of the compilation of the total group's responses to the Intergroup Scorecard. (This compilation is put on a sheet of newsprint by the leader during the small-group

discussions.) The leader should direct the discussion to examining the feelings Jews have with respect to non-Jews and to their fellow Jews. Two important Jewish concepts should be explored with respect to the data: (a) "All Israel are responsible for one another;" and (b) Hillel's dictum: "If I am not for myself, who is for me? and if I am only for myself, what am I? and if not now, when?" (*Pirkei Avot* 1:14).

❀   ❀   ❀

THE JEWISH SURVIVAL GAME

INTRODUCTION
The aim of this game is to stimulate a discussion on "The Perfect Society", to discover what attitudes members have to the running of society, morality etc.

The group is told a few facts which are the basis of the game, and must be accepted by everyone.

"The group, along with 100 other Jewish people of all ages, were on a cruise, but the boat was wrecked in the storm. Fortunately nobody was lost and all landed on a desert island, with only the clothes they were wearing, and a Bible."

The group is asked to assume that they have no hope of escape for at least a year and that everybody has expressed the desire to survive as a Jewish community, i.e., everyone wants to maintain their inborn Judaism.

Then split into small discussion groups which are the groups which will decide how their brand new society will be run. The suggested groups are Education and Religion, Social and Family Structure, and Law and Order.

Two things are important:

a) Stress that they can't conjure up people, e.g., rabbis for religion or African hunters for catching animals for food. The other 100 people are simply people in their families so there may be, for example, a teacher or a doctor, but no trained Robinson Crusoes!

b) Very important to stress that they should ignore the rules of the society from which they came and approach things with a fresh viewpoint. For example, the education system need not necessarily be only for 5- to 18-year-olds, and the curriculum need not necessarily be taught by adults—what part might people of their age play in the society?

It is important that, at the end, the whole group is brought together and each group presents its conclusions, and discuss the consequences of making such decisions.

THE JEWISH SURVIVAL GAME

THE SITUATION

All of you along with 100 other Jewish people of all ages were on a cruise, but the boat was wrecked in a storm. Fortunately nobody was lost and all of you have landed on a desert island, with only the clothes that you were wearing and a Bible. As you have no chance of rescue for at least a year, people have expressed the desire to organize some form of community. It is essential that you do not delude yourselves, you must accept the facts, however bleak they are. Also it is important to remember that you are in a totally new community and that the standards of your old community do not necessarily have to be applied.

EDUCATION AND RELIGION

Your Task
It is your job to discuss what kind of education system (if any) there should be in your new society. You must also decide how religion is taught and practiced.

1) What should be the aims of your education system?
2) What would be taught?
3) Who would it be taught to?
4) How are you going to teach it?
5) Should there be any Jewish education? If so, what?
6) Will Shabbat be celebrated in your new community? If so, how?
7) Should there be any religious activities and if so how should they be organized?

SOCIAL AND FAMILY STRUCTURE

Your Task

It is your job to discuss the social structure of your new community and the role of the family within that structure.

1) Should members of your society live in family groupings, age groupings, or in some other way?
2) Will marriage have a function in your new society? (Is adultery acceptable?)
3) Does the responsibility for bringing up the children lie with the parents or with the community?
4) How will old people be treated in your community?
5) Will women and men be given different roles in your new social structure?
6) Will the fact that you are all Jews affect the social organization of your new community? If so, how?

LAW AND ORDER

Your Task

It is your job to discuss how the new community should be governed and if and how the community should be controlled.

1) Who should have ultimate power in your new community?
2) Should there be a hierarchy within the government (either one leader or a small group)? If so, how should it work?
3) What power should the community have to enforce its decisions on individual members?
4) What kinds of punishment (if any) should be used in your new community?
5) At what age should children be regarded as full members of your society?
6) In what way, if any, should the fact that you are all Jewish affect the government of your community?
7) What actions, if any, should be regarded as criminal offenses?

(Submitted by Simon Klarfeld)

❀   ❀   ❀

THE FLOOD

Purpose:

Often conceptions of the organized Jewish community are determined by the existing pattern of institutions and services: what exists is what should be. This activity seeks to help people move beyond the status quo and view the Jewish community from the perspective of need, with no prior commitment to any institution or service. Adapting the budgetary concept of zero-base budgeting, this process might be thought of as zero-base social planning.

Group:

High school age or older; 12–30 people, to be divided into small discussion groups of 6–10 people.

Setting:

Any meeting room.

Materials:

A list of Jewish communal institutions (see below) and a pencil for each participant.

Time:

40–50 minutes.

Instructions:

1. The leader provides the following background information: Several years ago a flood occurred in Pennsylvania which had particularly devastating effects on the Jewish section of the city of Wilkes-Barre. Most of the Jewish communal institutions were seriously damaged and a major rebuilding was required. Suppose a similar catastrophe occurred in your community and all the Jewish communal institutions were destroyed. Soon

after the flood a meeting is called to plan the rebuilding of the Jewish communal institutions. This group has been organized as the committee to recommend the priorities to be followed in going about the task of rebuilding.

The committee is reminded that financial resources are limited, and they must confront the difficult task of coming up with a ranked listing of eight institutions in the order in which they should be rebuilt.

___ Jewish community center   ___ Jewish home for the aged
___ Jewish day school   ___ Jewish hospital
___ Jewish family service   ___ Jewish newspaper
___ Jewish federation   ___ synagogue

2. The leader suggests that each participant individually complete his/her ranking. When all the lists are completed, discussion groups of 6–10 are set up and each group is asked to achieve consensus on a single list, which will be their recommendation to their community. The full group is assembled and the groups give their reports, with some explanations of the basis for their decisions.

3. The leader concludes the activity by relating the discussion of the Jewish organizations in the hypothetical incident to the "real world." Is there a correlation between the value people afford to the Jewish organizations, as reflected in their rankings, and the priorities actually afforded these organizations in the Jewish federation budget allocations? Do any implications arise from the activity which suggest action by the participants in their communities?

TEN CRITERIA FOR STRONG JEWISH COMMUNITIES

Purpose:

This activity seeks to get people to think about the basic objectives of Jewish community organizations today. It is an activity appropriate for participants who are of high school age or older.

Below is a list of ten criteria which have been identified by Jewish leaders as basic to sustaining the future interest and commitment of American Jews. The objective of this activity is for you to reflect on these criteria and decide on their order of priority for future planning.

Your task is to rank these ten criteria in the order of importance you believe they have for ensuring Jewish continuity in America (1 is most important, 10 least important). Thinking about the relative importance of these ten criteria will be helpful to leaders of the American Jewish community as they decide on future priorities and programs for their communities.

TEN CRITERIA FOR JEWISH CONTINUITY

A pluralist Jewish community (includes Jews of diverse beliefs and backgrounds)
Tikkun Olam (Repair the world)
Stable Jewish families
Absence of anti-Semitism
High-quality Jewish professionals: rabbis, educators, communal workers
Observing Jewish customs, Shabbat and holidays
Active synagogue membership
Jews marrying other Jews
Engaging in study of Jewish texts
Trips to Israel

AMERICAN JEWISH COMMUNITY: A TIME CAPSULE

Purpose:

To identify representative symbols of various times in the American Jewish communal experience and to make comparisons across time periods.

Group:

Teenage and older; maximum 8 persons per group, with 3 groups meeting simultaneously.

Setting:

Facilities large enough for the small groups to meet without disturbing one another.

Materials:

Newsprint, marker, paper, pencils, tape.

Time:

45–60 minutes.

Instructions:

1. Each participant is given a sheet of paper and a pencil. The leader introduces the activity by talking about history-what is recorded in history books, what is left out, the notions of heritage, legacy, roots, etc. S/he also explains the purpose of creating a time capsule to capture the main ideas, values, and developments of a historical period.
2. Participants divide into three groups. Each group is assigned a different historical period. The three periods might be "1880–1920: Immigrant Experience", "1920–1950s: Acceptance", "1960s and 1970s: Questioning."
3. The participants in the three groups are asked to think about and list those items they would include in a time capsule to represent their time periods. The list of items may include objects, symbolic representations of experiences or values, slogans, etc.
4. The challenge to the groups is to be imaginative in their choice of items so that someone digging up the capsule a hundred years later would obtain a good sense of the period. A recorder is designated for each group and given newsprint and a marker. The groups have 15–20 minutes to compile a list of up to 20 items that they, as a group, wish to include in their capsule.
5. The leader reassembles the groups; they in turn post their newsprint list and a representative of the group presents the lists. The group members react to the three lists. The leader summa-

rizes the activity, attentive to any significant voids or tendencies to idealize.

Variation:

A. SPECIAL TIME CAPSULES. Time Capsules can also be developed for the following situations: the local Jewish community, one's extended family, a Jewish organization, any historical event or period in Jewish life (e.g., the Zealots at Masada, the Jews in the "Golden Age" of Spain, the Jews of the shtetl, the early waves of settlers in Palestine).

Notes to Leader:

SUGGESTED ITEMS FOR INCLUSION IN TIME CAPSULE
Names of key leaders
Examples of representative publications: newspapers, books, pamphlets
Photographs, artifacts, cartoons
Work of creative artists: song, poetry, drama, paintings
Announcements and minutes of organizations

(Adapted from an idea submitted by Franci Reiss)

KIBBUTZ TOWN MEETING

INTRODUCTION

The goal of this program is to give participants a feeling for and insight into the dynamics of collectivism. The vehicle of a Kibbutz Town Meeting brings to life the varying viewpoints of people involved in a process of change.*

The whole group constitutes the Town Meeting, and everyone is encouraged to participate, but fourteen members are selected in advance and given particular roles to play. During the course of the meeting, several issues will be brought up for the Kibbutz members to discuss, running the gamut from the philosophical to

---

*The Town Meeting is set in the year 1980.

the mundane, from the public to the personal. The roles which certain people play represent the constituent factors in the dynamics of change: the old-time pioneers, the native-born, the immigrant, the Ashkenazim and the Sephardim, the young and the old.

The participants who are assigned roles are given biographies which supply them with background information. Given the roles, it is then up to the participants to supply the dialogue. It is important to choose suitable people for the roles.

The Kibbutz General Secretary will present the agenda. It may be handled in two ways: either one item at a time, each discussed and decided in turn, or the whole agenda presented together, with brief explanations of each item followed by a free-flowing discussion on all of them. The latter has proved to be an exciting technique, for it allows the whole group to see the complexities and inter-connections of the problems. Eventually the whole group should be involved through committing themselves by vote to a particular solution.

The program may be followed by small group discussions addressing what happened in the meeting, how each person's style influenced the meeting, and perhaps on the history of the Kibbutz Movement and the Kibbutz Lifestyle.

KIBBUTZ TOWN MEETING CHARACTERS

Ya'akov is the General Secretary of the Kibbutz (i.e., President). He is in his late sixties and one of the founding members of the Kibbutz, having come from Russia in 1925. He was an ardent supporter of strict Zionist principles of collectivism, but with the change in times, he has also mellowed with the realization that Israel is a modern nation. He conducts the meeting, calling on people to speak, generally remaining objective, but speaking out when he feels strongly.

Agenda for the meeting: Ya'akov presents the following meeting agenda.
1. Treasurer's report—Rachel
2. Market Agent's report—Yitzchak
3. Work Manager's report—Shmuel
4. Items by individuals—a) Reuven b) Shimon

Rachel is the Treasurer of the Kibbutz. She is in her late sixties. Coming from Poland in the early 1920s, she was one of the founding members of the Kibbutz, and still has a great deal of nostalgia for the "good old days" when there was much more personal sacrifice and a smaller, more tightly knit group who believed very strongly in the strict principles of collectivism. She runs the treasury of the Kibbutz with an iron hand, being very critical of every expenditure of money and expecting that money should only be spent on items that will help the Kibbutz be more economically stable.

> *Treasurer's report:* Rachel indicates that the Kibbutz has accumulated a *small* surplus of revenue, but the exact figures are not available yet. A full report will be forthcoming in the near future.

Yitzchak is the Market Agent for the Kibbutz. He is in his late thirties, a native-born Israeli (but born on a different Kibbutz) who joined this Kibbutz about five years ago. He is not as concerned with the internal principles of collective living as he is with making the Kibbutz a modern economic enterprise with all of the latest machinery and techniques. He is in favor of greater diversification in the economy of the Kibbutz, and particularly in the construction of an electronics factory. He points out that this is a new opportunity to open up a market for this equipment, which can be sold not only in Israel, but also among the nations of the Common Market. He feels the Kibbutz must take the initiative to open new areas, regardless of any ideological commitments others may have. This new source of income will greatly benefit the Kibbutz in the long run.

> *Market Agent's report:* Yitzchak proposes building a new factory. He is aware, because of the year's sales, that there is a surplus of 750,000 Israeli shekels in the Treasury, though Rachel has tried to hide it.

Shmuel is the Work Manager for the Kibbutz. He is responsible for assigning jobs and recruiting additional help when necessary. He is in his late thirties and came to the Kibbutz as part of Youth Aliyah from Germany after the War. Contrary to many other members, he feels it is good to hire outside help, especially young teenagers and college students from abroad, even if only for the summer, so that they may be exposed to Israel and the Kibbutz

Movement. He also wants the Kibbutz to diversify in its various functions, but he has a severe labor shortage, especially in the Kibbutz's huge agricultural undertaking. The oranges and grapefruit are about to be picked and most of the other Kibbutzniks are already busy in other areas (taking care of various animals, harvesting the wheat, working in the canning factory, working in the kitchen, or on leave to the army). He is sympathetic to people and their problems and wants everybody to be happy, but gets very frustrated when things don't work out right.

Work Manager's report: Shmuel proposes taking on 75 American and British students for the summer. He also mentions that Shimon, the Kitchen Manager, has had a problem in the kitchen and has asked that one of the workers be reassigned, but that he will bring that up himself.

Shoshanah is an old-time Kibbutznik, having been born on this Kibbutz, and is about 40 years old. She remembers the good old times of dedication to the collective principles, and the sacrifice, but also feels that times have changed and it isn't necessary to subject the younger generation to the same kind of deprivations just for the sake of ideology. She is a teacher in the Kibbutz elementary school, and feels very strongly that the facilities for the children, including both housing and educational rooms, are very inadequate. They are old and crowded. Her priorities definitely are in favor of giving the best the Kibbutz has to its children. She disagrees with the proposed expenditure on a factory and asks that instead a new children's building be built.

Although there has been a change in attitude at many Kibbutzim, she still feels that housing children separately is the best contribution the Kibbutz has made. Shoshanah believes she can do a better job of taking care of and educating children than most parents because she is a professional, and she devotes her full time to it. Turning over more responsibility to parents would take away from their involvement in the Kibbutz and destroy the role women have come to play.

Reuven is in his 80s and a founding member of the Kibbutz, having originally come from Russia in the early 1920s. He is retired now (having driven the tractor and worked in the fields) and is not quite sure he enjoys the inactivity. He feels somewhat out of touch with what is happening nowadays, and is very much against the modernization that has taken place. He feels the original ideals of the founders are being eroded. The new cultural center is near his living quarters, and the noise of people playing music, dancing and talking keeps him awake at night. This center is a symbol to him of how the Kibbutz has changed: people have too much leisure and are not dedicated to their work.

Minka is in her 50s, having come from Iraq in the early 1950s. She is a cook in the kitchen. She feels somewhat alienated from many of the others because there are so few Oriental Jews at the kibbutz. She thinks that everything which is done or said that affects her in some way is because she is Sephardic. She thinks more Orientals should be brought to the kibbutz, especially during Harvest time, when help is scarce. She has been arguing with Shimon because she thinks he demeans her and asks her to do things in the kitchen that he doesn't ask of anyone else. Most recently, when he asked her to mop the floor because another person was out sick, she told him to mop it himself and then she chased him around the kitchen with a butcher's knife yelling and screaming.

Shimon is in his late 50s, having come from Germany after the war, via a concentration camp. He is the kitchen manager, responsible for assigning tasks and making sure everything runs smoothly. He also carries his load in the kitchen by washing dishes. He harbors no grudges against Sephardic Jews, though his patience has been particularly tried by Minka. When he asked her to do more than her usual job, she got angry because he was picking on her, though in fact, he does hand out jobs fairly. When she told him to do it himself, he told her he would bring this behavior up to the Kibbutz meeting, and she went after him with a knife. In fact, he had to restrain her. Now he wants her out of the kitchen as a safety risk, and he asks the Work Manager to assign her to another area of the kibbutz.

He thinks that cultural activities at the Kibbutz are essential and very good. He himself likes to play the clarinet, and he enjoys telling loud jokes long into the night. He doesn't understand why other members would complain about the cultural center.

Dov is a young Sabra, just returned from military service. He works in the canning factory, and likes the idea of building another factory for electronics. He thinks that the Kibbutz has to develop along technological lines, for agriculture alone will not suffice. However, he does not like the idea of outside help, people who will come in for a short time and then leave and not be fully integrated into the Kibbutz. Rather, he proposes taking in more members, particularly from the Oriental countries, to make the Kibbutz more representative of Israeli society.

Moshe is in his middle 50s, having come to the Kibbutz from Yemen. Though he is a Sephardic Jew, he feels perfectly at home among predominantly European members. He has given up his Yemenite background in favor of Israeli life, and even likes to think of himself as a Sabra. He thinks that Minka is being a fool by taking so personally Shimon's remarks, and that she is too self-conscious of being Oriental. He thinks the Kibbutz is large enough as it is, and would like to see the money spent on internal improvements either for the children or the adult living quarters rather than on expanding the economy.

Ruth is an American immigrant, in her middle twenties, who has joined the Kibbutz in the last three years. She is very idealistic about life on the Kibbutz. She works in the barn feeding the animals, milking the cows, etc., and finds great pleasure working with her hands, leading a simple life and close to nature. She does not like the idea of building factories, because she came to Israel, at least partially, to get away from a technological society. She likes the small numbers and doesn't wish the kibbutz to expand, because she also wanted to get away from the big city life with all its pollution, crime, and impersonality. She takes Minka's side because she feels that Oriental Jews are discriminated against in Israel.

Sara is the mother of two children, in her 40s, who came to Israel on Youth Aliyah after the war. Her children were born at the Kibbutz. She doesn't feel that a new children's building should be built because she would rather see her children living with her. She thinks the time has come for the Kibbutz to change its ways, and have families live together. She is a cook in the kitchen, and she feels she has enough time to care for her children as well as do her job. She'd rather see the money spent on larger and more modern family housing.

Working in the kitchen, she witnessed the fight between Minka and Shimon, and she thinks Minka reacted too strongly. Shimon is a fair boss, and she, too, has had to mop the floor when someone was absent. She likes Minka, but thinks it would perhaps be better for her to work elsewhere, since there is a personality clash with Shimon.

Dan is in his 40s, and came to the Kibbutz 15 years ago from France. He is a carpenter and does most of the repair work and building around the Kibbutz. He has seen a lot of growth and changes in the Kibbutz during this period, and is happy to be a part of it. He feels he has made a significant contribution by helping to build it. He feels a challenge ahead in building either the new factory, or more living quarters. . . . it doesn't matter which. Just don't let the progress stagnate.

He feels the Kibbutz must not take on more members, but that it should hire temporary outside help to tide it through. This help should be drawn, however, from the unemployed within the country itself, and not from foreign visitors who have no commitment to Israel. If they have so much interest in Israel, why don't they make Aliyah? Visitors are only here for a good time and for the curiosity. There are many others in Israel already who need the work.

Rivka is in her 90s, a real old-time pioneer who came to Israel at the turn of the century, worked in the city for a number of years and joined the Kibbutz in the 1930s. She is now retired, having been the supervisor of the young children for many years. She does not feel bored or out of touch now that she is retired. She is enjoying life even more, because she can listen to music and attend lectures. She thinks the cultural center is the best thing that ever happened at the Kibbutz, and she spends most of her day there. She thinks Reuven is only spiteful, and that if he would take advantage of the center, he, too, would enjoy it.

She definitely supports the idea of better facilities for the children, and thinks the present system is basically sound. She suggests a compromise of letting parents spend more time with their children in the special children's quarters.

She has heard the story about whether or not to hire outside laborers before, and she is tired of listening to it again. Why don't they decide it once and for all?

(Submitted by Simon Klarfeld)

THE "GAME" OF TEMPLE POLITICS

Purpose:

To give students or others an experience of decision-making in a synagogue setting, including various organizational roles, priority setting and budget allocation.

Group:

Junior high school age and older; 20–40 participants.

Setting:

Five adjacent small rooms or one large room where five subgroups can meet separately.

Materials:

Paper and pencils.

Time:

1–1½ hours.

Instructions:

1. The participants are divided into five subgroups of 4–8 persons per group. One group will function as the Board of Directors and the others as four committees—all of the same synagogue.

The committees comprise the education and welfare functions of the synagogue. They are: Adult Education, Youth Department, Religious School, and Elderly Services. The leader gives each subgroup a slip of paper outlining the task (see below).

2. The four committees make their presentations separately to the board. Approximately 5–10 minutes should be allocated for each committee. Then the board meets briefly and announces its recommendations for the coming year's budget.

3. The leader assembles all the participants for a concluding session in which the discussion focuses on the factors involved in operating a synagogue or a similar Jewish organization and how effective different positions were.

ASSIGNMENTS FOR THE FOUR COMMITTEES AND THE BOARD OF DIRECTORS

Adult Education: You must convince the board that educating the adults of your community should be the number-one priority. Explain the importance of well-read, educated parents, and state exactly how you feel the money would be used. Last year your committee received a budget of $6,700.

Youth Department: You must explain to the board why you feel that the youth group is most deserving of a larger portion of the available funds. Give specifics showing the importance of a strong youth program, and how you intend to utilize the funds. Last year your committee received a budget of $12,500.

Religious School: You must explain to the board why you think that the Hebrew school is most deserving of a larger portion of the available funds for the coming year. Explain the importance of Jewish education, and show specifically where the money could be used. Last year your committee received a budget of $37,000.

Elderly Services: Try to show the board how important it is for us to take care of those in the community who are too old or too poor to take care of themselves. Explain why your committee needs a larger portion of the available funds, and show exactly what services would be developed with this money. Last year your committee received a budget of $9,000.

Board of Directors: Each committee will be submitting a proposal explaining why it feels it deserves a larger portion of the available funds for the coming year. As members of the board, you must set your priorities based on effectiveness, need, long-term results, etc.

The education and welfare section of the synagogue's budget for the last fiscal year for these four committees was:

Adult Education	$ 6,700
Youth Department	12,500
Religious School	37,000
Elderly Services	9,000
TOTAL	$65,200

The Board of Directors must decide, based on each committee's presentation, whether allocations should remain the same or be altered to meet the, expressed needs of various committees. Your total budget for education and welfare must remain the same ($65,200) although you have the right to adjust the committee's figures as you see fit.

(Submitted by Alan Teperow)

QUOTES

The alternatives were the ghetto and the melting pot. Jews were being called on to segregate or assimilate, and there seemed to be no third option.

Chief Rabbi Jonathan Sacks

We must resist the flight into solitude, for we are called on neither to forsake nor to accept the world but to change it, creating in its midst a society of justice and compassion, equity and moral integrity, never yielding to despair even after a succession of failures.

Chief Rabbi Jonathan Sacks

You shall not stand idly by the blood of your neighbor.

Leviticus 19:16

Ye shall have one manner of law as well for the strangers as for the homeborn.

Leviticus 19:34

Let justice well up as waters, and righteousness as a mighty stream.

Amos 5:24

Oppress not the stranger, the fatherless, and the widow, and shed not innocent blood . . .

Jeremiah 7:7

Justice, justice shalt thou follow, that thou mayest live, and inherit the land which the Lord thy God giveth thee.

Deuteronomy 18:20

Rescue the poor and the needy

Psalms 82:4

Judge the fatherless, plead for the widow. Seek justice, relieve the oppressed.

Isaiah 1:17

He that hath a bountiful eye shall be blessed; for he giveth of his bread to the poor.

Proverbs 22:9

Upon three things the world rests: upon justice, upon truth, and upon peace. And the three are one, for when justice is done, truth prevails and peace is established.

Ta'anit 4:2, *Megilla* 3:5

This is the fast I desire:
To unlock the fetters of wickedness,
And untie the cords of lawlessness.
To let the oppressed go free;
To break off every yoke.
It is to share your bread with the hungry . . .

Isaiah 58:6–7

If you feed the hungry and satisfy the needs of the poor
Then your light will rise like dawn out of darkness
And your dusk will be like noonday.
The Lord will be your guide and will satisfy your needs
He will give you strength.
You will be like a well-watered garden
Like a spring whose waters never fail.

Isaiah 58:10–11

One who robs a non-Jew must return the article to the non-Jew;
stealing from a non-Jewish person is worse than stealing from a
Jewish person, because it constitutes a desecration of God's name.

Tosefta, Bava Kamma 10:8

If thine enemy be hungry, give him bread to eat. And if he be
thirsty, give him water to drink.

Proverbs 25:21

A hungry person should be fed as soon as possible. The angels can
wait to be greeted.

Chofetz Chaim (1838–1933)

Adonai, May it be Thy will to annul wars and the shedding of
blood from the Universe, and to extend a peace, great and won-
drous, over the world. Nor again shall one nation raise the sword
against another and they shall learn war no more. But let all earth-
lings know the innermost truth: that we are not come into this
world for quarrel and division, nor for hate and greed, perversity
and violence; but we are come into the world as a chariot of Thy
divinity, to keep Thy sanctity, and to dwell in peace, and to learn
the bounty of Thy eternal goodness.

Rabbi Nachman of Bratslav
(1722–1811)

Our generation is realistic, for we have come to know man as he
really is. After all, man is the being who has invented the gas chambers of Auschwitz; however, he is also that being who has entered
those gas chambers upright, with the Lord's Prayer or the "Shema
Yisrael" on his lips.

Viktor E. Frankl (1905–1997),
Man's Search for Meaning

Whoever saves a single life is as one who saves the entire world.

Talmud

It is curious that physical courage should be so common in the world and moral courage so rare.

Mark Twain (1835–1910)

It takes a village to rear a child.

Chinese proverb

The struggle of man against power is the struggle of memory against forgetting.

Milan Kundera (1929–)

Those who execute charity and justice are regarded as though they had filled the entire world with kindness.

Talmud

That which is hateful to you, do not do to your neighbor. That's the whole Torah. The rest is commentary. Go study.

Hillel (30 B.C.E.–10 C.E.)

Man does not live by bread alone, but also by the nourishment of animosities and the objects of our animosities are crumbling.

George Will (1941–),
The Morose Liberals

Am I my brother's keeper?

Genesis 4:9 (spoken by Cain)

And Abraham said unto his servant, the elder of his house, that ruled over all he had: "Put, I pray thee, thy hand under my thigh. And I will make thee swear by the Lord, the God of Heaven and the God of Earth, that thou shalt not take a wife for my son of the daughters of the Canaanites, among whom I dwell. But thou shalt go up to my country, and to my kindred, and take a wife for my son, even for Isaac.

Genesis 24:1–4

Neither shalt thou make marriages with them of the seven nations:
thy daughter shalt thou not give his son, nor his daughter shalt
thou take·for thy son. For he will turn away thy son from following Me, that they may serve other Gods: so will the anger of God
be kindled against you, and He will destroy thee quickly.

Deuteronomy 7:3–4

The messiah will come when we no longer need him

Franz Kafka (1883–1924)

9

LEADERSHIP

Leadership is the ability to articulate a compelling vision, communicate it to others, and mobilize others in support. The most important aspect is the relation between the leader and those who are led. Effectiveness is measured by the willingness of those led to support the vision. The quality of leadership is measured by the degree to which authority is used responsibly, relations with those led are democratic, and those led are enhanced by their support of the organizational enterprise.

Leadership can be exercised by persons, groups or institutions, which may or may not have been formally designated.

Many people have some degree of leadership responsibility in the workplace. Most relevant for informal Jewish education is leadership in such contexts as voluntary organizations, synagogues, or area planning councils. Examples would include leader of a youth trip to Israel, chair of a fundraising committee or lay member on the board of a synagogue. Even those who do not serve in a leadership capacity of a group or organization can play valuable roles through participation as committee members, volunteers, citizens, and examples to others.

The skills of leadership are largely those of group dynamics and social relations. Such skills will be of use to individuals as they assess their functioning within organizations and in any aspect of daily life where they are called upon to take initiative.

This chapter contains activities that consider the ideal qualities that leaders should possess, activities that promote description and assessment of actual leaders or organizations, and activities that address specific organizational structures, including synagogues and relations between lay boards and professional staff.

THE IMPORTANCE OF DELEGATING RESPONSIBILITY

This book has many activities focusing on the role of the group leaders. Most of this material is drawn from the realms of psychology, sociology, and organizational behavior. This activity, also offering important information for leaders working with groups, comes from a less traditional source: *The Bible.*

This activity is based on advice given to Moses by his father-in-law Jethro. Jethro was commenting on Moses' single-handed leadership of the Israelites following the exodus from Egypt.

"The thing thou doest is not good. Thou wilt surely wear away, both thou, and this people that is with thee; for the thing is too heavy for thee; thou are not able to perform it thyself alone. Hearken now unto my voice, I will give thee counsel, and God will be with thee: Be thou for the people before God, and bring thou the causes unto God. And thou shall teach them the statutes and laws, and shall show them the way wherein they must walk, and the work they must do.

"Moreover, thou shall provide out of all the people, able men, such as fear God, men of truth, hating unjust gain, and place such over them to be rulers of thousands, rulers of hundreds, rulers of fifties, and rulers of ten. And let them judge the people of all seasons; and it shall be that every great matter they shall bring unto thee, but every small matter they shall judge themselves; so shall they make it easier for thee, and bear the burden with thee, but every small matter they shall judge themselves; so shall they make it easier for thee, and bear the burden with thee.

"If thou shall do this thing, and God commands thee so, then thou shall be able to endure, and all this people shall go their place in peace." (*Exodus* 18:17–23)

Your challenge is to assess the advice given by Jethro. Why do you think that Moses, the greatest leader the Jews have ever known, needed the advice? How did the Israelites benefit? How would you phrase Jethro's advice in the language of today?

LEADERSHIP REQUISITES FOR THE JEWISH COMMUNITY OF THE 21ST CENTURY: VALUES, SKILLS AND POLICIES

Being conscious of the values, skills, policies and other qualities that are desired for leaders of the Jewish community will enable community members to select and maintain leadership that is attuned to the needs and expectations of the community. Periodically reassessing what are the most important criteria will help the community ascertain whether its expectations are realistic.

In this activity, participants list up to ten values, qualities, skills or policies that they would like Jewish community leaders to possess, and rank them in order of importance. Responses should be about attributes of leaders, rather than specific programs they would undertake.

After people have completed their lists, results are tabulated and posted, and the top ten or so responses identified. It would be interesting to analyze the consensus of the group in terms of characteristics of the group, such as age, education, religious affiliation, need for services and other factors. It would be useful to retain the list of top choices as a reminder when decisions regarding leadership need to be made.

It might be valuable to compile a database of the responses for comparison with responses in future years. In subsequent years discussion could address stability or change in what are considered leadership requisites.

REQUISITES FOR JEWISH LEADERSHIP

Purpose:

The objective of this activity is to consider requisites for leadership in the Jewish community: criteria for leadership, the process of how leaders are chosen, and responsibilities of leaders.

Group:

High school and older; any size is manageable, since smaller discussion groups will be formed.

Setting:

An open meeting room.

Materials:

Sheets of newsprint, markers, masking tape, pencil, and Leadership Ranking Sheets (see below) for each participant.

Time:

45–60 minutes.

Instructions:

1. Each participant is given a Leadership Ranking Sheet and pencil, and is asked to complete the rankings.
2. After the ranking sheets are completed, groups of 4–6 people are formed. These groups can either be formed at random or by bringing together people who have similar priorities (e.g., people who have chosen the same item as their # 1 priority are grouped together, etc.).
3. Group members discuss the basis of their selections and seek to come up with a list which all can agree upon. These lists are compiled on sheets of newsprint which are posted around the room; they can serve as the focus for a full-group discussion.
4. The leader summarizes with the full group on the consensus reached on the valued characteristics for Jewish communal leadership. The leader asks the group to relate these criteria to the existing leadership of Jewish communal organizations. If the participants are members of the same Jewish communal organization, it may be appropriate for them to compile a set of criteria for actual use in their organization. If such a list is generated, it could be utilized by a nominating committee, or whichever group is charged with the task of selecting leadership.

LEADERSHIP RANKING SHEET

Below is a list of 10 attributes which are pertinent to the exercise of Jewish communal leadership. You are asked to determine the relative priority of these so as to produce a set of guidelines that might be used by the Jewish organizations in your community in choosing lay leaders for the community's social, civic, and religious organizations. Rank these items from 1 to 10, with 1 being the most important attribute, 2 next important, and so on.

___ Maturity
___ Jewish knowledge and commitment
___ Prestige in the non-Jewish community
___ Organizational know-how
___ Personal assertiveness
___ Wealth
___ Youth
___ Political connections
___ Intelligence
___ Prominence in Jewish organizational life

Variations:

A. BOARD OF DIRECTORS. The following instruction sheet is given to each person: You live in Newtown—a newly built community to which all the families have moved within the past 6 months. The Jewish families have met together several times and decided to form a Board of Directors for their emerging community. The board will oversee the religious, educational, and social services of the community. The Planning Committee has mailed you a ballot that offers the following brief descriptions of candidates for the board. You must now vote for 6 out of the 10 candidates.

1. A wealthy, retired man who has no previous involvement in Jewish communal life.
2. A young married woman with two children who teaches in a nearby high school. Previously she had worked as a religious-school teacher.
3. A 70-year-old former postal employee who is very learned Jewishly.
4. A Jewish writer who dislikes "organized religion".
5. An ambitious young lawyer in a prestigious law firm.

6. A social worker who works in a Jewish community center in the nearby city.
7. A manager of a large, successful business enterprise.
8. A famous local artist who was recently divorced.
9. A man who owns a construction business and is active in reviving Yiddish.
10. A mother of 4 children, active in her synagogue sister-hood.

B. A MODERN SANHEDRIN. In ancient times there existed an organization called the Sanhedrin which functioned as a ruling high court in Jewish life. In 1806 Napoleon convened a modern Sanhedrin to help define the status of the Jews in France in the wake of emancipation.

Suppose the major organizations in Jewish life today were to agree to form a Sanhedrin to provide leadership for the American Jewish community. You are appointed to a committee which has been given two tasks: (a) define the procedures for electing the members of the Sanhedrin, and (b) select the names of 18 prominent American Jews who will serve as a Steering Committee to provide leadership to the American Jewish community until the Sanhedrin is elected and can assume office. In choosing people for the Steering Committee, well-known individuals can be listed or incumbents of an organizational position (e.g., president of the United Synagogue of America, executive director of the Council of Jewish Federations and Welfare Funds, etc.).

An alternative to choosing people for the Steering Committee is to make this an international body whose task is to provide leadership for world Jewry. Accordingly, representation may come from any country in the world.

C. ALL-STAR LEADERS. Another alternative, which is more imaginative and perhaps less practical, is to come up with a historical "all-star" Jewish leadership group. The participants are asked to draw up a list of 18 Jews, from Biblical times through the present, who would constitute an ideal Jewish leadership group. These should be people who in their own historical era demonstrated a capacity to provide effective leadership in Jewish life.

D. COMPARING LISTS. A final alternative, which might be especially appropriate as an educational unit, is to have a second session for the activity. After drawing up their leadership lists, the participants seek out comparable lists from resources within their Jewish community, e.g., rabbis, educators, social workers, one's own family. These lists are brought back and, at a subsequent session, the participants compare their own list with the lists of the community representatives.

QUALITIES AND SKILLS OF EFFECTIVE PROFESSIONALS

Purpose:

This activity is designed to help people identify the skills of leadership by reflecting on their observation of good professionals at work. Through the process of sharing observations of effective leaders in action, people can conceptualize in a practical sense the skills of leadership and requisite personal qualities.

Group:

Human service professionals.

Instructions:

1. Participants are given newsprint and markers and are instructed as follows. "Think of the top human service professionals you have known. What are the qualities and skills that account for their effectiveness? Come up with a list of a dozen words or phrases that best describe leadership skills or personal qualities of those professionals. Then, rank them in order of importance from 1 to 12."
2. After every participant has completed a ranked list, participants post their lists, then the group seeks to produce a consensus list from the individual reports. If there are more than 20 participants, divide into groups of 8–12. Consensus lists will be developed within each group, and then each group's list should be discussed.
3. The leader concludes the activity by summarizing the findings.

The leader should encourage participants to attempt to incorporate some of the themes brought up in this activity in their own professional work.

Note to Leader:

The list below provides examples of skills and qualities that could be used to characterize effective professionals. After the consensus list(s) are presented, suggestions of alternatives might be made from this list.

EXAMPLES OF SKILLS AND QUALITIES OF
EFFECTIVE PROFESSIONALS

Disciplined
Sets limits
Prompt
Visionary
Able to delegate
Articulate
Mediator
Innovative
Willing to risk
Creative
Sensitive
Listener
Supportive
Efficient
Follow-though
Advance planning
Well-organized
Jewishly knowledgeable
Jewishly committed
Pluralistic
Decisive
Good sense of humor
Manager
Researcher
High energy
Intelligent

❀   ❀   ❀

BEYOND TRIBAL WISDOM

Here is a clever approach to opening a meeting or retreat whose purpose is organizational review. The humor of "Tribal Wisdom" actually points up common pitfalls affecting organizations and the rationalizations employed in accepting them. Discussion of these absurd strategies may reduce defensiveness and self-congratulation and help participants become comfortable with looking critically at their own organization.

Begin by having participants read "Tribal Wisdom". Alternatively, the leader may read it to the group. The point may be self-evident. If not, the leader should note that everyone is prone to overlooking faults and seeking panaceas. A successful organizational review requires objectivity and willingness to ask probing questions and accept unflattering answers.

TRIBAL WISDOM

Indian tribal wisdom says that when you discover you are riding a dead horse, the best strategy is to dismount. However, in business/government/education we often try other strategies with dead horses. See if any of these look familiar.

- Buy a stronger whip.
- Change riders.
- Appoint a committee to study the horse.
- Move the horse to a new location.
- Provide status reports daily on the dead horse.
- Rename the dead horse.
- Create a training session to increase our ability to ride.
- Add more managers/supervisors per dead horse.
- Hire a consultant to give their opinion on dead horses.
- Promote the dead horse to a supervisory position.
- Terminate all live horses to redefine productivity.
- Arrange to visit other sites to benchmark how *they* ride dead horses.
- Provide an incentive bonus for the jockey.
- Schedule a meeting with the dead horse to discuss his productivity problems.

- Do a cost analysis study to see if contractors can ride it cheaper.
- Hire another consultant to refute the first consultant's opinion that the horse is really dead.
- Form a team positioned to shift the horse's paradigm.
- Finally, if all else fails, prop the horse up, put ribbons in his mane and tail, and see if you can find a buyer.

JUSTICE: AFFIRMATION AND/OR IMPLEMENTATION

"Justice and only justice shall you follow." *Deuteronomy* 16:20

The concept of justice is highly valued in Judaism and is reinforced in many of its basic texts. Does the Jewish tradition make clear specific ways individuals should act justly in their day to day lives? Below is a statement about how a South African tribe deals with an individual who behaves unjustly.

A Model of Justice from South Africa

"In the Babemba tribe of South Africa, when a person acts irresponsibly or unjustly, he is placed in the center of the village, alone and unfettered. All work ceases, and every man, woman and child in the village gathers in a large circle around the accused individual. Then each person in the tribe, regardless of age, begins to talk out loud to the accused, one at a time, about all the good things the person in the center of the circle has done in his lifetime. Every incident, every accuracy is recounted. All his positive attributes, good deeds, strengths and kindnesses are recited carefully and at length. No one is permitted to fabricate, exaggerate, or be facetious about his accomplishments or the positive aspects of his personality. The tribal ceremony often lasts for several days and does not cease until everyone is drained of every positive comment he can muster about the person in question. At the end, the tribal circle is broken, a joyous celebration takes place, and the person is symbolically and literally welcomed back into the tribe."

From Joanne Olshansky Hammil, Watertown, MA, 1998

What do you think about this tribal value/custom of responding to a member of their tribe who has acted irresponsibly or unjustly?

Think about how we today in our Jewish communities respond to a neighbor or friend who behaves irresponsibly. Individuals should share experiences. Then the group should contrast the approach of our American Jewish communities to those of the African tribe.

"When justice is done, it is joy to the righteous." *Proverbs* 21:15.

"There are times when a man must use force to seek justice." Max Nordau, Zionist leader (1849–1923)

LEADERSHIP PERFORMANCE: IDEAL-ACTUAL

Purpose:

To get people thinking about the leaders of the American Jewish community, either as a general category, or separately, as volunteer lay leaders and as professionals. The group leader should define in advance the specific group of leaders the participants are to review.

Group:

High school age or older.

Setting:

An open space, big enough to accommodate the number of participants. People should be assigned to small groups of between six and eight individuals.

Time:

1–1½ hours.

Instructions:

1. At the outset, the participants should be asked to define the ideal qualities they want their leaders to have. Then they should be asked to define the actual qualities they believe describe

most of the lay or professional leaders they know in their own community.

2. After about 20–25 minutes discussion in the small groups, the groups report on the ideal and actual leader qualities they come up with. The group leader should write on a blackboard or newsprint the two lists. Then, the group should rank qualities in each list. Ideal qualities should be ranked by importance and actual qualities by frequency of occurrence.

3. The leader should encourage the participants to discuss the qualities they have chosen for the community leaders. Are these realistic, achievable qualities? What are initiatives that might be taken to acquire the desired leadership qualities, and thereby, to diminish the gap between the ideal and the actual leader performance?

4. The leader should summarize the assessment of the leaders. What are the implications for leadership selection and training?

FIVE MOST IMPORTANT QUESTIONS

Purpose:

This activity would be used with members of a particular organization or community, who are interested in evaluating the effectiveness of their organization. The eminent organizational consultant Peter Drucker recommends that assessment of an organization begin with discerning questions. Specifically, he suggests formulating the five questions most germane to organizational functioning.

Group:

High school age or older. Participants are assigned to small groups (6–10 people), preferably comprising people from different backgrounds or with different perspectives.

Instructions:

1. Each group is to come up with their "five most important questions" to ask of their organization or community. Allow 20–25 minutes for groups to deliberate on their choice of questions.
2. Each group then shares its questions with the entire group. Results might be posted on a sheet of newsprint or blackboard. The leader then leads a discussion about similarities and differences among the several lists, and seeks to establish general principles for evaluating groups, organizations, or communities.

TEAM WORK

Purpose:

To help groups within an organization or larger community get to know each other better and especially to learn more about their respective agendas, values and style of work.

Group:

A workshop or meeting that brings together distinct groups of people from a larger community. For instance: people who work in different departments in a large organization; people who live in different neighborhoods in the same city; or people who belong to different synagogues or other religious institutions in the same community.

Instructions:

1. Ask people from the several different organizations or sub-populations present to come together in their natural "affinity groups"—to find the people present who are from their primary organization/community. These should be groups (teams) of between 6–10 individuals. The assumption is that the people on these teams know each other well and have previously worked together, while they have little or no familiarity with the people on other teams.

2. Teams are given up to 20 minutes to discuss the following questions:
   a) *Composition*: Who are we? What are our similarities, and our differences, from the people on the other teams(s)? What are our major strengths as a team or group? What are our weaknesses or problems? As a team are we representative of the larger Jewish population in which we live?
   b) *Action Plan*: What is the major task or problem facing us? What are the problems/obstacles we have to overcome? Has our group set priorities for each of those tasks? Then, delegate responsibilities so there is a clear understanding of who is to do what. Establish a time-line for your work by defining how much time is needed to ensure that the assigned tasks are completed.
3. Each team is paired with another team. (With an odd number of teams it will be necessary to form one group of three.) A team should be paired with one that is as unlike it as possible. This allows both for learning from and about people with whom there typically is less interaction, and provides an opportunity for enhancing relations among people in the larger community.
4. The objective of pairing up teams is to have them share their experience in "team work." Despite having different agendas or perspectives, the two teams have in common the exercise done in step 2. How well did each of the teams work together? Did they accomplish their team objectives? What worked well and what didn't work too well in each of the groups? How was leadership defined? Was the leadership effective? Finally, what principles of effective team work were learned that might apply to leadership within the Jewish community?

SYNAGOGUES OF EXCELLENCE—BEGINNING A SPIRITUAL AND RELIGIOUS JOURNEY

Purpose:

This activity is designed for lay and professional leadership of a synagogue to clarify the overarching objectives of the congregation and to develop an action plan.

Group and Setting:

The ideal format for this activity is to convene the board and the professional leadership of the congregation in a retreat. The intention is for the leadership to engage in self-introspection about the major components of the congregation and design a set of strategies to move the congregation forward.

Time:

A minimum of three hours should be devoted to the exercise with follow-up action plans to be formulated.

Instructions:

1. The facilitator asks each participant to consider the current state of the congregation and rate the following items for *current importance* within the congregation. You should stress that we are not looking for the "ideal" congregation, but rather a current description of where the congregation is on the religious spectrum. Participants should fill out the Synagogues of Excellence Questionnaire according to the following instructions:

   For each of the following items note its current importance within the congregation on a scale of "very important" to "not at all important." Under each item explain your answer, indicate if you would like to change this situation, and explain how you would go about modifying the current state of affairs.

2. The group should reconvene and determine the items with the highest number of very important scores. The leadership should discuss the rationale for how they voted to determine the top items, review the explanations, and determine a going-forward plan. In determining the implementation strategy, consideration should be given to answering the following questions with respect to each item:

   • Who will have responsibility?
   • What will be done?
   • How will it be accomplished?
   • What will be the cost?

- What are the blockages to moving ahead in this area?
- How will the effectiveness of the response be assessed?
3. Before the group breaks up, an implementation committee should be established of approximately 10 to 15 leaders of the congregation with specific responsibilities to implement the identified action items.

Notes to Leader:

This activity, while developed for synagogues, could easily be adapted for other Jewish educational and communal organizations by modifying the items asked.

The rationale and historical background for this activity are provided in an article by Steven Huberman, Ph.D. entitled "Synagogues of Excellence" that appeared in the Spring/Summer 2001 issue of *Journal of Jewish Communal Service.*

SYNAGOGUES OF EXCELLENCE QUESTIONNAIRE

For each item . . .

1. What is its *current* importance in your congregation?
   a) Very Important
   b) Moderately Important
   c) Slightly Important
   d) Not At All Important
2. Why do you feel this way?
3. Do you feel the current situation ought to be changed? How would you go about changing the situation?

1. Sustain quality worship and programs that bond the congregants to Judaism and create a caring community.
2. Be enriched, not imprisoned, by the history and practices of the synagogue.
3. Encourage Hebrew literacy and acts of *gemilut chassadim.* Social action should permeate the congregation.
4. Have congregants who incorporate Judaic values into their homes, workplaces, and community.
5. Develop productive lay and professional leadership who work in a partnership of mutual trust and respect.

6. Welcome and integrate new congregants and newcomers to the community. Become "user friendly."
7. Manage controversy in a civil and respectful manner. Have dialogue with other denominations and federation-agency leadership.
8. Actively engage in the broader Jewish and non-Jewish communal agenda.
9. Aim to achieve a Judaic learning community based on *mitzvot* and lifelong Jewish education. Day school and quality congregational education are both viable options.
10. Use best practices in administration, cost control, financial resource development, and management information systems. Maintain the physical plant. Incorporate federation-agency management best practices.
11. Maintain a healthy sense of humor. Reflect the joy and beauty inherent in Jewish observance.
12. Assume a shared responsibility for congregations and agencies with fewer resources and engage in inter-congregational/agency collaboration.
13. Promote and support the national, international, and other institutions of the UJC-Federation system, such as the Jewish Agency, World Zionist Organization, and American Jewish Joint Distribution Committee.
14. Actively support Israel.

(Submitted by Steven Huberman, Ph.D., Director of Regional and Extension Activities, The United Synagogue of Conservative Judaism.)

ASSESSING RELATIONSHIPS BETWEEN TOP PROFESSIONAL STAFF AND MEMBERS OF BOARDS OF DIRECTORS OF JEWISH COMMUNAL ORGANIZATIONS

Purpose:

Virtually all Jewish communal organizations, schools and synagogues have a Board of Directors which defines the policies and oversees the operation of the organization. The Board members serve voluntarily and function in collaboration with the professional staff members.

This activity has been designed to help the lay board members and the professionals assess their mode of operation. It might be used as a prelude to a joint board/staff retreat or meeting to begin the process of board/staff evaluation.

This activity can be used in one of two ways:

a) With professionals and board members from *the same Jewish communal organization*. In this case the relationship between the board members and professionals in that organization would be the focus of the activity, and the questionnaire would be completed based on the working relationships between those board and staff people. The issue of confidentiality of responses must be stressed.

b) With a diverse group of lay people and professionals from a wide variety of *different Jewish communal organizations*, and perhaps from different communities around the country. In this case, each person would respond in terms of the Jewish organization in which they are most actively involved. Since the responses of the lay people and professionals in this situation would be based on so many different organizations, and the responses are aggregated, confidentiality is less of a concern, but nevertheless, must be respected.

All board members and professional staff who have working relations with board members would be asked to complete the following questionnaire. All responses will be treated with confidentiality. Where there are enough different professionals completing the questionnaire it would be interesting to compare separately the total responses of the professionals and the lay people.

Allow time between completing the questionnaires and compiling a summary of the responses for discussion between the board members and the professional staff.

When the activity is used for board and staff of the same organization, consideration should be given to having prior board members and upper-level professionals from that Jewish organization complete the questionnaire, thus providing a larger data base, the benefit of more points of view, and greater confidentiality.

The Board members and professionals would have to consider

in advance whether the results of the questionnaires should be considered as confidential.

QUESTIONNAIRE FOR PROFESSIONALS AND LAY PEOPLE ON THE ROLE AND FUNCTIONING OF THE BOARD OF DIRECTORS OF YOUR JEWISH COMMUNAL ORGANIZATION

Respond in terms of the Jewish communal organization (JCO) in which you are, or have been, most actively involved, and in which there is an active volunteer Board of Directors and Professional Staff.

1.

a) In this Jewish communal organization (Jewish school, Federation, JCC, Jewish family agency, etc.) are you primarily involved as a: (check one)

_____ volunteer, lay person

_____ paid professional staff member

b) What type of Jewish communal organization is the one on which you will respond? (check one)

_____ Jewish school   _____ Jewish family service

_____ Jewish Federation   _____ Jewish youth services

_____ Jewish Community   _____ Jewish community
        Center   relations

_____ Jewish fund-raising   _____ Services to Jewish elderly

_____ other _____

QUESTIONS 2 AND 3 ARE ONLY FOR BOARD MEMBERS:

2. While you have been a JCO board member have you held any office?

_____ no

_____ yes, if so which office _____

        and for how long? _____

3. During the years you have served on the JCO Board, which one of the choices below best describes your pattern of attendance at Board meetings?

_____ I seldom missed a board meeting

_____ I missed one or two meetings a year

_____ I missed about three or four meetings a year

_____ I missed about half of the meetings

_____ I missed about 3/4 of the meetings

QUESTIONS 4–15 ARE FOR BOTH LAY PEOPLE AND PROFESSIONAL STAFF:

4. Rate your reaction to each of these statements based on your participation at the JCO Board meetings.

Scale: 1 = strongly agree; 2 = agree; 3 = disagree somewhat; 4 = strongly disagree

a) The JCO board meetings reflect good advance preparation. _____
b) The JCO board meetings are conducted very efficiently by the chair. _____
c) The JCO board meetings regularly start and end on time. _____
d) A small minority of JCO board members dominate discussion at board meetings. _____

5. In your opinion, would it be better if a smaller Jewish Community Organization Board Executive Committee were to assume more responsibility in decision making, and if the larger overall Board of Directors were to serve in more of an advisory consultative role?

(Choose one)

_____ strongly agree

_____ agree

_____ disagree

_____ strongly disagree

6. How would you describe the nature of your personal relation-ships with the members of the JCO Board:

(Choose one)

_____ I only see Board members when I attend Board meetings, and I have no personal ties with other JCO Board mem-bers.

_____ I know, to some extent, something about many of the members and have close ties with only one or two.

_____ I know most of the members fairly well and have close ties with about half or more of the members.

_____ I have close ties with most of the Board members.

7. What have you found most satisfying about your participa-tion as a member of the JCO Board?

_____

_____

8. What have you found least satisfying about your participation as a member of the JCO Board? _____

_____

9. Compared to other communal organizations (Jewish and other), in which you have been involved as a Board member, how would you rate your JCO Board service?

(Choose one)

_____ JCO board service has been more gratifying to me.

_____ JCO board service has been less gratifying to me.

_____ JCO board service is about the same as other boards.

_____ I have not served on other boards.

10. How would you evaluate the respective roles and collabora-tion between the JCO Board members and the professional staff person(s)?

Rate each item on the following five-point scale:

1) very good; 2) good; 3) fair; 4) poor; 5) very poor

a) advance planning for the meetings _____
b) the participation of professionals at the meetings _____
c) the participation of lay people at the meetings _____
d) the level of mutual respect between the lay people and the professionals _____
e) the promptness and thoroughness of follow-up on decisions reached at board meetings _____

11. Please offer one suggestion for improving the collaboration between the JCO professional staff and board members: _____

_____

12. What one word comes to mind which would be most descriptive of your impression of the JCO Board? _____

13. Overall what is one suggestion you would make to improve the way the JCO Board operates? _____

FOR BOARD MEMBERS ONLY

14. Having had experience serving on the JCO Board, if you were asked to serve another term as Board member, would you:

(Choose one)

_____ Accept with pleasure

_____ Accept, because I have trouble saying "no"

_____ Definitely refuse to serve another term

_____ I have not served on other boards

15. Any other comments or observations about your service on the JCO Board?

Thank you for completing this questionnaire.

❀   ❀   ❀

A SELF-RATING SCALE ON BOARD-STAFF RELATIONS

Basic to the leadership structure of virtually all Jewish communal organizations is the collaboration of professional staff and lay volunteers. The professionals provide a range of organizational and educational services, while the lay volunteers generate and oversee financial support and define priorities and operating policies for the organization. Effective operation of the lay/professional team requires initiatives to help the two leadership elements develop and maintain good collaboration.

This Board-Staff Self-Rating scale is a useful activity to be used by agency professionals and lay volunteers to assess how well the two entities collaborate. This scale was developed by Professor Gerald B. Bubis, the founding director of the Irwin Daniels School of Jewish Communal Service in Los Angeles, California and Professor Emeritus of Jewish Communal Studies at Hebrew Union College in Los Angeles.

Thanks to my long-term colleague, Gerry Bubis, for permission to include the scale in this book.

Both board and professional staff members should complete the 26 items on the scale. Allow time to tally and post the results, which would then serve as the basis for analysis and discussion between the staff and board members of the Jewish communal agency.

These compiled data should be saved to allow for subsequent use and analysis plus discussion of any changes. Do the changes show any improvement in the quality and effectiveness of the collaboration?

SELF-RATING SCALE ON BOARD-STAFF RELATIONS

	1 (low)	2	3	4	5 (high)
Job descriptions exist for staff and board.					
Board members and their staff counterparts mutually develop annual goals in descending order of importance.					

(continued)

	1 *(low)*	2	3	4	5 *(high)*
Board members and their staff counterparts mutually develop contracts of expectations they have one from the other.					
Notices for meetings are sent out 10 to 14 days before the meeting.					
Information in the agency is shared in a timely way and in usable form.					
Minutes are kept regularly and shared in a wide and functional circle. Thus executive committee members receive all committee minutes and reports.					
Board members receive executive committee minutes and at least quarterly financial reports.					
Committees have staff representation with voice and vote except those committees requiring only board membership (contract and salary negotiations).					
Agendas are developed mutually by board and staff.					
Objective criteria exist for board membership.					
Board and staff are evaluated regularly against mutually developed criteria.					
Board membership is rotated regularly.					

(continued)

	1 (low)	2	3	4	5 (high)
Committees nominate committee chairs for ratification by the volunteer agency head (sometimes called chief volunteer officer, president, or board chair).					
Boards and committees are diverse and representative of the community which the agency or organization serves.					
Constituents have easy access to officers and senior staff.					
Board meetings are open to the public.					
In organizations serving large geographic areas key meetings are rotated so as to expedite access to meetings.					
Communications to constituents encourage opportunities for communication from constituents.					
In organizations whose functions include fund raising, planning and programming recognition of volunteers is not confined to major fiscal supporters.					
The organization is gender neutral in board and officer membership.					
The organization is gender neutral in its hiring and promotion functions.					

(continued)

	1 (low)	2	3	4	5 (high)
Debate and discussion are encouraged at board and committee meetings as a tool for achieving consensus.					
Staff are not fired as a result of the actions or desires of any one volunteer.					
Trust between board and staff members exists in ways that are easily observable.					
There is respect between board and staff for each others' contribution to the fulfillment of the agency's or organization's mission.					
Both board and staff members are proud to be serving the agency or organization.					

Scoring:

The highest single rating is 130; the lowest is 26. Ask all board and staff to fill out the rating scale. Add the ratings of each form and divide by the number of people filling out the scale.

26 to 40   There is much work to be done across the board in work with board and staff.

41 to 60   Examine the areas of agreement and disagreement to see if special attention is needed to any particular dimensions of board staff relations.

61 to 80   The agency is moving in the right direction and should continue to emphasize the positives.

81 to 100   The agency has much to be proud of and should build on its achievements.

101 to 130   Eureka! The place to continue to invest one's treasure, abilities, and future.

References:

Carver, John, *Boards that Make a Difference: A New Design for Leadership in Non-profit and Public Organizations*, San Francisco: Jossey Bass, 1990, pp. 33–34, 912.

Geffen, Rela, "Fundamentals of the Jewish Political Tradition: Constitutional Principles of the *Edah*", in *Serving the Jewish Polity: The Application of Jewish Political Theory to Jewish Communal Practice*, Jerusalem Center for Public Affairs, Jerusalem, Philadelphia and Los Angeles, 1997, pp. 55–56.

Mitroff, Ian, *Mission Impossible? Teaching Corporate America to Think Strategically*, Unpublished Manuscript, 1985.

(Taken from: Michelle K. Wolf (Ed.) with Ellen Rabin, *Growing Jews: Selected Writings of Professor Gerald B. Bubis*, Hebrew Union College Jewish Institute of Religion, Cincinnati, OH, 2001, pp. 491–493.)

ASSESSING LAY-PROFESSIONAL RELATIONS

Jewish communities in the Diaspora are voluntary communities. They are directed by a dual pattern of leadership: (1) Professionals, with special skills in Jewish education and community organization, and (2) Lay-people, parents and volunteers who have a commitment to creating and maintaining a strong Jewish community.

For these Jewish communal organizations to function at optimum capacity it is vital that the lay and professional leaders develop a positive working relationship. The task of your group is to critically evaluate the current level of collaboration between lay and professionals in the Jewish schools and communal organizations in your community.

In what ways do you think lay and professionals are or are not working together effectively? Is there an appropriate division of labor, collaboration, and mutual respect? Is it clear who does what? Are communications clear, consistent and understood by the recipients? Is there mutual trust?

These questions could serve as the basis for a training workshop for lay and professional leaders, either from the same organization or from several organizations.

QUOTES

In a place where there are no men, strive to be a man.

Mishnah

It must be considered that there is nothing more difficult to carry out, nor more doubtful of success, nor more dangerous to handle, than to initiate a new order of things. For the reformer has enemies in all those who profit by the old order, and only lukewarm defenders in all those who profit by the new order, this lukewarmness arising partly from fear of their adversaries, who have the law in their favor; and partly from the incredulity of mankind, who do not truly believe in anything new until they have had actual experience of it.

Niccolo Machiavelli (1469–1527),
The Prince

So long as human beings have any desire to change their situation, we will cherish those individuals who can point us in a new direction and show us how to get there.

Howard Gardner (1943–)

If you can't stand the heat, get out of the kitchen.

Harry Truman (1884–1972)

Under favorable conditions, practically anybody can be converted to practically anything.

Aldous Huxley (1894–1963)

Only those who attempt the absurd will achieve the impossible.

Albert Einstein (1879–1955)

Never doubt that a small group of thoughtful, committed citizens can change the world; indeed it's the only thing that ever has.

Margaret Mead (1901–1978)

Every production of genius must be the production of enthusiasm.

Benjamin Disraeli (1804–1881)

It is better to be making the news than taking it; to be an actor rather than a critic.

Winston Churchill (1874–1965)

I have nothing to offer but blood, toil, tears and sweat.

Winston Churchill (1874–1965)

If you want to kill any idea in the world today, get a committee working on it.

C. F. Kettering (1876–1958),
American industrialist

I did not come to the Maggid of Mezritch to learn interpretation of Torah from him, but to watch how he tied his shoelaces.

Hassidic Rabbi Lieb

Good philosophers fly alone, like eagles, not in flocks like starlings. A single Arabian steed can outrun a hundred plow-horses.

Bertholt Brecht (1898–1956)

Community facilitators may be a modern necessity, individuals who organize social activities in which interpersonal and social bonds can be initiated.

Amitai Etzioni (1929–), *Spirit of Community*, 1994

I tried never to forget who I was, where I came from, and where I'd go back to.

Harry Truman (1884–1972)

I'd rather please one intelligent man, even if it means displeasing ten thousand fools.

Moses Maimonides (1135–1204),
Guide for the Perplexed

Power tends to corrupt, and absolute power corrupts absolutely.

Lord Acton (1834–1902),
English historian

O! It is excellent to have a giant's strength, but it is tyrannous to use it like a giant.

> William Shakespeare (1564–1616)

So much of what we call management consists in making it difficult for people to work.

> Peter Drucker (1946–)

Charismatic leaders make us think, "Oh if only I could do that, be like that!" True leaders make us think, "If they can do that, then . . . I can too."

> John Holt (1923–1985), educator

What is this thing that thou doest to the people? Why sittest thou thyself alone, and all the people stand about thee from morning unto even?

> *Exodus* 18:14

The thing that thou doest is not good. Thou wilt surely wear away, both thou and this people that is with thee; for the thing is too heavy for thee; thou art not able to perform it thyself alone. Hearken now unto my voice, I will give thee counsel, and God be with thee: be thou for the people before God, and bring thou the causes unto God. And thou shalt teach them the statutes and the laws, and shalt show them the way wherein they must walk, and the work that they must do. Moreover thou shalt provide out of all the people able men, such as fear God, men of truth, hating unjust gain; and place such over them, to be rulers of thousands, rulers of hundreds, ruler of fifties, and rulers of tens. And let them judge the people at all seasons; and it shall be, that every great matter they shall bring unto thee, but every small matter they shall judge themselves; so shall they make it easier for thee and bear the burden with thee. If thou shalt do this thing, and God commanded thee so, then thou shalt be able to endure, and all this people also shall go to their place in peace.

> *Exodus* 18:17–23

Judges and Officials you are to provide for yourselves, within all your gates that your God is giving you, for your tribal district;

they are to judge the people with justice . . . You are not to take a bribe . . . Justice, Justice you are to pursue in order that you are to live and possess the land that God is giving you.

Deuteronomy 16:18–20

Leaders Are Made—Not Born.
A short course in human relations:
The six most important words: I admit I made a mistake.
The five most important words: You did a good job.
The four most important words: What is your opinion?
The three most important words: If you please
The two most important words: Thank you
The one most important word: We

Anonymous

A leader is a dealer in hope.

Napoleon (1769–1821)

Don't do for others what they can do for themselves.

"The Iron Rule of Organizing"

A leader is:
Best when people barely know that he exists,
Not So Good when people obey and proclaim him,
Worst when they despise him.

Lao-Tse (604–531 B.C.E.),
The Way of Life

Fail to honor people, they fail to honor you. But of a good leader, who talks little, when his work is done, his aim fulfilled, they will say: "We did this ourselves."

Lao-Tse (604–531 B.C.E.),
The Way of Life

Leaders are ordinary people with extraordinary determination.

Unknown

Nothing gives one person so much advantage over another as to remain always cool and unruffled under all circumstances.

Thomas Jefferson (1743–1826)

He who speaks without modesty will find it difficult to make his words good.

Confucius (551–479 B.C.E.)

And they who are wise shine like the brightness of the firmament, and they who turn many to righteousness like the stars forever and ever.

Daniel 12:3

To be worthy of offering advice to another one need not be an expert. It is sufficient to be a trusted friend.

Rabbi Yerachmiel Yisrael
Yitzchak Danziger (1853–1910)

Let us now praise famous men, and our fathers that begat us.

Ecclesiastes 43:11

If the disciples know that their teacher is able to answer them, then they may ask. Otherwise they may not pose the question [and embarrass their teacher.]

Babylonian Talmud, Hullin 6

10

PERSONAL AND PROFESSIONAL VALUES

A core emphasis of experiential education is on values and personal growth. Personal reflection is a valuable undertaking both for individuals in their daily lives and for professionals who seek awareness of their strengths and weaknesses in their work. The activities presented in this chapter are not specifically on Jewish values. However, the activities can readily be employed for bringing out questions of Jewish identity and relationship with the Jewish community.

The participatory, flexible and non-judgmental orientation of the experiential approach makes it well-suited to helping individuals learn to introspect. By interesting and engaging the individual, experiential learning increases the likelihood that the individual will internalize and act on the lessons learned.

Our institutions, Jewish or otherwise, have an important part to play in enabling individuals to grow personally. For religious institutions this function is self-evident. Other institutions—voluntary organizations, formal educational institutions, even workplaces—can also profitably devote efforts to the improvement of their constituents. In the workplace, particularly in human service professions, clarifying professional values leads to improved ability to perform work effectively and to cope with stresses and demands of the job, as well as to derive more satisfaction from the work.

The subject matter of this chapter is inherently challenging for those participating. Participants are challenged to consider matters pertaining directly to themselves, rather than impersonal facts. Many individuals may be unaccustomed to discussing personal matters with relative strangers. Finally, the act of introspection may lead to uncomfortable self-realization.

Group leaders may find the material difficult for similar reasons. In addition, a group leader may experience doubts as to his/her ability to lead these activities in a natural and credible manner. Success in conducting activities on Personal and Professional Values requires application of the same principles and commitment that are generally employed in experiential education. Most important is to "trust the process", i.e., to place reliance on the strength of a well-designed activity and on people's general predisposition to enjoy a novel and insight-bearing experience. In a Jewish context, people's pride in their identity and desire to serve the community may also be assets.

It is particularly important with these activities to establish an open, non-judgmental tone. The group will be most receptive when warm-ups or activities of a less personal nature lead up to activities related to values. Consideration should be given to choosing an activity appropriate for the particular group at the particular time. The best learning and growth will be achieved when the activity is pitched at a level that is challenging and exciting without being too threatening.

❀   ❀   ❀

PYRAMID

This activity focuses on the imagery and underlying messages represented by the figure of the pyramid, as an analogue for the "underlying mysteries" of the human personality. What are the issues, ideas, or tensions that are buried within the individual? What does the individual keep privately stored in his/her memory?

Instructions:

1. Prior to the group entering the meeting room, the group leader should post a large drawing of a pyramid on the wall in front of the group. In addition, each participant should be given two copies of the pyramid figure with six subdivisions (see figure.) Participants are to compile lists of their positive and negative

characteristics, using one pyramid for each list. Characteristics should be listed in the order of their emotional significance for the individual, with #1, the top, being most significant and/or personal.

2. After all participants have completed their pyramids, the leader assembles the group. The leader explains the symbolism of the pyramid as a place where private possessions or memories are stored. The leader also reminds the participants that, up to now, the self-reflection has been a private and solitary search, but that the reflective process can be significantly deepened if people are ready to share their reflections with others in the group. The leader offers two ground rules: first, each person chooses which of their self-reflections they are willing to share with the other group members; and second, personal reflections shared in the activity are to be treated as confidential. These ground rules encourage participants to be forthcoming in sharing their self-reflections.

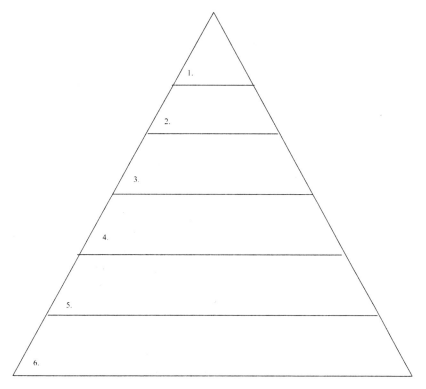

3. The full group is divided into groups of six. It is wise to separate people whose presence in the same sextet might affect the general spirit of openness. Within the sextet, members take turns sharing the self-reflections noted on their pyramids. Others in the group are to ask probing questions and to encourage the member to give an honest self-appraisal. Each member of the sextet is allowed approximately eight minutes for the interactive exchange.

4. It is recommended to take a break of half an hour or more at this point. When the activity resumes, the group re-assembles and discusses ways in which the activity contributed to greater individual or collective self-awareness. Sample questions to consider include:

- What did I learn about myself?
- What did I learn about people I knew already?
- Were people being forthright in what they were sharing?
- What might have been done differently in the activity, which would have added to the forthrightness of what people shared, and the insights generated?
- Any comments or suggestions about the leader's role in the activity?

5. In concluding, the leader should commend the participants for their readiness to explore and share their personal qualities openly.

WHO ARE YOU?

The Sunday edition of *The New York Times* from February 13, 1994 contained an article by James Barron that was in essence an experiential activity presented to New York notables. Barron considers, "Is it possible to define oneself in just a single word? Can one sort out all the complicated, complicating factors of public and private life, measure all the facets of one's personality, cast off what's extraneous and then name an essential, identifying characteristic?"

Participants are asked to identify one word that best defines them and to supply two or three sentences that amplify that choice. The additional explanatory sentences can make the exercise more substantive and enlightening and provide a basis for other people to understand a person's self-definition.

EXAMPLES

1. Ed Koch, former Mayor of New York: *CANDID* "I don't obfuscate, I don't dissemble, I tell you the truth painful or pleasurable."
2. David Dinkins, former Mayor of New York: *CARING* "I care about all people, especially the most vulnerable . . . like children, and seniors, and the disabled."
3. Donald Trump, real estate developer and casino owner: *DOER* "Life is the game. We're here for an average of 72.3 years and have to do something with the time—something that is productive, preferably important, and if possible, fun. I like to play hard and I like to play well—whatever inning it is, whatever the score."
4. Eartha Kitt, singer: *EARTHY* "I was named appropriately because I am of the earth, and as long as the earth is under my feet I will always be confident of who I am."
5. Rush Limbaugh, radio and TV show host, author, conservative pundit: *MISREPRESENTED* "There are two Rush Limbaughs. The real one broadcasts 12½ hours a week, has 7 million books in print, and a newsletter with 400,000 subscribers. Then there's the one who is written about and reported on. Rarely are they the same person."
6. Mary Gordon, novelist: *SEEING* "Everything that I do seems to come back to trying to see more clearly, widely, deeply, richly, from my writing to teaching to relationships with my children."

ME!

Purpose:

This activity is especially useful in enabling people to learn more about others with whom they are involved in a joint endeavor. It is a good initial activity for an extended workshop or for a committee that will be working together for a period of time.

Group:

Junior high school and older; groups of any size.

Setting:

Adequate space for individualized work and then for the full group moving about.

Materials:

Paper and pencils for each participant; half-sheets of newsprint, masking tape, marking pens.

Time:

45 minutes.

Instructions:

1. Participants are each given a sheet of paper and a pencil. They are asked to sit by themselves and compose an inventory of words or phrases that most effectively describe them.
   - What defines "me"?
   - What roles or responsibilities do you occupy?
   - What adjectives accurately describe your personality?
   - Are you a member of any group(s) that give direction to your life?
   - Are there certain characteristics or traits which are typical of you?

After writing down the various key words or phrases, they should rank them in the order of their importance in giving definition to themselves and their lives.

2. After completing individual lists, the group members use a marking pen to write on another piece of paper the word or phrase that they ranked #1 and in smaller print their names. These papers

are posted on the walls. By looking at the posted signs, the participants search for others with similar key words or phrases. Those individuals form a subgroup and share their lists, discussing similarities and differences. Participants who do not find others having similar key words should all go into one group.

3. After the members of the subgroups have talked with each other for 15 to 20 minutes, the leader asks the groups to focus their comments in a total discussion. This discussion will generate a list of the key phrases that were most frequently noted as shaping participants' lives. The leader might note these items on a blackboard or a sheet of newsprint. The leader should note absent items as well as those brought up by the group. What consideration is given to the participants' Jewishness?

Note to Leader:

The subgroups may serve as the work unit for the next activity

VALUES SWAP

Purpose:

To demonstrate vividly that every person has different priorities and to clarify for participants the priorities they place on different values.

Group:

High school and older. 20–25 participants eventually separated into groups of 6–8.

Setting:

A room with chairs and a space large enough for people to move around and hold the values swap.

Materials:

Slips of paper with values written on them (see below), enough for each person to get three slips; a hat or bag; newsprint and a marker.

Time:

40–50 minutes.

Instructions:

1. Start by defining what is meant by values. Stress that values are standards chosen by individuals.
2. Place the slips of paper in the hat. Each participant takes three slips of paper from the hat and examines them.
3. Participants now get up and move around the room. They try to trade values with other people until they are satisfied that the values in their possession are among those they consider most important. All trades must be one for one. Participants are encouraged to call out what they are willing to trade or to inquire what values are in another person's possession. The tone can vary from sedate to raucous as appropriate for the group. Trading should go on for 10 to 15 minutes or until it stops on its own.
4. Break into groups of 6 to 8. Participants report on their satisfaction with the set of values they ended up with and how their preferences compared to those of people with whom they traded. Then participants pool their values slips and attempt to pick the five most important values.
5. Assemble in the full group. Each subgroup reports on the values it selected and the process of reaching consensus. The leader records the selections on newsprint. The group looks for what the chosen values have in common (spiritual vs. material, general vs. specifically Jewish, etc.) Finally, the full group discusses how representative the values chosen are. Would most people be satisfied with them as values for themselves? Are there such things as universal values? What did people learn during the swapping exercise?

VALUE LIST

Dating someone Jewish
Marrying someone Jewish
Liking your work
Being successful
Making lots of money
Saving or investing money

Following current events
Educating the younger generation
Theater
Education
Studying Jewish texts
Volunteering at a hospital

Decorating your home
Having a Jewish home
Raising your children as Jews
Protecting the environment
Helping the sick
Learning about your ancestors
Helping the poor
Supporting Israel
Keeping kosher
Being involved in the Jewish community
Understanding Judaism
Learning Hebrew
Visiting Israel
Making *aliyah*
Learning about different cultures
Staying in touch with old friends
Admitting mistakes
Having a sense of purpose
Enjoying nature
Having a family and raising children
Being involved in diverse activities
Awareness of multicultural issues
Volunteering in a soup kitchen
Expanding your music collection
Giving 5% of your salary/income to charity
Believing in G-d
Dreams
Spirituality
Supporting America
Friendship

Maintaining good health
Not complaining
Making people laugh
Self-confidence
Travel
Taking care of animals
Pursuing a hobby
Spending time with relatives
Reading
Being politically active
Praying
Tzedakah
Taking pride in being Jewish
Setting goals
Supporting new technology
Movies
Showing respect for the elderly
Planting trees in Israel
Supporting the arts
Watching TV
Overcoming your prejudices
Owning an expensive car
Being punctual
Sports and fitness activities
Celebrating holidays
Keeping an open mind
Exercising your creativity
Voting
Joining a synagogue
Capitalism
Socialism
Vegetarianism
Spending time by yourself

(Adapted from an idea submitted by Emily Saffer)

CHOOSE THE LIFE

Rabbi Jerome M. Epstein, the Executive Vice-President of The United Synagogue of Conservative Judaism, wrote a pamphlet at the time of the New Year entitled "Choose THE Life". It starts with the familiar injunction from *Deuteronomy* 30:19 to "choose life." Rabbi Epstein states the importance of not just choosing life in the abstract, but choosing the most meaningful life for oneself. In his words, "Our challenge is to choose *the* life we want to live: a life that is meaningful; rewarding; fulfilling."

The pamphlet poses ten questions to consider when assessing the ultimate achievement of one's life. These questions may be of value to anyone interested in reflecting on their life and contemplating steps to change it.

1. How will we spend the time that God has given us?
2. How will I spend my resources?
3. How will we enrich the lives of God's creatures?
4. What will we learn?
5. How will we grow as Jews?
6. What values will I teach my family?
7. What will our legacy be?
8. How will we become more God-like?
9. What memories do we want others to have of us?
10. What will I do to make this truly a New Year?

(Source: "Choose THE Life" is available from The United Synagogue of Conservative Judaism, Rapaport House, 155 Fifth Ave., New York, NY 10010. Telephone: 212–533–7800.)

"DEAR ME—DON'T OPEN FOR 10 YEARS"

This activity would be especially effective with children aged nine to thirteen. It needs a coordinator, preferably a person associated with an organization such as a school, synagogue or JCC to gather and store the letters for 10 years, and then to mail them to the original writers.

The activity has three components.

1. Writing a letter: The group leader or teacher explains to the children in the group that they should each write themselves a letter in which they are to describe their current interests and values, their future expectations and ambitions, and how likely they

are to achieve those expectations and ambitions in 10 years. The letters should be put in stamped envelopes addressed to the student at his/her family address with a note on the bottom of the envelope: "Not to be opened until (list a date 10 years later)." The letters should then be stored in a sealed box in the organization. The students should also give the leader an alternative address or that of a close relative—in case the student's address changes in the course of 10 years.

2. Ten years later: Now, it is time for the teacher/leader (or the designated replacement) who 10 years ago stored the letters, to unpack and mail the letters to the original letter writers.

3. Assessing accuracy: The final task is for the individual who wrote the letter to read it and to assess the extent to which s/he accurately anticipated his/her personal development. How does the letter writer explain the actual outcome as compared to the expectations of 10 years ago? If feasible, it would be interesting if the initial teacher/group leader could convene the original group of letter writers to discuss together their reactions.

"BIG" QUESTIONS

A simple discussion of significant personal or philosophical questions can be a fruitful group exercise. Sharing of ideas will help participants see that these heavy or difficult questions can be answered or at least grappled with. The interaction and variety of perspectives may provoke new insights. A supportive group setting may encourage individuals to explore new ideas.

The following lists offer a number of thought-provoking questions.

Before starting the discussion, be sure to provide some time for participants to think about the questions. It may be useful to distribute questions in advance of the activity, so that participants can think about the challenging issues involved.

HEALTH AND LIFESTYLE

1. What is one good practice/habit you follow that contributes to good health and your likelihood to live a longer life?

2. What is one bad practice/habit you have that might shorten your life?
3. Try to be realistic and estimate how old you will be when you die.
4. In the same spirit of realism, what do you think will be the cause of your death?
5. What is a piece of wisdom that has helped to guide you or to make sense out of life's challenges? Where did that wisdom come from?

TWENTY QUESTIONS FOR HELPING YOU WRITE YOUR SPIRITUAL AUTOBIOGRAPHY

1. What are your memories of your earliest religious experience?
2. What were your formative experiences, influences, associations?
3. Who were significant or less significant people who had religious impact on you?
4. What religious communities and organizations have you been involved in?
5. What has been your spiritual path?
6. What changes have occurred in your religious life and thought over the course of your life? Why have these changes occurred?
7. What have been your happiest religious experiences?
8. What have been your unhappiest religious experiences?
9. Are there some religious people who influenced you?
10. Were there some religious people who became role modes for you?
11. What part have you played in organized religion? What part have you declined to play?
12. Have you experienced epiphanies? (*Webster's Ninth New Collegiate Dictionary* defines epiphany as "a sudden manifestation or perception of the essential nature or meaning of something.") Did this change your life?
13. If you have children, do/did you provide them religious education and immersion? If so, how?
14. Can you reflect upon your life odyssey and discern any theological issues that have informed you?

15. Has religion been a major, minor, or no influence on your life and actions?
16. Use a time line to look at your religious life in the past: How did your parents, grandparents, other family members influence you?
17. How did world events influence you religiously or spiritually?
18. What, if any, are the religious edifices in which significant things have happened to you?
19. What kind of key choices have you made in your life? Did your religion play a part in these choices?
20. What does the word "spirituality" mean to you?

("Twenty Questions" was taken from the curriculum for a course offered at the Brandeis University Adult Learning Institute in 2001 by Ruth Harriet Jacobs, author of *Be an Outrageous Older Woman*, New York: Harper-Collins, 1997.)

SPECIAL AWARDS: DEEDS OF COMPASSION

Purpose:

To explore ways to give encouragement and recognition for ethical achievement, especially among adolescents.

Group:

Children ages 13 and older and their parents or teachers.

A refreshing perspective on encouraging ethical practices was offered in an op-ed piece by Rabbi Sandy Eisenberg Sasso of Congregation Beth-El Zedeck in Indianapolis ("Honor the Hard Work of Compassion" in *The Christian Science Monitor*, June 15, 2000.) She notes the challenges that adolescents face in choosing to perform "deeds of compassion", actions concerned with the well-being or emotional comfort of others. Adolescents worry about fitting in with the majority. They want reassurance that by choosing to expend effort on others' behalf they are not missing out on something and that their choice will be accepted by their peers.

Writing at the time of high school graduations, Rabbi Eisenberg Sasso speculates about using graduation ceremonies as an occasion to honor ethical achievement in the same way that academic or athletic achievement are now rewarded. She also lists opportunities for deeds of compassion that commonly present themselves to adolescents, specifically:

1. Offering comfort to a friend who is having trouble in school or at home.
2. Refusing to use or accept derogatory statements about people of other ethnic backgrounds or religions.
3. Following through with a commitment, even though it is inconvenient.
4. Serving as a volunteer in the community.
5. Showing respect to teachers, parents, and peers.
6. Extending a hand of friendship to someone who is not part of the popular crowd.
7. Being honest when others cheat.

A discussion between adolescents and parents or teachers could serve to identify forms of encouragement and support that would promote ethical behavior among young people. Discussion could start with evaluation of the seven deeds described above and consideration of what behaviors to add or remove. What kinds of awards for ethical behavior are appropriate at a graduation? Discussion could then focus on questions of implementation. Specifically, how might ethical behavior be acknowledged at graduation? Is it reasonable to single out the top achiever in this area, or is there some way of honoring several people or even everyone? What other ways are there for a school to give more importance to deeds of compassion? How could other institutions, for instance, family or youth activities, offer more support to young people in achieving a balance between benefiting themselves and serving others?

BEING A MENSCH

Purpose:

To encourage people to think of concrete ways to perform good deeds.

Instructions:

1. At the outset, the leader introduces the notion of *mensch*. This simple Yiddish word embodies the notion of doing small good deeds without expectation of any reward or recognition, just because it is "the decent thing to do."
2. Each participant is asked to think of three or four acts of kindness they have recently performed or would be ready to perform. After people compile their mental lists, the individual acts are compiled on a large list by the whole group. Communally listing good deeds may provide support and encouragement for people to carry them out.
3. The group may wish to schedule another meeting a month or so later to follow up. To what extent did people carry out good deeds like the ones listed? How did people feel about their efforts to behave as *menschen*? Would those people who were not successful be willing to try again?

Notes to the Leader:

Acts of kindness are often overlooked in favor of more overtly ethical behavior. The leader may draw connections to the variety of *mitzvot*, commandments given in the Torah. Some pertain to religious ritual, but others pertain to everyday social relations.

A *MITZVAH!* SOME MODEST SUGGESTIONS

- Befriend someone.
- Visit a housebound or hospital-bound person.
- Help someone find a job.
- Do a favor for someone you don't usually get along with.
- Volunteer for a charitable organization.
- Visit or call Mom and Dad, just because.
- Spend time with your extended family. Tell them how much you appreciate them.
- Make up with someone you don't talk to. Even if it's your brother.
- Seek out a long-lost family member.

- Take your child to cheer up the *bubbies* and *zaidies* (grandmas and grandpas) at the retirement home.
- Have guests over for Shabbat.
- Smile at your spouse.
- Hug your kids.
- Make generous contributions to your community's Jewish federation campaign and its United Way campaign.

(From a list distributed by Chabad House of Cleveland, 4481 University Parkway, Cleveland, OH 44118. Their rallying cry is: "Together we can change the world, one *mitzvah* at a time.")

THE 11ᵀᴴ COMMANDMENT

Purpose:

To encourage participants to think about one of the central concepts of Jewish ethics and how it affects their lives.

Group:

All ages from elementary school children to seniors.

Setting:

This activity is best conducted in small groups; the size of the group would determine the size of the room needed. It is recommended that the participants be divided into small groups with six to eight people in each group.

Instructions:

The leader should begin by discussing the biblical sections which refer to God giving the Commandments to Moses (*Exodus* 20:2–14, *Deuteronomy* 5:6–8). The core motif to establish in this opening session is that Commandments are viewed as guidelines and supports meant to help people lead more meaningful and responsible lives.

After briefly reviewing each of the Ten Commandments, the leader explains the basic educational goal of this activity: to come up with an 11th Commandment—one additional expectation that is appropriate for people today and the challenges they face.

After about 20–30 minutes of discussion in small groups, each group should report on its 11th Commandment. The report can be delivered orally, with a skit, or in a creative visual presentation (which should be posted.) The leader should write on a blackboard or on newsprint all of the suggested commandments. If possible the group should seek to achieve consensus on the preferred 11th Commandment.

The activity should conclude with a summary of the discussion with two foci: 1) how the Ten Commandments were central in shaping the uniqueness of the Jewish people at the time of the Exodus and, 2) how the Ten Commandments do or do not influence Jews today.

Note to Leader:

In 1996 a book was published that featured representative responses to this activity. See *The 11th Commandment: Wisdom From Our Children*, compiled by the Jewish Lights Publishing staff.

EXAMPLE

At the time of Shavuot, a creative kindergarten teacher at the Solomon Schechter Day School of Greater Boston asked her students to come up with a code of behavior consisting of ten statements. This was the kindergarteners' version of the Ten Commandments:

- Be nice to other people.
- Never be destructive.
- Never say you hate a friend.
- Do not kill nature.
- Don't tell a lie.
- Always be friends.
- Never hurt someone's house.
- Always keep your baby safe.

- Never push other people.
- Never give up.

❀ ❀ ❀

UNFINISHED BUSINESS

Purpose:

This activity is designed to help people experience concrete means of resolving interpersonal tensions. It would be especially useful for addressing tensions among people within an organization, particularly in a retreat setting where participants might be more receptive than they would be in the workplace.

Group:

Young adults and older.

Time and Setting:

Depending on the available time and interest level of the group of participants, this activity can occupy from 60 minutes to 90 minutes. About half of the time should be spent in the small groups and the rest in reports from these groups and a concluding discussion and summary by the group leader.

Instructions:

1. The activity begins with people meeting in small groups consisting of 3–5 people. Participants are asked to review important relationships with friends, family, or work associates. Are there tensions or issues with any of those individuals that are unresolved?
2. Each participant describes one such piece of "unfinished business" that s/he would like to address and achieve closure on. Then the participant acts out what they would like to say or do with the other person, with one other member of the group playing the role of that person.
3. Then the total group discusses their experience of the role

plays, including general insights gained into resolving interpersonal tensions and whether individual participants felt that the activity was helpful for their particular relationship.

MY PROFESSIONAL INVENTORY

Whether you work as a human service professional or in the world of business, it is worthwhile to reflect on your effectiveness at work. Rate your effectiveness on each of the 18 work-related skills listed on "Professional Inventory".

Do a baseline scoring now. You may wish to add other aspects of leadership that are important in your work. This inventory will serve as an agenda for improving your weak areas and building on your strengths.

After some period of time, say half a year, assess yourself again, especially in areas that you found needed improvement.

PROFESSIONAL INVENTORY

(Score yourself using a 5-point scale, from 1 = "in need of much improvement" to 5 = "a definite asset".)

As I consider my professional readiness for my current and/or future career choice, I see myself in the following way:

Administration
Management
Budgeting
Coordination
Negotiation
Supervision
Consulting
Teaching
Creativity
Counseling
Designing Programs
Facilitation
Implementation

Judgment
Writing
Organization
Research
Human Relations
Other:

❀   ❀   ❀

PROFESSIONAL SELF-REFLECTION/ "USE OF SELF"

Purpose:

To help professionals reflect on their professional strengths and
weaknesses. Another basic professional leadership concept for
human service professionals which lends itself to being explored
with an experiential approach is "Use of Self".

The core idea of "Use of Self" is that human service professionals must be aware of their own psychological needs, values and
personal leadership style, as a prelude to defining how they
respond to their clients/members. The aim is not to make the professional self-conscious or defensive about his/her weaknesses. In
fact, self-reflection allows a professional to be more natural. Being
aware of oneself as a professional enables one to build on
strengths, control limitations, and recognize unconscious tendencies that may arise in the course of work.

Instructions:

1. Each professional is instructed to reflect privately on his or her
    professional work and to make note of strengths and weak-
    nesses. It should be stressed that this process and the notes are
    meant to be private.
2. Specifically, participants may be instructed as follows. "We
    encourage you to use this "safe space" to think about your
    characteristic style of professional work, focusing particularly
    on aspects of your work where you may not operate at your
    best:
    • where you avoid certain roles or situations

- relationships or personalities with which you are not comfortable
- other ways in which you "trip yourself up"

It is also important to be aware of your strengths, so that these personal and professional assets can be fully utilized in your work."

3. Divide the group into trios. No trio should contain people that are either close friends or have a work relationship in which one has a supervisory relationship with the other. Each trio should have a private space where they can meet and share their reflections. The leader should stress that each person chooses what to share in the trio; but participants are encouraged to respond frankly. At least 30–40 minutes should be provided so that each member will have an opportunity to report on their self-evaluation.

4. Following the sharing in trios, the leader convenes the full group and asks people to speak, in general terms, about the process of self-evaluation. Did they feel it was a serious and honest process? Did people gain any further insights about themselves and about professional self-reflection?

5. The leader highlights the key issues which have emerged, gives praise to the participants for their introspective work and concludes encouraging ongoing self-reflection as a basic requisite of top professional functioning.

Note to Leader: At the core of effective use of self is the readiness of the professional to be introspective. This is difficult because self-review poses a threat to one's status quo. Accordingly it is well to acknowledge at the outset that all people tend to resist change and seek to maintain their status quo.

USE OF SELF-INVENTORIES WITH PROFESSIONALS WHO ARE IN THE SAME ORGANIZATION

A requisite for any human service professional is the capacity to use him or herself in a disciplined way in serving the clients' needs, interests and agenda. To be effective in this non-directive mode of operation requires a combination of theoretical understanding of the helping process, plus self-awareness. Self-awareness by the human service professional is requisite to ensure that his or her own personal needs/interests do not impede his or her capacity to be most helpful to the individuals and groups with whom he or she works. A self-inventory is a valuable tool for providing the professional with a systematic assessment.

It is considerably easier for people to discuss their self-inventories with people they don't know than with colleagues working in the same organization. Nonetheless, by stressing confidentiality and ensuring that each person has the right to decide what personal information to share, the process can work with fellow staff members.

I have led several workshops based on self-inventories with professionals working in the same organization and these have worked out quite well. The key is at the outset to interpret clearly the confidentiality of the process. Specific sensitivity needs to be exercised in deciding with whom people share their self-inventories. Clearly no one should be asked to meet with any person with whom they would feel any inhibition. That would include people involved in any supervisory relationship.

The approach I have used is to assemble all the participants in a large open room. After stressing the importance of confidentiality, I ask people to circulate and form trios with others with whom they would feel comfortable sharing personal information. Then I ask each trio to find a section of the room that is removed from others.

It is helpful to share at the outset clear guidelines about how to productively use these trio discussions. The following are guidelines which I have found help people get engaged and assure that they are forthright and honest in sharing personal information. These guidelines apply after everyone has completed their self-inventory.

- Each individual in the trio has up to 10 minutes to present personal insights and perspectives.
- Then the other two individuals would offer their feedback, each having about 10 to 15 minutes to offer their reactions.
- Each individual will have about 30 minutes as the focus of discussion.

As a concluding component of the activity all the trios come together, and each person is asked to share their reactions to the activity, insights that emerged in the process of writing the self-inventory, and insights that emerged in the feedback experience in the trio.

It is important in concluding this activity that the leader give appropriate positive recognition to the participants for their willingness to engage in this process of self-reflection. Also, it would be important for the leader to indicate that he/she would be available if any of the participants wanted to pursue further personal issues which arose in the course of this activity. If such issues arise, the group leader might intervene directly or recommend a referral to an appropriate helping professional.

CODE OF ETHICS

1. Participants: This activity would be most appropriate for people who are involved in leadership responsibilities, either as professionals or as lay people. For the professionals, the educational objectives are to help the participants understand the nature and purpose of the Code of Ethics and see how the Code gives direction to their day-to-day work. For the volunteer lay people, the objective would be to understand how to shape organizational standards and practices of the social agency or school which are consonant with the code of ethics of their professionals and thereby to ensure quality programs and services.

   An experiential activity focusing on a code of ethics could be done in one of two ways: a) separately for professionals, or b) bringing together both professionals and lay people. The latter approach is preferred since it is likely to result in a greater impact on the organization's standards and quality of service.

2. Setting: A discussion of a Code of Ethics would be ideally explored at a retreat or training meeting of several days duration, which would allow adequate time for exploring the concept and specific ways the principles and practices enunciated in the Code would shape the policies and practices of the social agency.

An alternative approach would be a discussion with only professionals present, either those working in the same organization, or from multiple organizations.

3. Program: Two approaches to exploring the concept would be:
   a) Have participants at the meeting read the enclosed Code of Ethics and, perhaps in small groups, discuss their reactions to the concept in general and the relative importance of the individual items in the Code.
   b) A more elaborate program might begin with a discussion of the concept, followed by participants writing their own codes of ethics—either individually or in small groups. Conclude by having the full group try to agree on an ideal code of ethics, drawing from the several lists produced by the group.

4. Conclusion: The leader would seek to highlight the values reflected in the Code and encourage the participants to consider ways of introducing or upgrading codes of ethics in their social agencies or their professional associations.

Note to Leader:

A leader cannot elicit the interest and support of their constituency unless they consistently represent in their own practice the values and skills they espouse. Ideally, the group leader is a role model.

Early in my career as a university teacher of men and women preparing for careers as Jewish communal workers, I realized that those professionals needed a code of ethics no less so than traditional professionals, doctors, lawyers or architects. I set out to define such a code. That code, "A Jewish Communal Practitioner's Code of Ethics" incorporates standards from other human service professions as well as the values and disciplines that I drew on to be a responsible and effective helping practitioner.

A JEWISH COMMUNAL PRACTITIONER'S CODE OF ETHICS

In my professional practice I will seek to:

. . . Answer all phone calls within 24 hours.

. . . Answer all letters within three days.

. . . Make sure there are introductions at the start of all meetings and social occasions.

. . . Make sure to summarize at the end of meetings, both what occurred and steps that are needed for follow up.

. . . Personally greet and help connect strangers who enter groups of which I am a part.

. . . Give recognition to people for their special achievements as well as for their consistent and dependable performance.

. . . Be diligent about monitoring my own ego and ways it gets in the way of my empowering others to grow and assume responsibility.

. . . Seek to risk and be creative rather than to be conservative and cautious.

. . . Do my homework in preparing for all meetings and programs in terms of a clear agenda, knowledge of the issues and the participants.

. . . Be prompt and thorough in following up on all decisions arrived at in meetings where I am the professional.

. . . Concentrate on learning and using people's names.

. . . Start and end meetings on time.

. . . Demonstrate a commitment to pluralism in Jewish life with respect for the several religious denominations and other ways Jews identify with the community.

. . . Be a "boundary crosser," someone who sees the "larger picture," rises above parochial identifications to broader perspectives: beyond the department to the total agency; beyond the agency to the Jewish community; beyond denominational or ideological loyalties to a concern for *K'lal Yisrael*.

. . . Concentrate on listening to people in an open and non-judgmental fashion.

. . . Be attentive to my own psychological and physical well being so that when I am at work I have available physical and emotional energy.

. . . Finally, I am a role model. I am aware that I will have my greatest professional impact on the people with whom I work in the manner in which I conduct myself, both professionally and as a Jew.

VOLUNTEERS

At the core of the communal life of Jewish communities, particularly in the Diaspora, and especially in America, are volunteers—those countless individuals who choose to give of their time, energy and money to develop and sustain the Jewish community.

Yes, these Jewish communities have a cadre of well-trained professionals who perform the day-to-day tasks of providing services in religious, educational, social welfare and fraternal organizations. But that network could not function without the no less vital presence of volunteers. Indeed, this leadership partnership of professionals and volunteers is the essence of the American Jewish community. While the professionals receive special education to develop the specific knowledge and skills necessary to fulfill their leadership duties, their lay compatriots come from many diverse educational and vocational backgrounds. Recognizing this disparity, the Jewish communal organizations invest considerable resources in training programs for their volunteers.

The activity "Volunteers" is a useful opening or advance activity to include in a training for current or prospective volunteers in Jewish communal organizations.

Each person is given a sheet of paper with the word "volunteer" spelled out vertically along the left edge of the paper:

V
O
L
U
N
T
E
E
R

The task for each person is to come up with a word beginning with each of the nine letters that represents a key quality of volunteerism.

The American Red Cross is an organization that typifies the

essence of volunteerism. A recent brochure from the organization lists these nine words using the letters of "volunteer":

Versatile
Outstanding
Loyal
Understanding
Nurturing
Tireless
Enduring
Enthusiastic
Reliable

BRIGHT DREAMS, BIG WORLD

Purpose:

To decide on a group social action project in a participatory fashion, and to give participants a chance to fantasize about one action they might take to improve the world.

Group:

Ages 10–17; 12–25 participants.

Setting:

Open space.

Materials:

Writing materials.

Time:

30 minutes or more depending on number of participants.

Instructions:

1. Briefly discuss the concept of *tikkun olam*, repairing the world through social action. After participants present their views,

the leader may wish to fill in points that were not brought up. Each participant should spend 5 minutes thinking about what act of *tikkun olam* s/he would carry out if they could go anywhere in the world for twenty-four hours.

2. Divide into small groups. One way to do this is in terms of the area where participants would perform their act of *tikkun olam*, e.g. one group for local community, one for this country, one for foreign countries. Within each group, members should select one plan and consider steps necessary to bring it about.

3. Re-assemble. Have one person from each group present the plans. The total group should choose one plan as a project. A next step, such as a next meeting date, should be set in order to follow up on this project.

(Submitted by Julie Shumofsky)

HOW TO BRING ABOUT CHANGE

"We have the power to change things. It doesn't take much to start a revolution of thought and spirit. It takes one person and then another and then another. We have to have the willingness to be respectful of each other and not to let differences become obstacles. It's a responsibility and a chore. But when it works, it's a work of art." Lenny Zakim, 1978–1999 Executive Director New England Region Anti-Defamation League

The above words of wisdom are from a great social activist, Lenny Zakim, former Executive Director of the Anti-Defamation League of B'nai Brith in Boston from 1978–1999.

Lenny was a wonderful, committed social activist who unfortunately was struck with cancer and died much too young. The quote above, taken from the eulogy he wrote for himself, illustrates the spirit that enabled him to bring about so much social change in his years of community service.

What are your ideas about achieving constructive change in your own organization, local community, or larger societal constellations?

Do you consider yourself a social activist? Do you think about ways to improve the effectiveness of the social or communal organizations of which you are a member?

What is your philosophy of achieving change? And what are the strategies you would utilize to help make a more effective organization or community?

Compare your leadership credo with that of Lenny Zakim or other community activists who have inspired you and have helped make the communities and the world in which we live a better place. Who have been your heroes or models of leadership?

"How to Bring About Change" is an activity that can be the basis for a different type of meeting or weekend retreat for the leadership of your synagogue or communal agency. Perhaps such an approach to leadership might help extend people's expectations and vision and even bring about constructive change.

QUOTES

The world stands on three foundations: on Torah, on worship, and on deeds of loving kindness.

Pirkei Avot, Shimon the
Righteous, 1:2

There are three crowns: the crown of Torah, the crown of Priesthood, the crown of royalty. The crown of a good name is superior to them all.

Pirkei Avot 6:17

A good name is preferable to great wealth.

Proverbs 22:1

Tzedakah is not an easy word to translate. It isn't charity. Charity is optional: *tzedakah* is obligatory.

Rabbi Mitch Chefitz, Havurah of
South Florida, 1999

What doth the Lord thy God require of thee, but to fear the Lord, thy God, to walk in all his ways, and to love Him, and to serve the

Lord thy God with all thy heart and with all thy soul; to keep for thy good the commandments of the Lord, and His statement, which I command thee this day?

Deuteronomy 10:12–13

What doth the Lord require of thee: Only to do justly, and to love mercy, and to walk humbly with thy God.

Micah 6:8

Hate the evil, and love the good, and establish justice in the gate, . . .

Amos 5:15

Happy are they who maintain justice and righteousness at all times.

Psalms 106:3

You shall judge your fellow man with righteousness.

Leviticus 19:15

Which is the path of virtue a person should follow? Whichever brings honor to his Maker and brings him honor from his fellow human beings.

Pirkei Avot, Hillel 2:1

To leave the world a bit better, to know even one life has breathed easier because you have lived. This is to have succeeded.

Ralph Waldo Emerson (1803–1882)

It is best to do to another what will strengthen you even as it will strengthen him—that is, what will develop his best potentials even as it develops your own.

Erik Erikson (1902–1994),
Insight and Responsibility

All you need is love.

The Beatles, 1967

I still believe people are good at heart.

Anne Frank (1929–1945)

For this reason man was created alone, to teach you that if anyone destroys one human life, Scripture charges him as though he had destroyed a whole world; and anyone who rescues one human life, Scripture credits him as though he had saved a whole world. Furthermore (man was created alone) for the sake of the human race, so that a man should not say to his fellow, My father was greater than your father.

Sanhedrin 4:5

The world is a tree and human beings are its fruit.

Rabbi Solomon Ibn Gabirol
(1020–1057)

If you do not care for one another, who will care for you.

Buddha (565–483 B.C.E.)

Based on genuine human relations—real feeling for each other, understanding each other—we can develop mutual trust and respect. From that, we can share other people's suffering and build harmony in human society.

14th Dalai Lama (1935-), Tibetan
Buddhist spiritual leader

Better to violate a biblical command than to embarrass another human being.

Rabbi Nachman of Bratslav
(1772–1811)

Where there is no wisdom, there will be no reverence; where there is no reverence there will be no wisdom. Where there is no understanding, there will be no knowledge; where there is no knowledge, there will be no understanding. Where there is no bread there is no Torah; where there is no Torah, there will be no bread.

Pirkei Avot, Elazar ben Azariah, 3:21

Study with all your heart and with all your soul to know God's ways and to watch at the doors of the Divine law. Keep God's law in your heart and let divine reverence always be before your eyes.

Keep your mouth from sin and purify and sanctify yourself from trespass and iniquity and God will be with you in every place.

Babylonian Talmud, Berachot 17a

Who is wise? The man who can learn something from every man.
Who is strong? The man who overcomes his passion.
Who is rich? The man who is content with his fate.
Whom do men honor? The man who honors his fellow man.

Pirkei Avot 4:1

A man seldom thinks with more earnestness of anything than he does of his dinner.

Samuel Johnson (1709–1784)

It is with narrow-souled people as with narrow-necked bottles; the less they have in them the more noise they make in pouring it out.

Alexander Pope (1688–1744)

An ignoramus cannot be a righteous person.

Hillel (30 B.C.E.–10 C.E.)

He is happy who has his health. But nobody knows it until they get sick. And when they get well, they forget it. Everything else is nonsense; all this stuff about unhappiness and love and loneliness, it all evaporates when you get sick.

Erich Maria Remarque (1898–1970)

Give a man health and a course to steer, and he'll never stop to trouble about whether he is happy or not.

George Bernard Shaw (1856–1950)

So much has been given to me; I have no time to ponder over that which has been denied.

Helen Keller (1880–1968)

Every generation must find new methods to fight the evil impulse, because he becomes familiar with the old methods, and he knows how to defeat them.

Rabbi Aryeh Leib,
the grandfather of Shpoli

Where all are guilty, no one is.

Hannah Arendt (1906–1975), 1972

Without evil, goodness would not be possible either.

Eliezer Berkovitz (1908–),
American Orthodox rabbi

I prefer a wicked person who knows he is wicked to a righteous person who knows he is righteous.

The Seer of Lublin

Derekh Eretz (decency or acceptable behavior) which cannot be translated adequately into any other language, went a long way towards influencing the behavior pattern of the Jewish family. For a young person to be reminded of these key words when he became a bit too brash was often sufficient to put him back on the right track. The youth needed no other reprimand. To recall the concept alone was sufficient. "*Derekh Eretz!*" He had no difficulty in understanding the "code language" common to all members of the family.

Simon Glustrom, 1975

My generation of radicals and breakers-down never found anything to take the place of the old virtues of work and courage and the old graces of courtesy and politeness.

F. Scott Fitzgerald (1896–1940)

How often could things be remedied by a word. How often it is left unspoken.

Norman Douglas (1868–1952),
English author

It has been my experience that folks who have few vices have very few virtues.

Abraham Lincoln (1809–1865)

Know! A person walks in life on a very narrow bridge. The most important thing is not to be afraid.

Rabbi Nachman of Bratslav
(1772–1811)

If I am not for myself, who is for me? And being only for myself, what am I? And if not now, when?

Hillel (30 B.C.E.–10 C.E.)

It is better that we look inside of ourselves and see what is going on in here, than to look to the heavens to see what is going on up there.

Rabbi Shalom Shachna of Prohobitch

Throughout my life I never regretted telling the truth.

Rabbi Menachem Mendel of Kotzk
(1787–1859)

This above all: to thine own self be true, and it must follow, as the night the day, thou canst not then be false to any man.

William Shakespeare (1564–1616),
Hamlet, Act I, Scene 3, Polonius'
farewell to his son

Victory creates hatred, defeat creates suffering. Those who are wise strive for neither victory nor defeat.

Buddha (565–483 B.C.E.)

The meaning of life is that it ends.

Franz Kafka (1883–1924)

II

RELIGION AND CULTURE

The period at the end of the 20th and the beginning of the 21st century may be defined as the generation of seekers. We are seeking a source of meaning beyond what is in our lives at the moment. Questions abound. Is there a God? If so, what role does God play in my life today? What does the term "spiritual" or "spirituality" mean to me? What makes one community meaningful and another not? How important is ritual in my life? How important is it for me to feel connected to those who have a similar history or philosophy? Conversely, how important is it for me to maintain a sense of individuality?

These questions may seem an odd juxtaposition to questions regarding religion and culture. After all, religion and culture conjure up images related to assumptions we hold about rituals, ceremonies, prayer, God, the continuity of values from history and the history of that religion in particular. Yet, within the Jewish tradition the notion of questioning—our relationship to God, the way we lead our lives, how we connect both to this world and to the world that recognizes powers beyond human control—has been encouraged since biblical times.

When the forefather Jacob changed his name and turned what had been up until then a family of Jews into a people, the name chosen for him was "Yisra-el", which means to struggle with God. This is a profound statement.

What does this tell us about the function of the informal Jewish educator? The role of the educator is not to provide "the Jewish answer". Rather it is to assist participants to ask questions and begin to articulate their own responses, to inject Jewish viewpoints into that discussion, and ultimately to facilitate members of the group—as individuals and not through consensus of the group as a whole—to develop ways for creating meaning in their lives through ritual and the conduct of daily life.

The task of the informal educator is not to suggest that participants emulate the facilitator. We need to remember that in the Talmud a dissenting voice is always written, as we can never be certain of one human being's knowledge and interpretation of life's questions. In this regard, the saying from *Pirkei Avot (Ethics of the Fathers)*, "Who is wise, one who learns from everyone," is fundamental. This further suggests that the facilitator must be open to epiphanies or revelations of their own as the result of interactions with the members of the group.

The activities in this section provide opportunities for participants to experience Jewish ideas and practice personally and directly. Evaluation and reflection after the experience will enable participants to find personal meaning.

ROSH HASHANAH PUZZLES

Purpose:

To teach children about the holiday of Rosh Hashanah.

Group:

Ages 7–10; 20–25 participants.

Setting:

A classroom with tables and chairs.

Materials:

Index cards with pictures of objects associated with Rosh Hashanah—for example, shofar, round challah, apples and honey, wine, candlesticks, honeycake, and calendar. These cards will be used to divide people into groups of 3 or 4.

Puzzles on which are written statements about the holiday.

Blank puzzles can be obtained at an art supply store. Alternatively, puzzles can be created out of oaktag. Envelopes in which to place the puzzle pieces. Examples of statements:

a) Rosh Hashanah celebrates the birthday of the world.
b) Rosh Hashanah is the Jewish New Year.
c) On Rosh Hashanah we dip apples in honey for a sweet New Year.
d) *"L'shanah Tovah"* means "Happy New Year".
e) *Tashlich* is a service where we throw bread into the water to represent the sins we have committed in the past year.
f) The round challah represents our hope for a full and happy year.
g) The shofar is blown to welcome in the New Year.

Time:

10–15 minutes.

Instructions:

1. Distribute one index card to each child. Instruct the children to find the others who have the same symbol and form into a group.
2. Give each group an envelope containing the pieces of a puzzle and instruct the members to assemble it. When all puzzles are completed, one representative from each group should go to the front of the class and read what the puzzle says.

(Submitted by Emily Saffer)

SCRUMPTIOUS SUKKOT

Purpose:

To learn about the components of a kosher sukkah in an engaging and literally appetizing manner.

Group:

Children in 2nd–4th grade.

Setting:

A setting where eating is permitted. Tables and chairs. There should be sufficient space for participants to spread out all of their materials on the table.

Materials:

(Quantities are for ten participants.) Paper plates; two boxes of graham crackers; three containers of frosting; a large bag of Pull-N-Peel Twizzlers; one pound of raisins; two bags of chocolate chips; a one-pound bag of M&M's; bowls; ten knives for spreading frosting.

Time:

30 minutes for the process of building the sukkot. Allow an additional 10–20 minutes for eating the sukkot.

Instructions:

1. Participants will construct a model of a sukkah using food items. The leader presents various facts about the sukkah's structure. For each group of facts there are associated food items that are incorporated into the sukkah.
2. Paper plates are distributed for use as the base.
3. Leader describes requirements for sukkot:
   • It is a mitzvah to build a sukkah.
   • It is an obligation for each individual to build a sukkah.
   • A sukkah should be built after Yom Kippur.
   • A sukkah is erected in the open air under the sky, not in a room or under a tree.
   • Number of walls: minimum requirements are two complete and part of a third, but it is customary to use four.

- A sukkah consists of walls with a removable cover (*skhakh*).
- A sukkah is a temporary structure. (Point out to the children that this is the reason the sukkot are being built on paper plates.)
- Sukkah should be strong enough to withstand ordinary winds.
- Walls should be no more than 30 feet high (a sukkah is no longer considered temporary if the walls are higher) and no less than three feet (minimum space for one person.)

4. Four graham crackers are distributed to each child for use as walls. A container of frosting is put on each table. Each child is given a knife to spread the frosting in order to hold the graham crackers in place.
5. Leader describes requirements for *skhakh*:
   - It needs to grow from the soil.
   - It needs to be detached from the ground.
   - Sitting on top of the sukkah, *skhakh* needs to be loose enough so a person can see the sky.
   - It should be thick enough so the amount of shadow cast on the ground exceeds the light thrown by the sun.
   - It must not consist of grass or leaves, since they dry up quickly.
   - The materials that make up the walls and *skhakh* should not have an offensive odor or shrivel within seven days.
6. Pull-N-Peel Twizzlers are distributed for use as *skhakh*. Individual pieces of twizzler are laid on top of the graham crackers.
7. Leader points out the teaching that states that all commandments should have aesthetic appeal.
8. Bowls of raisins, chocolate chips and M&M's are placed on each table. Children can decorate their sukkot with these items, using frosting to attach them.
9. Leader states that Sukkot is a time for celebration, then encourages children to eat some or all of their sukkot.

Note to Leader:

In programming this activity, in particular planning following activities, the leader should bear in mind that the mood will become lighter as soon the eating starts.

(Submitted by Jennifer Wolinsky)

HUMAN TORAH

Purpose:

To give children an appreciation for the Torah scroll.

Group:

Children ages 6–10 years; 10–15 participants.

Setting:

A classroom with a long table and chairs. If a long table is not available, the floor can be used.

Material:

Two very long lengths of paper, 2 or 3 ft. wide, for instance, a roll of brown wrapping paper; supplies for decorating, such as crayons, scissors, colored tissue paper, glitter, and glue.

Time:

25–30 minutes.

Instructions:

1. Start with a discussion of Simchat Torah. What does the holiday celebrate? How is the holiday observed? Contributions should come from the children, with the leader filling in any key points that have been missed. The leader mentions the importance of the Torah scroll and the care that is taken in handling it.
2. Have the children decorate one of the lengths of paper for use as a wrapper for a Torah. Allow 10–15 minutes. The leader may suggest appropriate subject matter.
3. Two volunteers, who will represent the Torah scroll, take either end of the other length of paper and stretch it out. Those people turn inward toward the middle of the paper, winding them-

selves in the paper like the poles of a Torah. Now, two other volunteers wrap the human Torah scroll with the Torah cover made by the group.
4. If there is interest, unwind the cover and scroll, then repeat the process with another set of volunteers.
5. At the conclusion of the activity, be careful to unwrap the Torah in a suitably respectful manner.

(Submitted by Emily Saffer)

CREATIVE PURIM EXPRESSIONS

Purpose:

To determine, as a group, the most relevant aspects of the holiday of Purim; to create costumes that reflect holiday themes.

Group:

This activity is designed for adults, students, or families that have a basic familiarity with *Megillat Esther*. It could be modified to be used with younger children.

Setting:

This activity requires a place where groups can spread out to work privately and a central meeting area.

Materials:

Sheets listing aspects of Purim; supplies for making a costume, such as fabric, markers, craft materials, pencils, carves, pins, scissors, and other craft supplies.

Time:

45 minutes.

Instructions:

1. Leader briefly reviews the Megillah and identifies several aspects of Purim.

2. The group is divided into smaller groups of 5–10. Each group is given a list of aspects. The group chooses the aspect or aspects it feels are most important or revealing. Those aspects will be expressed in a costume developed by the group.
3. Roughly 20 minutes is allotted for making the costume. One member of the group will wear it.
4. The entire group re-assembles. Each group presents its costume. One person models it and another person explains its significance.

(Submitted by Leann Shamash)

PURIM FUN

Purpose:

To act out the story of Purim in imaginative ways.

Group:

Children or teens. This activity could be used with many participants divided into groups of five to seven people.

Setting:

There needs to be a "stage" or an area set aside for the groups to present their skits. There also should be room for people to develop their skits.

Materials:

Large paper bags or garbage bags containing assorted props and items for costumes. Contents of each bag can be different. Some objects should be directly relevant to the Purim story.

Time:

45 minutes or more depending on length and number of skits.

Instructions:

1. The leader divides everyone into small groups.
2. Each group is given a paper bag. The group must develop a

rendition of the Purim story that uses as many of the articles in the bag as possible. The leader will be available to provide assistance regarding the original story in the Book of Esther.
3. The groups come back together and present their skits.
4. It may be desirable to vote on the skits. Categories might include best acting performance, most (or least) faithful to the facts, best use of the resources supplied.

(Submitted by Shannon Stein)

THE SHABBAT TABLE

Purpose:

This activity is an enjoyable quiz designed to enhance knowledge and appreciation of Shabbat.

Group:

If this activity is conducted on the Sabbath, those who keep it more strictly can be comfortable participating, as the activity does not require writing. The participants are divided into small groups. It does not matter how many there are in each group or how many groups there are. There needs to be a designated leader in each group.

Setting:

An ideal setting would be a large gathering or summer camp. Best time for the activity would be before or during Shabbat.

Materials:

In preparation for the activity the leader must devise six appropriate tasks to be done by a small group. Examples: arrange members in a line from oldest to youngest, do an Israeli folk dance, form a human Star of David.
    Each group will receive:

- six envelopes. A question about Shabbat (see Sample Questions below) is written on the envelope and a slip of paper listing one of the group tasks is placed inside.
- a copy of the questions with answers, for the group leader.
- six pictures of items that are significant for Shabbat. Suggested items are challah, a bottle of wine, candlesticks, candles, and a prayer book. One of the items should be a large sheet of white paper, which represents a tablecloth.

The difficulty and content of questions should be adapted to the age and level of knowledge of the participants. It is not necessary that each group receive the same questions.

Instructions:

1. The aim is for the group to complete their Shabbat Table with religious articles (wine, bread, candlesticks, etc.) They receive the objects by answering questions and completing tasks.
2. Split the participants into small groups. Make sure there is a leader for each group. All the quiz materials are given to the group leader.
3. The group leader reads one of the questions to the rest of the group. When the correct answer is given, the participants open the envelope and perform the task specified. The group leader should participate in this task. After correctly answering the question and performing the task, the group receives the object. The group that completes their Shabbat Table first is the winner. The "prize" is the opportunity to present their views on the meaning of Shabbat and its importance in their lives.
4. Extra fun can be added by the overall leader stealing objects from the group. The leader can then "sell" that object to anyone—e.g., first person to hand in a blue shoelace gets the object.

Note to Leader:

If this activity is conducted before the start of Shabbat, actual objects might be given as rewards for correct answers, rather than pictures.

SAMPLE QUESTIONS

1. What does the word "Shabbat" mean?
   a) Seven
   b) Day of rest
   c) Creation

2. Who celebrated the first Shabbat?
   a) Abraham
   b) Moses
   c) G-d

3. What does Shabbat remind us of?
   a) Creation of the world
   b) Redemption from Egypt
   c) both a) and b)

4. How many days did it take G-d to create the world?
   a) 1
   b) 6
   c) 10

5. Which of the Ten Commandments deals with Shabbat?
   a) 1st
   b) 3rd
   c) 4th

6. What do we do at home to bring in Shabbat?
   a) Light candles
   b) Have a last cigarette
   c) Read Torah

7. How many candles do we light?
   a) 1
   b) 2
   c) 10

8. Why do we light two candles?
   a) For the two commandments of the Sabbath (to "keep" and "remember")
   b) To make it special
   c) One for Moses and one for Aaron

9. Why do we make Kiddush on Friday night?
   a) To make the day holy
   b) To remember those that have died
   c) To get drunk

10 Why do we make it over wine?
   a) To get drunk
   b) It is a symbol of joy
   c) It is an important drink

11. How many loaves of bread do we have on Friday night?
    a) 1
    b) 2
    c) 4

12. Why two loaves?
    a) For the two commandments of the Sabbath
    b) To remind us of the double portion of food the children of
       Israel received in the desert
    c) One for Moses and one for Aaron

13. How many meals should we eat on Shabbat?
    a) None
    b) 3
    c) 4

14. During the Friday night service we sing to welcome the bride.
    Who is the bride?
    a) G-d
    b) The Torah
    c) The Shabbat itself

15. How do we refer to the Sabbath apart from "the bride"?
    a) King
    b) Queen
    c) Prince

16. On Shabbat we sing songs during the meal times. What are
    these called?
    a) Zemirot
    b) Tefillah
    c) Kiddush

17. "_____ on Shabbat is a delight". What is a delight?
   a) Learning
   b) Praying
   c) Sleeping

18. What service do we have at home at the end of Shabbat?
   a) Kiddush
   b) Tefillah
   c) Havdallah

19. What does "Havdallah" mean?
   a) Separation
   b) End
   c) Restart

20. What objects are needed to make Havdallah, in addition to wine?
   a) Bread
   b) A plaited candle and spices
   c) Matzoh

21. How many categories of forbidden work are there on Shabbat?
   a) 9
   b) 39
   c) 139

22. Why are these types of work forbidden?
   a) To make the day difficult to keep
   b) To give us something to learn about
   c) To create a true day of rest

23. Can we ever break these laws?
   a) No, never
   b) Yes, if it is difficult
   c) Yes, to save life

24. According to Jewish Law, what is the punishment for breaking these laws willfully?
   a) Death penalty
   b) Fine (money)
   c) Prison sentence

25. How long does Shabbat last?
    a) 12 hours
    b) 24 hours
    c) 25 hours

26. When do we know that Shabbat is over?
    a) When it gets dark
    b) When there are three stars in the sky
    c) Sunday morning

Answers:

1—b; 2—c; 3—c; 4—b; 5—c; 6—a; 7—b; 8—a; 9—a; 10—b; 11—b; 12—b; 13—b; 14—c; 15—b; 16—a; 17—c; 18—c; 19—a; 20—b; 21—b; 22—c; 23—c; 24—a; 25—c; 26—b.
(Submitted by Simon Klarfeld)

OBSERVING SHABBAT: AGAINST AND FOR

Purpose:

To help participants gain insight into the extent to which they accommodate observance of Shabbat in their lives.

Group:

Teens and adults, any size with the option of splitting into small groups.

Setting:

Any room with comfortable seating.

Time:

45–60 minutes.

Materials:

Sheets printed with the list of "Ten Plagues Keeping Us from Observing Shabbat" (see below); paper and pencils.

Instructions:

1. Leader introduces the activity by describing the list of "Ten Plagues . . ."

2. Suggest that the group think about the "For" position. What are the reasons that might *attract* one to observing Shabbat? Instruct the group to come up with ten reasons for the "For" Shabbat observance position. They may also have others to add to the list of "Plagues". After the "For" list is compiled, participants should debate the relative strengths of the forces for and against observance.
3. To conclude the activity the leader should ask for insights from the participants as to their own beliefs or practices that get in the way of religious practice.

TEN PLAGUES KEEPING US FROM OBSERVING SHABBAT

1. "I can't, I won't, I don't know how."—This is the fear of embracing our tradition, knowing that we will make mistakes but striving for meaning nonetheless.
2. "We all go our separate ways."—This is the disengagement of our family from one another. To celebrate Shabbat together is to affirm our sense of family.
3. "I work late on Fridays."—This is about priorities and use of time. Can the time be rearranged to allow for time with our friends and family?
4. "That's our night out."—Can we be in the culture without being completely of the culture?
5. "I have too much to do."—When will we slow down?
6. "It's not for me."—If we refuse to bring meaning to our lives then none will come by itself. If we take the time for meaning, our lives will be made richer. Shabbat is about meaning.
7. "It's too much of a hassle."—Once it becomes a part of our routine, it is easy.
8. "The telephone never stops ringing"—Turn it off; the silence will be radiant.
9. "I don't have time to make dinner."—Ordering out is okay!
10. "I'm not that religious."—If we judge ourselves by the standards of others, we will never be satisfied. Religiousness is deeply personal and always changing.

(From the newsletter of Temple Israel in Tulsa, Oklahoma.)

FINDING TIME FOR RITUAL

Purpose:

To consider how to structure household life to allow for more ritual and to emphasize importance of home-based rituals.

Group:

This activity is appropriate for parents, particularly those with young children. Activity is conducted in groups of 8–12 people and each group requires a facilitator.

Setting:

A space large enough to allow for comfortable discussion.

Materials:

Masking tape and newsprint or a dry easel; paper; pencils.

Time:

30–40 minutes.

Instructions:

1. After introduction of the facilitator(s) and participants and an overview of the activity, participants are divided into groups of 8–12. A facilitator is assigned or designated for each group.
2. The first discussion is about the atmosphere and activities in the home around dinnertime on Friday night. Paper and pencils are distributed. Participants are asked to write a short description of the scene or draw a picture. When people have finished preparing their descriptions (3–5 minutes) they share them with the group. The facilitator records the responses on the newsprint.
3. It is important for the facilitator to acknowledge and validate the practice in each household. Pointing out aspects of the situation that get in the way of a relaxed, spiritual feeling can also be useful.

4. The second discussion is about rituals that participants experienced in their homes when they were children. Participants are asked to write down up to five rituals that they experienced as children. The facilitator may need to give encouragement to help them recollect. Then, participants share their lists. The facilitator records the answers. Discussion centers on common threads among the rituals. In what setting did they occur? Did they pertain to food? bedtime? holidays? reading?

5. The third discussion is about rituals that are currently practiced. Participants are asked to write down up to five rituals that are currently practiced in their homes with the family. Once again participants share their answers and the facilitator records them. Are there any patterns? Are any of the rituals that the parents participated in as children being continued today? This is an important time for the parents to share and take pride in the rituals that are now relevant in their lives.

6. In summary, the facilitator draws together themes that emerged during the discussions and connects them to observance of Shabbat.

(Submitted by Leann Shamash)

THE QUEST FOR MEANINGFUL JEWISH PRAYERS

There is a growing number of highly educated, sophisticated Jews who have drifted away from attending formal religious services and yet wish to satisfy their religious inclination. Often those inclinations are expressed in terms of "spirituality", implying something beyond the purely rational. Many of those people view synagogue services as too mechanical, routinized and authoritarian. One response has been the creation of informal religious networks, *minyanim* or *chavurot* (fellowships).

Other searching Jews are experimenting with devoting time to meditating or praying on their own. I would urge those among the religious searchers to reflect on what they can do to make prayer more meaningful.

Is there a prayer that you find especially meaningful? Discussing this question with friends, or as part of a workshop or retreat would certainly help the participants get different perspectives on religious interests and shed light on the oft-mentioned, but seldom defined, realm of *spirituality*.

If you really want to be bold and expand your own spiritual inclinations, try to create your own prayer. Combining the best of traditional Jewish prayers with your own creations would make for a creative spiritual experience.

It might be useful to have an exchange on views of prayer on a broader level. It might be interesting to hold a conference on prayer that brings together members of the informal Jewish networks with members of various denominations.

EXPERIENCING LITURGY: THE SH'MA

Purpose:

To experience liturgy, especially the *Sh'ma*, as a meaningful link to our inner spirituality, prayer, and the people and issues in our lives.

Group:

Any age; any size.

Setting:

Enough space with enough chairs to accommodate the group.

Materials:

Art supplies.

Time:

15 to 45 minutes, depending on interest in the group.

Instructions:

1. Conduct a guided experience on the *Sh'ma* using the instructions provided below. Read them slowly.
2. At the conclusion of this experience, pause for a short silence. Then either lead a discussion of the experience or ask participants to draw their vision of any of the following concepts:

God, wishes that arose during the visualization, people who appeared during the visualization, some other aspect of the experience.

INSTRUCTIONS

Sit comfortably and place your weight equally on your sitting bones. Place your feet flat on the ground to stay in touch with the earth. Keep your back straight so your lungs are not crowded with the weight of your shoulders. Put your hands palms down on your lap or thighs to be enclosed in your private experience. Pretend that a Force greater than you makes you straighter by holding a string from the crown of your head to the heavens. Align your body and spine with this imagined string. Do not force your posture into discomfort.

Breathe evenly and shallowly. Not too deeply nor with too much exertion or noise. Breathe naturally until the breath breathes you.

Hear the breath breathing in and out from your lungs.

Listen to the pause between the breaths.

Again let the breath breathe you. . . . This is *Ruach*.

Listen to the silence in the room. Let us be ONE in this silence. Each one of us helps the silence of the other.

Each one of us helps the concentration and the focus of the other.

We are now a *chavurah*, a fellowship of souls breathing and letting the spirit breathe us. Each one of us has a spark, a holy spark, a holy spark of light. Locate that spark now somewhere in your chest. (Pause.) Now, with each breath, expand that spark to fill your torso, (pause) your legs, (pause) and your head. (Pause.) Relax your jaw. You are now a body of light held in by your skin. (Pause.) We are a minyan of light, reflecting the Holy Light, the *Ruach HaKodesh*. (Pause.)

Enjoy this. This is a good thing.

Now, we'll say the *Sh'ma* together. I'll say each word first; then you'll repeat the word.

Leader: SH'MA
Group: SH'MA
Leader: YISRAEL

Group: YISRAEL
Leader: ADONOY
Group: ADONOY
Leader: ELOHEINU
Group: ELOHEINU
Leader: ADONOY
Group: ADONOY
Leader: ECHOD
Group: ECHOD

Now listen to the silence silently.

ECHOD is ONE. Picture a ONE, or an ALEPH. It is full of light. Let the light fill the world.

Now we will try to use this light to help us.

Think of things that you need or that your family or friends need. Things that money can't buy. Maybe someone is sad, or poor, and without comfort or food or money. Maybe there is someone who isn't near you and you need that person near you.

Picture yourself and these people. Bring the people you love to the light.

Bring the people you like to the light.

Bring the people you don't yet love to the light.

Bring the people you want to forgive to the light. Watch them become full of light.

Bring the people who you find hard to forgive to the light.

Bring the people who have harmed you to the light. Don't strain—just do what you can.

Now bring yourself to the light.

Bring everyone together to the light. To the light of the ONE.

Keep breathing.

Let the light heal you and them.

This is comforting. Remember this as a good feeling. Etch it in your hearts. Remember this when you are going to bed at night. You can do this yourself. You can say the *Sh'ma* anywhere. You tell your secrets to the light. Bring them to the light, all the questions that need resolving. I don't have to know them. They are your secrets.

You can come back to this quiet place, this good feeling, anytime. During a bedtime *Sh'ma*, during the day, or anytime in a crowd or together with others.

Now let's say the *Sh'ma* again together.

Remember, I'll say each word first; then you'll repeat the word again as a group.

Leader: SH'MA
Group: SH'MA
Leader: YISRAEL
Group: YISRAEL
Leader: ADONOY
Group: ADONOY
Leader: ELOHEINU
Group: ELOHEINU
Leader: ADONOY
Group: ADONOY
Leader: ECHOD
Group: ECHOD
Leader: And let's all say AMEN!

Breathe again as before. The *Ruach* is still here breathing in us as ONE, by ourselves and together.

Listen again to the silence. You can pray like this again. Only listen to the silence after the prayer. Sometimes you'll be thinking the answer to your prayer.

Feel your feet on the ground and your sitting bones in the chair.

Open your eyes slowly, slowly, and don't look at anybody else until you're ready.

(Submitted by Rosie Rosenzweig, Resident Scholar in Women's Studies at Brandeis University.)

BRACHA WALK

Purpose:

To become awake and fully alert to each other and our surroundings. In a Jewish context, through a "bracha walk", we will achieve a high level of awareness about our surroundings.

Group:

Any age; any size.

Setting:

A quiet natural setting. The leader should determine a walking route that will be free of distractions.

Materials:

Copies of traditional blessings in Hebrew, English or English transliteration according to participants' needs.

Time:

30–45 minutes.

Instructions:

1. On a bracha walk, participants are encouraged to notice as many things as they can through all of their senses—sight, smell, touch, taste and sound. The idea is to be as aware as possible. Participants are encouraged to make blessings, either traditional or original. However, making blessings is not required to get meaning from this activity.
2. Before going on the walk, the leader explains the nature of the activity and the appropriate mood. The challenge to participants is to notice as much as they can. The leader should make available copies of traditional blessings and carry them along on the walk.
3. On the walk, people should not talk or interact and should try to move quietly. By staying silent, they will be completely available to observe sensations and stay with them. Though everyone is going on the same walk, each person experiences something completely different.
4. At some point during the walk, allow the participants to move apart for a minute or two and just sit or stand alone to see what they notice.

5. At the end of the walk, the group should process what they have experienced. Each participant might mention something s/he experienced that inspired saying a blessing. Other questions for the debriefing:

- How many things were you able to notice and experience? Are you surprised by how many?
- What would you be like if you said blessings more often?
- What is another way of staying mindful if you are not comfortable reciting blessings that address God?
- How does saying a *bracha* affect how you perceive your world?
- What does this activity have to do with building community?

Notes to Leader:

Judaism provides an opportunity for constant mindfulness through blessing. There are blessings for seeing rainbows and hearing thunder, for eating food and excreting waste, for smelling flowers and sighting the first buds of spring, and for witnessing sights of extreme ugliness and beauty. The opportunities for blessing are constant, and one must therefore be constantly alert. In fact, Rabbi Meir expected Jews to recite as many as 100 different blessings per day. Imagine how awake to the world we would have to be in order to say 100 different meaningful blessings! Thus, not only can a Jew experience the world and respond with a blessing, but the habit of reciting blessings can cultivate sensory awareness, enabling one to truly experience the world.

The traditional format of a blessing acknowledges the Source of Life (God) and refers to the specific experience that prompted one to say it. The experience comes first, the *bracha* second.

Encourage participants to take saying blessings seriously. It is okay to have a joyous attitude, but levity is not acceptable. There is the concept of *bracha levatala*, a wasted blessing.

Blessings should be said quietly so as not to disturb others. While saying a blessing loudly may allow a person to "share the moment," the purpose of blessings in this activity is to heighten the individual's connection to and awareness of the natural environment.

CREATE A PERSONAL PRAYER

Purpose:

To explore traditional and alternative ways through which Jews have communicated with God and to allow participants to create their own personal prayer.

Group:

Appropriate for elementary school through high school. This can be adapted for adults. Five participants and up.

Setting:

A large room with enough space for participants to spread out.

Materials:

Pens; paper; various inspirational sources, including traditional siddurim, camp siddurim, alternative siddurim from the Chavurah movement, and other sources of songs, poetry, or inspirational writing by Jewish and Israeli authors; examples of personal prayers (see below.)

Time:

45–60 minutes.

Instructions:

1. The leader provides an introduction to purposes of prayer and a brief exploration of the range of prayers or ways of praying that different Jews have used.
2. Each participant is asked to create a prayer. Source materials will be available for reference. There are no specifications as to length or style. Prayers can address God in whatever way the author chooses.
3. Fifteen minutes will be allotted for creating prayers. Paper and

pens are distributed to participants. During this time, the leader should be accessible to answer questions or offer pertinent source materials.

4. Reconvene. Participants share their creations. Follow-up discussion should focus on how participants felt about creating a prayer of their own and how it relates to their customary prayers. Discussion should examine whether there are differences in attitude between more traditional and more liberal Jews regarding creating new prayers.

5. Following the activity, the facilitator may choose to publish a collection of the groups' personal prayers. If the group is part of an organization that has ongoing services, such as a camp or religious school, selections can be incorporated into those services.

EXAMPLES OF PERSONAL PRAYERS

The examples below were written by 7th graders at Temple Concord, Binghamton, NY, in 1994.

PRAYER

Love Adonai your God with all of your heart.
with all your soul,
with all your strength. Take these words, which I command you
today.
Teach your children well,
these words which I command you this day.

(Untitled)

I pray for world peace, happiness, an end to world hunger,
that the Republicans will all resign from office,
all those people in Israel will stop fighting
and for myself
that Macaulay Culkin's allowance for a month
will be mistakenly sent to me.

THANK YOU

Thank you for making me live in Binghamton,
and please help me deal with my step-mother,
world peace.

Thank you for making a little girl feel better.
Please watch over her
so she stays better.

Thank you for giving me
a happy life and food.
Thank you for giving me
a loving family who cares about me.
Thank you for giving me
friends who are there for me.
And thank you for giving me life.

(Submitted by Allison D. Halpern)

JEWISH SURVIVAL KITS

Purpose:

To stimulate discussion of the personal relationships of individuals toward Jewish symbols; also, a learning exercise focusing on the attainment of group consensus.

Group:

Junior high school and older; 20–30 participants meeting in smaller groups of 5–6 participants.

Setting:

A room large enough to allow for separate discussions in small groups.

Materials:

A list of Jewish articles (see below) and a pencil for each person.

Time:

1½ hours.

Instructions:

1. Each member of the group is given a sheet of paper with up to 10 Jewish articles listed. The leader asks members to imagine that they are confronted by the following situation: They are prisoners in a labor camp in some barren and remote part of the world. Because of their active roles in Jewish life, they have been sentenced to extended periods of labor-camp confinement. Their sole consolation is an offer by the camp commander to bring into the camp a limited number of "Jewish objects." The members are asked to rank, according to their personal feelings of priority, the items on the sheet, in order to assure their "Jewish Survival."

JEWISH ARTICLES

Rank the 10 Jewish articles listed below in order of importance for the Jewish survival of the group of Jews in the labor camp.

_____ Candles   _____ Mezuzah

_____ Dreidel   _____ Wine

_____ Haggadah   _____ Siddur

_____ Jewish history book   _____ Tanach

_____ Lulav and etrog   _____ Tefillin

2. Allow 10 minutes for individual ranking, and then divide the group into subgroups (5 or 6 per group). The subgroups are presented with the task of arriving at a group decision concerning the ranking to be presented to the camp commander. The function of the subgroup is to negotiate among themselves, on the basis of each member's individual ranking, a group consen-

sus that must be reached. At this point the leader reiterates the importance of:

a. the difficult situation for them in the camp

b. each individual in the subgroup expressing an opinion

c. arriving at a single list for their group in order to assure the receipt of the items

Approximately half an hour should be allowed for this part of the activity.

3. The members are then reconvened, and each subgroup is asked to communicate to the larger group the following points:

a. their final group ranking

b. how they arrived at that decision (reference to the group dynamics)

c. feelings of individual members about the experience.

4. In summarizing, the leader focuses on two levels: individual perceptions of what is needed for Jewish survival and the dynamics involved in reaching group consensus.

Variation:

A. JEWISH SURVIVAL-GROUP DYNAMICS. The individuals in the subgroup are asked to record their rankings, both individual and group, from when they first come together and when they finish their group deliberations, and to obtain difference scores so as to represent the extent of change for their subgroup. This will be a reflection of the extent of group accommodation. In addition, the groups may be artificially structured to have contrasting styles of leadership. This contrived situation would provide interesting material for discussion, based on the different leadership styles and ensuing group processes, e.g., authoritarian, democratic, laissez-faire.

Note to the Leader:

This activity is a modification of the NASA (National Aeronautics and Space Administration) experiment widely used in experiential learning. Reference to the original NASA experiment may be useful to the leader in utilizing this activity.

(Adapted from an idea submitted by Barry Judelman)

ENCOUNTERS WITH JEWISH RITUAL OBJECTS

Purpose:

To give participants a chance to test their knowledge of Jewish ritual objects, and to explore the importance of these objects for individual and collective Jewish life.

Group:

Ages 8–16; 10–20 participants.

Setting:

A classroom or similar setting.

Materials:

A handkerchief (for blindfolding), a table, and Jewish ritual objects: Kiddush cup, menorah, Torah ornaments (pointer, breastplate, crown), Havdalah candle, dreidel, mezuzah, spice box, tefillin, shofar, tallit, tzitzit, pushke, lulav and etrog.

Time:

30–35 minutes.

Instructions:

Participants take turns being blindfolded and are given a Jewish ritual object by the leader which they try to identify. To add interest the group may be divided into teams. In that case time is kept to see how long it takes team representatives to identify their objects.

Variations:

A. JEWISH RITUAL CHARADES. The group is divided into several teams, and each team is situated in a corner of the room. The leader has a box of Jewish ritual objects in the center of the room. Each team sends up a representative to the leader, who shows them one of the objects. (The leader must be careful that only the representatives see the object.) The representatives quickly race back to their teams and, without using any words, act out or use gestures to communicate what the object is. The leader keeps score of which team first guesses the Jewish ritual object.

(Submitted by Sol Yousha)

B. PERSONAL REACTIONS TO JEWISH RITUAL OBJECTS. The leader places several Jewish ritual items on a table in the center of the room. S/he asks the group members, without speaking, to examine the Jewish ritual objects before them. People are encouraged to touch or use or involve themselves as fully as they can in any or all of the objects. The leader may have Jewish background music playing while people are silently experiencing the objects. After about 15 minutes, the leader asks the group members to speak of any reactions or emotional associations they had with the Jewish ritual objects.

C. IMPROVISED JEWISH RITUAL OBJECTS. The group is divided into smaller units of 6–8 people. The leader distributes to each group a paper bag, in which s/he has placed a number of everyday household items (e.g., ballpoint pen, ashtray, light bulb, eraser, string, paper cup, a balloon, spoon, dice, matches, rubber band, thread, etc.). The group is asked to figure out creative ways in which each of these objects can be used for some Jewish ceremonial purpose. For example, a ballpoint pen, covered with aluminum foil, would serve as a Torah pointer. A paper cup could be used as a Havdalah spice box, etc.

(Submitted by Susan Olshansky)

D. AUCTION OF JEWISH CEREMONIAL OBJECTS. The leader divides the participants into small groups (about 6–8 people) and explains that they will be the representatives of a Jewish community at an auction of Jewish ceremonial objects. This is a new community that needs to buy Jewish ceremonial objects for use in the community. They have allocated $1,000 to their representatives to spend at the auction. (Each small group is given $1,000 in play money.) Each group is aware that other groups will be at the auction and they will be bidding against each other.

In preparation for the auction, the groups are given a list of the Jewish objects which will be auctioned (see list above in Materials). The group is to decide, in advance, on their priorities-how they will allocate their $1,000. They should discuss the reason for their priorities in terms of the needs of their community, as well as bidding tactics, such as the maximum amount to be spent on a particular item. Also, they should choose a leader to be their spokesperson at the auction.

(Submitted by Fran Ginsburg)

E. OBJECTS FROM HOME. In advance of the session, participants are asked to bring a Jewish ritual item which has special meaning for them or their family. The item may be a family heirloom or an object that has some story connected with it. At the session they present their object and explain its unique meaning.

F. OTHER RITUAL OBJECTS. In addition to including the Jewish ritual objects described above, the activity can take on a different dimension through the introduction of non-Jewish objects. Some suggestions include: a crucifix, a Catholic religious medal, a Christmas card, a Thanksgiving platter, Halloween decorations.

HOW ONE SHOULD GIVE TZEDAKAH

Purpose:

To educate fundraisers on aspects of charitable giving (*tzedakah*).

Group:

Volunteer solicitors or professional staff working in a fundraising environment. 20–40 people to be divided into groups of 6–8.

Setting:

A space large enough to accommodate separate small group discussions and a wall where Maimonides' Ladder of Charity can be posted for all to see.

Materials:

A copy of Maimonides' Ladder of Charity printed large enough for everyone to read; masking tape; a marker. One set of eight scenarios (see below) for each group. Each scenario should be printed on a separate sheet of paper. Because the activity requires the group to place the scenarios in order, they should not be numbered or distributed in the order in which they are presented below.

Time:

30–45 minutes.

Instructions:

1. Divide into groups of 6–8. Distribute a set of scenarios to each group.
2. Each group must arrange the scenarios in order of how well they embody the spirit of *tzedakah*, from most to least virtuous. Each group should arrive at their own criteria.
3. Reconvene the entire group. Post Maimonides' Ladder of Charity. Introduce it as a widely recognized system used in Judaism for assessing and thinking about the spirit underlying giving behavior. Review the description of each level of the Ladder, then determine where each scenario fits. Write a shorthand description of the scenario in the appropriate place on the ladder. For example, scenario #1, which belongs on level 1, might be "newly arrived mother and child".
4. Discuss the system of Maimonides. Questions to consider might include:
   • Is it useful or even possible to compare acts of *tzdekah*?
   • Why does Maimonides consider the highest level to be enabling others?

- What is the role of differing relationships between giver and receiver?
- Is it important to make a distinction between anonymous giving and getting recognition? What are the pros and cons of anonymous giving?
- What roles are played by size of donation or the means of the giver?
- What other criteria might be proposed for judging the spirit of giving?

SCENARIOS

1. A mother and her daughter have recently arrived in the U.S., fleeing war in their native country. Since the woman is good with computers, you put her in touch with a friend who has a small consulting business and is looking for help.
2. Clothing is donated to the Hadassah Thrift Shop and it is distributed to people in need.
3. Your neighbor just lost her job and has a sick child. You collect donations from the neighborhood and anonymously leave the money along with a basket of food on the front steps of her house.
4. A major donor establishes a scholarship fund to send Jewish children to Israel. The money is distributed by the fund administrator. Although the recipient never meets the donor, he/she is aware of the origin of the scholarship.
5. Upon hearing news of the successful heart transplant performed on your best friend, you make a substantial contribution to the American Heart Association.
6. A face-to-face fundraiser solicits you for the New Israel Fund. In response to his convincing solicitation, you immediately make out a check for $1,000,000.
7. You attend a United Jewish Appeal pizza party. You are asked by one of your classmates to donate $36 to the Annual Campaign. You smile and hand them $36 cash.
8. A panhandler accosts you on the street. You tell him you don't have any change, but he continues to follow you for several blocks. Annoyed, you hand him a dollar bill and walk quickly away.

MAIMONIDES' LADDER OF CHARITY

Steps of Charity Arranged from Highest to Lowest

1. The person giving helps the person receiving to become self-sufficient
2. The giver does not know the person receiving, and the person receiving does not know who gave.
3. The giver knows the receiver but the person receiving does not know the giver.
4. The giver does not know the receiver but the person receiving knows the giver.
5. A direct donation to the hand of the needy, given without being asked.
6. A direct donation of sufficient size, given after being asked.
7. A direct donation of small size, given cheerily (after being asked).
8. A direct, small donation given grudgingly (after being asked).
   (from *Mishneh Torah: Hilchot Matnot Aniyim* 10:7–12)

(Submitted by Tracy Kimball)

THE JEWISH MORALITY GAME

Purpose:

To increase the moral and ethical awareness of the participants and to encourage them to find out how the "Jewish viewpoint" affects their views.

Group:

Children or adults. Care should be taken to provide moral dilemmas that are suitable for the maturity and interests of the group.

Instructions:

1. The leader chooses a set of moral dilemmas that is appropriate for the group and the time allotted. (See below for examples.)
2. The leader reads each dilemma to the group. The participants

are asked to decide their opinion on the dilemma. The leader should acknowledge that these dilemmas usually offer no attractive alternative but stress that each person must come to a decision. Then, participants present their opinions. Finally, the leader offers the "Jewish viewpoint" and the participants must explain why they agree or disagree with that viewpoint.

THE JEWISH MORALITY GAME

(a) You have been captured by your enemies. They are brutal enemies. They want information from you concerning your friends. If you tell them all they wish to know you will go free. If you do not, they will humiliate, terrorize and torture you in every way they know.

You are aware that should they catch your friends they will do the same thing to at least some of them, perhaps all of them.

Whom will you betray?

(b) You and your friend are lost in the desert, miles from civilization. You have a large flask of water but if this water is shared between the two of you, there will be an insufficient amount for either of you to return alive. However, if only one has the water, he will certainly return alive to civilization. What would you, as owner of the water, do?

(c) A girl you know has become pregnant. You are the father. The girl is not certain whether she wants the baby or not. She asks you to help her to decide.

Would you try to convince her to have an abortion? Would you try to convince her to have the baby? Would you offer to support her if she had the baby? Would you tell her that the decision was entirely up to her and decline to state an opinion?

(d) You are a leader of a small country which is at war with a neighboring state. At a crucial stage of unofficial moves towards peace, a band of enemy terrorists have snuck into your country and are holding hostage a group of children. They threaten that unless you release a number of their compatriots being held prisoner in your country, they will kill themselves together with the hostages. You are given only 24 hours to decide. What would you do?

(e) You are a prominent politician. Many years have passed

since the abolition of the death penalty in your country. However, recent years have seen an alarming increase in murder and violence. You have personally felt the effects of this with the recent murder of a close friend. Mounting public pressure has forced members of Parliament to vote on re-introduction of the death penalty. What would you do?

(f) War breaks out and you are asked to enter the army and fight for your country. However, you are in a dilemma. On the one hand you are committed to the ideal of pacifism and are against all forms of violence; yet all your instincts tell you that you have no right to plead conscientious objection, when your country's very survival is at stake. What would you do?

(g) You are returning home late one evening. On the way you meet a beggar. He approaches you and asks you for some charity. You feel obligated to give charity when requested; however, you also know that this man has made no effort at all to find work and make a living. You feel that by giving him money you are contributing to his reliance on begging, and therefore hesitate. What would you do?

(h) You are one of the two top candidates for a managerial position in a large firm. You have heard that the firm discriminates against Jews and African Americans. During the final informal interview with the "big boss" he makes an apparently joking side remark about how Jews are pushy and are taking over everything. You also know that you have to complete a form that asks about your religion. Should you work in this setting? Should you say anything to the boss at once or ignore what he said? When you complete the form, should you list your religion or say something else, knowing that this could make a difference to your getting the job? What would you do?

(i) For two years you have been dating a non-Jewish woman. Your parents have continually objected to this, but you have kept insisting that there is nothing wrong with interfaith dating. Now, the two of you have decided to get married despite your parents' strong objections. But you are still in a dilemma: Should you ask her to convert? Or is your love for her the most important factor, and if she doesn't want to convert, it won't matter anyway. You now have to make a decision. What would you do?

(j) Your teenaged son tells you that his school will be running a social club every Friday night. You have always insisted that Friday night is a time when the whole family should be together and no one should go out. However, your child now insists that if he is not allowed to go, he will feel left out at school and his firmly established circle of friends will ostracize him for "being too proud" to join them. The matter is obviously causing your child some distress. What would you do?

(Submitted by Simon Klarfeld)

MITZVAH MAN

Purpose:

To teach the importance of *mitzvot*. To learn how to integrate *mitzvot* into everyday lives

Group:

Ages 4 and up; groups of any size.

Setting:

Any set-up that is conducive to a participatory theater experience.

Materials:

Mitzvah Man costume: neatly dressed, with a cape displaying the number 613
    Evil Averah (sin) costume: dishevelled or flowing clothing

Time:

Each vignette takes approximately 20–30 minutes.

Instructions:

The storyline for this participatory theater program always follows the same pattern:

Volunteers from the group act out a scene where the action of performing a mitzvah was either missed or ignored. Upon seeing this missed opportunity to perform a mitzvah, "Mitzvah Man" transforms himself from an innocent bystander into a super-hero with the words: "There are 613 commandments in the Torah—I see one that is not being followed. This is a job for . . . Mitzvah Man!" Miztvah Man rights the wrong by chasing off Evil Averah, the temptress who caused the infraction in the first place.

The program ends with Mitzvah Man teaching about the particular mitzvah and showing how easy it is to incorporate these little acts into our every day lives. The exit line always remains the same: "Wherever there is injustice . . . I'll be there! Whenever there's the threat of Averah . . . I'll be there! I am . . . Mitzvah Man!"

The following is a sample list of themes for Mitzvah Man skits:

Ahavah Re'ut	love and friendship
Bikkur Cholim	visiting the sick
Derech Eretz	decency, acceptable behavior
Emet	truth
Gemilut Chasadim	deeds of loving-kindness
Hachnasat Orchim	hospitality
Hekdesh	community shelter for the needy
Kavod	granting honor
Kenah	jealousy
Keren Ami	Fund of My People
Leshon Hara	gossip, slander
Mensch	a good human being
Nekamah	revenge
Rachamim	mercy, compassion
Tikkun Olam	repairing the world
Tzedek	righteousness, justice

Variations:

For a more mature group, a text study and discussion could follow that was centered around the commandment played out in the skit.

(Submitted by Joe Levin with assistance from Jeff Ripps and Jay Sherwood)

TEN JEWISH IDEALS

Purpose:

Throughout Jewish belief, both in religion and cultural norms, there is an emphasis on principled behavior. This activity challenges participants to consider the importance of various Jewish ideals. In the course of considering which values are most important, the individual may also learn about what is of importance to other people.

Group:

Teenagers through adults.

Setting:

Comfortable setting with seating for all.

Time:

45–60 minutes.

Instructions:

Below is a list of Jewish ideals. How would you rank them in their importance for your day-to-day life? The process of considering this list of 10 ideals challenges people to think about their own values and behavior.

In the discussion of the responses it might be interesting to ask the participants to think of other ideals beyond the ten identified in this listing.

TEN JEWISH IDEALS

1. Devotion to *Tzedakah*
2. Devotion to furthering Jewish culture and language
3. Observance of *Mitzvot*
4. Commitment to work for Israel

5. *Tikkun Olam*
6. Spirituality and Godliness
7. Learning of traditional Jewish Texts
8. Commitment to teach Judaism to others
9. Commitment to provide leadership for local Jewish organizations and schools
10. Commitment to build a more inclusive and egalitarian Jewish community

(Submitted by Professor Joseph Reimer of Brandeis University)

THEOLOGY PARK

Purpose:

To help participants express their beliefs and feelings about God metaphorically.

Group:

Family units with children above the age of 10.

Setting:

A room equipped to accommodate several crafts projects.

Materials:

Ample craft material including string, tin foil, toothpicks, modeling clay, cardboard, construction paper, boxes, matchboxes, streamers, glue, pencils, markers, rulers and masking tape.

Time:

1 hour or more.

Instructions:

Distribute "A Guide to Theology Park" and follow the instructions.

A GUIDE TO THEOLOGY PARK

Each of us during our lifetime understands his/her relationship with God differently. An interesting metaphor for this relationship involves the image of a theme park. A theme park affects us in many powerful ways, for example:

At a theme park we can. . . .
be dizzied by the rides and sights
be propelled up and down on a roller coaster
be gently swayed by the merry-go-round
be bumped and crashed into by the bumper cars
soar upward on the rocket ships
climb
ascend
crash
be frightened
be thrilled

Feel free to add more of your own ideas.

How do you feel as you read these comparisons and replace the theme park concept with the concept of God? Do they make you angry? Lonely? Satisfied? Indignant? Surprised? Certainly all of the thoughts we have about God are personal and sensitive. You as families or as individuals may or may not be willing to use this list as a guide to direct you to the construction of your theme park "experience". Share as you feel comfortable with your group and enjoy the opportunity to express artistically a subject that we often find difficult to find the words to express.

What to do to construct your ride:

1. As a family or a group decide upon the name and the concept of the ride that you would like to construct. If you cannot think of a ride that you might find in a theme park, then make one up that describes your relationship with God.
2. Using the crafts supplies provided, put together a three-dimensional model of a ride or a picture depicting your ride.

Make sure that on the papers provided you record the name of your ride and a description of it for the visit to the "theme park" following the completion of construction.

Following the visit to the theme park, the group will reassemble in small groups to discuss the different themes of the rides and their meaning to the participants.

(Submitted by Leann Shamash with assistance from Monika Kupfelberg, Family Educator at Temple Isaiah, Lexington, MA)

PROPHETS FOR PRESIDENT

Purpose:

To expose participants to the ancient prophets and their views. By structuring a contemporary context, it is hoped that a broader insight into the work of the prophets will be provided. This is a good activity for a religious-school special event or a day program for a camp or a retreat.

Group:

Junior high school and older; 30–60 people in groups of 8–12.

Setting:

A large open room with space for the small groups to work separately without disturbing each other. Since the activity is a political convention, the room becomes a convention hall, in which the participants can engage in crafts activities, post signs on the walls, etc.

Materials:

At least one Bible for each group plus other readings on the prophets. Groups will need a full kit of crafts supplies: poster board, newsprint, paint, brushes, marking pens, tape, strips of wood (for signs), noisemakers.

Time:

Approximately 3 hours: 1½-2 hours for preparation, 1 hour for the convention.

Instructions:

1. The leader assigns one prophet per group and explains that each group will try to get its prophet elected president at a convention, which will follow later. To prepare for the campaign, each group should set up three committees:
   a. public relations-makes vote-influencing posters, hats, handbills, buttons, etc.
   b. speech writers-writes speeches for candidates
   c. campaigners-organizes demonstrations
2. The groups should begin by investigating each candidate's life history; his major areas of concern and the major issues of his lifetime; and the main ideas expressed in his writings, especially those which may be used as campaign slogans. (See suggested readings below.)
3. After all research and campaign arrangements are completed, the several groups are called to the convention hall. Time is allowed for distribution of banners, buttons, hats, posters, circulars, delivery of speeches, and, finally, voting.
4. One person is designated as the spokesperson and s/he will be called on to give a 5-minute election speech, embodying the major thoughts and ideas of his/her prophet.
5. The convention concludes with a vote on the prophets; participants cannot vote for their own candidates. The winner is appropriately honored.

SUGGESTED READING LIST

Chapter	Theme
Jeremiah	
chap. 4	"If you will return, O Israel"
chap. 7	"Amend your ways, your doings"
chap. 12	"Wherefore do the ways of the wicked prosper"
Ezekiel	
chap. 2	"The mission of Ezekiel"
chap. 16	"Ingratitude and unfaithfulness"
chap. 22:23–31	"The sins of all classes"

Isaiah
chap. 2: 1–11   "The messianic era"
chap. 6   "Isaiah's call to prophecy"
chap. 42   "Characteristics of God's ideal person"

Amos
chap. 2   "Description of evils committed by people"
chap. 8:1–7   "In the End of Days"
chap. 7   "Sin, repentance, salvation"

Note to the Leader:

For the convention hall to have an appropriately authentic atmosphere, and for the convention itself to run smoothly, a coordinating staff will be required. It is desirable at the introduction of the
activity that the leader recruit three or four participants to serve as
the convention staff. This staff will coordinate decorating the hall
and help the leader, who will serve as the convention chairperson.

(Adapted from an idea submitted by Deborah Goldstine)

A QUIZ ON THE BIBLICAL STORIES OF CREATION
AND OF NOAH AND THE FLOOD

The first *parashah* (portion) of the Bible, *Genesis* 1:1—6:8, presents the story of Creation. The second *parashah*, *Noah*, *Genesis*
6:9—11:32, presents the story of Noah and the flood.

    This is a quiz based on the details provided in those *parashot*.
Answers are provided for the group leader/teacher following the
listing of the questions.

Eight Questions:
1. In how many days did God create the world?
2. What were the creations on each of those days?
3. How many children did Adam and Eve have, and what were
    their names?
4. How many children did Noah and his wife have, and what
    were their names?
5. How many animals of each species did Noah take on the ark?

6. For how many days and nights did it rain while Noah was on the ark?
7. What type of bird did Noah send out from the ark to see if the waters from the flood had abated?
8. What heavenly sign did God bring forth to indicate that the flood had ended?

Eight Answers (If you get 8 correct answers you are entitled to a free ticket on Noah's ark, the next time he launches it.)

1) seven days
2) God's creations:
   Day 1—light and darkness
   Day 2—earth and heaven
   Day 3—sea, land and vegetation
   Day 4—heavenly bodies
   Day 5—fishes and birds
   Day 6—animals and man
   Day 7—The Sabbath ("God rested")
3) Adam and Eve had 2 children: Cain and Abel
4) Noah and his wife had three sons: Shem, Ham and Japheth
5) Of the "clean beasts"—7 males and 7 females; of the "beasts which were not clean"—2 males and 2 females.
6) It rained 40 day and nights
7) A raven
8) A rainbow

Variations:

Quizzes could be developed focusing on other key figures and events in the Bible. Other examples from Genesis include:

- Abraham and Sarah
- Isaac and Rebecca and their sons, Jacob and Esau
- Jacob, Rachel and Leah
- Joseph and his Brothers
- Joseph and Pharaoh

Two other major subjects for developing quiz questions would be Jewish history and the contemporary Jewish world.

UNDERSTANDING PARASHAT SHEMINI

Purpose:

The goals of this activity are two-fold: 1) To help the participants gain insight into the human interactions and personal relationships involved in the situation which occurred in parashat Shemini, and 2) to help the participants understand how certain values espoused in this parasha (kashrut, high standards) apply to us in the modern world.

Group:

This program may be used for any small group setting (teens, families, junior congregation, etc.). The activity can accommodate between 10 and 20 people, which would allow for two to four people in each of the smaller, break-out groups.

Setting:

A very large room where small groups can work without being disturbed by other groups, or a series of rooms (or hallways, etc.) around a larger room, where small groups can work in seclusion. The chairs in the large room should be arranged in a circle, or, where appropriate, participants could sit on the floor.

Materials:

Scenarios, instruction sheets, and synopses of the parasha should be photocopied for everyone. Each scenario should be given only to members of the group that will be performing it. Tape three large, blank pieces of newsprint to the front wall of the large room. Write numbers 1–5 on the top of the synopsis sheets which you will hand out. Those numbers will be the basis for forming the groups to act out the skits. Also, number the small break-out locations 1–5 in advance by putting numbers on the wall.

Time:

1–1½ hours, depending on how much time is spent in discussion and preparing the skits.

Instructions:

People will understand and identify with the characters and situations in the parasha if they confront the issues on a personal level. They can do this in several ways. They can "become" the character in question (e.g., Moses, Aaron), and challenge the character according to their own values and beliefs, or they can apply the concepts and values delineated in the parasha to their own lives in the modern world. If the protagonists in the Torah "live" for people, they will internalize the values, remember the stories, and confront the issues in a way that they would not be able to by just reading the parasha in the traditional manner. This activity is an attempt to turn the study of a parasha into experiential education.

Have everyone sit in a circle. Hand out the synopsis of the parasha. Ask everyone to read the synopsis silently. Then, solicit a volunteer or two to read the synopsis aloud. Ask for questions of clarification. Using one piece of the newsprint, have the group construct a time line of the events which occurred in the parasha. (The facilitator should decide if he/she is comfortable writing and soliciting input at the same time, or if he/she prefers to ask one of the members of the group to do the writing). After the time line is complete, elicit from the group members themes or values that they learned from the parasha so far. Write their answers on the second piece of newsprint. Divide the people into five groups, based on the numbers on the tops of their synopsis sheets. (If there are adults and children in the group, you may want to be sure that they are equally divided.) Explain the direction, and then hand out written directions and the scenarios, and ask people to form their smaller, break-out groups. Allow about twenty minutes to one half hour for people to prepare their skits. Then, reconvene and allow each group to perform. Ask each group to read its scenario before they perform their skit so that the rest of the people will understand what is happening. After all of the skits are acted out, ask the group what ideas, values and themes they learned from the parasha after acting out, and viewing, the skits. Write those ideas on the third piece of newsprint.

Summary:

Briefly review the time-line of the parasha. Show the differences and similarities between the values and concepts that people were able to glean from the parasha, before and after they performed the skits. Show the connection between what was being taught in the parasha, and the scenarios which dealt with modern times. We should be careful not to judge others (either in the Torah or today), because we probably don't have a full emotional understanding of the situation. Also, as mere human beings we can not expect to understand G-d's actions or plans. By putting ourselves into situations akin to those in parashat Shemini, we can gain emotional and intellectual understanding of the ideas and the values of the people involved in the situation.

SCENARIOS

1. Nadab and Abihu are standing outside of the Tent of Meeting, trying to decide whether or not to go in.
2. Aaron is having a discussion with G-d about the fact that He killed his sons. (Remember: discussion means that G-d answers.)
3. Your very religious Catholic friends can't understand why you can't go to McDonald's with them to eat a cheeseburger. He/She says that Catholics are holy too, so why shouldn't everyone be able to eat the same things. He/She wants to know if you think that Jews are more holy than Catholics.
4. After Aaron's sons are killed, Moses berates Aaron for not fulfilling his duties by eating the required part of the sacrifice. How does Aaron feel? What would a private discussion between Moses and Aaron sound like?
5. You are the president of your class. The requirements for becoming president are high academic grades, involvement in social action, popularity, honesty, and integrity. You are supposed to be a role model for the rest of your class. You were up late last night helping your sick mother, and you did not get a chance to study for you math midterm. When you come to school, you discover that your friend (who is not a class officer) also did not study for the test. The two of you work out a way to cheat on the test, but you are both caught. Your friend's punishment is that she will flunk math this semester. You, however, are expelled from the school. You argue with the principal

that this is not fair, since you both committed the same transgression. What would this argument sound like?

DIRECTIONS FOR ROLE PLAY-PARASHAT SHEMINI

1. Choose one person to act as the director. Have this person read your acting assignment out loud.
2. Discuss how you will act out your skit. Your skit should convey ideas and values as well as action.
3. Your skit should be between three and five minutes long.
4. Remember, not everyone has to act. There may be other important roles, such as sound effects, narrator, etc.
5. Rehearse. You will have one-half hour to practice.
6. You will present the skit in front of the whole group.

(Submitted by Andrea Ilsen)

WRITING MIDRASH: JEWISH TEXT STUDY USING INFORMAL METHODOLOGY

Purpose:

To study Jewish texts in an informal setting, in a fun and interactive way. The activity is meant to be informative and educational, while engaging and hands-on.

Group:

College age and beyond; group of 16–20 people.

Setting:

Room should be set up with moveable chairs in a circle or square for introduction; chairs should then be moved to form small groups when it is time for the groups to split up.

Time:

1 hour: 15 minutes for Introduction, 30 minutes for Midrash writing, and 15 minutes for Wrap-up.

Materials:

Paper and pens for each group; "Tips for Writing Midrash" handout (see below), copies of text to be studied (in Hebrew and English), samples of midrashim.

Instructions:
I.   Introduction (15 minutes)
     A. What is Midrash? Leader should facilitate a brief discussion of what Midrash is, where it comes from, what role it plays in Jewish text study, and how we use it today. Leader should encourage the class to volunteer and provide information to as large an extent as possible. If class members cannot provide information, or they provide incomplete information, leader should fill in the voids.
     B. Samples of Midrash and the texts to which they are related. Leader should research and present one or two well-known texts and Midrashim and use them as examples for the class. Leader should encourage class members to read aloud the midrashim that have already been distributed to them.
     C. Introduction to Exercise. Hand out text and have someone read it out loud. Leader instructs group that this is a creative activity, with no right or wrong answers. The aim is to look at Torah study in a fresh way. Leader reviews "Tips for Writing a Midrash" (see below.)
II. Writing Midrash (30 minutes)
     A. Break group into smaller groups of 4 people each.
     B. Leader should move from group to group, helping participants get started and offering guidance. Note: It may be necessary for other staff besides the leader to perform this task.
     C. Leader should encourage the groups to begin getting some ideas down on paper within the first 10 minutes of the exercise. Groups that finish quickly may try to write another midrash.
     D. Leader should give a warning 5 minutes before the ending time.

III. Wrap-up (15 minutes)
  A. The small groups should reconvene. Leader should ask one person from each group to share the group's midrash.
  B. After each group has presented, leader should facilitate a brief discussion of how the midrash-writing process worked, what group members liked and disliked, and what this taught them about different views and understanding of texts.
  C. Leader should close by explaining advantages of text study in this fashion.

Below is the handout "Tips for Writing a Midrash." This can be modified according to the leader's preferences. Attached are samples of midrashim and the primary text for the biblical Tower of Babel story. The text chosen should be appropriate for the background and education of participants. The context and background of the text should be given during the introduction.

TIPS FOR WRITING A MIDRASH

Carefully read each line. The midrashist is primarily concerned with explicating a particular verse or set of verses in the biblical text, not a whole book or even an entire narrative.

Is there one idea you want to expand on? Is there an open-ended question you would like to answer? Is there a troubling problem? Are there different ways of interpreting certain words/phrases/ lines? Can you give the story a context? Can you suggest a deeper meaning? Is there one character who you would like to write about?

Be creative! There are no "wrong answers."

(Submitted by Sharon Janowitz and Melissa Braverman)

THE TWO CHAIRS: CONVERSATIONS WITH BIBLICAL PERSONAGES

Purpose:

The "Two Chairs" activity is meant to afford the students the opportunity to explore questions or dilemmas they have about particular biblical stories or people.

Group:

This activity is designed for students age 13 and older who have had prior exposure to commentaries on biblical texts. Since the participants/students are expected to do some advance preparation and to meet with the group leader/teacher, a school class would be the ideal setting for this activity.

Everyone is asked, in advance, to think about any biblical individual or story that has had some special emotional meaning for them. This might be a negative or a positive reaction, or it might be a lingering curiosity about the what or why of the biblical tale.

Also, in advance of the session students are asked to list the most appropriate biblical figure(s) who they feel might be the right person(s) to provide the relevant information or insight about their selected biblical story.

The group leader puts two parallel columns on a sheet of paper: one includes the important biblical events/stories, identified by the students; the other includes the biblical figures with whom the student would like to have a conversation.

In advance of the session, the leader circulates the parallel lists to the students, and asks them each to volunteer to serve as the biblical respondent to one of the biblical stories or dilemmas posed by one of the other students. This is where the two chairs fit in. The two chairs should be facing each other and are situated in the center of an outer circle of chairs. The two students having the conversation sit in the center and the others sit in the outer circle and observe and listen.

Students come to the class prepared to have two conversations: one, in which they present their questions or reactions to a particular biblical story/personage(s), and a second conversation in which each student assumes the role of one of the biblical personages, and responds to the questions/dilemmas posed by one of the other students.

Advanced preparation is important, if this is to be a serious, educational activity and not become a parody. This caution should be communicated by the teacher/leader. Further, it would be helpful if the teacher met in advance with each student to discuss content of the biblical event to be presented and the response they have prepared for one of the other student's questions/dilemmas.

Examples of situations for conversation:

What went through Eve's mind when she chose to eat the forbidden fruit? (*Genesis* 3:6)

What went through Adam's mind when Eve chose to eat the forbidden fruit? (*Genesis* 3:6)

How did Cain feel when God accepted Abel's offering and not his? (*Genesis* 4:3–5)

What were the thoughts of the two rivals, Sarah and Hagar, as they vied for Abram's attentions? (*Genesis* 16; Genesis 21:5–10)

What was Abram thinking as he was about to sacrifice Isaac? (*Genesis* 22:1–19)

What was Isaac thinking as he was about to be sacrificed by Abram? (*Genesis* 22:1–19)

What were Isaac's thoughts in his final days as he prepared to meet with his two sons, Esau and Jacob? (*Genesis* 22:1–40)

What was Jacob's reaction when he discovered that he had married Leah instead of Rachel? (*Genesis* 29:16–25)

What were Dinah's feelings as her brothers negotiated with Shechem, the Hivite, who had defiled her but then sought her as his wife? (*Genesis* 34)

What were Moses's reactions when he discovered that while he was away at Sinai, the Israelites created and began worshipping the golden calf? (*Exodus* 32:1–32)

JEWISH CLASSIFIEDS

Purpose:

Fun with Jewish history. An opportunity to combine one's knowledge of Jewish history with one's wits in developing clever classified advertisements based on Jewish themes.

Group:

Junior high school age and older; any number of participants.

Setting:

Any class or meeting room.

Materials:

Paper and pencils and a list of Jewish classifieds (see below.) Individual ads should be written on separate slips of paper and placed in a container such as a hat or box.

Instructions:

1. The leader places folded slips with the individual classified ads in a container. Participants take turns picking out, reading and trying to guess the person from Jewish history or the situation referred to in the ad. An alternative is to divide the group into teams and keep score of correctly identified ads.
2. After the group has gotten a taste of the activity, the leader asks the group to develop their own classified ads. For younger groups it may be useful to suggest some Jewish historical figures and events. For example: Jacob and Esau, Judah Maccabee, David and Goliath, Samson and Delilah, Esther and Vashti, Hillel and Shammai, the Sanhedrin, the Essenes, the Marranos, the Kabalists, the excommunication of Spinoza, the false messiah Sabbetai Zevi, the *Protocols of the Elders of Zion*, the Falasha Jews, the Haganah, David Ben-Gurion.

JEWISH CLASSIFIEDS

Personals
1. Large family wishes to rent spacious three-story boat for extended trip. Prefer gopherwood construction. Must be able to weather rough winds and high waters. Minimum size 300 x 50 x 30 cubits. Animals must be welcome.
2. Urgent: Seeking information as to the whereabouts of my eleventh son, last seen in vicinity of Dothan, wearing multi-colored sports jacket. Anyone with information please write _____
3. My husband is often away. Seeking young man to share apartment. Call before 6 p.m.
4. Lost: Ten tribes. Last seen in Assyria. If found please notify Government House, Jerusalem, Israel.

5. Desperate: Need 7 cruses pure olive oil by 25th of Kislev. Will pay top shekel. Contact _____

6. Elegant French gentleman wishes correspondent to exchange experiences with. Have much leisure time to write at length; can tell many stories of life on tropical island. Write

_____

For Sale

7. For Sale: Almanac in six volumes. Advice on crops, farm animals, marketing arrangements, prices on Jerusalem exchange. Also includes care of wives, guide to native festival celebrations, sunrise approximations, exotic stories, words of wisdom, and current gossip. More complete than the *Farmers' Almanac*—a real collector's item!

8. Must sell: pair of ram's horns, slightly scratched by thorns. A real sacrifice. Write _____

Help Wanted

9. Speech therapist for private lessons for aspiring national leader. Contact _____

10. Interpreters needed urgently. Must have good speaking knowledge of Ugaritic, Akkadian, Phoenician, Moabite, and Hurrian. Experience in construction helpful but not necessary. Write _____

Announcements

11. Wanted: Contributions of old gold, rings, coins, for refabrication into contemporary sculptural form to be dedicated at forthcoming communal worship service. Contact _____

12. Thursday night wrestling match: the Mauling Malach vs. Jacob the Jew. Best of 5 rounds. No holds barred, may go all night. Winner will receive blessing and name change. A real thigh-grabber. 7:30 p.m., The Other Side of the River Arena

13. Spectacular singles' weekend! Out-of-this-world entertainment, complete with fireworks. The fun never ends at our resorts in the twin cities on the lush, green shores of the Dead Sea.

Services Available
14. Demolition expert. No job too big. Special experience with walls and fortifications. Contact _____
15. Interior decorator for religious structures—capable, talented artisan, excellent references. Free estimates. Write _____
16. Make your next party a hit! Your guests will love my talking ass. Write—c/o King Balak, Royal Palace, Moab.

People or situations referred to in the Jewish Classifieds
1. Noah and the flood
2. Joseph sold by his brothers as a slave
3. Wife of Egyptian official Potiphar, seducer of Joseph
4. Israelite tribes exiled in 719 B.C.E.
5. Oil needed for the Temple after the Maccabean revolt
6. Alfred Dreyfus after his exile to Devil's Island
7. The Mishnah compiled by Judah the Prince
8. The ram sacrificed by Abraham in place of Isaac
9. Moses and his lisp
10. The many languages which appeared at the time of the Tower of Babel.
11. The golden calf built while Moses was on the mount and Aaron was in charge of the Israelites.
12. Wrestling between Jacob and the angel
13. Sodom and Gomorrah
14. Joshua breaking down the walls of Jericho
15. Bezalel the biblical artisan
16. Balaam the biblical prophet and his ass

(The 16 Jewish classifed ads were taken from the March 4, 1977 and the April 1, 1977 issues of *Sh'ma*, where they first appeared. Thanks to the original contributors and Editor Eugene B. Borowitz for permission to reprint them.)

WHO SAID IT?

In this activity, group members must attempt to identify which Jewish historical figure might have said one of a series of imagined statements. (Make the statements as colloquial as possible so that the group members can relate to the characters while at the same time be amused at the thought of a historic figure using modern terms of speech.)

The more advanced the group, the more information you should require in their answers (e.g. to whom would the statement be said, in what context was it said).

These statements may be presented in a variety of ways but it is important to note that it can be used as a "trigger" for discussion and further activities rather than simply as a complete activity. After using the statements, have participants create their own "Who Said It" statements; perhaps using drama/costumes.

Examples:
1. "You were told not to turn around!"
2. "G-d, this people seems always to be complaining."
3. "We disagree, those residents aren't so huge, we would overcome them."
4. "You mean I've been chosen as the first king?"
5. "I've got to make myself look really pretty, since the future of my people may be at stake."
6. "I'm proud to say I love my mother-in-law."
7. "Yes, it is true that people called me by a different name, but that was before my all-night wrestling match."
8. "Look at that cute little boy floating in a box in the river."
9. "You would look so much better if you would let me cut your hair."
10. "Well, perhaps it would be more practical to consider Uganda"!

Answers:
1. LOT to his wife, who disobeyed G-d by turning around to look at the destruction of Sodom and Gomorrah and became a pillar of salt.
2. MOSES, speaking to G-d about the frequent complaining by the Jewish people during the Exodus.
3. CALEB and JOSHUA disagreeing with the other ten spies sent out by Moses from the desert to scout the land of Canaan.
4. SAUL, upon being selected by the prophet Samuel as the first king of Israel.

5. ESTHER preparing herself for the search by King Ahasuerus to find a replacement for Queen Vashti.
6. RUTH speaking about her decision to remain with her mother-in-law, Naomi, after the death of her husband, Boaz.
7. JACOB became "Israel" after wrestling with the angel.
8. PHAROAH'S DAUGHTER speaking to her handmaidens as she discovers the baby Moses in the bulrushes.
9. DELILAH, who betrays Samson by cutting off his hair, thereby depriving him of his strength.
10. THEODOR HERZL, after experiencing early difficulties in trying to establish a Jewish state in Palestine, briefly considered the African country of Uganda as an alternative.

Variation:

JEWISH GEOGRAPHY (or JEWISH YEARS). Pick slips of paper from a container on which are written names of geographic locations (or critical years), and tell in what way that place (year) is connected to Jewish history.

Examples of Places
1. Ararat
2. Machpelah
3. Shushan
4. Devil's Island
5. Basel, Switzerland
6. Kishinev
7. Petah Tikvah
8. Damascus
9. Cincinnati
10. Castle Garden
11. Evian
12. Nuremberg

Examples of Years
1. 586 B.C.E.
2. 70
3. 135
4. 1492

5. 1654
6. 1948
7. 1967
8. 1973

Answers to Geographic Places
1. The resting place of Noah's Ark after the flood. Also, the colony to settle Jews proposed by the American Jew, Mordecai Manuel Noah, in 1825 in Grand Island, above Niagara Falls.
2. The cave in Hebron bought by Abraham as a burial place for himself, his wife, and other Hebrew patriarchs.
3. The city in Persia in which the Purim story occurs.
4. The French penal colony to which Alfred Dreyfus was sentenced after being falsely accused of treason.
5. The city in which Herzl convened the World Zionist Congresses in 1897–1903.
6. The site of the Russian pogrom in 1903 where many Jews were killed or injured.
7. The agricultural settlement established in Palestine in 1878 by the Hovevei Zion (Lovers of Zion), the first Russian Jewish immigrants.
8. Site of the "Damascus Affair" in 1840, in which a number of Jews were imprisoned and tortured for allegedly killing a Christian monk.
9. Location of the Hebrew Union College, seminary for training Reform rabbis, established in 1875 by Isaac M. Wise.
10. The immigration station in New York City where immigrants to the United States during the nineteenth century first arrived.
11. A city in France in which a conference was held in 1938, organized by President Roosevelt, to consider the plight of the refugees from Nazi Germany.
12. In 1935 the Nazis promulgated their anti-Semitic doctrines at Nuremberg. After the war the trials of the Nazi war criminals were held in the same city.

Answers to Years
1. Destruction of the First Temple by the Babylonians.
2. Destruction of the Second Temple by the Romans.

3. The defeat and end of the Bar Kochba revolt at Betar at the hands of the Romans.
4. Expulsion of the Jews from Spain.
5. First settlement of Jews in America.
6. Establishment of the State of Israel.
7. The Six-Day War in Israel.
8. The Yom Kippur War in Israel.

EXPRESSING THE ESSENCE

Purpose:

To help people to relate more fully to Jewish personalities, holidays, and events by using analogies.

Group:

Junior high school and older; to be conducted in small groups and can be done with several groups simultaneously.

Setting:

A classroom or meeting room with chairs and with adequate space for the number of participants.

Materials:

Paper and pencil for each person.

Time:

50–60 minutes.

Instructions:

1. The leader explains the exercise to the group, pointing out that through the use of analogies we can extend our understanding of certain events and people, and thereby get closer to their

"essence". For example, "If you were to describe Moses as a color, what color would he be? What object of nature (e.g., plant, animal, natural setting, etc.)?" Or, "Letting your imagination flow, what fantasies come to mind as you think expansively about Moses?" The leader should try a few analogies, with the whole group volunteering answers, until it is clear that the group understands the mood of the activity.

2. Ask the group to form triads or quartets. Give each cluster a list of Jewish events, holidays or personalities, and ask them to experiment expressing the "essence" together.

3. Ask the clusters to take one or two Jewish persons or events not listed, and to develop appropriate analogies.

4. When the group reassembles, go around the circle and ask each person to give one of the analogies they especially liked. The leader concludes the activity by asking the participants to indicate whether their understanding of the Jewish individuals or concepts has been broadened through this creative exercise.

LIST OF ANALOGIES

	Color	An Object of Nature	Fantasy Image
Purim			
Abraham			
Noah			
Israel			
Chanukah			
Havdalah			
Herzl			
Yom Kippur War			
Local Synagogue			
Passover			
Yom Kippur			

(Submitted by Jeanne Maman)

WATERSHED EVENTS IN JEWISH HISTORY

Purpose:

To discuss major events in Jewish history and to understand the long range importance of each one on the Jewish people.

Group:

Teens 13 years and older or adults.

Setting:

One large room that can be used for both large and small groups. One area should have chairs arranged in a circle. Another part of the room should be prepared for smaller group work. There should be enough space so that the groups can not hear one another work.

Materials:

One sheet of newsprint and marker for each group (4–6 people)
Fact sheet for each group listing events in Jewish history (see attached)
Index cards that each have one event in Jewish history written on it (can be color coordinated to be used to form groups after mixer.)
A complete set of event cards for each group (Can be color-coordinated as well for group recognition.)
Newsprint for summary

Time:

1 hour.

Instructions:

1. Facilitator should welcome everyone and explain purpose of activity.

2. Introductions: Everyone should go around, say their name in English and Hebrew and describe where one of the names came from (i.e., who they were named after). After sharing personal family history, explain that the group will look more broadly at events in Jewish History.

3. Mixer: Each member of the group receives a slip of paper that has an event from Jewish history written on it. Everyone needs to form a time-line, standing from the earliest event to the most recent event, in a straight line. Anyone who is not sure of when or what the event is, should ask other members of the group. Once everyone is in a line, have the participants read their event and briefly describe what it was starting from the earliest event.

4. Small group ranking activity: Each group receives a set of cards. On each card is written one event in Jewish history. Groups are instructed to use the events that are offered (and make up their own as well if they deem necessary) and choose the top five events that have had the largest impact on the Jewish people. Each group should also receive a fact sheet that briefly describes each event. The group should write them on newsprint, appoint a group reporter and hang them at the front of the room.

Creation
The Six-Day War
The Enlightenment (Haskalah)
The Destruction of the First Temple
Assassination of Yitzchak Rabin
The Holocaust
The Akedah
Oslo Accords
The conquest of Canaan
The Destruction of the Second Temple
The completion of the Babylonian Talmud
Jerusalem Talmud
The Exodus
Massada
The Establishment of the State of Israel
The Spanish Inquisition
God gave Moses Ten Commandments and the Torah

5. The entire group then reassembles, and each group leader should explain a little about their group process and final decisions. Discuss any events that were added by any group. Facilitator should point out interesting differences or similarities, and allow for discussions/debates among participants.
6. Conclude by ranking the top five events with the entire group. Finally, evaluate what they have learned from this exercise.

Variation:

This activity could be used in numerous other ways. Try ranking most important Jewish people or Jewish texts/books, or aspects of Judaism.

MAJOR WATERSHED EVENTS IN JEWISH HISTORY

Listed below are important events from throughout Jewish history. Please add events that you feel are very important. You are asked to choose the five events that have had the largest impact on the Jewish people.

1. Creation
   First chapter of *Genesis*.
2. Patriarchal Period (2000–1800 b.c.e.)
   The Akedah: When Abraham was commanded by God to offer Isaac as a sacrifice. At the last moment God told Abraham to desist and declared "Now I know that you fear God."
3. From Slavery to Sinai (1800–1250 b.c.e.)
   The Exodus: Moses led the Jewish slaves out of Egypt.
4. From Slavery to Sinai (1800–1250 b.c.e.)
   On Mount Sinai, God revealed the Ten Commandments and the Torah to Moses, who delivered them to the assembled people.
5. Conquest and Kingship (1250 b.c.e.)
   The conquest of Canaan led by Joshua, beginning the existence of the Children of Israel living in the Holy Land in a loose federation of tribes.
6. Destruction of the First Temple (586 b.c.e.)
   The Jewish people were exiled to Babylonia. The center of

Jewish study and Jewish life was in Babylonia. Many believe that this is where the synagogue, a major institution in Judaism today, was first established.

7. Destruction of the Second Temple (70 c.e.)
   Many Jews died during revolts against the Romans. The remaining Jews were exiled from Jerusalem, never to rebuild the Temple.

8. Massada Shall Not Fall Again (72 c.e.)
   The Zealots of Massada did not allow the Romans to take them as slaves, but rather chose to take their own lives in dignity. This event has become a symbol of strength for many.

9. Completion of the Babylonian Talmud / Jerusalem Talmud (5th century)
   After the destruction of the Second Temple, the center of Jewish life moved to Yavneh (West of Jerusalem near the western shore of Israel), the Galilee (northern Israel) and Babylonia.

10. Spanish Inquisition (1492)
    While the Babylonian center of Jewish life declined, the communities in North Africa and Spain flourished. However, when Christians supplanted Muslim rulers, the Jews lost their prominent position in society. Finally, in 1492, the Jews were given the choice of converting to Christianity or leaving the country. The result: dispersion of the Jewish population.

11. The Enlightenment (Haskalah) (18th century)
    A philosophical movement spread by Napoleon which held that human reason and not divine revelation was the source of authority. This was accompanied by the assimilation of Jews into general society. Moses Mendelssohn, the leader of the German Haskalah, translated the Bible into German to make it more accessible to German Jews. This eventually would lead to new movements within Judaism.

12. The Holocaust (1933–1945)
    The death of six million Jews by the Nazis.

13. Establishment of the State of Israel (1948)
    Following a struggle for statehood and the War of Independence, the Zionist dream of many became a reality.

14. Six-Day War (1967)
    Changed view of the world to regard Israel as a powerful nation. Affected Jewish Diaspora feelings toward Israel,

changing the nature of the relationship. For the first time, placed another population under Israel's control.

15. Oslo Accords (1993)
    Yitzchak Rabin and Yasser Arafat shake hands on a new peace plan designed in Oslo. This is the beginning of the Peace Process in the Middle East as we know it today.

16. Assassination of Yitzchak Rabin (1995)
    Jew killing Jew.

(Submitted by Liz Kaufman-Taylor)

QUOTES

To do righteousness and justice is more acceptable to the Lord than sacrifice.

Proverbs 21:3

Where man meets the world, not with the tools he has made but with the soul with which he is born; not like a hunter who seeks his prey but a lover to reciprocate love; where man and matter meet as equals before the mystery, both made, maintained and destined to pass away, it is not an object, a thing that is given to his sense, but a state of fellowship that embraces him and all things.

Rabbi Abraham Joshua Heschel
(1907–1972)

The first directive to man in the Torah is not what one might expect in a divine text. It does not focus on interaction between God and man, nor on fraternal interaction between man and man. Rather the first directive to man is pru urevu, "Be fruitful and multiply." (*Genesis* 1:26). The first directive to Noah after the flood is the same (*Genesis* 9:12). Fulfillment of creator potential is a holy thrust of the cosmos, flowing directly from the core of the divine essence.

Unknown

The Yiddish language is a language of exile, without a land, without frontiers, not supported by any government, a language which possesses no words for weapons or war tactics.

Isaac Bashevis Singer (1904–1991)

What in other faiths was achieved through architecture—visible symbols of the order and majesty of creation—was achieved in Judaism through the life of the Holy community, constructed according to the plans of the Torah.

Chief Rabbi Jonathan Sacks

"They tried to kill us. We won. Let's eat!"

Anonymous (nine-word summary of meaning of all Jewish holidays.)

Hospitality is more important even than encountering God's intimate presence.

Talmud Tractate Shabbat 172a

I am unable to imagine the universe and human life without some guiding principle, without a source of spiritual warmth, that is nonmaterial and not bound by physical laws.

Andrei Sakharov (1921–1989),
Memoirs, 1989

The world of our experience seems chaotic, disconnected, confusing. We do not know what to do with ourselves. We seek the awareness of our being anchored in the earth and the universe, the awareness that we are not here alone, nor for ourselves alone, but that we are an integral part of higher mysterious entities, against whom it is not advisable to blaspheme.

Vaclav Havel (1936–)
President Czech Republic, 1994

Divinity designates those energies and activities which sustain us and elevate our lives. Such an understanding of divinity requires no justification in the presence of evil.

Rabbi Harold Shulweis

Biblical descriptions of God are couched in human terms so that we might understand them, not because God is adequately described in that way.

Rabbi David J. Wolpe, 1990

Where there is no God, all is permitted.

Fyodor Dostoevsky (1821–1881)

Spirituality is a search for meaning in an age that supposedly has seen the "eclipse" or "death of God".

Theodore Roszak, social historian, 1968

Only someone who submits to the authority of the universal order can genuinely value himself and his neighbors, and thus honor their rights as well.

Vaclav Havel (1936–), former President
of Czech Republic

God is the ultimate mystery of being and is beyond thinking.

Joseph Campbell (1904–1987),
The Power of Myth

God is the source of inspiration, hope, energy, the capacity to rise beyond despair and to feel a sense of security and confidence that there is a purpose and order to the universe.

Rabbi Harold Kushner,
Who Needs God?, 1989

God is an almost imageless conception, a dark light, a light darkness, that is caring and compassionate, has deep feelings about us . . . and is always available.

Archbishop Desmond Tutu (1931–)

Silence is the language that God speaks and everything else is bad translation.

Trappist Father Thomas Keating
(1923–)

Through my scientific work, I have come to believe that the physical universe is put together with an ingenuity so astonishing that I cannot accept it merely as a brute fact. Whether one wishes to call that deeper level "God" is a matter of taste and definition.

Paul Davies, physicist (1946–),
Mind and God, 1992

God stands for the good in life—for justice and love. Behavior needs to be sanctified, if it is to affect adherence to ideals. . . . The worship of one God is the negation of the worship of men and things.

Erich Fromm (1900–1980)

God created man in his own image, in the image of God created he him.

Genesis 1:27 (the notion of *imitatio Dei*)

Ye shall be holy, for I the Lord your God am holy.

Leviticus 19:2

Of all that the Holy One created in the world, God created nothing without a purpose.

Shabbat 77b

The East and the West is God's; therefore whichever way ye turn, there is the face of God: Truly God is immense and knoweth all.

Koran, Sura 2: 109

Now I shall explain something to you that you should know, namely, that the entire act of creation was for the purpose of man in accordance with the commandment of God. . . . Accordingly, since man's rational soul never dies it is comparable in its eternity to God. . . . And, therefore, the prophet states that he "saw the Glory of God as the appearance of man."

Abraham Ibn Ezra (1089–1164)

The Almighty, desiring to lead us to perfection and to improve the state of our society, revealed to us His laws which are to regulate our actions. These laws . . . presuppose an advanced state of intellectual culture. We must first . . . have a knowledge of metaphysics. But this discipline can only be approached after the study of physics. . . . Therefore, the Almighty commenced Scripture with the description of Creation, that is, with physical science.

Moses Maimonides (1135–1204)

Beauty is in God's handwriting—a wayside sacrament. Welcome it in every fair face, in every fair sky, in every fair flower and thank God for it is as a cup of blessing.

Ralph Waldo Emerson (1803–1882)

Religion is an illusion, a lingering childish desire for a Father substitute—the fruit of oppressed desires and infantile impulses.

Sigmund Freud (1856–1939)

If to believe in God means to be able to talk *about* him in the third person, then I do not believe in God. But if to believe in him means to be able to talk *to* him, then I do believe in God.

Martin Buber (1878–1965)

I believe in Spinoza's God, who reveals himself in the harmony of all being, but not in a God who concerns himself with the fate and actions of men.

Albert Einstein (1879–1955)

God is the power in the cosmos that gives human life the direction that enables the human being to reflect the image of God.

Rabbi Mordecai Kaplan (1881–1983)

To the prophet . . . God does not reveal himself in an abstract absoluteness, but in a personal and intimate relation to the world. . . . This notion that God can be intimately affected, that he possesses not merely intelligence and will, but also pathos, basically defines the prophetic consciousness of God.

Rabbi Abraham Joshua Heschel
(1907–1972)

Awe is an act of insight into a meaning greater than ourselves. . . . The beginning of awe is wonder, and the beginning of wisdom is awe. . . . Awe is a way of being in rapport with the mystery of all reality.

> Rabbi Abraham Joshua Heschel
> (1907–1972)

Everything hints at something that transcends it; the detail indicates the whole, the whole its idea, the idea its mysterious root.

> Rabbi Abraham Joshua Heschel
> (1907–1972)

God is in need of man for the attainment of His ends.

> Rabbi Abraham Joshua Heschel
> (1907–1972)

It matters very little how we conceive God, as long as we so believe in God that belief in Him makes a tremendous difference in our lives.

> Rabbi Mordecai Kaplan (1881–1983)

. . . the quest for perfection, which is the most idealistic striving of our nature, directs us to seek the higher unity that must finally come in the world. In that day—God will be one and His name one.

> Rabbi Abraham Isaac Kook
> (1883–1935)

The person who does not believe in miracles is not a realist.

> David Ben-Gurion (1886–1973)

Creation finds its expression in man's fulfilling all of his tasks, causing all the potentiality implanted in him to emerge into actuality, utilizing all of his manifold possibilities, and fully bringing to fruition his own noble personality. . . . Realize, actualize yourselves, your own potentialities and possibilities, and go forth to meet your God. The unfolding of man's spirit that soars to the very heavens, that is the meaning of creation.

> Rabbi Joseph B. Soloveitchik, 1965

The question of whether the world is nothing but a physical accident or whether there is a plan, this is the main question of every human being. Because the only answer to our suffering would be that there is a purpose in it, that there is a spirit behind it. If these would not exist, our life would be a hopeless business.

Isaac Bashevis Singer
(1904–1991), 1991

In saying "God" in prayer, I give the object of my wonder a name. . . . We attach the word "God" to our search for meaning, to our desire to find a word for that which evokes our sense of awe and wonder, for that which humbles and inspires us, for that which calls us to its service.

Professor Arthur Green (1941–), 1992

Humanistic Judaism is incompatible with theism. There is no evidence that a supernatural conscious being exists who responds to the personal problems of human beings and who deliberately intervenes in the affairs of humanity in response to prayers or to ensure justice.

A Guide to Humanistic Judaism, 1993

Unable to believe in the God of their fathers or to invest their emotional piety unreservedly in Israel, Jews born after 1945 discover themselves to be atheists in search of a synagogue, at least in the sense of a place of common recognition.

Frederic Raphael, 1994

Spirituality is surrounded by superstition. It is a permanent siege.

Leon Wieseltier (1952–)

Seek the answers to eternal and ultimate questions about life and death, but be prepared not to find them. Enjoy the search.

Professor Morris Schwartz (1907–1995)

We need to reconstitute Judaism as a religion friendly to the notion of quest, to a vision of life as an unending voyage in search of truth or God or Oneness.

Professor Arthur Green (1941–), 1994

The believer asks no questions while no answer can satisfy the unbeliever.

Traditional Jewish saying

12

PLURALISM

The body of this chapter on Pluralism was adapted by Alan Tep-erow from an article he wrote entitled "One Jewish People? How One Community Addresses the Issues That Divide Us" that originally appeared in the Summer, 1998 issue of the Journal of Jewish Communal Service.

This chapter discusses the challenge and context around achieving religious pluralism among Jews of different denominational backgrounds. Pluralism has become an "in" word for today's American Jewish community. It refers to the goal of achieving mutual recognition, understanding and cooperation among the denominations. While most leaders acknowledge the idea of pluralism, the real question is what the strategy should be for creating a pluralistic American Jewish community. This chapter details efforts in that direction by the Synagogue Council of Massachusetts and other local bodies. Presented first is a strategic analysis of the problem of achieving pluralism, then description of local efforts, and finally activities that are being used in those efforts.

One Jewish People? How One Community Addresses the Issues That Divide Us[1]

"Nature's topography is rich in its variety, which is the essence and source of its beauty. No gardener will plant flowers of only one color; it is the multicolored garden that appeals to our esthetic sense. The same holds true for the topography of humankind. As

1. The author wishes to express his gratitude to Toby Gutwill, Synagogue Council Assistant Director, for her help with the article.

Thomas Carlyle (1795–1881) once observed, 'God does not rhyme his children.'

The Talmudic sages said: Man stamps many coins with one dye and they are all alike, one with the other. The King of Kings, the Holy One, blessed be He, has stamped all humankind with the dye of the first man and yet not one of them is like to his fellow.

The strength and pride of our nation lie in its many ethnic groups, each contributing its special gifts to the enrichment of the entire community. I think of the United States as a beautiful mosaic, each part of which represents an ethnic group. When one of the parts is dull, colorless or flawed, the work is diminished. It is good for the mosaic that each part shine its brightest, most luminous colors."

Mario M. Cuomo
Former Governor of New York[2]

So, too, Jewish life is a rich tapestry. In those communities where there is an understanding of, and appreciation for the variety of Jewish religious expression, *K'lal Yisrael* is strengthened. Taking pride in individual differences, practiced most universally through the denominational movements or "streams" of Judaism, while nurturing a healthy acceptance of the collective of the Jewish people is, in my view, a formula for effective community-building.[3]

However, most Jewish leaders, and far worse, the marginal and unaffiliated among us, observe that the current state of interdenominational affairs, both in North America and abroad, has declined precipitously in recent years. We face growing divisiveness over such topics as patrilineal descent, the ordination of gay and lesbian rabbis, and the status of non-Orthodox conversions—all variations on the recurring themes of "who is a Jew?" and "who is a Rabbi?"

We witness the increasingly isolationist practices of the fervently Orthodox bumping up against the vocal and highly visible rituals of Jewish feminists and their supporters. Too often these clashes

2. Brown, Cherie R. *The Art of Coalition Building: A Guide for Community Leaders.* American Jewish Committee. 1984, p. vii.

3. For the purposes of this chapter, *religious* pluralism will be the primary focus of discussion, dealing with the four major movements of congregational expression within Judaism.

of culture and ideology lead to shocking acts of violence. Public statements and proclamations by segments of American Orthodoxy deligitimate the authenticity of Jews from the other streams. Counter attacks from the religious left condemn the Orthodox, often failing to distinguish between those who have made discrediting statements and those who have repudiated them. American Jewish leaders attack Israel's Orthodox establishment with threats of pulling their organization's financial support. And the demise of the Synagogue Council of America, not to be mistaken for our local Synagogue Council of Massachusetts[4], is just one more indicator of both the importance and difficulty of achieving—and sustaining—dialogue and cooperation across denominational lines.

Are we rapidly approaching a time of complete separation between segments of Orthodoxy and the rest of the Jewish world? Has "Yitz" Greenberg's prophecy of a fundamental split in the Jewish world already become a reality? Is there cause for hope in a society both numbed by terror and fanaticism and skeptical about any "good news" in communal or political life?

Answers to many of these issues that confront world Jewry are, indeed, beyond the conceptual and strategic reach of most individuals, myself certainly included. But I am convinced that, working in a mode of cooperation and respect, individuals and communities *can* change. From the outset, it should be understood that workable solutions to tough issues often give rise to feelings that each group occasionally "gains" and occasionally "loses." Collaborating in an atmosphere of mutual respect gives coalition partners the sense that "we are all in this together." In healthy coalitions the organization's agenda is not owned by any one group, but by the collective. In a truly pluralistic environment, the integrity of each coalition partner is highly valued, regardless of his or her denominational leanings, and it is assumed that the discussion is *L'shem Shamayim*, for the sake of heaven.

How do these principles play out in the actual trans-denominational work, in the community, of a group or organization that promotes, and actually lives with a pluralistic mindset? Although

---

4. The Synagogue Council of Massachusetts is a trans-denominational organization with more than 120 member congregations, headed by the author of this chapter since its inception in 1982.

there is no absolute formula for building bridges across denominational lines, it is patently and strategically easier to remain within
the "safe zone"—the window of programming opportunities
within which everyone can come to common agreement. It is my
contention that we have to do more.

If enough of us working at the grassroots level are able to
change attitudes and bring people from the polarities together in
dialogue and friendship, we will eventually build a foundation for
future discussion on the really tough issues. It is far easier to snub
institutions than friends; much simpler to dismiss the beliefs and
practices of amorphous groups than individuals with whom there
has been serious human contact.

Where does all this leave us? Can individuals be significantly
changed, in their Jewish attitudes and behaviors, as a result of
their participation in such trans-denominational programs? Every
indicator, including studies in the early years comparing attitudes
before and after the Synagogue Council's Unity Mission, suggests
that the experience does affect participants' views and practices in
significant ways. As the dialogue is enhanced, so too is the desire
to grow together, as individuals and as a community, committed to
the ideals of pluralism, *derech eretz* and self-pride. I am absolutely
convinced that regular and sophisticated use of experiential education in structured learning environments can change attitudes, help
people grow Jewishly, and build bridges across denominational
lines.

Seven Principles of Religious Pluralism[5]

Given the many different threads that make up *our* trans-denominational tapestry, what are the principles that enable those with
whom we interact, with disparate ideologies and institutional priorities, to come together in unity?

Let me share some of the overriding principles that guide my
work, and the work of the Synagogue Council of Massachusetts.

5. I would like to acknowledge the impact of CLAL (the National Jewish
Center for Learning and Leadership), and its founding President, Rabbi Irving
"Yitz" Greenberg, on the conceptualization of these principles—and on much of
my work as Director of the Synagogue Council of Massachusetts.

1. Neither single group nor ideological branch has a monopoly on Judaism's fundamental truths. We, as individuals and institutions, are all partially correct, sometimes dead wrong, and often too self-centered. But only the Almighty has the right to ultimately judge who is living his or her life in God's image.

2. Pluralism is not caving in to other denominational groups for the sake of unity; it is not the acceptance of other positions without serious struggle and dialogue; it is certainly not compromising on widely held fundamental beliefs and practices. As pluralists, we accept *ab initio* the existence and communal validity of our coalition partners, although we may, and often do disagree on many religious issues. We recognize that we need each other and are enhanced by the existence and success of the other streams of Judaism.

3. We acknowledge the inherent spiritual dignity and integrity of each movement and the respect that must be afforded its leadership. Those who do *not* accept the other's legitimacy will, nonetheless, reap the benefits of our democratic, pluralistic society.

4. Communal leadership needs to concentrate on what *can* be accomplished, rather than on what divides us. Serious obstacles to Jewish unity and organizational integrity must be addressed head on, enabling each of the coalition partners to be heard. We try to set our sights on achievable goals, with full recognition that not every disagreement can be resolved and that conflict resolution invariably requires some degree of compromise, but never at the expense of any group's basic ideological or theological underpinnings.

5. We offer a hand in friendship and unity, with the hope that it will be accepted in the spirit in which it was extended. We embrace each individual, congregation or denominational group at whatever level it finds most comfortable, remembering that *the goal is unity, not uniformity.*

6. We deal with human beings—not institutions, and attempt to develop a level of trust and mutual concern, which must be sustained over time through consistency in thought and action. We help people establish friendships, relationships and alliances across all lines. We have learned that disagree-

ments are best resolved slowly and without fanfare, public announcements or proclamations.

7. We have fun together; we study together; we bring humor into our deliberations. At programs such as the Synagogue Council's annual Shabbaton we sing loud and *daven* with *kavannah*, even as we lower the decibel level of rhetoric by assuring each individual that he or she is being heard. And, perhaps most importantly, we stress the common values, practices, celebrations and beliefs shared by all Jews.

I. Unity Mission as Paradigm

"When Mission participants met before the trip, I was struck by the diversity. One participant, brought up in an Orthodox home, now considers himself Conservative. Another, once an atheist, is now Reform, and so on. Barriers are fluid, not rigid, and people change. Individuals are always more complex than categories, and more interesting than ideological platforms."

Dr. Avi Rockoff, Unity
Mission Participant

In 1987, the first Unity Mission of the Synagogue Council of Massachusetts became reality, with thirty-two eager participants representing a very broad and diverse group of men and women who were the *halutzim* of this now institutionalized annual excursion. The Unity Mission includes two full days of travel, study, dialogue, prayer, spiritual renewal and introspection for congregational leaders from the Greater Boston area. Two meetings are held prior to the Mission to enable participants to meet one another and learn from local rabbis about the background and philosophy of the four major movements. At the first of these pre-Mission meetings, the dialogue begins in full force, with attendees sharing in small groups how they came to their current religious philosophy and level of practice. At the second meeting, participants are grouped by denomination and asked to articulate what perceptions they believe others have of them, and what aspects of their particular philosophy make them most proud.

II. Unity Shabbaton Opening Session

"We rejoice because we have come together from all denominations, and we're living together in peace. Perhaps today we are lighting a small candle. And when other Jews hear about it, that light will burn brighter and brighter, fulfilling the words from the Shacharit service—ohr chadash al tziyon tair, may a new light shine upon Zion."

Rabbi Norbert Weinberg, member of
the Shabbaton faculty

The Synagogue Council of Massachusetts' Unity Shabbaton is a celebration of Shabbat across the denominations. Many of the participants are leaders of their congregations; many are involved regionally and nationally in their own movements. And many are simply committed Jews desirous of celebrating Shabbat with people from other backgrounds, with a faculty as diverse as the attendees themselves. People come together with a sense of pride in their individual denominational affiliations, recognizing that the boundaries between groups are fluid and that each individual has a responsibility to break through the walls of separation.

In this context, the Shabbaton celebrates diversity in an environment that embraces differences. It is an experiment in living and praying and studying together. The weekend provides an opportunity for growth through an observance of Shabbat in a spiritually-rich environment.

III. GENESIS Informal Educational Training

"Seeing the Community Informal Educators (CIEs) as seven very different, serious Jewish role models shatters the students' pre-conceived notions of a single definition of what it means to be Jewish."

"I now have a greater appreciation for the need to tackle issues relating to pluralism . . . head-on."

Community Informal Educators

GENESIS at Brandeis University is an exciting residential summer experience for high school students interested in the arts, humanities, Jewish studies, and social action. The counselors or *madrichim* are known as CIE's (community informal educators) who, in addition to working with the students one-on-one and in groups, are Jewish educators and rabbinical students who are responsible for building community and helping the teens develop their sense of Jewish identity and commitment.

As part of the overall training and mentoring of the CIEs, group conversations as well as individual contacts proved to be quite powerful, ranging from frank and open discussions together as a group to individualized learning and supervision during one-on-one sessions. Through experiential activities and small group learning exercises, each CIE had the opportunity to reflect on his or her own work-style, relationships with the other CIEs and students, the group process, spirituality, programming, and individual growth patterns. These conversations also considered implications for future applicability (both personal and communal), and assisted the CIEs in understanding and ultimately articulating GENESIS' unique vision.

IV. General Education Program on Religious Pluralism in America

"Every dispute which is in the name of Heaven,—its end (or—in the end it) is to be permanently established. And [every dispute] which is not in the name of Heaven,—its end (or—in the end it) is not to be permanently established. What is [an example of] a dispute in the name of Heaven? It is the dispute between Hillel and Shammai. And what is [an example of a dispute] not in the name of Heaven? It is the dispute of Korah and his band."

Pirkei Avot 5:17

This program was developed at the request of the rabbis at Temple Emanuel of Newton, Massachusetts, the author's home congregation, for a Yom Kippur afternoon "break" discussion on religious pluralism. The challenges were many: exhaustion and hunger on the part of both the audience and speaker, a sanctuary venue in which pews were stationary, and a large number of attendees (approximately 250 individuals). Not to be deterred, interactive, experiential learning became the mode of transmission. This program may—daresay, should—be adapted to other settings, large or small, but can be used for a sizeable audience at a conference or other public venue.

Conclusion

The prophets of doom hear our words with deaf ears. What about conversion, patrilineal descent, *gittin*, they ask? What about the *real* issues that divide us? To this I respond: "I'll deal with my little corner of the world, you deal with yours. If enough of us working at the grassroots level are able to change attitudes and bring people from the polarities together in dialogue and friendship, we will eventually build a foundation for future discussion on the really tough issues. It is far easier to snub institutions than friends; much simpler to dismiss the beliefs and practices of amorphous groups than individuals with whom there has been serious human contact." As the dialogue is enhanced, so too is the desire to grow together, as individuals and as a community, committed to the ideals of pluralism, *derech eretz* and self-pride.

"So this year, let us remember what we share: A love of the history of our people; a responsibility to be a link in the chain of stories that has carried us through generations; a pursuit of learning; and a desire to celebrate the seasonal and life cycles in ways that connect us to our tradition. And above all, we share in the commitment to treat one another with the consciousness that we are all created in the image of the Divine."[6]

PRIDE AND PERCEPTIONS[7]
(Unity Mission Pre-trip Activity[8])

"We were a very disparate bunch. The journeys that had brought us to this place in our lives were varied, as were our conceptions of Judaism, and of our own Jewish identities. Nonetheless, we all

6. Taken from a CLAL message entitled, "This Year Pray For Peace" distributed for the 5761 High Holiday season.

7. Adapted from an exercise developed by Cherie Brown of the National Coalition Building Institute. My gratitude to Wendy Aronson, Hornstein '02 [Hornstein Program in Jewish Communal Service at Brandeis University] and a student intern at the Synagogue Council, for assisting with this exercise.

8. The exercises in this chapter, although designed with particular programs and constituencies in mind, are highly adaptable to other settings—and have been used by the author in a variety of educational modalities.

believed that the work of the laity is essential to any rapprochement between our various movements."

Deborah Bernstein, Unity
Mission Participant

Objective:

To enable individuals to articulate concerns about ways in which they are perceived by the "other" and to crystallize their thinking about what makes them feel good about their particular denominational affiliation.

Time:

1 hour.

Setting the Stage:

This is the only time during the Unity Mission that we break into denominational groups. For some, this may be uncomfortable or untenable, given a reluctance to identify with one specific group, but we believe this is a very useful and important tool in beginning the dialogue process. This activity is only valuable if group members are honest in their answers, and respectful of the opinions that will be voiced.

Instructions:

1. Break the group into three or four smaller groups according to denomination. Each group will meet in separate parts of the room, or separate rooms, where large pieces of newsprint and markers will be set out.
2. Each group chooses a secretary to record the group's thoughts and ideas on the newsprint and someone who feels comfortable presenting the group's ideas to the larger group when we reconvene.
3. The secretary uses two pieces of newsprint to record the group's brainstorming session, one entitled "Perceptions" and the other "Pride." On the Perceptions sheet, each group lists

words or phrases that describe how they feel they are perceived by individuals from the other movements. Since this is a brainstorming session, the groups list all of the ideas that arise, whether they are positive or negative perceptions.

4. On the Pride sheet, the groups respond to the following statement: "The things that make me most proud to be a (Reform, Orthodox, Conservative or Reconstructionist Jew) are . . ."

5. After brainstorming, the groups come together to present their findings to the larger group. If possible, the newsprint should be taped on the wall so that everyone can read the responses while they are presented. The "Perceptions" section is presented first. The facilitator plays a key role in this section. To assist in the discussion, the facilitator should ask group members to further explain or elaborate upon their responses.

Facilitator's Comments:
Do people in the room agree or disagree with a particular perception?
Is there any truth or reality to these perceptions?
How does it feel to learn that some people feel this way about you?
As we are about to embark on our journey, it is important to remember this moment, and the ways in which people are deeply affected by the negative stereotypes others have of them. It is apparent that we have barely touched the surface of a conversation that will continue throughout our time together.

6. Each group then presents their "Pride" section, with little explanation. It is important for the facilitator to emphasize the extent to which people are proud of their denominational affiliations, and to point out that the negative perceptions of one group might be elements of pride for another.

Facilitator's Comments:
The facilitator wraps up the activity on a positive note:
We hope that this exercise was eye opening and has allowed you to express pride in your own movement, while being open to the ideas of the other movements. This synergy is what brings us together, and allows for a successful dialogue process.

You may leave here tonight with lingering thoughts that we hope you will pursue while on the Mission. This exercise was designed to push you to think about your relationship to your particular denominational group, about what you are really proud of and what you think it means to be an active (Reform, Orthodox, Conservative or Reconstructionist) Jew. Hopefully, this activity also highlighted a number of common threads that are shared by all the movements.

STEREOTYPING: A REFLECTION OF OUR SOCIETY?
(Unity Mission Bus Discussion)

"This was an empowering and transforming experience which proved that dialogue is possible. The Mission gave us an opportunity to shed our denominational skins and to relate to each other as fellow Jews. The two days in New York City demonstrated that it is our fundamental Jewishness that counts and not arbitrary labels. We saw that Jews of diverse persuasions can sit together, study together, daven together, share thoughts and aspirations without the expected awkwardness and sense of separateness. As we linked arms in a wide circle—Reform, Conservative, Reconstructionist and Orthodox Jews—singing "Hinei ma tov u mana'im", I felt at that moment, that the walls which divide us can be brought down."

Dr. Ken Tucker, Unity
Mission Participant

Objective:

To consider how widespread and potentially damaging stereotyping can be in our society, and especially within the Jewish community.

Setting the Stage:

I would like to begin today's discussion by discussing "baggage"— not the kind of baggage you take on a trip or vacation, but the kind of baggage we all carry every day of our lives. As we all know, this baggage gets heavier and heavier with the increased stereotypes and generalizations we carry from our childhood throughout our adult lives.

If we are to be truly honest with ourselves, we all have biases, which begin forming at an early age. I hope that, as we participate in today's program, each of us will try very hard to shed some of that baggage and gain new insights and understandings. Ultimately, we may gain greater respect for each other and our respective congregations—not only for the ones we pray in but for the ones we may have never stepped foot in prior to this venture. It isn't easy! We may not always feel comfortable—but I ask you to let go of YOUR BAGGAGE and enjoy the ride!

Time:

1 hour.

Instructions:

1. Utilizing Jackie Mason's videotape, entitled, "Jackie Mason On Broadway" (1998), show approximately 20 minutes of Act IV on Jews and Gentiles. This tape elicits a variety of responses—from laughter to shame to offense—and is a wonderful trigger for discussion on group pride, shame, diversity, self-hate, societal norms, stereotyping, etc. Break the large group into smaller groups, from 3–15 people per group, and encourage discussion of the following key questions:

   Questions for small group discussion
   As a Jew, what kind of feelings does Jackie Mason engender (i.e. pride, embarrassment?)
   What kinds of stereotypes about Jews can you identify with—either from the tape or from your own experience—and how do you feel when someone uses these to describe you, or someone you know?

2. After bringing the large group back together, the facilitator should guide a summary discussion asking how people reacted to the tape and whether there was agreement, or not, within

the smaller groups about the value and/or danger of this kind of humor. There will be strong feelings, and probably some disagreement, about how concerned we should be about stereotyping based on the tape. Let the discussion take its own course, finally asking if anyone found the tape offensive. This should carry the conversation in a direction in which a concern for the "offended" is articulated by many of the participants.

Facilitator's Comments:
It is obvious that we watch Jackie Mason with mixed emotions. Many of us find him hilariously funny and, in certain ways, identify with the man and his humor. For others, there is a sense of discomfort and embarrassment. But, as we all know, there is an element of truth and reality in most stereotypes. And that's where the danger lies. People who have suffered mistreatment or persecution find little humor in the proliferation of ethnic jokes or stereotyping which becomes internalized in our psyche and ingrained in our society (e.g. "JAP" jokes).

3. Pose the following question: Why do we utilize this tape as one of the Mission's educational tools? (Wait for responses.) During the Mission, try to get to know the person behind the label. Try to learn about the "other", getting beyond those pre-conceived notions you may have been harboring for a lifetime. And most importantly, make personal contact with individuals, not institutional representatives. Through these personal contacts the barriers will begin to fade away.

4. Share the following document with the group, emphasizing several of the most salient points.

Guidelines for Respectful Conversation[9]

1. Everyone enters the discussion with dignity and leaves with the same dignity.
2. Everyone is assumed to be well-intentioned and sincere.
3. No one is put down for choices he or she has made.

9. These guidelines are excerpted from an educational piece written by the NCCJ, (National Conference of Christians and Jews, now referred to as the National Conference for Community and Justice) New York, NY.

4. No one is pressured to do or say anything that he or she does not wish.
5. We all work together for a cohesive Jewish community.

Rights, Responsibilities, and Skills of Dialogue

1. Each person has the right to define him/herself without being labeled by others.
2. Each person has the right to express his or her beliefs, ideas and feelings.
3. Each person has the right to ask questions—respectfully—that help him/her understand what someone else has said.
4. Each person must be willing to seriously question his/her assumptions about "the other."
5. Each person must accept the other as equal partners in the dialogue, even (or especially) in times of conflict or disagreement.
6. Each person should learn to *temporarily* set aside his/her own views and feelings in order to be more sensitive to what the other is saying.
7. Each person should learn to deal with different points of view while maintaining his/her own integrity.

"SHABBAT: A PANOPLY OF RELIGIOUS PERSPECTIVES"[10]
(Unity Mission Bus Discussion)

"Experiential learning will trump Briefings anytime and I think this Mission uses that notion to great effect. What better way to get people to confront their preconceived notions than to confront spiritual beauty in unexpected places and unfiltered feelings among their peers."

Alan Leifer, Unity Mission
Participant

10. This exercise was originally developed by Nicole Schuller, Hornstein '00, for students at Boston's New Jewish High School in a first-year internship. As a second year student at the Synagogue Council of Massachusetts, this program was adapted by Nicole for the 2000 Unity Mission.

Objective:

To develop a realization of and appreciation for the scholarship, wisdom and spiritual richness that transcends institutional affiliations.

Time:

30–40 minutes.

Instructions:

1. Make enough copies of the selections (below) on Shabbat and distribute them to the entire group. Ask people to work together in smaller, denominationally diverse groupings, and to determine which statement(s) comes from which movement (Reform, Orthodox, Conservative, Reconstructionist; or *Havurah*). In most cases, the statement is the philosophy of an individual rabbi or scholar who is generally identified with one of these groups, but his/her quotation is not necessarily *the* definitive statement on Shabbat of that group or movement.

    "On Shabbat there is neither anxiety or bad news . . . Jews travel through time in order to enter a perfect world for a day and a night. The goal is to create a reality so complete and absorbing that these time travelers are caught up in its values and renewed. The Shabbat is the foretaste of the messianic redemption."

    "[Shabbat] is a day on which we are called upon to share in what is eternal in time, to turn from the results of creation to the mystery of creation; from the world of creation to the creation of the world . . . The seventh day is a palace in time which we build."

    "[Shabbat is] a sanctity, that through it man should be continually reminded of his appointment by God in God's world to be God's servant and that he should devote himself to that capacity . . . [The Shabbat] thus became the symbol of man's appointment by God; symbol of God's rule and man's destiny."

    "By keeping Shabbat the Jew becomes, as our sages say:

['*domeh l'yotzro*'- like G-d Himself]. He is, like G-d, work's master, not its slave . . . Shabbat is thus a weekly-reoccurring divine protest against slavery and oppression."

"The flickering candles themselves possess a power to transform us because of the *kavvanot* (meanings) that past generations attributed to those candles: for example, the identification of that light with the *Shekhinah* (divine presence) or the experience of receiving a *neshamah yeterah*—an additional soul that enables the Jew to reach greater spiritual heights on Shabbat."

"[Shabbat] gives us the opportunity to begin to let ourselves feel intense love and joy and appreciate that which we are often too busy to notice during the week. We can let our emotions come out, acknowledge them, examine them, know them so intensely that each moment becomes a complete experience."

"If the Jewish home is a miniature sanctuary during the ordinary days of the week, how much more so on Shabbat and festivals. Shabbat and festival dinner hours should be prolonged and should include *zemirot* (table songs), study and discussion, and *Birkat Hamazon*."

2. Bring the group together for a processing of the smaller group discussions. We have found that, even with adults, turning the exercise into a slightly competitive game adds humor and enjoyment to the deliberations. Using one statement at a time, in no particular order, ask how many people thought that the following quote was made by someone from the movement (correct answers may be found below). Did the small groups come to consensus on some of the statements? Does anyone know which philosopher made the statement, and in what text or context?

The Jewish Way, Rabbi Irving Greenberg (ORTHODOX)

The Sabbath, Dr. Abraham Joshua Heschel (CONSERVATIVE)

Horeb, Rabbi Samson Raphael Hirsch (ORTHODOX)

The Sabbath, Dr. Isidor Grunfeld (ORTHODOX)

Exploring Judaism, Rebecca Alpert & Jacob Staub (RECONSTRUCTIONIST)

The Jewish Catalogue, Richard Siegel, Michael & Sharon Strassfeld (HAVURAH)

Gates of Mitzvah, Central Conference of American Rabbis (REFORM)
3. Ask the following question: "Did the group find this exercise interesting? Surprising? Why?"

Facilitator's Comments:
We thought it would be important to explore the richness of our heritage from different religious perspectives and to dispel some common myths. As I hope you've learned from our prior discussions, it may be possible in certain cases to identify *a* philosophy with *a* movement, but attempting to do so universally is tricky, if not harmful, business. Is *Kavvanah* the exclusive purview of *Hasidisim*? Are Shabbat *Zemirot* and *Birkat Hamazon* recited in only Orthodox homes? Are social values such as fighting slavery and oppression found only in the Reform movement? Is it so surprising that reaching spiritual heights by seeing the *Shekhinah* in the light of the Shabbat candles is a Reconstructionist value?

As we are about to meet with some of the scholars and leaders of the major movements within Judaism, I hope you will remember this discussion and acknowledge that ideological platforms, important as they are in defining institutional philosophies, are also fluid. Our approaches to Torah, God and Israel may differ, but at the core of each group's belief system is a commitment to these fundamental principles within Judaism.

REACHING BENEATH THE SURFACE
(Shabbaton Opening Exercise)

Objectives:

To enable Shabbaton attendees to become acquainted, relieve the tension of "newness", set a tone for openness and sharing, and to get to know the human being and committed Jew beneath the façade that might otherwise identify him/her as "liberal", "traditional", "religious", "secular", or *"frum"*—among others.

Time:

20–30 minutes.

Instructions:

1. Before arrival of the attendees, structure the chairs to facilitate dialogue in pairs and that allows for easy movement into new pairs after each question [inner circle facing out, with outer circle facing in; rows of chairs facing each other]. The group leader explains that this exercise is designed to help people get to know one another and begin exploring important questions of identity in a welcoming and safe environment.

2. The facilitator asks people to always share who they are and where they are from, and then to talk together about each of the questions below. When the noise begins to subside, invite people in the inner circle, or rows 1, 3, 5 etc., to move one seat to the right so that everyone will be facing someone new. The facilitator should also, as appropriate, ask people to share with the entire group how they responded to certain compelling questions and encourage discussion around those responses.

   a) What made you decide to come on this weekend? What do you hope to get out of it?

   b) As you reflect on your life up to now, what is the one achievement about which you feel most proud?

   c) Talk to each other about your personal and spiritual journeys. That is, as a Jew, how did you get to where you are today?

   d) If someone walked into your home, would he or she know that you were Jewish? How?

   e) When you were younger, what person or incident most influenced you as a Jew?

   f) What was the most important advice you ever received, and from whom?

   g) As a Jew, what single incident that you've experienced in your own life would you hope that children today would never have to experience? Explain.

   h) What is your favorite Jewish holiday? Why?

VALUES CLARIFICATION EXERCISE
(Shabbaton Group Discussion)

Objective:

To help people from across the denominational spectrum engage in conversation about critical Jewish values and to elucidate which of these values are primary and fundamental, given the variety of backgrounds and opinions within the group.

Time:

45 minutes.

Instructions:

1. Break the large group into several smaller, denominationally diverse groupings. Each individual should be given a packet of cards with one Jewish value (below) typed on each card.
2. First in pairs, and then in the small groups, participants should try to rank the top three Jewish values that they, as individuals, think are most important to them (not what is most important to Jewish survival and continuity). The facilitator should walk around the room, clarifying questions that may arise and generally listening to the conversations.
3. When the groups have completed their work, ask everyone to turn their chairs and face the front. Each group then reports its findings, explaining how they came to consensus (or if consensus was impossible, why) and opening the discussion to the entire audience.

BELIEF IN GOD
SHABBAT OBSERVANCE
HESSED (SOCIAL ACTION)
TORAH STUDY
SUPPORT FOR ISRAEL
KEEPING KOSHER
SYNAGOGUE ATTENDANCE
FAMILY

JEWISH EDUCATION
JEWISH CULTURE (e.g. music, food, dance)

Facilitator's Comments:
The organizers of this weekend felt that a discussion on Jewish values might be a useful and interesting approach for encouraging people to really talk to one another about core values. Although coming to consensus was not our ultimate goal, and may have been difficult in your small group discussions, understanding the positions of other Jews and how devoted they are to those positions is an important way to begin the Shabbaton. Although our approaches to Torah, Jewish Education, God, Social Justice and Israel may differ, we believe that at the core of each individual and group's belief system is a commitment to these fundamental Jewish values.

OUR SPIRITUAL SELVES[11]
(GENESIS Staff Training)

Objectives:

To help the CIEs get "in touch" with their own spirituality, share their views and concerns with one another, and consider the ultimate relationship between one's personal spirituality and his or her communal responsibility as a Jewish educator and "spiritual role model".

Time:

1 hour.

Instructions:

1. In pairs, discuss the following questions about spirituality and your relationship with God. One person serves as interviewer while the other responds, and then switch roles.

11. Special thanks to Simon Klarfeld, Hornstein '94 and Director of Genesis, for his help in creating this exercise.

a) What does "spiritual" mean to you?
b) How has your image of God evolved during your life?
c) How does your current image/belief of God propel you to live, interact with others, and treat yourself?

2. Share what you heard from your partner, trying to accurately introduce his/her spiritual self to the group. Does the interviewee want to add to, or correct anything that was said?

3. Using the following questions, the group leader should facilitate a discussion on the relationship between one's individual beliefs and his or her role as a Jewish educator or communal professional:

a) To what extent does your image of, and relationship to God impact on who you are as an educator/Jewish professional?
b) If you don't believe in God, or are fuzzy about your beliefs, is it possible to be effective in your work in Jewish settings? What does it mean to be a "spiritual role model", and are you comfortable with that role—in general—and at Genesis in particular?
c) How is your image of God reflected in your observance of mitzvot, and how does this impact on your role as a Jewish educator/communal professional?

Facilitator's Comments:

Based on your comments, and the wonderful sharing of personal thoughts and sometimes gut-wrenching concerns, it is evident that each of us is on a spiritual journey. The very fact of being on a journey implies that we are somewhere "along the way"—in a not-so-comfortable abyss between where we think we are, and would like to be. I think this struggle is great. In fact, if we were not struggling with our relationship to God, our definition of spirituality, and our role as "spiritual role model", could we be possibly be "spiritual role models"?

Perhaps we can be most supportive and helpful to the kids by *not* having—or pretending to have—all the answers, but by engaging, *with them*, in asking the right questions. And, perhaps, spirituality will be found in the struggle itself, and in those transcendent moments of helping others, or *davening*, or simply swaying together to the sounds of our own voices.

The other thing I hope you derived from this exercise is the power of experiential education in helping people get to, and articulate some of their deepest thoughts and concerns. How did it feel being interviewed by your partner? What was it like being the interviewer? Share your thoughts with the group regarding how it felt listening to your partner express—on your behalf—some of your innermost feelings about God and spirituality. It would be beneficial to utilize the variety of informal educational strategies and exercises you've experienced this week in your work here at Genesis, and in your future work in the Jewish community.

POST-GENESIS EXERCISE ON "OUR SPIRITUAL SELVES" (GENESIS Staff Training)

Instructions:

1. At the end of the month, the group leader facilitates essentially the same exercise as during the orientation session, with a few changes in the sharing questions.
   a) After Genesis, what does "spiritual" mean to you, and how did you experience spirituality during the program?
   b) How did you support students' individual or group quests for spirituality? Were there any moments you can share in which you guided an individual/group's search for God, and how did it feel taking on the role of "spiritual mentor"?

Facilitator's Comments:
Now that the month is over, it will be interesting to discover how your relationship with God and spirituality changed as a result of the Genesis experience, if at all, and how your own spirituality affected those around you. In pairs, discuss the following questions about spirituality, your relationship with God, and the impact Genesis may have had on your thinking. One person serves as interviewer while the other responds, and then switch roles.

2. Share what you heard from your partner, trying to accurately introduce his/her spiritual self to the group. Does the inter-

viewee want to add to, or correct anything that was said? The facilitator takes a passive role, allowing the flow of thoughts and feelings to speak for themselves.

"THESE AND THOSE ARE THE WORDS
OF THE LIVING GOD"
(General Education Program)

Objective:

To engage a group, not necessarily predisposed to supporting pluralistic causes, in text study and interactive conversation about the values, principles and practicalities of religious pluralism

Time:

1 hour.

> *Facilitator's Comments:*
> For the benefit of everyone involved, I would like to establish some guidelines for our time together: (a) I'm not going to talk *at* you the entire time, but rather, would hope to engage us all in interactive and collaborative discussion; (b) Today's topic is confined to the American scene, although we are obviously affected by what goes on in Israel; (c) There is bound to be some disagreement amongst us, which is great, but I hope it will be approached in a spirit of respect and personal growth; and (d) During the next hour or so, we will be involved in several components of learning—small group text study, a discussion about the *principles* of religious pluralism, and reviewing a case study to help us understand the *practicalities* of religious pluralism.

Instructions:

1. **Text Study:** Distribute enough copies of "*Hevruta* Discussion on *Elu V'Elu*" (below) so that at least every other person has a copy. The facilitator should explain that we will be taking about 15–20 minutes in small group, *hevruta* study to put into

context how our tradition helps us deal with differing points of view on issues that affect the Jewish people. The facilitator either reads the selection aloud, or asks for a volunteer, and instructs everyone to break into groups of two or more people. Read the selection over again in your small groups and then discuss the two questions at the bottom of the page.

HEVRUTA DISCUSSION ON "ELU V'ELU"
CHAPTER ONE   ERUVIN

אָמַר רַבִּי אַבָּא אָמַר שְׁמוּאֵל – **R' Abba said in the name of Shmuel:** שָׁלֹשׁ שָׁנִים נֶחְלְקוּ בֵּית שַׁמַּאי וּבֵית הַלֵּל – **For three years, Beis Shammai and Beis Hillel debated each other.** הַלָּלוּ אוֹמְרִים הֲלָכָה כְּמוֹתֵנוּ – **These said that the halachah follows their view,** וְהַלָּלוּ אוֹמְרִים הֲלָכָה כְּמוֹתֵנוּ – **and these said that the halachah follows their view.** I.e. each side insisted that its own view was correct. יָצְאָה בַּת קוֹל וְאָמְרָה – **A heavenly voice went forth and declared:** אֵלּוּ וְאֵלּוּ דִּבְרֵי אֱלֹהִים חַיִּים הֵן – **These and those,** i.e. both views, **are the words of the living God,**[13] וַהֲלָכָה כְּבֵית הַלֵּל – **but the halachah in practice follows Beis Hillel.**

For discussion:
If a heavenly voice declared that both views "are the words of the living God", why do we follow the *halacha* of Beit Hillel?
Is it possible to have two equally valid and legitimate views on questions of Jewish law? If so, how is this reconciled in modern American Jewish life?

2. **Large Group Discussion:** When the room starts getting quiet, reconvene the entire group, asking for responses to the following questions. The facilitator, using a portable microphone, moves up and down the center aisle repeating people's responses and generally guiding the conversation along.
   a) Can there be two equally valid and legitimate views on questions of Jewish law?
   b) Why do we follow the *halacha* of *Beit Hillel*?

Facilitator's Comments:
In the *Mishna* that immediately precedes the *Hillel/Shammai* discussion, there is an argument about the ritual purity of an

obscure animal or reptile known as a *sheretz*, including conflicting views in the *Gemara* about its status and how purity is
defined. It seems pretty clear to me that the passage we've just
studied is placed *directly* after that argumentative discussion as
a response, not only to the thorny question of the purity of a
sheretz, but as a guide for all times and circumstances, providing a formula for dealing with *halachic* conflict. *Hillel* and
Shammai were friendly and collegial, although they seemed to
disagree on nearly every issue. But their disagreements were
L'shem Shamayim (for the sake of Heaven), their followers
engaged in earnest argument, and they never separated into
two distinct communities. Most importantly, the children of
the house of *Shammai* were able to marry the children of the
house of *Hillel*—despite their occasionally bitter differences.

What is perhaps most instructive for our time is that the
Gemara tells us that the *halacha* is fixed according to *Beit Hillel*
because they were "easy and forbearing and they would study
their opinion *and* the opinion of *Beit Shammai*." And not only
that, the *Gemara* continues, but they (the house of Hillel)
would mention the matters of *Beit Shammai* before their own."
I would submit to you that Hillel's humility ultimately caused
his viewpoint to prevail.

3. **Principles of Religious Pluralism:** Using the "Seven Principles
   of Religious Pluralism", in the opening section of this chapter,
   the group leader should read the most important points aloud,
   encouraging limited discussion so there will be ample time for
   the case study.

4. **Practicalities of Religious Pluralism—A Case Study:** In order
   for this discussion to be most effective, it is suggested that the
   facilitator use a case study from within his or her own community. The study must show the principles of religious pluralism
   in action, honestly sharing some of the challenges that Jewish
   leaders face when they listen to varied and diverse points of
   view while attempting to strengthen community. In our program, I used the concept of a community *mikveh* as the basis
   for open and animated discussion.

5. **Community *Mikveh* as Paradigm:** I introduced the case study
   as follows. In the Newton area, and in our neighboring sub-

urbs, there is a growing need—especially among the non-Orthodox—for a *mikveh* that has easy and equal access. A small exploratory committee of rabbis and key community leaders from across the denominational spectrum has been meeting for approximately six months to consider the feasibility of establishing a new *mikveh* in the western suburbs. I would like to use this process as a case study for our conversation on the practicalities of religious pluralism.

Principles of Common Purpose[12]

Halacha (Jewish law)—Commitment to *halachic* standards for building and maintaining the *mikveh*.

Tzniyut (modesty)—Privacy, propriety and confidentiality for all users with separate use by men and women.

Ahavat Yisrael (love for all Jews)—Respect for, and sensitivity toward individual Jews and their practices regardless of Jewish affiliation.

K'lal Yisrael (the totality of Israel)—Shared ownership of the *mikveh* by a cross-communal board, respecting the authority of rabbis and their congregants using the *mikveh* for conversion and personal use.

Chinuch (education)—Educational opportunities for students and adults.

Hiddur Mitzvah (beautifying the occasion)—Creating an aesthetic setting for ritual observances.

Petichut (openness)— Accessible hours including evenings, weekends, and daytime.

6. After explaining the guiding principles of the *mikveh*, as well as the many details, difficulties and sensibilities involved with its creation, the group leader facilitates a discussion with the entire group around the values and challenges of working in a pluralistic communal environment.

Facilitator's Comments:

As I think you can clearly see, the creation of a *mikveh* under one denomination's auspices (usually Orthodox, though in recent years within Conservative and Reform settings) is a

---

12. Created by Rabbi Barbara Penzner, one of the founders of *Mayyim Hayyim*, as an overriding philosophy for a communal *mikveh*.

much easier strategy for simply "getting the job done". But we are committed to the enterprise of *K'lal Yisrael* and the notion that communal institutions, to the extent possible, should be open and accessible to the totality of the Jewish people. We should remember that the question of a communal *mikveh* has been presented today as a case study . . . to help us look at the bigger picture of religious pluralism.

QUOTES

It was in the synagogue that Jews were able to keep alive the three things on which their existence depended, *torah* or Jewish study, *avodah* or Jewish worship, and *gemilut chasadim*, acts of social welfare. It was their school, their miniature Temple and their social center.

Chief Rabbi Jonathan Sacks

The story of modern Jewry is the fragmentation of a once coherent people into contending sects.

Chief Rabbi Jonathan Sacks

Judaism is not a religion of the lonely man or woman of faith. It is a covenant which calls into being a community of faith.

Chief Rabbi Jonathan Sacks

Judaism sees the person within a network of relationships, as part of a family, a community and a society. It is society as such that must be sanctified if the individual is to find God in the daily life of the world He created and pronounced good.

Chief Rabbi Jonathan Sacks

This is what the Holy One blessed be God said to Israel,
My children, have I deprived you in any way?
What do I want from you?
I only ask that you should love each other,
and treat each other with dignity,
and stand in awe of each other.

Midrash, Seder Eliahu Rabbah 26

Are we not formed, as notes of music are, for one another, though dissimilar?

> Percy Bysshe Shelley (1792–1822)

I do not want my house to be walled in on all sides and my windows to be stifled. I want all the cultures of all lands to be blown about my house as freely as possible. But I refuse to be blown off my feet by any.

> Mohandas K. Gandhi (1869–1948)

One glorious chain of love unites us all.

> Rashi Chanukah Tamhui 5759

Nothing Jewish is alien to me.

> Franz Rosenzweig (1886–1929)

Do not separate yourself from the community.

> *Pirkei Avot*, Rabbi Tzadok 4:7

All Jews are responsible for one another.

> *Babylonian Talmud*, Shevu'ot 39a

All Jews are relatives and friends.

> *Midrash Tanhuma*, Neso 1

Those who work to fulfill the needs of the community are as if engaged with Torah.

> *Talmud Yerushalmi*, Berakhot

We are not independent, but interdependent.

> Buddha (565–483 B.C.E.)

One should always associate oneself with the congregation.

> Rabbi Abaye, *Talmud Mas.*,
> Berakhot 30a

Let respect for the congregation be always upon thee; for behold, the Kohanim had their faces towards the people and their backs towards the Shekhinah.

> Rabbi Isaac, *Talmud Mas.*, Soteh 40a

RESOURCES ON PLURALISM AND DIVERSITY

Brown, Cherie R. *The Art of Coalition Building: A Guide for Community Leaders.* Published by the American Jewish Committee, 1984.

Cohen, Steven M. "The One in 2000 Controversy", *Moment Magazine*, March, 1987.

"E Pluribus Judaism", special issue on Jewish Diversity, *Hadassah Magazine*, March, 1998.

Elcott, David M. "The Four Denominations", *Perspectives*, published by CLAL, April, 1986.

Eron, Lewis John. *"The Four Major Religious Movements in Contemporary American Jewish Life"*, prepared for the 1988 CLAL Critical Issues Conference, April 28, 1988.

Fetterman, Towvim & Shevitz. *"Challenge & Response: Varieties of Jewish Religion in America"*, published by Boston's Bureau of Jewish Education, 1982.

Friedman, Samuel. *Jew vs. Jew: the Struggle for the Soul of American Jewry*, 2000.

Gillman, Neil. "Four Basic Religious Issues that Divide Us", *Moment Magazine*, 1988.

Greenberg, Irving. "Will There be one Jewish People in the Year 2000?", *Moment Magazine*, June, 1985.

Greenberg, Irving. "The One in 2000 Controversy", *Moment Magazine*, March, 1987.

"Is American Jewry Unraveling?" *Reform Judaism*, Summer, 1995.

"Jewish Moderate Urges Believers to Take Stand", *New York Times*, March 24, 1988.

Librach, Clifford E. "Reform Judaism: A Call to the Center", *Sh'ma*, April 28, 1995.

Lubarsky, Sandra B. *Tolerance and Transformation: Jewish Approaches to Religious Pluralism*, Hebrew Union College Press, 1990.

"Modern Orthodox Rabbis Claim Assault from RCA Right Wing", *The Jewish Week*, July 13, 1990.

Rosenblatt, Gary. "Judaism's Civil War: How Deep is the Rift?", *Baltimore Jewish Times*, January 29, 1988.

Siegel, Danny. *Family Reunion: Making Peace in the Jewish Community*, Town House Press, Spring Valley, NY, 1989.

"To Be One People" (a dialogue between Rabbis Gottschalk, Lamm & Schorsch), *The Jerusalem Post*, May 18, 1991.

Twersky, Aaron. "Open Letter to Dr. Norman Lamm", *The Jewish Observer*, April, 1988.

Wertheimer, Jack. *A People Divided: Judaism in Contemporary America*, Basic Books, A Division of Harper Collins, Inc., 1993.

"Who Is a Jew?", CLAL special issue in conjunction with the *Long Island Jewish World*, 1984.

13

JEWISH IDENTITY

"What does it mean to be a Jew?" Every Jew has a unique identity and life history that have been shaped by things Jewish, to a greater or lesser extent. One's memories, beliefs, values, attitudes and lifestyle are affected. An important aspect of identity, particularly in the context of informal Jewish education, is the relationship between a person's Jewish identity and his/her other identities. How influential is being Jewish compared to other sources of identity? Is the person proud of being Jewish? Is the person comfortable with the distinctiveness of being Jewish?

The activities in this chapter will help participants understand their identities as Jews. Through discussion, debate, role-playing, and shared experience, each person is called upon to clarify what being Jewish means to him/her and to become aware of how other Jews define themselves. There are no right or wrong here; the aim is to become aware of aspects of oneself that are often taken for granted. As Rabbi Hillel admonished us, "If I am not for myself, who will be for me? If I am only for myself, what am I? And if not now, when?"

JEWISH IDENTITY BINGO

Purpose:

To learn about the Jewish identities of group participants; to become comfortable with differences and similarities.

Group:

Elementary school through college age and older. Can accommodate groups of 10 to over 100. The discussion portion should be held with groups no larger than 50.

376

Setting:

Open space in which participants can move about and a clean, comfortable floor where group can reconvene.

Materials:

Bingo sheets consisting of a grid of boxes with statements that describe an affiliation, practice, experience or belief, such as "I have been to the Western Wall," "My family lights candles on Friday night." (See attached sample for elementary school children.) Pencils.

Time:

30 minutes (5 min. introduction, 15 min. for filling in Bingo sheets, 10 min. for discussion).

Instructions:

1. Leader distributes a Bingo sheet and pencil to each participant. Participants are instructed to attempt to fill in the entire sheet by asking questions of the others and finding people who can say "yes" to statements on the sheet. Leader notes that some individuals will find that many statements apply to them, while others will find that none apply. That is fine—each member of the group has a different identity and each identity is accepted.
2. Participants mingle, asking relevant questions about the Jewish identity of other participants to complete their sheets. For example, "Have you been to Israel?"; or "How do you observe Shabbat?" If the answer to the question is represented by a box that has not been filled in yet, the fellow participant should initial the box.
3. When at least one individual has filled every box with initials, the group reconvenes for a discussion. For each statement, the group reveals, by a show of hands, how many people found a representative for each statement. Take note of what that indicates about the importance and prevalence of that characteristic within the group. After all statements have been discussed, summarize the experience of participating in the activity: How did it feel to share your Jewish experiences with the other group

members? What statements would you have added to the game? For group members who could not sign any box, how did they feel; what statements would they make to characterize their identity?

Variation:

A. GROUPS FROM BINGO BOXES. After the group has reconvened, form a subgroup of all participants for whom a particular statement is true. The subgroup makes a presentation of what that aspect of their identity means to them.

Note to Leader:

Content of this activity can be changed to suit various programmatic needs. For instance, statements on the Bingo sheet could be focused on a single topic relevant to the overall program, such as Jewish ritual practices. The activity can be adapted for different age groups by changing the seriousness and complexity of statements. Length of time required for the activity can be shortened by specifying that participants need to fill in just a line of boxes (across, down or diagonal) rather than filling in the whole Bingo sheet.

JEWISH IDENTITY BINGO
(sample sheet for elementary school children)

I can read Hebrew.	I enjoy learning about Jewish history.	I often get together with my relatives.	I believe in God.
I feel proud when I learn that a famous person is Jewish.	I have made hamentashen.	Passover is my favorite holiday.	I know who Abraham was.
I have been to Israel.	My family lights candles on Friday night.	Most of my friends are Jewish.	People in my school know I'm Jewish.
I like to eat bagels.	I admire my rabbi.	Hanukkah is my favorite holiday.	I have given money to charity.

(Submitted by Allison D. Halpern)

OBJECTS OF JEWISH IDENTITY

Purpose:

To help a group of people become acquainted and express something about their Jewish identity. To reach this goal, individuals will express the significance of particular Jewish objects and religious articles for their own Jewish identity.

Group:

Teenagers and older; between 10 and 20 participants.

Setting:

A room set up with a circle of chairs and a low table in the center of the circle for holding the Jewish objects. The table should be low so that it does not block the vision of the individuals sitting in the circle.

Time:

15–25 minutes. Allow five minutes for preliminaries plus one minute per participant.

Materials:

Objects that have a strong association with being Jewish. Suggested items include: tallit, tefillin, prayer book, mezuzah, kiddush cup, shabbat candles, challah cover, havdalah candle, spice box, matzoh, menorah, dreidel, tzedakah box, Jewish cookbook, wig, black hat, shroud, map of Israel, Israeli flag, picture of the Western Wall, book about the Holocaust. There should be as many objects as there are participants.

Instructions:

1. The group leader asks each participant to take a Jewish object. After each person, including the leader, has selected an object,

the leader asks the participants to think about what the object means for their Jewish identity, whether it be positive or negative. Each person states his/her name and presents the Jewish object and what it means for their Jewish identity.

2. The group leader goes first to illustrate. For example, if the leader selected the Israeli flag he/she might say: "To me, this flag represents a homeland for all Jews throughout the world. When I see this flag I think about the struggle the Jewish people have gone through in establishing the State of Israel and the innocent lives that have been lost in the process. This flag also makes me think about the Law of Return which states that all Jews have the right to immigrate to Israel. Knowing that I have a homeland that I can always go to gives me a great sense of safety. When I see this flag I feel a deep sense of pride and connection to my Jewish heritage. My Jewish identity is deeply connected to Israel."

3. When everyone has introduced themselves and their object, the leader concludes with a brief summary of patterns seen in the nature of Jewish identity of the group.

(Submitted by Melissa Braverman and Sharon Janowitz)

A JEWISH SOUND SHOW

Purpose:

To arouse Jewish cognitive or emotional responses through the sense of hearing. Using selective musical pieces or other recorded sounds, the object is to stimulate new insights and expand Jewish consciousness.

Group:

Junior high school and older; up to 50 people; conducted in smaller units.

Setting:

Three adjacent rooms of small size and reasonably good acoustics.

Materials:

Three cassette or CD players plus selected cassettes and/or CDs (see suggestions below) placed in each room; paper and pencil for each participant.

Time:

50–60 minutes.

Instructions:

1. In preparation for the activity, the leader prepares three sound presentations on CD or tape. Each presentation should run about 8 minutes and should have a theme. Examples include: (a) Yiddish Sounds—poems or songs; (b) Israeli Sounds—songs of Naomi Shemer, such as "Jerusalem of Gold" and "Machar" (Tomorrow) or "Mayim" (Water); (c) Sounds of Alienation—speech of Adolf Hitler, church bells, Christmas carol; (d) Jewish Religious Sounds—cantorial selections, chanting of the Four Questions at Passover, the Kaddish, blowing the shofar. Three of these recorded presentations are to be set up in three rooms and are ready to play. One person in each of the three groups should be prepared to run the stereo equipment.

2. The group is divided into approximately three equal groups. The leader explains that they will be listening to a series of CDs and/or tapes in three different rooms. They are asked to listen carefully to what is played and to remain silent throughout the time they are listening to the sound presentations and until the leader instructs otherwise. They will remain in each room for about eight minutes. After they have been to each of the rooms, they return to the original room. Before they depart, the leader explains the location of the three rooms and the sequence in which the three groups will visit them. The plan is for one

group to be in a room at a time. Prior to moving to their first room, the leader again reminds the people not to speak but rather to listen carefully to the CDs/cassettes and let the sounds fully envelop them.

3. After the participants have heard the three sound presentations and are reassembled in the original room, the leader asks them to continue to remain silent, so as to savor the sounds they have just heard. Then the leader gives each person a piece of paper and a pencil, and asks them to write down the thoughts and emotions they associated with each of the three sound presentations.

4. Now the participants speak, sharing their associations and reactions to the sounds they have heard. Did the medium of sound bring forth any new aspects of Jewish awareness or any insights about one's Jewishness?

Variation:

LISTEN! A simplified version of this activity is to conduct the activity in one large group (up to 25 individuals) and remain in one room instead of going from room to room. The participants are each given a sheet of paper and a pencil and asked to note their thoughts or emotions as they listen, without speaking, to the recorded sounds. When the CD or tape is completed, the participants discuss their reactions.

BAROMETER

Purpose:

To clarify Jewish values and beliefs and to explore the range of views and identifications within the Jewish community.

Group:

Elementary school age through young adult; conducted in groups of 15–20; several groups can meet simultaneously.

Setting:

An open room with a noncarpeted floor on which a paper "barometer" can be taped.

Materials:

Masking tape, newsprint, magic markers, and straight chairs.

Time:

1 hour.

Instructions:

1. Using masking tape, the leader creates a long "barometer" on the floor. This is easily done by placing the tape in one long line along the entire length of the room. Divide the tape into equal sections by placing strips of masking tape perpendicular to the main line. Number the gradations in intervals of 10, from -50 through 0, and then up to +50. Place as many chairs as are needed around the barometer, leaving enough room for people to move on the barometer.
2. Ask two-thirds of the group to stand on the barometer; the rest of the group should remain seated and observe the proceedings. The leader should explain that he/she will say a word or a phrase. The people on the barometer should express their reaction to the word or phrase by moving to a position they select along the barometer: a -50 position indicates a very negative feeling to the word; 0 indicates a neutral feeling; +50 demonstrates a very positive feeling.
3. The observers should be instructed to be attentive to the choices of those on the barometer. Are there any words that produce a polarized response? Are certain people making similar choices? Are there evidences of inconsistencies in choices? Are there categories of words people respond to in similar ways? What patterns of response seem to emerge?

4. Words or phrases should be used which relate to a theme (e.g., Jews and non-Jews, Israel, Jewish observances, etc.) Examples of words within the theme of Jewish observances might include: Kashrut, Chinese food, lighting Shabbat candles, prayer, shopping on Saturday, God, *birkat ha-mazon*, wearing tzitzit, putting on tefillin, sin, having a Christmas tree, giving Chanukah gelt, etc. After the leader has called out all the phrases in a unit, the group of observers is asked to comment on any patterns they noted among those moving to the positions on the barometer. This can be followed by a full discussion involving the entire group.

5. At least three themes should be used so that everyone has a chance to be on the barometer and also to function as an observer. In the summary discussion, the leader should focus on the expressions of diversity within the group. What is the basis of the differences? What are the implications of these differences for developing and sustaining a sense of Jewish community? Is there an underlying ideological basis to the choices people made?

(Submitted by Alan Teperow)

JEWS AS CHOSEN

Purpose:

To encourage participants to consider the meaning of the concept of the Jews as the Chosen People and to provide a forum for participants to express a personal response. This is a concept that is often misunderstood or taken for granted.

Group:

Teens and up.

Setting:

A room comfortable for a group discussion.

Time:

30 minutes to 1 hour.

Instructions:

1. The leader begins by introducing the concept of the Jews as the Chosen People. Key aspects of this central tenet of Judaism are as follows. God has singled out Jews to represent divine teachings in their individual behavior, families and communities; Jews should be a principled and disciplined people whose lives are focused on their sacred mission; and they should be conscious that this special relationship with God has both benefits and obligations.
2. There follows a discussion of this concept. Each participant is urged to express his/her opinion. Participants should respond to the following questions:
a) In your opinion what is meant by "the Chosen People"?
b) Is it a concept you take seriously? What do you find appealing or unappealing about it?
c) Is it more beneficial or more harmful to the Jewish people as a whole?
d) How do you perceive Jews who take the Chosen People notion seriously and who act accordingly?
e) Are you ever aware of being "chosen" as you conduct your daily life? Can you give examples of choices you made that were influenced by thinking of yourself as "chosen"?
f) Have you ever felt life would be easier for you, or the Jews, if the Jews had not been chosen?
3. After each person has spoken, the floor is opened for general discussion.

FOUR CHOICES

Purpose:

Four Choices is one of the first Jewish experiential activities that the author helped design, and it has become one of the most widely used. It is an ideal activity for aiding people to clarify their ideas about a range of issues in Jewish life. Because of the physical movement involved, the shifting clusters which form, and the active participation called for, this is also a good activity for setting an appropriate tone early in an experiential program.

Group:

Junior high school and older; 15 to 50 people (to allow for representation of the four positions while assuring full participation in the subgroups.)

Setting:

An open room with movable chairs and walls on which signs can be posted. Also, it is preferable that the room not be too large, so that if the four subgroups are seated in the four corners of the room, they can talk to the other corners without having to shout.

Materials:

Each Four Choices set requires five signs: one sign that defines the issue or question, and four other signs, each of which is a potential response. These sets of signs should be prepared in advance on sheets of paper approximately 15" × 30". Suitable adhesive is needed to post signs on the wall.

Examples of Four Choices sets pertinent to Jewish identity:
"I am a . . ." — Jew; American; human being; man/woman.
"I observe Jewish holidays . . ." — for warmth and nostalgia; because they are prescribed by the Torah; because they help my children know they are Jewish; because others expect me to.
"For me, being Jewish means" — working on behalf of the Jewish community; observing Jewish law and rituals; being ethical in my relations with others; working to improve the lot of the disadvantaged.

Time:

Each set of a Four Choices activity requires 20–30 minutes. At any one time a maximum of three sets would be appropriate or a maximum of 1½ hours.

Instructions:

1. In advance of the activity, the leader chooses an issue to explore and determines the four choices. The "Four Choices" format is suited to a vast range of issues. Each of the four choices should be unambiguous and clearly different from the others. Together, the set should cover the spectrum of opinion on the topic.

2. The leader posts in front of the room the sign that indicates the issue being explored (e.g., attitudes to Israel, views about God, etc.). He/she then posts, in the four corners of the room, the four signs that offer alternative responses to that issue. Participants are asked to think about the Four Choices, pick the one that most closely approximates their thinking, and physically move to that corner of the room.

3. In the four corners the participants are instructed to discuss why they chose that particular response. After 5 or 10 minutes, the leader opens up the discussion across groups. If the subsequent discussion convinces anyone of the merits of one of the positions other than his/her first choice, that participant should switch corners.

4. The leader concludes the activity by summarizing the points made in the discussion.

Variations:

A. GRANDPARENTS AND CHILDREN. After the participants have discussed their personal choices in a particular set, ask them to respond to the choices their grandparents might have made. Follow the same procedure, with participants explaining the choices on behalf of their grandparents. Then, put the same Four Choices before them, with the request that they respond as their children or grandchildren might respond a generation hence. Following these two variations, the group explores differences in response across the generations and the bases for these.

B. FOUR CHOICES IN PICTURES. Instead of posting four signs for a particular category, the leader, in advance, prepares four pictures or collages to represent the alternatives. For example, for the category, "What I think is most vital to sustain Jewish life in America is . . . ," pictures would be put together to depict: (1) the Holocaust; (2) Jewish family and religious life; (3) local Jewish community activities; and (4) Israel. These pictures are posted in the four corners, and the activity proceeds as in the regular manner.

Notes to the Leader:

1. The requirement for moving to one of the four corners immediately obliges each individual in the group to get involved in the subject. If the person does nothing else, he/she has, at least, had to think about the subject and decide his/her preference among the four alternatives. The subsequent discussions, both within the smaller group and then across the four groups, challenge the individual to think further about the basis of his/her decision. Introducing the possibility of changing corners following the across-group discussion adds an incentive for the groups to present their positions coherently and convincingly, and also opens people up to changing their initial ideas based on new information. This becomes an ideal example of peer learning.

2. The critical discipline required of the leader of Four Choices is to avoid favoring one of the positions. If in any way the leader communicates the idea that one position is "right," it jeopardizes the dynamic that makes Four Choices an exciting educational vehicle. The participants should sense that they are shaping their own and other people's views from among several valid alternatives. This is not to foreclose a role for the leader in expressing points of view; in fact, the leader's role is quite important. But it should be consistent with two key considerations: (1) comments should be expressed in non-subjective terms; and (2) comments should be directed at ensuring that any pertinent view, not otherwise articulated, gets into the arena of ideas.

3. That no sense of closure is felt at the conclusion of any particular Four Choice discussion is in itself an issue worthy of being pursued further. This points up the diversity of beliefs and opinions that exist among Jews. By interpreting this diversity

as both a strength and a potential weakness with respect to Jewish continuity, the leader helps the group deal with their differences in a constructive manner.

4. Inevitably, in the course of the activity someone in the group will tell the leader that he/she doesn't like any of the choices. The leader can respond in one of two ways: (1) a reminder that life is full of imperfect options and one needs to make choices among less than ideal alternatives; (2) permitting participants to take a position in the middle of the room, forsaking the posted Four Choices, but only if they are willing to present their own alternative.

5. The leader should count and record the number of participants choosing each corner. Not only is this of interest in comparing responses of various groups, but it starts a data bank which the leader can use for future comparisons across groups and over time.

THE THREE CHILDREN

Purpose:

To address what defines a "good Jew". You may have heard the comments: "Yes, he is a member of the synagogue but look at the way he runs his business!"; or, "I don't have to go to synagogue to be a good Jew. What's important is my sense of ethics." The story of the "Three Children" is a program technique that is an exciting way for the group to become involved in trying to find an answer.

Group:

Up to 50. Groups larger than 25 should be broken into two after the characters make their presentations. Discussions should be held separately. The two groups should come together again only at the end to compare their findings.

Setting:

A large room with comfortable seating.

Time:

At least 1 hour.

Materials:

Documents used in the role play (see below.) Depending on the creative abilities of the group and the time available for planning, this program can be developed to a full-scale dramatic presentation using costumes and lighting, without much preparation. The group may decide to follow up by inviting a local rabbi or teacher to present to the group their views on what is a good Jew.

Instructions:

1. The leader informs the group that this activity is a performance of the reading of the will of the late "Selma Cohen". Presentations will be made by her three sons to determine who Mrs. Cohen would have considered worthy of her inheritance in living as a "good Jew". The leader may post, in advance, the "Invitation to the Reading of the Will" or distribute it to group members at this point.
2. The leader should assign the roles of the sons to three group members prior to the start of the session. Each should be given their written biographical background information to read prior to the role play. They will sit at the front of the room. The leader should act as the attorney and the discussion leader. The meeting should begin with no introduction or explanation. The leader should begin immediately in the role of the attorney and read the statement about the will.
3. After the reading of the will, three members assigned to play the roles of the sons should each be called upon by the attorney to speak for a couple of minutes to justify their claims to the money. The audience is then asked to vote on their first impressions of which child is the best Jew.

4. The attorney then throws the discussion open to the floor: this can take the form of group discussion, or direct questions and cross-examination of the three children. To prevent confusion it is best to interview the three children one at a time. No more than thirty minutes should be allowed for this part of the proceedings; then, a vote should be taken and the decision announced to the audience.

Note to Leader:

Remember that each group must determine for itself which child shall be eligible for the bequest. Before voting, remind the group that there is the possibility of rejecting all three children and dividing the estate among various philanthropies.

INVITATION TO THE READING OF THE WILL

YOU ARE ASKED TO ATTEND
THE READING OF THE WILL
of the late
SELMA COHEN

which will take place at _____ on _____

BECAUSE of a strange request which appears in this Will; and

BECAUSE implementation of this Bequest is only possible with the earnest assistance and considered judgement of a selected group of citizens, including yourself,

The Community's Leading ATTORNEY will read the Will in the presence of

THE THREE CHILDREN of the deceased.

ANNOUNCEMENT BY ATTORNEY

"I have an unusual document in my hand. It is the last Will and Testament of the late Selma Cohen. Now, Mrs. Cohen is a completely fictitious character, but you are asked to pretend that she was a leading Jew in our community, who died only one week ago. I am her attorney and it is my duty, in the presence of her three children, to read you her Will.

THE LAST WILL AND TESTAMENT OF THE LATE SELMA COHEN

This will is made by Selma Cohen of Miami, Florida. I wish that my entire belongings shall be given to whichever of my children be deemed to be the best Jew. My attorney shall select a committee of representative Jews to make this determination. If this committee decides that none of my children is worthy to be called a good Jew, or if the committee cannot agree on a selection, my belongings are to be divided equally among the following charities . . .

This much of the will is relevant. You have been selected as the committee to make the required decision. I hope that you will pay close attention as the basic facts are presented to you by the three children—David, Aaron and Joshua Cohen."

Background of DAVID COHEN

David Cohen, the oldest child, is also the wealthiest. He is the chief executive of an automobile plant. He is married and has three children. David Cohen is an observant Jew. He is a member of the synagogue and has been for a decade its most generous single contributor, as well as donating to Jewish charities. David Cohen always attends Friday evening services, even when he is travelling in other parts of the country on business. In addition, Shabbat and Jewish holidays are observed in the home. All the children attend Hebrew school.

Apart from faithful attendance every Shabbat, David does not participate personally in other phases of the synagogue's activities or the work of other organizations in the community, except for free legal advice to members of the community; this is his particular interest. When asked to serve on committees of the synagogue or other groups, he replies, "I'm sorry, my business and Legal Aid work take all my time. I don't have time to give. There are many who have the time. You know that I give generously to all worthy causes in the community. That's all I can do."

David recently became a controversial figure when he refused to make any safety improvements at the plant following an accident that killed three workers. David issued the following statement: "The demands of providing the lowest cost product possible have unfortunately made it unrealistic to make changes in our plant's operations."

Background of DR. AARON COHEN

Dr. Aaron Cohen, the second child, is an atheist. An intellectual and a scholar, Aaron teaches philosophy at a university. He has contempt for his older brother's religious views, which he terms "blind religious conformity."

When Aaron was a young boy, approaching Bar Mitzvah, his best friend was struck by a hit-and-run driver. Aaron prayed for his best friend to recover. After lingering in a coma for days, the boy died. Aaron decided "there is no G-d" and refused to go through with his Bar Mitzvah. Since that day, Aaron has had no interest in religion. He will not belong to a synagogue, and does not send his two boys to Hebrew school. His wife shares his views on these matters. Despite this attitude towards Jewish religious life, Aaron has always been active in secular Jewish groups concerned with the welfare of Jews in and outside the community.

Several years ago, Aaron suffered a stroke, and his teaching hours have been greatly reduced. His brother David has gone out of his way to help Aaron with the cost of private medical treatment and make arrangements for therapy.

In gratitude to David, Aaron refused to turn his back on his brother after the controversy over the fatal accident. To the extent that his injury allows, he is also active politically in the civic life of the general community.

Background of JOSHUA COHEN

Joshua Cohen, the youngest child, married a non-Jewish woman. She converted to Judaism and has become an active member of their synagogue. Joshua, although a member of the synagogue, is not active and does not attend services regularly. He explains that he is trying to clarify his own religious views and his conceptions of G-d, Judaism, Zionism, etc. He is presently learning Hebrew.

Joshua is serious-minded and has read the Bible in its entirety five times and reads Jewish literature voraciously. He has had running arguments for ten years with his older brother David, who always says: "Aaron—I can understand he doesn't believe. At least he knows where he stands. You just never grew up. You're confused, and you'll always be confused." Joshua is active in civic and political life within the general community.

Joshua, at one time, served as a financial consultant in his brother's business. After the accident, Joshua wrote a letter to David, saying, "While I am still uncertain as to just what I believe in terms of ritual and theology, I believe that if my being Jewish means anything at all, it means doing the right thing. I am therefore resigning from all association with the factory."

David has not spoken to Joshua since this incident occurred. Joshua and his wife have had a series of rows as a result of this because she disapproved of his resignation. "You like to be a hero," she said. "But if you're such a social reformer, why did you wait until now? You knew all the time that conditions were unsafe, didn't you? When did David's money get dirty to you?"

(Submitted by Simon Klarfeld)

ON BEING DIFFERENT

Purpose:

To help people explore how comfortable they feel about acknowledging their Jewish identity and priorities, especially in settings where most people are not Jewish.

Group:

Teenagers through adults. Four participants needed for the role play and up to 25 for observers.

Setting:

A large room with four chairs lined up in front and enough seating for the remainder of the group.

Materials:

Paper and pencils for the observers, written character descriptions for those in the role play.

Time:

45 minutes.

Instructions:

1. The facilitator chooses four volunteers to stage the role play; assigns the roles; and passes out the written character descriptions. The activity is conducted as a role play that takes place at the 5th reunion of the Butte Montana High School. One of the students, Rachel, is Jewish, the other three are Christian. Rachel's "coming out" as a Jew occurs at a roundtable discussion in which the Butte graduates are discussing their career plans.
2. Instruct the remainder of the group to observe the role play and imagine themselves in Rachel's place.
3. Have the participants sit in the front of the room and enact the role play.
4. Following the role play, the observers are asked to discuss the character of Rachel. How would they have responded if they had been in Rachel's situation? After considering this scenario, people are asked to relate similar situations from their own lives, in which they were the only Jew in a discussion. How comfortable were they, or would they have been, in talking about their Jewish identity?

DESCRIPTIONS OF HIGH SCHOOL GRADUATES ATTENDING THEIR FIFTH-YEAR REUNION

RACHEL

When you attended high school you kept a very low profile about being Jewish. Since your family name is Green, you and your family were not recognized as Jews. After graduating, you have become positively identified with your Jewish background. This has contributed to a sense of belonging and direction that were lacking when you were in high school. As a consequence, you are studying at Brandeis University in the Boston area, with the aim of going into Jewish Communal Service.

You are seated at a table with people who were among your best friends during high school. There is discussion about their current activities. You realize that you are Jewish while the others are not. You feel somewhat uncomfortable mentioning your choice of attending a Jewish-oriented university and preparing for a career working with middle-class Jewish people. You try to avoid the subject and talk only in response to being prodded by John or the others.

JOHN

Your family background is WASP and you do not feel particularly identified with any ethnic or religious group. You start a discussion about your classmates' career plans. You talk enthusiastically about your pursuit of a career in social work. You are in a graduate program with students from many countries, representing many different religious, ethnic, and racial backgrounds. Embellish this stream of universalism and brotherhood. Also you feel good about serving culturally disadvantaged people. After a while, you realize that one person, Rachel, hasn't joined the discussion, and you try to get her to tell what she is doing. Prod her as needed to be forthcoming about her plans.

JANE

You recently graduated college and are in an M.B.A. program at the Harvard Business School. You are optimistic about your future prospects and mention that graduates of last year's class received starting salaries of $70,000 and up. You expect to be earning in six figures within five years. Moving to Boston has exposed you to a more cosmopolitan style of living, and you have become "fed up with small town life."

MARY

After graduating from a Catholic women's college in another state, you were happy to return to your home town. Now, you are working for an insurance company, but you get fulfillment from volunteering at a hospital several hours a week. You proudly mention that your twin brother Tom (who was in the same high school class) has decided to go to seminary to prepare for the priesthood. You listen with interest to the conversation with Rachel. When Rachel mentions that she is studying in a Jewish program, you interrupt the conversation to express your surprise that she is Jewish. You had just assumed that she, like almost everyone else, was Protestant.

WHERE DO YOU DRAW THE LINE?

Purpose:

To have participants reflect on their own identities as Jews living in America, by making comparisons with the Jewish community living under Greek rule 2,000 years ago. Specifically, to examine arguments for assimilating versus remaining separate.

Group:

High school and older. 10–30 participants; only 6 people will speak during the debate; with a large group it is possible that not everyone will be able to contribute to planning the debate.

Setting:

A room with signs labeled "pro-assimilation" and "pro-separation" posted at opposite ends.

Materials:

Copies of "The Account of a Jewish Family . . ." (see below.) Letters are written in the upper right-hand corner: "A" signifies assimilation, "S" signifies separation. Newsprint or blackboard, magic markers or chalk.

Time:

50 minutes.

(Debate planning, 20 minutes; the debate, 15 minutes; summary, 15 minutes)

Instructions:

1. Leader passes out "The Account of a Jewish Family . . ." to each participant. Based on the letter indicated on the sheet, participants will be assigned to one of the sides of the debate, assimilation or separation. Each side assembles under the appropriate sign.
2. Each side plans its case. The pro-assimilation group defends the viewpoint that it is permissible to allow the Greek culture and way of life to permeate the Jewish community. The pro-separation group defends a viewpoint that states it is important that the Jews remain a separate people untouched by the Greek culture and way of life. Arguments for the debate should use facts stated on the sheet as a starting point. Three people are chosen to present the different parts of the case.
3. The debate is held. The sides alternate, with each side having an opening argument, rebuttal and closing statement. Leader keeps careful track of the time: two minutes for opening argument and rebuttal and one minute for closing statement.
4. Discussion. What was persuasive in each side's case? Which side was more persuasive? Do you see similarities between the choices made by Jews 2,000 years ago in assimilating to Greek culture and the way Jews of today adapt to American culture (celebrating American holidays, intermarrying, working on Shabbat, eating nonkosher foods)? What is distinctly Jewish in your connection to American culture?
5. In concluding, the leader summarizes common threads about the challenge of assimilation for Jews that were brought out in

the debate and discussion. Leader may note the many periods in history when the opportunity for assimilation was great: Babylonian captivity, Spain during the 15ᵗʰ century, and Europe following the emancipation of 1789.

THE ACCOUNT OF A JEWISH FAMILY LIVING IN JUDEA UNDER GREEK RULE CIRCA 300 B.C.E.

You are a Jew who has grown up under the rule of Alexander, the current ruler of the Greek Empire. Alexander has conquered the land of Judah, the territory once controlled by the Jews, where you live with your family. Alexander permits the Jews to live in relative peace as long as the Jewish community pays a tariff to the Greek government. Although your father is fluent in Greek and Hebrew, because of the changing times, you are only fluent in Greek. Fortunately, the Torah has been translated into Greek. Under the auspices of the Greek government, you are required to learn the Greek letters. The first book you read in school was Homer. Your family often attends the festivals of your pagan neighbors to maintain solidarity within the entire community. Although you are allowed to bring kosher food and do not eat the food of the Greeks, these festivities often include the celebration of pagan gods, celebrations that go against the Jewish notion of monotheism. Your family has educated Jewish friends who are fortunate to have a job working in the Greek courts. However, because of their demanding work schedule, they are unable to observe the Sabbath and most of the Jewish holidays. Finally, last summer you went to the wedding of your first cousin, who married a non-Jewish Greek woman. Since the woman converted to Judaism, the marriage was permitted by the high priest of the Jewish community.

(Source: Bickerman, Elias J., *The Jews in the Greek Age*, Cambridge MA: Harvard University Press, 1988, pp. 237–256.)

(Submitted by Scott Kadish)

MY JEWISH SELF / MY AMERICAN SELF

Purpose:

To distinguish Jewish and American influences on personal values.

Groups:

Adults.

Setting:

Any room.

Materials:

Newsprint sheets printed with "Influences on Personal Values" (see below) and a marker.

Time:

30 minutes

Instructions:

1. The leader defines sources of influence on values. A person's values are shaped by the society he/she was brought up in, currently lives in, or aspires to be part of. This activity is concerned with the balance between Jewish and American influences.
2. For each value on the list, people respond with the source for their belief in the value: Jewish only, both Jewish and American, or American only. It is possible to respond that this value is not of importance. Responses for each value are tallied on the newsprint.
3. Look for patterns among the values. For what values is the influence primarily Jewish? Are there values for which the Jewish influence is not as strong as it ought to be? What is the extent of the American-only influence?

Note to Leader:

Remind participants that this activity is about the sources of their own values. It is not concerned with deciding which values are characteristic of Jews or Americans.

INFLUENCES ON PERSONAL VALUES

	Jewish	Both Jewish & American	American	not a value

Personal Traits

P1. Education
P2. Maintaining good health
P3. Not complaining
P4. Being punctual
P5. Admitting mistakes
P6. Having a sense of purpose
P7. Spirituality
P8. Understanding your religion
P9. Dreams

Relationships

R1. Having a family and raising children
R2. Marrying someone of similar ethnic or cultural heritage
R3. Spending time with relatives
R4. Loyalty to your country
R5. Friendship
R6. Being concerned about the values taught to your children
R7. Learning about your ancestors

Activities

A1. Being successful in your career
A2. Following current events
A3. Saving or investing money
A4. Decorating your home
A5. Supporting new technology
A6. Being involved in your local community
A7. Supporting the arts
A8. Learning about different cultures
A9. Celebrating holidays
A10. Enjoying nature

Kindnesses

K1. Helping the sick
K2. Taking care of animals

K3. Protecting the environment
K4. Making people laugh
K5. Being charitable
K6. Fighting injustice
K7. Showing respect for the elderly

(Adapted from an idea submitted by Emily Saffer)

MY CRITICAL BOOK

Purpose:

To reflect on factors that have shaped participants' identities, by focusing on the influence of books or texts. (This format is applicable to many themes; here, it serves to highlight whether influence on an individual's identity comes from Jewish or non-Jewish sources.)

Group:

High-school and older. 15 or more participants.

Setting:

A classroom or any open room with chairs, or an outdoor setting.

Time:

45 minutes—1 hour.

Instructions:

1. The leader asks the group to think of the one book or text they read that had the most influence in shaping their values and identities. Since an objective of this activity is to see the extent to which participants are influenced by Jewish or non-Jewish sources, it is important that the leader present the task in general terms.
2. In small discussion groups (for groups of 30 or more) or in a

plenary (under 30), each person explains his/her choice and the nature of its impact. The leader records on newsprint or a blackboard the book title and a key word or phrase summarizing the impact on the individual.

3. Following everyone's report, the leader conducts a discussion to explore the themes reflected. The key issue is the extent to which books chosen were of a Jewish nature. How often were Jewish authors mentioned? How often was the Bible or other basic Jewish text mentioned? Are participants surprised? What was the influence of Jewish texts relative to non-Jewish texts?

4. The leader's summary should address the mix of Jewish and non-Jewish texts. This mix reflects the ever-present tension felt by contemporary Jews between two attractive and competing cultures: the Jewish heritage and post-emancipation culture of Western society as reflected in America.

QUOTES

I am a Jew. Hath not a Jew eyes? Hath not a Jew hands, organs, dimensions, senses, affection, passions?

William Shakespeare (1564–1616),
The Merchant of Venice, 1597

Jewry is not merely a question of faith, it is above all a question of the practice of a way of life in a community conditioned by faith.

Franz Kafka (1883–1924)

Judaism is about joyousness, dedication to good works, love of learning, community solidarity, concern for justice.

Rabbi David J. Wolpe, 1998

I have always been far more pleased by my good fortune in being born a Jew than my critics may begin to imagine. It's a complicated, interesting, morally demanding, and very singular experience, and I like that. I find myself in the historic predicament of being Jewish, with all its implications.

Philip Roth (1933–), 1985

The pursuit of knowledge for its own sake, an almost fanatical love of justice, and desire for personal independence—these are the features of the Jewish tradition which make me thank my stars that I belong to it.

Albert Einstein (1879–1955)

It was to my Jewish nature alone that I owed two characteristics that had become indispensable to me in the difficult course of my life. Because I was a Jew I found myself free from many prejudices which restricted others in the course of their intellect; and as a Jew I was prepared to join the opposition and do without agreement with the compact majority.

Sigmund Freud (1856–1939), 1924

No reader of the Hebrew version of this book will find it easy to put himself in the emotional position of an author who is ignorant of the language of the holy writ, who is completely estranged from the religion of his fathers—as well as from every other religion— and who cannot take a share in nationalist ideals, but who has yet never repudiated his people, who feels that he is in his essential nature a Jew and who has no desire to alter that nature. If the question were put to him: "Since you have abandoned all these common characteristics of your people, what is left to you that is Jewish?" He would reply: "A very great deal, and probably its very essence," although he could not now express that essence clearly in words.

Sigmund Freud (1856–1939), 1930

I have often felt as though I had inherited all the defiance and all the passions with which our ancestors defended their Temple and could gladly sacrifice my life for one great moment in history.

Sigmund Freud (1856–1939)

The decisive factor in the present inner crisis of Jewish life is the Jews' necessity to live in two civilizations. These are Judaism and Americanism in this country, or Judaism and some other modern civilization elsewhere.

Rabbi Mordecai Kaplan (1881–1983),
The Future of the American Jew

Jews had to acquire the culture and manners of the wider society, and in many countries and individuals the experience of living in two worlds produced a crisis of identity.

Chief Rabbi Jonathan Sacks

. . . then you shall be My own treasure from among all the peoples . . . and you shall be unto Me a kingdom of priests and a holy nation . . .

Exodus 19:5–6

It is a people that shall dwell alone and shall not be reckoned among the nations.

Numbers 23:9

For thou art a holy people unto the Lord thy God: the Lord thy God hath chosen thee to be His own treasure, out of all peoples that are upon the face of the earth. The Lord did not set His love upon you, nor choose you, because ye were more in number than any people—for ye were the fewest of all peoples—but because the Lord loved you; and because He would keep the oath which He swore unto your fathers, hath the Lord brought you out with a mighty hand and redeemed you out of the house of bondage, from the hand of Pharoah, King of Egypt.

Deuteronomy 7:6–8

I, the Lord, have called you with righteous purpose and taken you by the hand; I have formed you, and destined you to be a lamp to all peoples, a light unto the nations.

Isaiah 42:6

All Israel has a share in the World to Come, as it is said: And your people are all righteous; they shall inherit the land forever; they are the branch of My planting, My handiwork, in which to take pride.

Isaiah 60:21

. . . since He has not made us like the nations of the world, nor placed us like other families of the earth, since He has not made our portion like theirs nor our destiny like that of all their multitude . . .

Aleinu Prayer

If the statistics are right, the Jews constitute but one percent of the human race. It suggests a nebulous dim puff of stardust lost in the blaze of the Milky Way. Properly the Jew ought hardly be heard of; but he is heard of, has always been heard of.

He is as prominent on the planet as any other people, and his commercial importance is extravagantly out of proportion to the smallness of his bulk. His contributions to the world's list of great names in literature, science, art, music, finance, medicine, and obtuse learning are also way out of proportion to the weakness of his numbers.

He has made a marvelous fight in this world in all the ages, and has done it with his hands tied behind him. He could be vain of himself and be excused for it. The Egyptians, the Babylonians, and the Persians rose, filled the planet with sound and splendor, and faded to dream stuff and passed away. The Greeks and the Romans followed and made a vast noise and they were gone. Other peoples have sprung up and held their torch high for a time. But it burned out, and they sit in twilight now or have vanished.

The Jew saw them all. Beat them all, and is now what he always was, exhibiting no decadence, no infirmities of age, no weakening of his parts, no slowing of his energies, no dulling of his alert and aggressive mind.

All things are mortal but the Jew. All forces pass, but he remains.

Mark Twain (1835–1910), Harper's
Magazine, 1899

The third generation seeks to remember what the second generation sought to forget.

Marcus L. Hansen (1892–1938)

We Jews have a shared history but not a common destiny.

A. B. Yehoshua (1936–)

14

INFORMAL EDUCATION: PRACTITIONERS' PERSPECTIVES

This chapter presents views of practitioners in North America, Israel and England on the definition, institutional needs and future of informal Jewish education. The authors consist of influential informal Jewish educators and students who have been beneficiaries of informal Jewish education programs. These individuals represent a range of backgrounds and organizational settings.

The articles here constitute the entirety of the May 2001 issue of *Sh'ma*, which was devoted to informal Jewish education.

Sh'ma is a monthly forum for independent, cross-denominational exchanges on Jewish cultural, social, religious and political matters.

To contact *Sh'ma*:

Address: P.O. Box 9129, 90 Oak St., 4ᵗʰ floor, Newton Upper Falls, MA 02464

Telephone: 617-965-7700

Web address: *www.shma.com*

Jumping Into the Currents: The Art of Informal Jewish Education
Joseph Reimer

Rafting down the Colorado River last May, I was hoping not to be the one who falls off. I was sitting on the raft next to the guide who had much to tell us about the river and how to ride the rapids. Indeed, as the rapids grew fiercer, I could see her considerable skill in handling the oars. I began to believe we would make it; and before long we had passed through all the rapids. I was starting to relax.

Suddenly Dusty, the guide, said we could all jump off into the river. Having spent my energy and concentration staying on the raft, why would I now jump off? But off went most of the others on our raft. I looked around and jumped.

Those first moments in the Colorado were filled with terror. The current was fast and powerful. I was definitely not in control. But all around me other people were happily floating. It had to be all right. I released my tension. Suddenly what terrified me was thrilling. I was in the grip of a power much greater than myself. If I could trust myself to that power, it would support me. Now I was meeting the river on its own terms.

Back on the raft, I realized I had thought the guide's job was to get us through the rapids and teach us about the river. But Dusty understood the power of surprise and never said a word in advance about jumping. She also knew the value of being in the river itself. It is one thing to be on a raft and hearing about the Colorado; it is quite another to be in the river carried along by its currents. It is the latter I will never forget. It is imprinted on my body and mind.

By analogy, much of formal Jewish education is like sitting on the raft and hearing about the river. The teacher tells the stories and the students absorb new information about the history of the religion and customs of its practitioners. But there is little opportunity to jump into the river itself, to feel the powerful currents of religion. There is no terror and no thrill, just more stories about God and our ancestors.

Until Dusty's surprise I was happy sitting on the raft. I needed to begin there. Left alone I would not have known what I was missing. I would have reached my "bar mitzvah," done everyone proud by not falling off, and left a satisfied customer. It just would not have made a lasting impression. And that is what recent research by Bethamie Horowitz tells us about much of formal Jewish education outside the day schools. It does not leave much of a lasting impression. "The strongest predictors of current Jewishness were to be found among voluntary experiences—ones that a person chose to undertake, like Jewish youth group, Jewish college activities or a trip to Israel." (See her essay in this issue for a fuller account of this research.)

We call these voluntary experiences "informal Jewish education." But the term "informal education" is problematic. What gives these experiences their power is not primarily their informality. What matters, in part, is that they are chosen rather than prescribed. But what really matters is that for many these are their first opportunities to be *in* the river, to experience Judaism as a live current that carries them along and leaves a lasting impression.

There is a mystery here that we barely understand. The human mind registers certain experiences in lasting ways while other experiences are scarcely remembered. Some experiences—especially when something happens to leave a lasting "memory trace"—are often remembered years later when more routine experiences have long been forgotten.

The power of informal Jewish education, I am suggesting, lies in the creation of lasting Jewish memories. When reluctant or ambivalent Jews get surprised and experience themselves—in the company of trusted peers—swimming in powerful Jewish currents, they take notice. Before they have the time to erect the usual defenses, they are standing before the Western Wall and finding its allure overwhelming. They are singing *Lecha Dodi* at camp and the Sabbath Queen is dancing before their eyes. They are holding their friends' hands in the dark as they bid farewell to Shabbat by the light of a hundred havdallah candles. They are talking about God at 2 a.m. They are crying at the gates of *Yad Vashem* as they take in the horror of the past. They are doing Jewish and not feeling strange or awkward about it. Is it any wonder these moments stand out and are not forgotten?

Such moments do not create themselves. They are as carefully designed as when Dusty told us to jump into the river. Informal education has its spontaneous moments, but on the whole its programs have to be as carefully and thoughtfully designed as lessons in a classroom curriculum. Informal educators—at their best—are artful designers of other people's experiences. They have to know enough about experiential learning to design programs that catch people a little off guard, and yet help them to take in and record the significance of what they have experienced.

The Jewish community is only now becoming aware of the full

educational potential of informal education. But that potential will be realized only when there is a complementary awareness of the craft of the informal educator. Designing powerful experiences that create meaningful Jewish memories is an art form that is not often appreciated. At the Institute for Informal Jewish Education at Brandeis, we are cultivating that art form, celebrating its practitioners, and preparing a next generation of artful designers. This is pioneering work that has significant long-term implications for creating the memories that will seed the Jewish identities of today's Jewish youth.

Dr. Joseph Reimer is Director of the Institute for Informal Jewish Education at Brandeis University and Professor at the Hornstein Program at Brandeis University.

Informal Jewish Education as Art Form
Barry Chazan

Dear Joe,

Your rafting trip sounds great! As always, you succeed so well in using life to teach us about life. And here I am stuck in my book-filled office trying to "understand" what informal education is. So let me take a stab at it and try to do some strait-laced analytic conceptualizing about the art form you so well describe. As we both know, most people think that "Jewish education" means schools and children. But that is not the whole story. Learning happens in many places: at camp, at a Jewish Community Center, on an Israel trip, at a retreat or Shabbaton, in an adult study group. Contemporary Jewish life shouts loudly that the campus of Jewish education extends much beyond the walls of primary or secondary school. Indeed, there is another "school" that has touched all of us—the "school" of informal Jewish education. I think this "school" has seven characteristics:

1. AUTONOMY: It's something that one chooses freely.
2. PERSON-CENTERED: It makes the person the center of education.
3. EXPERIENCE-CENTERED: It educates by enabling Jews to actually *have* Jewish experiences (rather than merely talking about them).

4. INTERACTIVE: It highlights the relationship between educator and learner as central to Jewish education.
5. A "CURRICULUM" OF JEWISH VALUES: The "curriculum" of informal Jewish education is about the Jewish values, behaviors, and beliefs that we want Jews to internalize. This curriculum is not carved in stone but is flexible; paper and pencil tests do not measure it.
6. FUN AND ENJOYMENT: It is fun and assumes that enjoyment enhances rather than inhibits Jewish learning!
7. DIFFERENT BREED OF EDUCATOR: Informal Jewish educators are living role models of the values, beliefs, and behaviors they teach, and they "teach" by showing, doing, and asking rather than by telling, lecturing, or posing. (They are also likely to wear shorts, t-shirts, running shoes, and sports uniforms!)

Informal Jewish education refers to an approach to education that is aimed at the personal growth of Jews of all ages. It happens through active participation in a diversity of Jewish experiences. It is rooted in basic Jewish beliefs, values, and behaviors. It requires careful planning—along with great flexibility. It requires educators who are very interactive and participatory, and who live what they teach. It doesn't take place in any one venue but happens all over.

The big question that we both wrestle with is how to make this happen?

There are two hefty challenges we face in this context. First, we need to professionalize the field. Our colleague Mark Charendoff writes well about this subject in this issue of *Sh'ma*; the Institute for Informal Education is an important step in this direction.

Our second challenge is to convince the contemporary Jewish world and its leaders that informal Jewish education is really significant. We must show them that it is not "secondary," "extra, " "fluff, " "window dressing, " or simply "fun" (these are all words we have both heard). We must ensure that informal education is as much a system and context in which people learn as are schools and syllabi. Our friends in general education have learned this lesson—hopefully we can teach the same lesson to our family within Jewish education.

Perhaps the way Jewish life was traditionally "taught" is the best to learn—utilization of the entire campus of life to educate. As we have told each other so often, maybe the real story of Jewish education is a story of a great informal educational system.

Joe, keep rafting and may we continue to ride the crests of this great new stream!

Best regards,
Barry

Barry Chazan is Professor of Education at the Hebrew University of Jerusalem and Education Consultant to Birthright Israel. He is the author of books and articles on moral education, informal education, Jewish education, and teaching Israel.

Jewish Community and the Informal Educator: A New Pact for a New Era
Mark S. Charendoff

I was struck recently, at a gathering of informal Jewish educators, by the passion and commitment of those in attendance. Unfortunately, that was not the only thing that struck me. The event, like many others I have seen in the world of informal Jewish education, lacked a certain discipline. People arrived to sessions late and left early. Some were sloppy, inattentive—even rude. What struck me most, though, was in contrast to other professional conferences the lack of professionalism here was even more stark.

No doubt, I will be accused of generalizing. These pages of *Sh'ma* include essays by informal educators who are models of professionalism, skill, and dignity. But here the exception serves to prove the rule. A historian would have to determine who is to blame, but I note a tacit agreement between the organized Jewish community and informal Jewish educators. The Jewish community does not take informal educators seriously as professionals, and the educators neither expect nor give cause to warrant such respect.

We are ready to negotiate new terms. We, the informal Jewish educators of the world, will become models of excellence and professionalism in the Jewish community. We applaud the recent growth of the day school field and hope that it is only a beginning. At the same time we know the areas that we own. Among them are camping, Israel experiences, youth groups, college program-ming, and adult education. We occupy an increasingly important space in communities' efforts to enhance Jewish identity. The great frontiers of Jewish education lay in our path. We are determined to keep the best and brightest among us in this field and are dedi-cated to attracting the best and brightest in the emerging genera-tion to join us in our quest. We believe that we can persuade them to abandon thoughts of investment banking and Internet start-ups to enter what we know can be a glorious career. To do that we pledge the following:

Literature: A profession needs its own literature. We will create a journal, web and print based, in order to ensure that our ideas are challenged by our peers and refined through open debate.

Certification: A profession needs to define its members, not to have members thrust upon them. To do that we will introduce mandatory certification of all informal Jewish educators. A defined curriculum and period of internship will precede acceptance to the field. An accumulation of in-service credits will be obtained through attendance at seminars, contributions to scholarly jour-nals, and service on national committees. Annual recertification will be necessary.

Standards & Censure: We will develop standards of behavior and conduct for our profession. We will take responsibility for withdrawing certification, or imposing less drastic measures, for those individuals who do not embody the high ethical standards of our field.

Dignity: We will conduct ourselves at all times in a manner that draws others to the field and gives our colleagues and constituents reason to respect this field of education. While we will continue to be comfortable sitting on the floor and playing a guitar, we will also be comfortable sitting at a table engaging in strategic plan-ning.

For their side of the bargain, Jewish communal institutions must give informal educators the means to do all of this and more. They will pay us salaries that are competitive with professionals in the not-for-profit sector when we are their equals in ability and experi-ence. Jewish communal organizations will hire educators who are committed to informal Jewish education as a career, not as a dis-traction. The Jewish community will fund our programs to a degree that provides for excellence—both in terms of delivery and content—and demand that new efforts be researched and piloted before being delivered and evaluated during and afterwards.

Jewish communal leaders may argue with us and disagree, but they will accept our informed opinion with the respect that we have earned. They will be proud when their children join our ranks.

As for me, I am eager to see which side signs first.

Mark S. Charendoff is Vice President of the Andrea and Charles Bronfman Philanthropies. He is proud to be an informal Jewish educator.

Frisbee with Dignity
Debbie Sussman

I am struck by Mark Charendoff's comment that what struck him at an informal Jewish educators' conference was *passion and commitment*. I agree; the rest is commentary! What do we want from the teachers who teach our children? Passion and commitment. What is it when an environmentalist takes our children into the woods and suggests they listen to God's creatures or enjoy an awesome sight from atop a mountain? Passion, commitment, and enthusiasm in action. Do we, as informal Jewish educators, believe that children learn from the experiential—the sound of spirited *zemirot* Friday night? A resounding yes.

Formal Jewish educators often try to duplicate the camp experience: the song festival, the Shabbat *ruach*, the *whither thou goest I will go* feeling inspired by camp leaders who are trusted and admired, and who engender emulation.

The head staff at Camp Yavneh are 20- and 30-year-olds, and have been coming to camp for 7 to 25 years. Jewish or secular teachers during the school year, they return each summer to make a difference in their campers' lives. Jewish camping is about learning to live in a community and getting along with your bunkmates. It is about learning to interact with adults of all ages who listen, take seriously your concerns, and then go play frisbee with you in the rain. What does this have to do with *dignity*? Everything!

Strategic planning must be done, and as Director, I must create a budget and assign bunks, purchase food and communicate with parents, staff, and boards. All this is accomplished in a very professional way. A thankless part of my job, it only becomes gratifying when the campers and staff want to come back to camp summer after summer to be part of a warm, loving, Jewish, (in our case Shabbat observant) joyful environment where—excuse the cliché—Judaism comes alive!

There already are professional camping organizations, to which most Jewish camp professionals belong. They publish a periodical, sponsor conferences, and help in many ways. Our camp just finished a five-year strategic plan, raised money for physical plant improvements, participated in a four-month task force envisioning our camp's future, sponsored teachers' meetings, new camper meetings, reunions, and the like. Do we need to be certified to make these things happen?

Can the Jewish community help the jewel of Jewish life? Yes. Provide support and funding. In the past few years the Foundation for Jewish Camping has emerged to help Jewish camps with small grants, staffing, and overall "we want to help" support. This is still too little. Informal educators and institutions need funds to improve aging facilities, to sponsor creative programs and scholars-in-residence, to support in-service training during the year (perhaps led by "formal and informal Jewish professionals working together"), and to pay staff for the jobs they do. Support for internships to train the younger staff for jobs with more responsibility would ensure the perpetuation of strong and meaningful Jewish camping. Eventually, a "superfund" should be set up to establish new camps in each region of the country to accommodate the thousands of Jewish children who are presently unable to attend camp.

To quote Mark: *Jewish communal leaders may argue with us and disagree, but they will accept our informed opinion with the respect that we have earned.* With all due respect, whether we are sitting on a dusty floor or standing on a bench singing our hearts out, respect *is* earned each summer and the results are felt throughout the year. Just ask the kids.

Debbie Sussman is Director of Camp Yavneh, a division of Hebrew College in Brookline, Massachusetts.

"Informal" Doesn't Necessarily Mean Unprofessional
Doron Krakow

Summer camp, youth group, kids' conventions. These words conjure up images of games, fun, and happy kids. These, along with programs in Israel designed to show children the wonders of our National Homeland, are the bastions of "informal" education. By informal, of course, we mean outside of the classroom. No lectures. No homework. Even books are few and far between. In fact, because informal education takes place in environments like "the country," a youth lounge, or someone's basement, there are those who believe that it should hardly be considered education at all.

Experiential education—that is, learning by doing—builds positive associations through culture, language, and the environment. Children develop pride in their identities and an enthusiasm for learning unfettered by the natural resistance they may feel to compulsory learning.

Often, in our zeal to maintain the informality that defines our field, informal educators maintain a commitment to informal *organization* as well. It is a widely held belief that the wellspring of great programming for the field is a working environment that connotes the very character of the programs it will produce. Thus, informal dress, flexible workspace, a highly interactive office culture, and the regular presence of young people routinely define the offices where informal educators spend their days. So far so good. This setup might just as easily describe the home offices of a high-tech company these days, and in fact these conditions do describe a healthy environment for the management of these types of programs.

However, educators often lack a willingness to juxtapose the informal agenda of their programs with the more formal context in which these programs reside. In fact, quite often informal educators resist the very notion of managerial professionalism because, by definition, that type of approach appears to contradict the very informality they so vociferously espouse.

Identifying talented professionals to staff our programs is one of the fundamental challenges facing our field. We seek a unique combination of skills and personal history. Managerial skills—including background in staffing, supervision, marketing, public speaking, bookkeeping, and computer knowledge—are skills that most talented people can learn. But when I sit across the table from a candidate seeking a key professional role in Young Judaea, I'm really looking for someone with charisma, energy, and a passion for our mission, including a personal history in informal education. I'm looking for someone who grew up in a youth movement or attended camp, and who has a strong connection to Israel. I want someone to engage young people and inspire trust, faith, and respect.

I am committed to professionalism in my work, and in the work of my team, because only through specific attention to detail, organization, and management can we consistently be successful in building a solid youth movement. While this might be more readily understood in a discussion of marketing and promotion, it is equally true in all other areas critical to our programs' success. Without a strong commitment to staff recruitment, assessment, training, and development, no program or collection of programs can possibly fulfill its potential. Our programs—that is, the direct contact points with young people—are wholly dependent on proper research, program preparation, and the training of facilitators, educators, and leaders. In fact, there are virtually no elements of our work that don't fundamentally depend on the outgrowth of a thorough and professional foundation. There is no reason why a commitment to this type of foundation needs to compromise the informal character of the programs and experiences we provide.

We must draw the distinction between our roles as educators with an innate desire to connect with children and teens, and our responsibility to manage and run a successful service industry. Too "professional" and it stops being "informal" education. Too "informal" and it's hard to remain viable. The answer is in the balance.

Doron Krakow is National Director of Young Judaea, the Zionist Youth Movement sponsored by Hadassah.

Reviewing Educational Paradigms
Zvi Bekerman

Little is known about Jewish education in general and even less is known about its informal counterpart. Our community leaders are still too busy promoting the needed outcomes of Jewish education (strengthening Jewish identity and fostering continuity), and promoting the so-called tools to achieve such aims as text-learning and ritual to even consider seriously what education—informal or not—really is.

I wonder what progress can be made when talk about informal education develops only in relation to its opposite—formal; in that case, we could say there is nothing more formal than the informal.

Though in principle I would agree with Doron Krakow's call to professionalize the field of informal education, I think we need first to reach a better description of what the field encompasses. Lacking such a description would mean not knowing what we are seeking to professionalize.

Doron's definition, suggesting experiential education (learning by doing) is not enough in a way of characterization. We should all readily agree that formal education works on the same premise; indeed at schools (the assumed bastions of formality) children learn what they do. Thus they learn to be subjugated or successful citizens working in and for the machinery of the sovereign state. It is by now common experience and knowledge that if we remember anything that we were taught at school, it had more to do with relationships than with Bible, physics, or geography (paradoxically we could say the disciplines become the *real hidden* curriculum).

Doron is the first to admit, honestly, that some of his suggestions might be better understood within the context of "a discussion of marketing and promotion"; this is exactly what I worry about. As a strong believer that language not only describes the world but primarily constructs it, I worry about the use of metaphor and its implications for the shaping of our consciousness and understanding—especially in terms of education.

What are the basic premises behind this world of marketing and professionalism? Are we aware that behind words such as *recruitment*, *assessment*, and *professionalism* stands a worldview of individuality, autonomy, measurement, and repression that is not necessarily a good fit for the educational aims of an ethnic/religious minority, dependent for its survival on community and trust?

In recent years new research has investigated ideas such as apprenticeship, distributive cognition, and activity theory. These fields of knowledge are uncovering a rich world of daily, natural human activity that represents approaches contrary to those implemented to date in either formal or informal education. They point to the need to refashion our educational understanding in order to return to embodied understandings of self as opposed to Cartesian abstraction—to pay attention to activity rather than intentions. For example, think about how we learn the most difficult thing ever to be learned by humans—one's primary language. Neither professionals nor institutions are involved in the process. We learn language by participating in a community (a family) that talks. We learn not in our isolated abstract minds but rather by interacting with others fully with mind and body. If and when we make mistakes, they are identified not as problems of the individual but rather as memories to recall lovingly in the future. Without interaction with others, there would be no learning of any language. In this sense, language is the outcome of participating in communities of practice—not a bad metaphor for learning in general and Jewish learning in particular. If we truly understood this, then "text" (our favorite tool for Jewish learning) would reclaim its etymological meaning (from the Latin) "to weave." Rather than being something that is transferred from teachers to the minds of individual students, text would become a social, interactive "weaving." Indeed these theories call upon educators to pay special attention to social processes as opposed to abstract ideas.

What we wrongly call "informal" seems to be characterized by gaiety—that is, working on the borders between play and reality. Characterizations such as a female perspective, caring and dialogue, an emphasis on making meaning through narrative and an inclusion and tolerance of difference—all point to directions different than those suggested by recent developments within formal education.

In short, I believe that developing so-called informal education agents has more to do with reviewing the present paradigms that guide our educational thinking than with recruitment, training techniques, and assessment, which seem to hide the paradigms that bind us.

Dr. Zvi Bekerman teaches Anthropology of Education at the Melton Center and the School of Education, Hebrew University, Jerusalem.

Informal Education and Jewish Identity Development
Bethamie Horowitz

For the past few years we've seen a lot of emphasis in both the Jewish press and Jewish communal policy on the importance of Jewish education as a way of influencing or ensuring Jewish identity and Jewish continuity. Certainly I believe that Jewish education plays a crucial role. However, much of what we hear is not about Jewish *education* in its fullest sense—it's about *schooling* and especially day schools.

There has been a blossoming of Jewish day schools around the country and that is a welcome communal development. But what is sometimes lost in the current climate is the very important impact and potential of what has come to be called informal Jewish education, especially its role in the Jewish identity development of American Jews who do not attend day schools.

Recent research supports the important role of Jewish education separate from formal schooling. Informal Jewish educational experiences such as summer camps, youth groups, Israel trips, and involvements in Jewish college programs among others, play an exceedingly important role in the Jewish development of Jewish individuals. We need to keep reminding the community that Jewish education is much bigger than schooling.

What role do "involuntary" and "voluntary" Jewish experiences play in the development of Jewish identity in adulthood? Although we typically differentiate Jewish educational experiences by calling them *formal* and *informal*, for the purposes of thinking about Jewish identity formation, I would like to redirect our attention to the issue of motivation. *Involuntary* experiences are those experiences a child has because of the circumstances of his or her background, *before the child has any say* in the matter. For example, parents make decisions about children's schooling and camp. And they create the emotional climate in the home (especially around holiday celebrations). *Voluntary* experiences, on the other hand, are those that a person *chooses* to undertake. These typically begin in adolescence and continue through adulthood. Teenagers choose to attend camp, to belong to a youth group, to go on a Jewish teen trip, to partake of Jewish college experiences. During adolescence and early adulthood, a child's parents cease to be the primary decision makers about their child's Jewish experiences. During this period a teenager's own motivation comes to play a central role in how or whether to be Jewishly involved.

I prefer to distinguish between involuntary and voluntary experiences rather than formal versus informal because the former focuses our attention to the core issue of Jewish identity development. The involuntary experiences can be viewed as what a person inherits by virtue of his or her upbringing, while the voluntary experiences represent the series of choices that a person makes with regard to Jewishness. The question of inheritance and desire lies at the heart of our challenge as American Jews today. Each of us needs to integrate both sorts of experiences in order to discover a Jewishness of our own.

Connections and Journeys, a recent UJA-sponsored study I directed, examines the relationship between these two Jewish educational experiences (voluntary and involuntary) and the current Jewish connection and engagement of American Jewish adults born between 1946 and 1976. Two broad swaths of people were included: those who had been raised in intensive Jewish settings (typically, but not exclusively, Orthodox) and those with a less intensively Jewish upbringing.

The pattern of Jewish education and socialization was quite different for these two groups. Those from more intensive Jewish backgrounds were more strongly influenced earlier in their lives. They typically came from families where the parents were deeply committed to Jewish life and conveyed this at home, in their educational choices (day school), and in their communal and synagogue involvement. This early training (involuntary) seems to have been the main factor shaping their Jewishness in adulthood. Later "voluntary" experiences (like youth groups, trips to Israel, and college activities) had less influence, because these people were already very involved in Jewish life; these later experiences did not create much "added value" over and beyond what had already been encouraged by day school (which in this population often continued through high school). We could call this the "early and often approach."

In contrast, the adults who came from less intensively Jewish backgrounds were most strongly influenced by later, "voluntary" experiences during their adolescence and early adulthood, includ-

ing being involved in Jewish youth groups, Jewish studies and Hil-
lel-like activities in college, or having a significantly positive
relationship or experience being Jewish.

What I learned through this study is that there is no one way to
raise a Jew. We tend to think that people who get their Jewishness
"early and often" (and, let us add, healthily—without emotional
trauma) are already on the road to internalized Jewish identity.
But it is important to understand that just because people miss out
on intensive Jewish exposure early in their lives does not mean
that they will not have such experiences during adolescence and
adulthood. In fact, what appears to have the greatest impact is the
voluntary experience.

Jewish identity development involves a process of exposure—
internalizing and ultimately reflecting on both the early involuntary experiences that happen to a child and become part of one's
inheritance (or baggage), and what a person acquires later out of
desire. In terms of identity development, both experiences are
important—what we are given and what we ultimately choose.
The mystery of Jewish identity formation is that we don't know
for any given person if and when desire will kick in. The best strategy, then, is to create a set of opportunities that maximize both
sets of experiences.

Bethamie Horowitz is the author of Connections and Journeys:
Assessing Critical Opportunities for Enhancing Jewish Identity,
published by the UJA-Federation of New York (2000).

What Page Are We On? Traditional Texts in Informal Jewish Education
Raphael Zarum

"Moshe isn't overreacting." "I think he's angry at their attitude."
"The two tribes didn't understand their responsibilities to the
whole People." It was a typical text study setup: a leadership training seminar for twenty teenagers—all potential youth leaders—
learning about teamwork; text handouts for everyone. Engaged,
their counselor (their madricha) decided to push them: "Look at
Moshe's speech, what's he actually blaming them for?" Divided
into pairs, they analyzed a selection of commentaries looking for

answers. Opinions flooded out, "Moshe is reminding them of times when they didn't listen to each other." "Like when you don't work as a team." Things were getting heated, "A leader has to say it like it is." "No, Moshe was just being spiteful, that's no way to lead." The madricha smiled, they were connecting with the texts, now the real issues were emerging . . .

A challenge often leveled against informal Jewish education is its lack of content. Camp counselors and youth workers may create an open, fun environment that engenders Jewish identity in young people, *but do these young people really learn anything?* To be sure, the grandeur of informal Jewish education is its "pedagogy of participation," which emphasizes asking many questions, carefully listening to answers, respecting diverse opinions, empowering individuality, and experiential learning. However, in the hands of under-educated informal Jewish educators, this approach masks an ignorance of basic bodies of Jewish knowledge, and tacitly justifies an inability to convey the depth and complexity of Jewish thought. Too many young leaders are severely deficient in confidence and skill in the arena of Jewish study.

The growth of traditional text study within informal education has begun to address this problem. The sight of young people huddled together, clutching sheets containing a select number of readable Jewish sources while voraciously debating and discussing them, is becoming commonplace. The bite-sized manageable nature of these texts, culled from Tanach, Talmud, midrash, and generations of commentators, coupled with their innate ability to stimulate and challenge even the marginally affiliated, have quickly captured the imagination of youth leaders allowing this form of study to gain credence in many informal settings.

Text study puts the content back into informal education. Rather than endless discussions around stock responses to open questions, text-focused education works from a core body of knowledge that can be manageable enough not to frighten apprehensive learners and open enough to serve as a warm induction into traditional Jewish learning. Instead of just cataloguing everyone's opinions—legitimizing each and thus not really prizing any—study with Jewish sources always fundamentally grounds perspectives in a recognizably Jewish framework. Interpretations are encouraged, but their validation comes if they lie well with the text. Also, texts act as addresses for eager learners to follow further study.

Indeed, text study is naturally suited to the informal setting. Just as informal Jewish education stresses the value of the "person" over the "subject," so text study encourages the active pursuit of multiple interpretive meanings over the passive recognition of the plain sense of a text. The Talmud, interpreting a verse in Jeremiah (23:29), expounds on this point: "Just as the hammer splinters a rock into many pieces, so does one text splinter into many meanings" (*Sanhedrin* 34a). The noisy interplay of study in *chavruta* (traditional learning partnership pairs) also highlights the informal and very person-orientated nature of text-based learning.

Texts need to be thoughtfully selected, faithfully transcribed, and kept within their conceptual context. They must also resonate with the learner, quickly spark their interest, challenge their unrefined notions, stimulate responses, and be practically readable (simple Hebrew, good translations, uncluttered layout, etc.). Educational facilitators need to be familiar with texts and their contexts, conceive of questions to help unpack the material, be conscious of different readings and understandings of the sources, and have a keen ability to bring out and develop the ideas of the group. It is therefore essential to train and prepare seriously the facilitators of text study if this approach is to survive beyond what could be just a short-lived fad.

At Makor-AJY, the Centre for Informal Jewish Education that services British Jewry, a "Text & Values Project" has been set up to "turn up the Jewish heat" by producing new materials and training courses to both respond to and encourage the desire for more text study in this sector. *Torat Hadracha*, an interactive study guide for learning about Jewish educational leadership through the study of traditional Jewish texts, is being piloted within the Zionist youth movements. As well, training for summer camp and trip personnel now includes a selection of pertinent texts on subjects such as *Tisha B'Av* and the summer Torah portions.

Jewish texts must be more sacred than the venerated pages of numerous leadership manuals, and facilitating the adventure of Jewish living must never be stifled by an unquestioning acceptance of authoritative Jewish texts. A dynamic equilibrium is essential. Informal Jewish education will then achieve a balance between learning and living, treasuring both content and consciousness. Traditional text study refocuses informal education toward the pages of Jewish tradition, just as the pedagogy of this educational genre has always taught us that we too have a place on those pages.

Dr. Raphael Zarum currently works for Makor-AJY, the London-based Centre for Informal Jewish Education, a project of the UJIA and the Jewish Agency. His book for Jewish teens, The Jampacked Bible, *can be found online at http://users.charity.vfree.com/a/aj6/jpbo. He can be contacted at Raphael@makor.org.uk.*

Living Jewish Lives
Elisa Spungen Bildner

At his bar mitzvah a few weeks ago, our son Eli led 300 congregants in our Conservative synagogue through *psukei d'zimrah*, *shachrit*, the Torah service and *musaf*. He chanted all seven *aliyot* of his Torah portion as well as the *haftorah* and delivered a scholarly 15-minute *d'var Torah*.

Another Jewish mother bragging? Yes. But for one particular reason: Eli—and our other two children whose *b'nai mitzvot* preceded his—accomplished what he (and they) did because of many summers spent at nonprofit Jewish sleep-away camps whose mission is informal Jewish education. The fact is, these camps offer a full Jewish life for the weeks a child is in attendance.

Don't get me wrong; the camps only minimally tutored our children for their *b'nai mitzvot*. But what they did—and still do—is instill in our four children—none of whom, I should mention, attend day school—a love for Jewish learning and living. To quote Eli: "Hebrew School and day school is Jewish teaching, which is fine, but Jewish camp is Jewish life."

Our children's joyful summers at camp, along with recent research showing that camp experiences increase Jewish identity, practice, and commitment, inspired my husband, Rob, and me, in August 1998, to found and provide seed money for the Foundation for Jewish Camping, a public charity. Its mission is to improve Jewish camping by providing support for:

- Advocacy—The Foundation makes the case for Jewish camping wherever leaders gather because the community focuses pitifully little attention and money on this precious resource.

- Scholarships—More need-based and incentive scholarships will attract children and families to consider Jewish camps.
- Increased Capacity—Jewish camps are out of space unless beds are added and camps built. Additionally, no Jewish music, art, sports or other specialty camps exist.
- Staff Recruitment—Camps desperately need well-qualified Jewish senior and summer staff.
- Programmatic Excellence in Secular as Well as Judaic Areas— Jewish camps must meet or exceed "state of the art" programs in general as well as Jewish areas of summer camping.

Asking my children to identify more specifically what it means to live a Jewish life at camp, Rafi, at age 7, our youngest and about to make the move from Jewish day camp to overnight camp, says: "I can't wait; it will be more Jewish. I love baking challah every Friday, all the sports and 'rabbi time,' when the rabbi tells Jewish folktales and *midrashim*."

My 14-year-old son Ari says that besides the sports and discussion groups ("I took a great elective last summer: We studied why bad things happen to good people"), daily *tefillah* is important. "Sometimes we hold services in the woods, and sometimes we use melodies I never hear in synagogue; it's a warm atmosphere."

The highlight for Eli last summer was a special Talmud study session the camp arranged for him and a friend with a visiting scholar. They studied *mishnaot* concerning Pesach. What if a camper is less studious? Eli responds: "Camp caters to all levels, and much of the learning is unstructured. While taking care of the pet rabbits and goats at camp, the counselor in charge of *teva*, or nature, explains why Judaism requires humane treatment of animals."

Elana's school friends are primarily not Jewish. Her email life best sums up one of the benefits of summers at Camp Ramah: She has a virtual teenage Jewish community of camp friends. Elana is constantly in touch online with former bunkmates despite the fact she last attended camp before freshman year.

But lest my kids give the impression that Jewish camp is nirvana, a few more quotes highlight an unfortunate reality. Says Eli, who loves doing Jewish but also relishes the sports and other pursuits that make being a kid fun: "Sometimes the quality of the secular activities made me really disappointed," Eli says. "Take the facilities. Two of the tennis courts looked like remnants of an old driveway with cracks all over. And some of the rackets were still wood. The *tzilum* (photography) shack is really a shack. You can't believe it." Or listen to Ari: "The dining room we ate in was really a tent with a gravel floor and the windows were broken." And listen to both of them: "We need more sports and instructors!"

Jewish educators, the Jewish community: Do listen. Jewish camping is Jewish education within Jewish life; to use today's lingo, 24/7. Let's trumpet the good and fix what needs fixing.

Elisa Spungen Bildner is Founder and Co-President (with Rob Bildner) of the Foundation for Jewish Camping, a public foundation supporting and promoting nonprofit Jewish camping throughout North America (www.jewishcamping.org). President of FreshPro, a New Jersey fresh-cut produce manufacturing company, she is currently national Vice-President of the American Jewish Committee and serves as a member of AJC Board of Governors.

Teenage Boys and Girls: A Jewish World Apart
Leonard Saxe and Shaul Kelner

Today's American Jewish teenagers are the first to grow up in an era when gender equality is both the law of the land and a principle of non-Orthodox Judaism. Just as our society has removed barriers to women taking leadership positions, so too have non-Orthodox Jewish movements removed barriers to women becoming rabbis and communal leaders. In the world of federations and Jewish philanthropies, gender neutrality is accepted at least in principle if not always in practice. The increasing prominence of women in visible public roles, however, has masked another important shift in the gendered experience of American Jewish life, one that is playing itself out among Jewish adolescents: teenage Jewish boys are rapidly exiting the playing field, leaving the girls to hold the ball.

Although young people in North America are perhaps the most studied and tested group of individuals who have ever lived, there is a surprising lack of systematic data about Jewish teenagers. We tried to redress the lack of information by surveying nearly 1,500 Jewish adolescents and their parents, asking about their lives, activities and attitudes about school, religion and family. Our goal was to understand how teens make sense of their Jewish and secular worlds and to examine how this changes over the course of adolescence. One of the most striking findings was that boys and girls often see their world in quite different ways. Consistently, we found that girls were more likely than boys to be active members of their Jewish communities, to espouse Jewish values, and to enjoy participation in the community; boys more readily bid farewell to Jewish involvement.

Affective versus Instrumental Orientations

Although both boys and girls were highly motivated to be successful, girls were more oriented to social activities and boys toward individual activities. These different orientations have been called affective versus instrumental orientation and reflect traditional views of women as nurturers and men as producers. Girls, in contrast to boys, place greater value on things such as family, finding meaning in life, working to correct social injustice, and, being Jewish. Girls were also more likely to be involved in volunteer work. They were also more favorably disposed to school, less often bored and less likely to blow off either their assignments or entire days of school.

Involvement in Judaism/Jewish Community

Boys expressed consistently less interest in things Jewish, held more negative opinions about past Jewish experiences, and generally considered Judaism more peripheral to their lives in comparison to the girls. Boys were twice as likely to say that they saw their bar mitzvah as their graduation from their Jewish schooling. Judging by their participation in post-bar/bat mitzvah Jewish education, youth groups, and Israel experience programs, it does not appear that they are merely more negative in expressing their views. Indeed, boys participate less and, even when they do participate, enjoy it less and find it less meaningful.

Overall, we found that by the end of high school, nearly half of those who had become bar or bat mitzvah had little involvement in the Jewish community. They neither participated in formal Jewish education, nor informal programs, such as youth groups, Jewish camps, or Israel trips. Although this trend applies to both boys and girls, it is more pronounced among boys and is accompanied by more negative attitudes. This should be a cause for concern.

Supporting Teenagers in the Jewish Community

The disproportionate withdrawal of teenage boys stems from a basic mismatch between their instrumental orientations and the Jewish community's affective presentation of self. Not everyone is looking for a Jewish identity-building experience, nor should one have to, in order to find an open door to Jewish life. Instead of demanding that teens first conform to a normative vision of Jewish involvement as an end in itself, the Jewish community can engage them by identifying and serving their needs.

The teenagers we studied, both boys and girls, live stressful lives; school, work, and social pressures are not trivial. Jewish organizations can help young people cope with the pressures of adolescence—providing physical outlets like sports and intellectual support like preparation for SATs. Some of these programs, like competitive sports, may attract more boys than girls and fill gaps in engagement that currently leave boys on the outside. Work contributes to teen pressures, as many teens are forced to choose between the jobs they love and the jobs that pay. The Jewish community can offer a better alternative: well-paying, meaningful employment within the Jewish community.

The disaffection of boys from Jewish life opens a window into a central fact of American Judaism: Except for a minority who make it their full-time profession, Jewish life in North America is primarily a voluntary activity, and meets affective rather than instrumental goals. In a society that defines itself by work, and judges success by material gains, Judaism is treated as something to be done in one's spare time, if at all. Boys are more likely than girls to take this as a cue to exit, but the problem transcends gender. It calls out for a response.

The authors are faculty members at the Cohen Center for Modern Jewish Studies at Brandeis University, and collaborated with Charles Kadushin to develop the recent study, Being a Jewish

Teenager in America: Trying to Make It. *This essay is adapted from the research findings. Leonard Saxe, Director of the Center, is a professor of social policy. Shaul Kelner is Research Associate and Wexner Graduate Fellow pursuing a Ph.D. in sociology at the City University of New York.*

Moving Along a Jewish Track
Yehiel E. Poupko

There is no such thing as informal Jewish education; only Jewish education. While Jewish *schooling* is a pediatric classroom activity, Jewish *education* is a lifelong process whereby Jews learn Jewish tradition and then integrate it into their inner life and daily activities. The Jewish community spends too much effort and too much focus on the pediatric activity of Jewish schooling.

Let's look at it from this perspective. Approximately 15 percent of American Jewish children receive their Jewish education in day schools. The other 85 percent—who receive a Jewish education—do so in the following way and in the following order: early childhood Jewish education, day and residential camping, and synagogue supplementary school.

But Jewish education does not begin in childhood. It begins when we create family as adults. Jewish educational efforts should mirror, therefore, the realities of families who, for the most part, do not become synagogue members until their children are ready for school. Synagogue membership is often a life-stage decision and not necessarily a matter of theological discretion. Programs that are geared to young adults, like "Young Leadership" activities sponsored by federations, should attempt to channel families into synagogue membership and early education programs, which would later flow into other educational opportunities.

Jewish educational providers must accept the principle that one important purpose of each and every Jewish educational experience is to build toward another one. When a family's participation in an early childhood program is about to end, the early childhood director should not only discus the child's next academic steps in kindergarten or first grade but also guide the family to its next Jewish educational provider.

This requires a tracking system whereby educational providers would work as partners, ensuring that when American Jewish families finish one education program someone guides and helps them move to the next step. Federations—capable of identifying a significant portion of young adults, singles, and young families— could help identify and track families along that path.

Such a tracking system will allow key educational providers to be accountable to each other. Each will depend upon the success, the quality, and the goodwill of the other providers. A centrally organized tracking system (such as the federation system) will supply the providers with the names, addresses, and phone numbers of potential students and participants.

Jewish education is not always the motivation for enrolling young children in Jewish preschools. Nor is this the motivation for many families who enroll their children in bar and bat mitzvah preparatory programs. Rather, realities create opportunities. Rather than focusing these two popular Jewish educational products exclusively on children, why not address the entire family? Why not be candid and develop a contract with each and every family? Why not say, You have two options:

Option 1. We will provide Jewish experience, Jewish education, and Jewish preparation of your child.

Option 2. In addition to the experience of the child you, the family, can contract to participate as well.

Schools or other institutions would develop a special set of family educational experiences just for those families who want it. Too many families are currently coerced customers of Jewish education. A contract between the institution and the family, however, will enable programs to separate those who get more than they want, and are thus frustrated, from those who do not get as much as they want and are frustrated.

Rather than being Conservative, Orthodox, or Reform— theologically speaking—most American Jews are "episodic Jews." They know they are Jewish, and at critical moments in the lifecycle, in the calendar year, and in response to Jewish history or to certain current Jewish events, they connect and seek something authentic.

Outcomes for "episodic Judaism" may be categorized in four groupings:

1) the individual and the family
2) community responsibility and interpersonal relations

3) Jewish peoplehood
4) the inner life

If the American Jewish community addresses Jewish education as a lifelong process and accepts the basic pattern established by families as they move, develop, and grow, then we can bring the providers together, develop a tracking system, and achieve agreement on content and desired outcomes.

Rabbi Yehiel E. Poupko is Judaic Scholar at the Jewish Federation/ Jewish United Fund of Metropolitan Chicago.

Nurturing Jewish Youth Through Their Teenage Years
Laurie Katz Braun

There is a rumor that teenagers are difficult. The rumor, my friends, is false. While no adult who shares her or his life with teenagers would fully object to this statement, it is fundamentally an unfair description. In fact, it is not teenagers themselves who are difficult, but rather the teenage years.

Teenage years are the most growth-filled, painful, exhilarating, impossible years of life. It is the age of between-ness. Between being a child and being an adult. Between knowing exactly who you are because others have always defined you, and knowing how you will define yourself. Between being a slave to the rules of parents and teachers and deciding what your own rules should be. In a sense, teenagers are like the Israelites in the midst of crossing the sea of reeds. They're not sure what's on the other side, but they're willing to make a break for it.

And it's our job to help them get to the other side safely.

What do we know about this strange and challenging journey? We know that crossing the sea is only the beginning—that the journey is long and requires certain tools. Most of all, we know that the journey involves leadership. If we don't provide leaders for the journey, the travelers will find their own—often leaders we rather they not choose.

Who are we empowering to lead our children through these years? When I started rabbinical school in 1992, there were very few full-time Jewish youth professionals serving congregations, so

I decided that I'd serve best in a non-congregational capacity. Initially I taught in a Jewish day school, loving especially the occasional moments of informal education on retreats and special trips. But working as a day school teacher by definition meant working in a structure of mostly formal education. When I became an administrator two years later, I found that only a small fraction of my time was spent with young people—the original focus of my rabbinate.

Eventually, I found exactly what I was looking for—an opportunity to create fundamental change in the youth community of Westchester Reform Temple in Scarsdale, New York. My mandate—to create new avenues for Jewish youth involvement beyond traditional models—was clear, as were the risks: How would I encourage young people to accept ownership for new programs? What if the youth population was not interested in having a "youth rabbi?" How would I know how much change is too much?

The synagogue's professional and lay leader team was fully aware that caring for youth is a communal responsibility. In fact youth leaders were part of the interview and selection process for my position. Soon I began to plant the seeds of a teen theater, teen chavurah, and teen healing service. I nurtured our youth group and student teacher program, accompanied our teens to Israel, and—in partnership with senior youth group members—created a student-led junior youth group. Most importantly, I spent three years building relationships with the synagogue youth. I have learned certain fundamental truths in the process:

The youth community is a microcosm of the larger community.

For every congregational issue there is a parallel in the youth community. While we strive toward meaningful adult education or prayer experiences, we need also to work on meaningful youth education and prayer services. And while we work to create an adult caring community, we need to think about caring for our youth community.

One size doesn't fit all.

We all say that our children are our future, but teenagers are one of the most absent constituencies from our synagogues. Why? Many congregations offer one or two paths for teenage involvement in Jewish life, and if they don't sign up they're considered synagogue drop-outs. Teenagers are as varied as any other cross section of our population.

If you build it together, *they will come.*

We can't build a youth community *for* our teenagers, but we can build it with them. We need to do a better job of listening to our teenagers and working together to create places they want to inhabit.

The Jewish community must raise the level of support for youth professionals. Hiring a youth rabbi/leader/director is only the beginning; caring for our youth is a communal responsibility.

My initial questions about Jewish youth work have changed and I no longer ask these questions in the first person. Now I ask: How do we manage growth successfully? How do we reach out to youth who have not yet found a door into the Jewish world? How do we convince adults not to judge success by numbers alone? And if not now, when?

Rabbi Laurie Katz Braun is a graduate of the University of Pennsylvania and Hebrew Union College (LA and NY) and serves as Youth Rabbi at Westchester Reform Temple in Scarsdale, New York. She is a Fellow at Brandeis University's Institute on Informal Jewish Education.

Book Review
The Jew Within: Self, Family, and Community in America
(Steven M. Cohen and Arnold M. Eisen, Indiana University Press, 2000, 255 pp, $27.95)

In the academic field of Jewish Studies, it has fallen to the social sciences to unlock the mystery of American Jews. Every new quantitative study, however, raises inevitable questions about what the numbers really measure, and what they capture about the lives of American Jews. Steven M. Cohen, a sociologist, and Arnold M. Eisen, a religious studies scholar, have set out to do just that in a highly readable and fascinating book titled *The Jew Within*. This collaborative work draws on fifty lengthy interviews and a national survey of more than 1,000 Jews. From this data, they learned what a significant sector of American Jews does and believes, as well as how, where, and with whom they practice their Judaism. What they learned about American Jews is provocative, perhaps not surprising, but neither is it simply predictable.

One of the unique features of this study is its focus on the group that they define as the most "typical" of American Jews, the "moderately affiliated." These baby boomers belong to Jewish organizations, most likely synagogues, which they attend occasionally. They are not leaders, nor are they among the more religiously observant. They are most likely to be married with children, and have a Jewish spouse.

Eisen and Cohen learned that the moderately affiliated Jews are deeply committed to their Judaism, but the nature of that commitment is precisely what calls for analysis. Their "subjects" describe their Judaism as a journey, and they travel through it overwhelmingly in the company of the nuclear family, both as children and as parents. Only "the sovereign self" is the arbiter of what happens on that journey, because these American Jews are little moved by the authority of God or the normative tradition in their behavior and attitudes. They seek a Judaism that is meaningful to them and, therefore, requires a degree of personal investment that is high in the private sphere of the family where emotions are deep.

The Jews of the new century are less committed than any previous generation to either communal expression of Judaism or the Jewish people. Although they continue to feel a special connection to other Jews, the boundaries that separate them from non-Jews are far more porous than previously experienced. While these Jews would oppose their children choosing another religion, that may be the last frontier of absolute difference for them in American culture.

The privatization and deep personalism of this Judaism seems to have effected a significant change in these Jews' attitudes toward Israel, which they regard with a mixture of criticism and attachment; that criticism has very much limited the extent of that attachment. Similarly, organizations that often linked Jews to Israel, like the Federations, are currently viewed by most as alienating and unappealing.

These Jews feel a strong attachment to God, but they do not

anticipate encountering that God in the synagogue. They are not disappointed, according to Cohen and Eisen, when God does not appear. The rituals, activities, and events from which they derive the most meaning involve family members. Their zeal to pass on this Judaism to their children is profound, but they do not want to be told what is an acceptable or legitimate form of Judaism.

The rich narratives that make up much of *The Jew Within* go well beyond these key findings. They are testimony to all that is involved in a journey, its struggles, power, and disappointments. What is even more significant than the nature of the journey is how it is different from their parents' sojourns. If both generations can be described as "pick-and-choose Jews," it is the baby boomers who are less concerned with consistency than their parents. Their expectation for personal meaning is greater and their experience of community and collective responsibility is far weaker.

The authors raise powerful questions and conundrums. Have they described a Judaism that is close to running its course, since nearly two generations that follow the baby boom are in or moving toward adulthood? *The Jew Within* emphasizes the link between Jewish identity and family perhaps more fully and complexly than any recent study of American Jews. It is a major contribution to the study of Jewish identity. Families, however, continue to change. Is the Judaism of journey tied to the rather traditional forms of family life described in this book, or will Judaism become the religion only of such families? While Jewish practice continues to grow in the soil of Jewish commitment and observance, the freedom to choose among *mitzvot* and the yearning for meaning have created not a new formulation of Judaism as much as a new version of an increasingly secularized Judaism,

It is precisely these powerful tensions, if not contradictions, that *The Jew Within* brings to our attention. This book will serve as a mirror into which American Jews will gaze for many years, if not decades, puzzling out who we are and how we got here.

Riv-Ellen Prell, an anthropologist, is Professor of American Studies at the University of Minnesota. She is the author, most recently, of Fighting to Become Americans: Jews, Gender, and the Anxiety of Assimilation.

Staying in Touch via the Internet

When I was younger I remember there was but one computer in my classroom—with a black screen and green writing, and it only took big floppy disks. By the sixth grade we had four computers with color monitors. Since then, my world has quickly become more high-tech. If it weren't for the Internet, I don't know how Jewish I would be. Of course I would still celebrate Rosh Hashanah, Yom Kippur, Passover, and Chanukah. But I would, in all likeliness, be a secular Jew.

When I say that I would be a secular Jew, I mean that without the Internet I wouldn't know any of the lore about Lilith, I wouldn't engage in discussions about Holocaust education, or study passages in the Torah. I love Web sites like Jvibe.com and MzVibe.com where I get involved Jewishly. When I attended the Genesis program at Brandeis University last July, I left miserable—not because I had hated the experience but because of how truly amazing it had been. I was terrified of losing the friends I had made.

Our promise to stay in touch worked because of the Internet. Whenever I go online I'm sure to talk to one of my new friends. Inevitably, conversation turns to some obscure topic in Judaism like what colleges have the most active Jews. I'm also more connected to politics via the Internet. I've taken out an Internet subscription to the *New York Times* so that I can keep up with Israeli/Palestinian issues. When the *New York Times* isn't enough, I go to the *Jerusalem Post* online, or *Ha'aretz's* English online edition. My experiences with the Internet make me a more informed person with much stronger views. They keep me connected to my Jewish friends and Jewish issues.

Jan Kushner is 16 years old and lives in Lawrenceville, New Jersey. She participated in the Genesis 2000 program at Brandeis University. (Disclosure: JVibe.com and MzVibe.com are published, like Sh'ma, *by Jewish Family & Life.)*

"Invigorating, Intriguing, Empowering"

I remember the high school program beginning memorably—a group of students being challenged to "define power." The activity was invigorating, intriguing, and empowering; an important question had been posed, and we had to come up with answers. Over two more days, we connected with peers from throughout the country, heard stimulating debates about civil rights, modeled a session of the Israeli Knesset, and grappled with economic issues as talmudic texts on *tzedakah* came to life in our hands. We met with leading thinkers and activists—people I would call years later, "dreamers, makers, and shakers."

Over those few days I began to develop a deeper regard for my Jewish heritage and a more profound gratitude for its penetrating insights. Ancient Jewish texts spoke to the very concerns that we raised as though the rabbis had heard our intense striving and were responding directly with discerning words of wisdom Our learning planted deep roots because the relevance coursing through it transcended the boundaries of any classroom. With our burgeoning sense of social justice and empowerment and a desire to mold our learning into action, we made *mitzvot* come to life. Engaging with Jewish ideas, when I was just beginning to feel empowered in the world, has made me appreciate the extraordinary value of Judaism and its myriad ways of teaching life.

Arielle Parker, who participated in Panim el Panim in high school, began rabbinical school at the Ziegler School of Rabbinic Studies in Los Angeles in September 2001.

Informal and Formal Education Work Hand-in-Hand

I have been immersed in Judaism since the day I was born. After years of Hebrew school, attending religious services, and keeping Jewish ritual, I identified myself as a Jew. I cannot, however, say with conviction that I had a strong connection to Judaism.

Nine years ago I became a member of Young Judaea, the Zionist youth movement sponsored by Hadassah, after attending Camp Young Judaea Sprout Lake in New York. Thus I began the long process of developing my own Jewish identity through informal education.

My experiences in the youth movement provided me with the opportunity to develop my own opinions, and, more importantly, a personal ideology. The casual and creative setting of camp turned learning about Israel and Judaism into a passion rather than an obligation. Under these conditions, I found an authentic connection to the Jewish people. Now, in my senior year of high school, I am serving the same movement that nourished my passion for Judaism and Zionism.

Educators often split education into informal and formal education. I, however, believe that the two work together, hand-in-hand. Without one to supplement the other, a student cannot possibly obtain a rounded education. Without a well-rounded education, it would be very difficult to develop a connection with Judaism. My personal experiences with formal and informal education have affirmed these beliefs.

Josh Scharff is 18 years old and National Mazkir of Young Judaea.